Transnati

This book investigates ... ıternational links of the extreme right in one of ... opean areas since 1945. Andrea Mammone details the long journey ... development of this political and cultural phenomenon in France and Italy, tracing the exchanges and the similarities among neofascist movements and thinkers across national borders from 1945 to the present day. Mammone analyzes the adaptation of neofascism in society and politics, the attempts to build international associations and pan-national networks, and its responses to the defeat of fascism, the Cold War, European integration, decolonization, immigration, and EU-led austerity politics.

Andrea Mammone is a lecturer in modern European history in the Department of History at Royal Holloway, University of London. He has published extensively on the European far right, modern Italy, transnationalism, and other themes in European history, politics, and society, including numerous articles, edited books, and journal editions. Mammone has notably written for the *International Herald Tribune*, *The Independent*, *Foreign Affairs*, *The Guardian*, Al Jazeera America, Reuters, the *New York Times*, and the *New Statesman*. He has been interviewed by Al Jazeera, the BBC, Voice of America, *The Observer*, Radio 24, *Il Fatto Quotidiano*, *To Vima*, *Weekendavisen*, the *New Zealand Herald*, LBC Radio London, Sky News, TIME, *O Globo*, *European Voice*, *The Economist*, Radio Rai, and *The Guardian*.

Transnational Neofascism in France and Italy

ANDREA MAMMONE
Royal Holloway, University of London

CAMBRIDGE
UNIVERSITY PRESS

CAMBRIDGE
UNIVERSITY PRESS

University Printing House, Cambridge CB2 8BS, United Kingdom

One Liberty Plaza, 20th Floor, New York, NY 10006, USA

477 Williamstown Road, Port Melbourne, VIC 3207, Australia

314-321, 3rd Floor, Plot 3, Splendor Forum, Jasola District Centre, New Delhi - 110025, India

79 Anson Road, #06-04/06, Singapore 079906

Cambridge University Press is part of the University of Cambridge.

It furthers the University's mission by disseminating knowledge in the pursuit of education, learning and research at the highest international levels of excellence.

www.cambridge.org
Information on this title: www.cambridge.org/9781108705851

First published 2015
First paperback edition 2019

A catalogue record for this publication is available from the British Library

Library of Congress Cataloging in Publication data
Mammone, Andrea.
Transnational neofascism in France and Italy / Andrea Mammone.
pages cm
Includes bibliographical references and index.
ISBN 978-1-107-03091-6 (Hardback)
1. Right-wing extremists–France–History–20th century. 2. Right-wing extremists–Italy–History–20th century. 3. Fascism–France–History–20th century. 4. Fascism–Italy–History–20th century. 5. France–Politics and government–1945– 6. Italy–Politics and government–1945–1976. 7. Italy–Politics and government–1976–1994. 8. Italy–Politics and government–1994– 9. Transnationalism–Political aspects–France. 10. Transnationalism–Political aspects–Italy. I. Title.
HN440.R3M327 2015
320.53′30944–dc23 2014027889

ISBN 978-1-107-03091-6 Hardback
ISBN 978-1-108-70585-1 Paperback

Ai sorrisi di Mariangela e di nonna Rosina

Contents

Preface

To find any sense in life it was pointless to search in
the places where people were instructed to look.
Sense was only to be found in secrets.

John Berger, "Here is where we meet"

Pour trouver un quelconque sens à la vie,
il était vain de chercher là où on nous disait de le faire.
On ne pouvait trouver du sens que dans les secrets.

John Berger, "D'ici là"

Se si vuole trovare un qualche senso nella vita
è inutile cercare nei posti dove ti dicono di guardare.
Il senso lo si può trovare solo nei segreti.

John Berger, "Qui, dove ci incontriamo"

Walking across Paris is an extraordinary experience and an irresistible temptation to avoid locking oneself up in a library. Springtime is especially fascinating and intriguingly romantic, even beautifully melancholic. This French universe appears full of veritable discoveries: from the Jardin du Luxembourg to the Centre Georges Pompidou, and from Parc de Belleville to Saint-Germain-des-Prés – these all portray a glimpse of the finest European architecture and culture, with a typical Francophone taste. But even Paris cannot be taken alone and decontextualized. Europe, its people, cultures, and many of its histories, are much closer and more tied together than had previously been thought. As the Dutch journalist and writer Geert Mak magnificently pointed out after his "journeys" across the old continent: "Berlin can never been understood without Versailles, nor London without Munich, Vichy without Verdun, Moscow without Stalingrad, Boon without Dresden, Vásárosbéc without Yalta."[1]

Europe then has always been a world full of discoveries and the starting point of further explorations. Indeed, at one point during the research for *Transnational Neofascism in France and Italy*, I felt like a little Cristoforo Colombo – although much less famous than my worldwide-known compatriot, and probably less happy-go-lucky than contemporary tourists visiting the *Ville-Lumière* (as they are not usually committed to go through archival catalogs). My own modest voyage of discovery in such a lovely city, often at the center of this interconnected European world, was in those rather modern *bâtiments* hosting the Bibliothèque Nationale de France. After years of working on the French and Italian extreme right, I accidentally came across a seemingly unimportant essay that had been published in one of the main neofascist periodicals in postwar Europe, *Défense de l'Occident*, on the fin-de-siècle Italian writer Alfredo Oriani (1852–1909), an author appropriated by Benito Mussolini's circles and included in the pantheon of his *fascismo*. The article apparently had no relevance to my main interests, namely, the transnational links, similarities, and the cultural and political transfer between French and Italian right-wing thinkers, activists, and movements. The author of the piece was Pascal Gauchon, at the time a twenty-four-year-old contributor to the journal and, later, strongly involved in some of the French right-leaning groups that were also looking at Italy as their major role model. He opened his article as follows:

> Italy and France live according to the same political rhythm. We have brought this evidence to light a number of times in *Défense de l'Occident*, evidence that deserves to be extended beyond historical realities, to a study of ideology. Revolutionary Italian union activists imitate their French counterparts. The thinkers behind Alleanza Nazionalista are the natural heirs of AF [Action Française], whether they intend it or not. It is no surprise to see that of the thinkers that most influenced Mussolini, we find three French figures like Bergson, Maurras, Sorel. We are not only talking about a simple level of influence here: there are also many similarities in life and style between Barrès and D'Annunzio, as there were with Doriot and Mussolini, Mazzini and the revolutionaries of 1848. … To summarize, nationalist ideology was created and developed in parallel in the two countries.[2]

[1] Geert Mak, *Europe: Travels through the Twentieth Century* (London: Vintage, 2008), p. XVI.

[2] Pascal Gauchon, "Alfredo Oriani, précurseur du 'fascisme,'" *Défense de l'Occident*, 118, 1974, pp. 10–11.

A little difference was in the impact of the Action Française's thinkers on early nationalism, an influence that, perhaps, could not find, Gauchon continues, an exact Italian counterpart. According to the French writer, this explains why, after the First World War, political ideologies developed more distinctly in Italy than in France: "in fact it was Italy that served as a model, and it would be the French thinkers who would seek their source of inspiration from these [Italian] fascist writers."[3] All this is hardly surprising. Historically, well before Napoleon, these neighboring countries experienced a long history of exchanges, mutual cultural influences, and transborder links. In fact, these links and the cross-fascination existed before the establishment of Italy's nation-state – when it was often a land geopolitically unified only in some literary landscapes of foreign travelers such as Alexandre Dumas and Stendhal.[4] Gauchon's statement was, nonetheless, at least for me, a sort of bolt from the blue: It was a near perfect synthesis of my own evolving methodological approach and even an excellent (potential) abstract for a book. It captured some of the key theoretical themes that I had been developing regarding the role of transnationalism in the development of recent Europe, the evolution of the extreme right, and the proximity of these two nations.

This neofascist writer was then wholly truthful: Italy and France in the interwar years had, in fact, an incredible number of ties. Extreme-right history experienced the borrowing of some relevant Italian fascist events by activists in France and of French fascistic intellectuals by like-minded fellows in Italy. It is true that there had been notable patterns of transnational associations and a transmission of doctrines and strategies across the Alps since (and even before) the First World War: from Tommaso Marinetti to Georges Sorel, from Charles Maurras's Açtion Francaise and Georges Valois's Faisceau to the March on Rome, from Benito Mussolini to the fascist leagues of Marcel Bucard and Jacques Doriot, and from the Italian Fasci in France to the newspaper *Je suis partout*. However, there was even more than this. A shared Franco-Italian nationalist space, and life, was also made by a web of artists, art critics, and modern aesthetics – all often strongly tied up with extreme-right politics and ideology. Given such a fruitful context, some scholars have pertinently

3 Ibid.

4 "In France alone 1,700 travel journals were written about Italy in the nineteenth century. Many of these books contributed to characterisation of Italian typologies even before a national identity had been elaborated." Paolo Varvaro, "European travellers in Italy," *European Review of History–Revue Européenne d'Histoire*, 4(2), 1997, p. 165.

suggested that "the common premises of fascist thought in France and Italy led to the development of shared ideological and cultural precepts; and these principles were often expressed and promoted by figures who maintained links with both countries."[5]

This cross-fertilization developed well beyond the fin-de-siècle and the interwar years. At the edge of the Second World War, which was to change Europe, Robert Brasillach, in a melancholic but imaginative frame of mind, envisioned that France and Italy would "meet" again after warfare. He summarized this feeling with a simple *Au revoir, Italie.*[6] In hindsight, he was right about this: Extreme-right France and Italy would find one another again, although Brasillach, of course, did not experience this new encounter himself. This war collaborationist, well-known intellectual, and literary critic, who labeled fascist Italy the "eternal country" and praised the Italian Duce, was executed for treason on February 6, 1945. He, nonetheless, represented an epitome of the fascist transnationalism with a life and an intellectual trajectory that "paralleled that of a generation of European youth caught up in the vision of a new type of man, *homo fascista*."[7] Admiration of Brasillach circulated widely among right-wingers over the postwar years, and Italian neofascists often paid tribute to him and also commemorated his figure.[8]

My own "discovery" of Gauchon was therefore very apt, for he fairly assumed the existence of a "same political rhythm" shared by France and Italy. These were, according to the neofascist press of the 1950s, two "sister" Latin nations, with the same "torments" and "fate."[9] For a long part of the postwar period, they really had a parallel destiny: a Catholic

[5] Matthew Affron and Mark Antliff, "Art and Fascist Ideology in France and Italy: An Introduction," in M. Affron and M. Antliff, eds., Fascist *Visions: Art and Ideology in France and Italy* (Princeton: Princeton University Press, 1997), p. 3.

[6] Robert Brasillach, "Au revoir, Italie," *Je suis partout*, May 26, 1939, pp. 1 and 3.

[7] William M. Tucker, "Politics and Aesthetics: The Fascism of Robert Brasillach," *Western Political Quarterly*, 15(4), 1962, p. 605.

[8] Ibid. On September 21, 1985, for example, the important neofascist newspaper *Il Secolo d'Italia* discussed the republication (in Italian) of a "quality work" such as Jean Madiran's book on Brasillach and interviewed the author. This work first appeared in France under the title *Brasillach* and was published by the Club du Luxembourg in 1958. "Jean Madiran" is one of the pen names of Jean Arfel. This latter was a nationalist and extremist journalist closely involved with the mentioned *Action Française* and very close to the leader Charles Maurras during the interwar years. He then backed a number of extreme-right movements and was among the founders of the daily *Présent* in 1982, a publication close to the Front National.

[9] "'Purtroppo la Francia mancava.' Commento di 'Rivarol' al congresso del MSI," *Meridiano d'Italia*, 9(30), January 24, 1954, p. 4.

culture with some effects on their sociopolitical life, a strong polarization between opposing symbolic (ideological) universes, the presence of the strongest communist parties in Western Europe, and a low degree of political alternation in power (with the exclusion of communist forces).[10] Nonetheless, as suggested before, this shared history and ground was especially true for the extreme-right ideology, developments, and forces in the twentieth century.

Politically and historically, France is indeed deemed to be the nation with the ideal-type of a contemporary right-wing extremist party, the Front National (National Front, FN) and its longtime leader Jean-Marie Le Pen, and now successfully (also from an electoral standpoint) led by his daughter, Marine. However, *the hexagone*, long before the arrival of the FN, has always been a land where extreme-right and proto-fascist "ferments" were lively.[11] Moreover, culturally and ideologically, the country produced noteworthy postwar intellectuals and schools of thought. For example, since the 1970s, the powerful, and truly transnational, group the Nouvelle Droite (New Right, ND), led by Alain de Benoist, influenced right-wing thinking well beyond France and outside the usual extremist fringes (an Italian permutation was, for instance, immediately formed after a meeting in Paris). Italy represents the other excellent reference point in Europe. Historically this *penisola* is the land that experienced the invention of the word "fascismo" and the twenty years of the fascist regime, then the advent of the Repubblica Sociale Italiana (Italian Social Republic, RSI – also known as the Salò Republic), and, subsequently, the birth of the Movimento Sociale Italiano (Italian Social Movement, MSI) in 1946.[12] Politically, it may be seen as the vanguard of right-wing extremism (at least in its electoral version) in

[10] Isabelle Sommier, *La violence politique et son deuil: L'après 68 en France et en Italie* (Rennes: Presses Universitaires de Rennes, 1998), pp. 23–24.

[11] Scholars such as Zeev Sternhell have even claimed that fascist ideology had some French roots, or at least that many ideals, later found in Italian Fascism and German National Socialism, first and foremost appeared in France. See Zeev Sternhell (with M. Sznajder and M. Asheri), *The Birth of Fascist Ideology: From Cultural Rebellion to Political Revolution* (Princeton: Princeton University Press, 1994); Zeev Sternhell, *La droite révolutionnaire (1885–1914); Les origines françaises du fascisme* (Paris: Gallimard, 1998); Zeev Sternhell, *Ni droite ni gauche: l'idéologie fasciste en France* (Paris: Seuil, 1983); Zeev Sternhell, *Maurice Barrès et le nationalisme française* (Paris: Armand Colin, 1972).

[12] Interestingly, the MSI, despite its isolation, and its anomalous position within the framework of a republic based on an anti-fascist constitution, managed to maintain visibility in the political system. As rightly suggested, the party was paradoxically "neo-fascist by identity" and "democratic from necessity." Roberto Chiarini, "Anti-Zionism and the Italian Extreme Right," *Modern Italy*, 13(1), 2008, p. 22.

Western European societies for roughly forty years. The MSI was a magnet for similar foreign groups, cultivating links with many of these groups along with authoritarian regimes across Europe. French neofascists undoubtedly perceived it as a "great party," the most important one among all the groups that, in their own words, "consider themselves the successors of a politics crushed in 1945."[13]

It will be shown how extreme-right movements in this significant European region built, since the interwar years, a wider network of exchanges. This friendship will be "confirmed" and very often renewed by the same protagonists of my story. The influential intellectual of the ND, de Benoist, for example, wrote at the edge of the past century: "No matter what we do or say, among other Europeans, the closest to us French and those we get on with most easily are the Italians."[14]

Some years ago, a French journalist, Frédéric Charpier, similarly remembered this connective framework linking neofascist France to its neighboring nation:

> The links between the French between the French and the Italian extreme right are old. They hark back to the Mussolinian era, to the role of Italy's secret agencies with their funding and armament of the Cagoule, the PPF [Parti Populaire Français, led by Doriot], and the [Bucard's] Parti franciste. These links were renewed after the war at the 1951 Malmö congress, where the MSI build a European alliance with some French, Belgian, and Swedish groups. At the moment of the Algerian war, these ties were strengthened, whether it was for a direct support to the OAS [Organisation Armée Secrète] or the connections between the Italian and French student organizations. The majority of [foreign] movements, in fact, sent their activists to attend the summer schools organized by the FEN [Fédération des Étudiants Nationalistes].[15]

What is probably surprising, however, is the fact that although French neofascists, as well as their intellectual and political newspapers and publications, were ready to accept and admit the proximity of France and Italy, much of the (mainly French) academic literature was reluctant to develop such paradigms. Consequently, neofascist sources became, from my own perspective, excellent portrait painters of the transnational framework; this is also one of the reasons why readers will find in these

[13] Fabrice Laroche, "Le M.S.I.: des origines à nos jours," *Europe Action*, 11, 1963, p. 20. Fabrice Laroche is known to be a pseudonym used by the mentioned Alain de Benoist.

[14] Alain de Benoist, *Dèrnière Annèe: Notes pour conclure le siècle* (Paris: L'Âge d'Homme, 2001), p. 73.

[15] Frédéric Charpier, *Génération Occident: De l'extrême droite à la droite* (Paris: Seuil, 2005), p. 212.

pages my commentaries and analyses of some historical processes and facts, but also what the same protagonists were writing at the time, often while looking at each other.

Is this another case of French-based *exceptionalisme*? The situation was certainly aggravated with the first electoral successes of Le Pen's Front National in the 1980s, followed over the years by other electoral achievements of similar parties across nations. This caused consternation in many sectors of European civil society, public opinion, the mass media, and academia. The sight of an extremist party gaining votes and popular credibility took many commentators by surprise and caused considerable confusion among those attempting to analyze it in the initial stages. What were the reasons behind the FN's success? Why in France? How was the FN to be classified in terms of European political history? I shall return to some of these questions later.

Italian scholars were probably less narrow, but, with very few exceptions, similarly less interested in analyzing the transborder stances and international dimensions of the postwar right. More generally, only a few of them were interested in the history of the MSI itself. Studies of this political phenomenon started quite late, mostly when the party had transformed itself and entered in a governmental coalition – and roughly the same can be said for works in the English language. Continuing interest in the fascist regime had probably diverted most scholarly attention toward the interwar phase of Mussolini's galaxy. This is bizarre because Italian neofascism (taken as a whole and not confining this universe to the MSI) often had a kind of "international aspiration" that has been overlooked by academics for a considerable number of years. This internationalism was mutually linked with the Italian neofascists' actual impact and influence on foreign like-minded movements and its attempts to build or participate in international blackshirt associations (such as the European Social Movement and the Euroright, which will also be discussed). Moreover, some Italian historians have recently pointed in the direction of another almost neglected dimension: this domestic right-wing extremism often had a fascination with some overseas thinkers and borrowed some nonnational authors and references.[16]

[16] This was, in reality, also made for some very practical reasons: It was to avoid any contamination with the prevailing antifascist national culture – and, I would add, it was a way to react against the military defeat of local fascism and its post-1945 "burdens" in terms of blame or shame. See Francesco Germinario, *Da Salò al governo: Immaginario e cultura politica della destra italiana* (Turin: Bollati Boringhieri, 2005), pp. 31–35.

Transnational Neofascism goes in a very different direction than much of this published literature on the postwar extreme right in Europe and on the extreme/radical/far right in general. First, it takes "history" very seriously. It covers, for example, a historical period from the end of the Second World War up to the late 1970s/early 1980s, which a number of other books – mostly written by political scientists, and only with some few exceptions – usually overlook.[17] This is somewhat curious, although to a certain extent understandable given the different approaches (and aims) of the various academic disciplines. On the other hand, the wrong belief that nothing relevant happened in the first postwar decades prevailed. These years are, in fact, often perceived like a sort of crossing of the desert, while the extreme-right saga started only with the first electoral successes of the FN. Yet the long postwar period is truly fundamental to understanding the evolution of the contemporary parties (and their ideology), particularly regarding the development of that cross-national web that is so relevant today. Second, my work has the ambition to widen the scholar's "lens of investigation" on this subject. The analysis encompasses political cultures, as well as party politics, looking at both the organizational and the intellectual dimensions of the extreme right. In doing so, it additionally goes beyond the usual well-known movements: The book certainly covers their stories but also narrates the trajectories of little groups and how they disappear or migrate in other political containers. It describes the influence of (important) thinkers such as Maurice Bardèche and Julius Evola but also how less renowned bulletins, and activists, operated like transnational vectors or (ideological and organizational) transmission belts from a decade to the other or from a country to its neighbor. I understand that other social scientists might be slightly worried by all this: What are the reasons and aims to (also) study some obscure groups and almost unknown extreme-right personnel? What is their actual impact? The answer is that obviously they all contributed to the making of this bigger neofascist "whole," including the most recent one, and, consequently, they help to clarify some of its inner dimensions and worldviews. Moreover, although radical, or – at least in some cases – marginal, we are not

[17] As suggested, there are a number of exceptions including David Art, *Inside the Radical Right: The Development of Anti-Immigrant Parties in Western Europe* (New York: Cambridge University Press, 2011); and Roger Eatwell, *Fascism: A History* (London: Pimlico, 2003) among others, but not many monographs take a long-term historical perspective, and none of them, to my knowledge, look at the transnational exchanges.

dealing here with a fringe phenomenon, but rather one at the center of European politics. More recently, the extreme right has influenced mainstream policies on immigration as well as ethnic relations in many countries. Studying this – and also in a historical perspective, considering the strong impact of some movements (like the MSI), ideals, and events (like colonization, among others) on contemporary phenomena and looking at the transnational interactions – is therefore essential to understanding the functioning of the contemporary western world and to (implicitly) contribute to the ongoing discussion on very popular concepts such as heritage and belonging, cosmopolitanism and national identity, multiculturalism and migration.

What seems to be peripheral might have deeper outcomes or influences than immediately expected. The extreme-right ideal of an uncontaminated and mythical Europe is one of the various examples here: It is still a relatively neglected page in the history books. In July 2011, after the tragic events in Norway, the extreme-right "terrorist" admitted that he acted to save Europe from multiculturalism and that he was part of a wider pan-European network. All this generated surprise in the media and among the general public. Was the extreme right only indissolubly linked to the preservation of its own nation and citizens? How can we then explain such references to "Europe?" How may some activists believe in the value of a pan-nationalism? *Transnational Neofascism* attempts to cover this ground. It shows the birth of this Euro-nationalist thinking in the 1950s and how it was also developed by some "obscure" and "fringe" streams; at the same time, it highlights the extreme right's efforts to balance national interests with a transnational, or even pan-European, agenda. Some of these cultures have remained and might clearly be seen in today's right-leaning variegated networks (from parties to marginal activists, and from music to the internet). History, in this sense, matters a lot, and it can elucidate contemporary processes.[18] In other words, even some of the apparent "little stories" narrated in the following pages fostered the modern transnational exchanges and the existence of a right-wing brotherhood that is still active today, and not only at the EU parliament level. On the other hand, nothing should, in theory, even stop us from studying fringe movements: This is also a book, as implicitly suggested before,

[18] See Andrea Mammone, "A Lesson That European History Can Teach Us," *The Independent*, July 25, 2011, p. 4.

on the adaptation of neofascism to the changing times and European contexts, and all discussed movements and people are part of this wider story.

Most interestingly, at least from a historiographical perspective, I attempt to build a somewhat innovative method for the study of the extreme right and European political history at large. I use the current case studies – despite their alleged centrality or marginality – as a methodological platform that may also hopefully generate new research frames and further writing tools for other scholarly explorers. In this specific case, the book adopts a transnational and historical analytical framework to show the porosity of geographical borders along with some of the mentioned broader, often neglected, extreme-right dimensions. This "transnational history" seems to me the only frame able to identify and examine some of the key processes of cross-fertilization and the circulation of extremist doctrines, strategies, and personnel across state borders, as well as a commonality of behaviors between neofascist France and Italy.

Readers will discover that politicians in one nation were, for example, well aware of the ultra-rightist political and intellectual developments taking place in the other, neighboring, nation, but, more generally, how the same people were, for example, aware of developments brought by more mainstream "nationalist" politicians, such as Charles de Gaulle, and by events and facts that were happening across the Franco-Italian border. Indeed, events in other countries mattered, as international politics were in play. The Algerian decolonization will be a significant example: Italian neofascists became involved with a foreign politics issue rather than with a strictly extreme-right one. By looking at the colonization process, the story narrated in these pages also crosses the boundaries of Europe's territorial landscape. In other words, this work takes a transregional stance by relating what was perceived as a narrow right-wing "localism" with a more global sphere.

In this sense, I might have certainly have included other international events, such as the rise of right-wing authoritarian regimes and leaders in Latin America, the impact and reactions to the policies of Soviet Russia in foreign nations, the Greek Colonels, and even the season of anti-communism in the United States among others, and have eventually highlighted how the French and Italian extreme right looked at them or if there was any of their "transnational" involvement in some of those processes. However, this monograph faces the usual inevitable limitations of spaces that force a selectivity of themes to be covered. Moreover, this could have affected the shape and narrative of existing sections and distracted readers from some of the book's aims. On the other hand, I accept that, in some cases, the intercontinental and global dimensions have an appropriate significance. This is what Federico Finchelstein has superbly done in his work on "transatlantic fascism," offering a global vision of the interwar extreme right in Argentina and Italy and the transnational reformulations of fascist ideology in different places – work that has further confirmed some of my beliefs.[19]

To summarize, a new and different way of looking at the extreme right will also fascinatingly show that, basically, even what is generally perceived as a narrow nationalism can take a non-national dimension and redeploys at a supranational or international level (even if the main feeling of blackshirted comradeship was almost always with their right-wing fellows and with their political and ideological projects). As suggested, looking at France and Italy offers some novel and clear gateways for research and historical investigations. Intriguingly, French neofascists very often shaped their own world visions according to events occurring in Italy, and Italians did the same on their part (and the outlook might have been really extended to other nations, and some of them are, at times, mentioned). The influence worked, in fact, both ways, sometimes with the prominence of a country, at other times with the impact of the other, while in some cases with an almost equal fertilization. The following pages explore these processes in detail. In doing so, I implicitly challenge, as also mentioned before, any assumption of the exceptionality of French and Italian history, as well as those who refer to a "special (domestic) path" followed by the nationalist extreme right. This is, nevertheless, not simply a challenge or criticism of extreme right-wing studies. Indeed, I prefer not to position myself into any nebulous literature or academic school of thought – albeit I take an evident strong stance in favor of "trasnationalism." The problem, as I see it, is wider: It is the overall lack of studies aiming to consider some European political movements as units of a much larger geopolitical, and cultural, space. This is often, I suspect, for issues of language proficiency, time, and funding. My work has, instead, other goals – some empirical, historiographical, and methodological ones. The belief is that the permeability of Europe should not be relegated just to a consideration of the European integration and its common market. In such a context, this monograph

19 See Federico Finchelstein, *Transatlantic Fascism: Ideology, Violence, and the Sacred in Argentina and Italy, 1919–1945* (Durham: Duke University Press, 2010).

hopefully aims to represent a new contribution to the "transnational history of Europe." Through discussion of postwar fascism, it further shows, in fact, the richness of Europe as a whole, its interconnected history and the porosity of its politics, cultures, and spaces.

The book therefore highlights the most salient cases of transmission of political ideals and their similarities, looking at the resurgence of the extreme right after the war, the various patterns of radicalization and pan-Europeanism, the extreme right's reorganization in the Cold War years, the establishment of international associations, the fascination with French Algeria across the Alps, the impact and the aftermath of 1968 on neofascism, the attempts to escape political and cultural marginalization, and the borrowing of a transnational xenophobia in recent years (along with the response to the austerity politics and anti–financial markets and anti-European Union discourse).

All this also implicitly reminds us that this monograph is placed into a transnational narrative. This means that the story frequently jumps from one case to another, from one source to another, from France to Italy, and vice versa, and the attention is brought to all the connective issues: how events, values, movements, and people were linked, perceived, and covered across nations. Like in a sport competition spectators will follow the ball ("history") moving quickly from one side to the other.

Acknowledgments

A book on the history of two countries, and grounded in a dissertation granted by a university in yet another nation again, needs incredible support. I would, first and foremost, like to thank the Department of French at the University of Leeds, which provided me with financial support through a Departmental Scholarship in the years 2003–6 and additional support for long periods spent in Paris and Rome. The entire School of Modern Languages and Cultures at Leeds also gave me the great chance to use excellent facilities and meet interesting people.

Imogen Long, Francesco Capello, and Tim Peace have been my intrepid fellows at Leeds University. I remember our long (often never-ending) conversations on PhDs, academic life, and jobs. They all made their suggestions available to me, along with comfort, irony, and, principally, their friendship. In Leeds, Jim House and Brian Jenkins supervised my doctoral research. They have been very supportive. In retrospect, what I have really appreciated was the fact that they never pushed me in a specific academic direction. On the contrary, I have been encouraged to explore a whole universe that was out there. This was the first lesson I learned in Britain. I will be never able to express my gratitude enough to them for this and for the incredible job they have done with a young southern Italian who was moving across academic and state borders – and with a life that brought me to live (sometimes for jobs and research) in nine cities, four nations, and two continents, in the past years.

This somewhat transnational life is reflected in the book, its genesis, and its theoretical frame: If, like countless other people, I was travelling across nations, and I had social, cultural, human, and intellectual links in different countries, was it possible that some of the protagonists of these pages had a similar cross-national outlook? This also means that the book has also moved substantially from the doctoral dissertation. This led to extensive additional research in France and Italy, in order to find further evidence of lives, ideals, and politics "in between" European nations. I naturally need to thank the personnel of a number of libraries and archives for their often invaluable help with my research. I specifically refer here to the Biblioteca Universitaria Alessandrina (Rome), Archivio Centrale di Stato (Rome), Bibliothèque Nationale et Universitaire (Strasbourg), Bibliothèque de Documentation Internationale Contemporaine (Nanterre), Biblioteca Nazionale Centrale (Florence), Fondazione Ugo Spirito (Rome), Biblioteca di Storia Moderna e Contemporanea (Rome), and Bibliothèque Nationale de France (Paris). The Biblioteca Universitaria Alessandrina also kindly offered one of the pictures for this book. I wish to thank all who hosted me in some of the mentioned places or simply offered me their support of the topic I was researching. It would be impossible to mention all of them, but my gratitude goes to all of them (as it goes to my other lifelong friends) who made my existence, in Rota Greca, Mongiana, Siena, New York, Florence, Rome, Strasbourg, Paris, London, and Paola, a much better one.

I also own a debt of gratitude to a number of other people who have made the book possible and shaped it along with, at times, my overall academic career. Paul Corner, at my alma mater Università di Siena, never lectured me in a university course, but, on the other hand, implicitly, he has taught me a lot. When I first met him in Siena as an undergraduate student, I was impressed by his kindness; therefore, I realized that England was the place that I had eventually to explore for postgraduate studies. I immediately recognized, even now that I work as a professional historian, that Paul was a significant example. In sum, if I became a historian, it was particularly because Paul was a historian. However, if I am a "transnational" historian, I should thank Gerd-Rainer Horn. I came across Rainer when he was working at Warwick University and I was looking for a PhD scholarship. He was a living academic example of transnationalism: born in Germany, university degrees in the United States, and fluent in an incredible number of languages. When we first met, he mentioned that we had the transnational history approach in common. I immediately answered, "Yes," even although I had never heard the word transnational being applied to history before. After some time, I read one of his books on the left-leaning world: It was, in some ways, what I was also trying to do with parties located on the other side of the spectrum. It was the perfect theoretical frame for my own goals. It was transnational history. I could also claim to be a transnational historian then.

Over the years, meeting people like Anna Cento Bull and Giuseppe Masi convinced me that I was doing "the right thing." This encouraged me to carry on my research with their same moral rigor and academic integrity. Colleagues like David Art, Tamir Bar-On, Sarah de Lange, Roger Eatwell, Christian Goeschel, Dan Stone, and Imogen Long, Anna Cento Bull, Rainer Horn, and Tim Peace have been generous readers of various drafts and chapters at some (very) different stages of the manuscript. Their feedback has been quite helpful in improving it. Loredana Guerrieri, Marco Cuzzi, Pedraic Kenney, Alain Bihr, Jean-Yves Camus, Roberto Chiarini, Emmanuel Godin, Pierre-Yves Saunier, Marco Tarchi, Guido Liguori, and Matteo Albanese have also provided me with material and/or offered me some very good advice. I am really grateful to all of them. I additionally need to express a debt of gratitude to John Schwarzmantel and Jim Wolfreys, who read and commented on my doctoral dissertation in an incredibly useful way. If the manuscript has now this shape, it is also because of their suggestions and, above all, their criticisms. I would also like to say thank you to the Department of History at Royal Holloway, University of London, and my colleagues, for the warm and nice welcome I received when I started working there. I similarly have to mention the generous support for the production of the book received from Isobel Thornley's Bequest to the University of London.

I am also very indebted to Jeff Goodwin because he convinced me that my work was worthy of a top publisher and for our long and pleasant discussions and soft drinks under the lovely Florentine sunshine at Villa Ulivi (owned by the Florence program of New York University where I was working at that time). Linked to this, the manuscript is published in the present shape because of the great patience and support of Lew Bateman and Shaun Vigil at Cambridge University Press in New York, as well as the very stimulating and motivating comments made by the reviewers. In general, all the production team has been excellent.

Some parts of the chapters were previously published (usually in very a different format) in *Contemporary European History* (2008), *Journal of Contemporary European Studies* (2009), and *Patterns of Prejudice* (2011), while some very sporadic sentences and intellectual elaborations appeared in some of my articles for various media outlets. I would like to thank the editors (and publishing houses) of the aforementioned journals. However, the material has been heavily reworked and reshaped with additional sources.

Needless to say, I cannot forget to thank my family at "home." Without my family I would have never carried out most of my studies nor have a transnational life: *un affettuoso grazie* to Angelo, Liliana, and Luca (along with the rest of the family, relatives, and cousins). My father, Angelo, would have been very proud of many things I have done in recent years. I know that our existence is very different without him. Antonio Storino, my father-in-law, a keen writer, will also not be able to read these pages. I am sure he would have loved to see my name on the front page of this book. We are missing his humble, true, and elegant style.

On a very personal note, Mariangela made my life much easier in these slightly hectic past years. She has stayed *al mio fianco*, and never questioned the nights spent writing, my silences, and when my mind seemed to be far from this world – a world that is, at times, unfair, although I am also learning it is really a fantastic adventure. She helps me with her *sorrisi* – "smiles" that remind me of those of my grandmother Rosina. It is to these significant women that this book is also dedicated.

Abbreviations

AEMN	European Alliance of National Movements
AN	Alleanza Nazionale
ARLP	Alliance Républicaine pour les Libertés et Progrès
DC	Democrazia Cristiana
DN	Destra Nazionale (see also MSI-DN)
EA	Europe-Action
EU	European Union
FANE	Fédération d'Action National et Européenne
FDJ	Front de la Jeunesse
FEN	Fédération des Étudiants Nationalistes
FLN	Front de Libération Nationale
FN	Front National
FUAN	Fronte Universitario d'Azione Nazionale
GRECE	Groupement de Recherche et d'Études pour la Civilisation Européenne
GUD	Groupe Union Droit/Groupe d'Union et de Défense
IND	Nuova Destra
JN	Jeune Nation
LN	Lega Nord
MNP	Mouvement Nationaliste du Progrès
MPF	Mouvement Populaire Français
MSE	Mouvement Social Européen
MSI	Movimento Sociale Italiano
MSI-DN	Movimento Sociale Italiano-Destra Nazionale
ND	Nouvelle Droite
NOE	Nouvel Ordre Européen
OAS	Organisation Armée Secrète
ON	Ordine Nuovo
PCF	Parti Communiste Français
PCI	Partito Comunista Italiano

PDL	Popolo della Libertà
PFN	Parti des Forces Nouvelles
PSI	Partito Socialista Italiano
REL	Rassemblement Européen de la Liberté
RSI	Repubblica Sociale Italiana
UDCA	Union de Défense des Commerçants et Artisans
UNIR	Union des Nationaux Indépendants et Républicains
UQ	Uomo Qualunque

Introduction

On the Extreme Right and Transnational History

Even though he was referring to the study of interwar right-wing extremism, Robert Paxton, in his famous *The Five Stages of Fascism*, had highlighted the importance of a non–nation-centered framework for analysis:

> Comparison works revealingly with fascisms, since every Western society has contained at least some marginal example. Their different fates across time and space in neighboring settings should help us to identify the principal factors in the varying success of specific cases, and even to isolate the constants.[1]

However, even the term "comparison" does not fully account for the scope of my book, including the convergence between French and Italian extremists in political attitudes and strategies and tracing the dynamics of what I perceive to be a genuine transnational actor. In essence, I also assume the existence of a common historical ground between the extreme right in these two neighboring countries – two nations that, as highlighted previously, shared a long and fruitful history of exchanges. The political and cultural phenomenon of right-wing extremism is hence taken and analyzed as a whole, focusing on patterns of commonality and ideological transfer. In such a perspective, the following pages do not focus simply on the history of the French and Italian neofascisms per se, but on what unifies them – in other words, on their transnational history.[2]

[1] Robert Paxton, "The Five Stages of Fascism," *Journal of Modern History*, 70(1), 1998, p. 10.

[2] For nation-based studies in the English language, see instead, for France, the informative work by James G. Shields, *The Extreme Right in France: From Pétain to Le Pen* (London: Routledge, 2007).

The natural outcome of this approach is, first, a rejection of the use of any narrow national label to classify parties and party-families. As we shall see, an example of this issue is the belief that a party like the FN is stemming from a local, French-based, national-populist tradition. To be fair, this is not a very uncommon reading of histories of the various forms of nationalisms. The historiography of nationalism

> still remains for the most part embedded within the overwhelming predominance of national (or regional) case-studies, while being increasingly well anchored in a theoretical perspective and often inspired by an (implicitly or explicitly) comparative perspective. The problem is not only that the nation(-state) continues to encapsulate most research on nationalism and the nation. National inferences also tend to impregnate research monographs with a comparative perspective.[3]

All this is here even aggravated, because the classic ultra-rightist doctrine has been often perceived to be indissolubly related with the concepts of nation and race. Parties and political cultures belonging to the right of the mainstream right might be consequently better analyzed only in given national contexts, as they are tied with some deep virtues of the fatherland and should be mainly seen as genuine products of single nation-states. Hence, these prominent features led some scholars to consider the extreme right as an exclusive national tradition, and profoundly different from similar foreign movements, regimes, and doctrines.[4]

For fascism in France and Italy, this has been evident in relation to the academic schools associated with famous historians such as René Rémond and Renzo De Felice. These scholars promoted an image of the extreme right linked with a domestic historical pathway and were followed in such efforts by a good number of historians. In 1954, Rémond published his famed *La Droite en France de 1815 à nos jours* (The French Right in France since 1815 to the Present), where he developed the well-known theory of *les trois droites* (basically, the three

[3] Xosé-Manoel Núñez, "Nations and Territorial Identities in Europe: Transnational Reflections," *European History Quarterly*, 40(4), 2010, pp. 675–76.

[4] Setting aside the recent Finchelstein, *Transatlantic Fascism*, for the interwar years, one of the exceptions to this trend is probably represented – at least partially – by Alexander De Grand's book on Germany and Italy, where he also tried to demonstrate the copious similarities between fascism and National Socialism. For the contemporary era, Jeffrey Kaplan and Leonard Weinberg have instead highlighted the common identity of a Euro-American radical right. See Alexander J. De Grand, *Fascist Italy and Nazi Germany: The 'Fascist' Style of Rule* (New York: Routledge, 1996); and Jeffrey Kaplan and Leonard Weinberg, *The Emergence of a Euro-American Radical Right* (New Brunswick, NJ: Rutgers University Press, 1998).

right-wing variants). To summarize, according to this approach, historically, France had not experienced a unique right-leaning momentum but three different rightist permutations: *légitimiste*, *orléaniste*, and *bonapartiste*. In such a classification there was space neither for fascism nor for the influence of non-French paradigms.[5] On the other hand, De Felice produced a monumental range of scholarly material, which was translated into different languages and included many volumes on Benito Mussolini. Just like Rémond, his approach tended to depict fascism as a purely local phenomenon, which could be understood only within a certain geographical context and alongside the role of Mussolini. All this, in De Felice's estimation, made, for instance, any comparison with Hitler's Nazism untenable.[6]

However, all this failed to acknowledge any fascist connections and exchanges across the whole of Western Europe and not merely the links between Germany and Italy. This similarly looks a bit paradoxical: trans-, supra-, and pan-national are, in fact, not obscure concepts in fascist history, nor, as I shall show, were they uncommon in the post-1945 period. They were certainly favored by the inner "universalist" tendencies of some fascist currents. This originally developed in interwar Italy (and in France with intellectuals such as Robert Brasillach) and gathered around the periodical *Antieuropa*; however, even the mainstream fascist journals *Critica Fascista* and *Gerarchia* contributed to a *fascismo universale* (universal fascism).[7] People such as Eugenio Coselschi, Alvero Gravelli, Herman De Vries de Heekelingen, and James Strachey Barnes

[5] For a challenge to this approach, and among the various contributions on French fascism, see Brian Jenkins, ed., *France in the Era of Fascism: Essays on the French Authoritarian Right* (Oxford: Berghahn Books, 2005); Michel Dobry, ed., *Le mythe de l'allergie française au fascisme* (Paris: Albin Michel, 2003); Robert Soucy, *French Fascism: The Second Wave, 1933–1939* (New Haven, CT: Yale University Press, 1995); Robert Soucy, *French Fascism: The First Wave 1924–33* (New Haven, CT: Yale University Press, 1986); and Robert Soucy, *Fascism in France: The Case of Maurice Barrès* (Berkeley: University of California Press, 1972).

[6] Some recent research in this field is instead suggesting the use of a more flexible approach for the study of Fascist Italy and Nazi Germany. One should, in fact, look at the "fascist entanglement" between the two nations: This would not be simply a history of transfer, but also of interconnectedness and mutual influences. See Christian Goeschel, "*Italia docet?* The Relationship between Italian Fascism and Nazism Revisited," *European History Quarterly*, 42(3), 2012, pp. 480–92.

[7] For example, *Gerarchia*, in October 1932 (no. 10), devoted a special issue to "Fascismo Idea Universale" (Fascism: A Universal Idea) that hosted articles by foreign fascists, including British fascist Oswald Mosley, and a good number of other analyses of foreign permutations of the fascist idea.

and organizations such as the Fasci Italiani all'Estero (fasci abroad), the International Center of Fascist Studies (also simply known as CINEF), and the Comitati d'Azione per l'Universalità di Roma (Action Committees for the Universality of Rome, the CAUR) played a significant role.[8] This also led to visits and transfer and a fascist conference that in 1934 that gathered some of the future representatives of European fascism. According to historian Marco Cuzzi, "The originality of universalism and of its practical application, namely, fascist internationalism, was grounded in the perception of a corporatist, hierarchical, totalitarian, antidemocratic, and deeply racist Europe."[9] This corporative Europe, along with the German pan-Europeanism and its mythology, were also all to be reformulated in the postwar years.

In line with this, this introductory section will specifically attempt to advocate (again) the importance of more rounded historical and cross-national analyses for the study of political phenomena, introduce readers to some of the relevant scholarship in this field, and, starting from the following section, discuss the use of some approaches, histories, and labels to classify and grasp the nature of extreme-right movements.

A CASE OF NATIONAL POPULISM?

Some of the interpretations of interwar history had an impact on the scholarship, the academic classifications, and the understanding of modern right-wing extremism (and probably influenced the public opinion and some of the media). One should wonder if this is, essentially, also a sort of *ars oblivionalis* (art of forgetfulness). There is, in fact, at times, a small and direct link between memorial and intellectual interpretations of the past and legitimization of the present and of contemporary ideologies and political movements.[10] In some intellectual circles in France, this

8 One of the few sources in English on fascist universalism is Michael A. Ledeen, *Universal Fascism: The Theory and Practice of the Fascist International* (New York: Howard Fertig, 1972). In Italian see Marco Cuzzi, *L'Internazionale delle Camicie nere. I CAUR, Comitati d'azione per l'universalità di Roma 1933–1939* (Milan: Mursia, 2005), and Marco Cuzzi, *Antieuropa. Il fascismo universale di Mussolini* (Milan: M & B Publishing, 2007). On the fasci abroad see Luca De Caprariis, "'Fascism for Export'? The Rise and Eclipse of the Fasci Italiani all'Estero," *Journal of Contemporary History*, 35(2), 2000, pp. 151–83.

9 Cuzzi, *Antieuropa*, p. 8.

10 On this relationship see also John Coakley, "Mobilizing the Past: Nationalist Images of History," *Nationalism and Ethnic Politics*, 10(4), 2004, pp. 531–60, and Andrea Mammone, "A Daily Revision of the Past: Fascism, Anti-Fascism, and Memory in Contemporary Italy," *Modern Italy*, 11(2), 2006, pp. 211–26. This is not an isolated

contributed to the adoption of the category of the *national populisme* (national populism) to classify parties such as the FN.[11] In some cases, even the label "extreme right" disappeared because it was regarded as vague for modern movements.[12] In other cases, the FN was considered in the context of other French populisms (the *populismes à la française*) such as *boulangisme* and *racisme fin-de-siècle*.[13] The common denominator of these works was the (intended or unintended) building of a scholarship that insisted on the exceptionality of the FN.

Paradoxically enough, a party such as the FN came to be analyzed in the terms provided by its own leader, Jean-Marie Le Pen, as a "popular, social, and national right,"[14] a definition that in some academic circles was perceived as the most accurate because Le Pen's movement would be a typical case of national populism.[15] According to this view, ideologically, this latter would endorse the contemporaneous presence of a protest dimension and, more notably, of a nationalist one

case. By way of example, the debates "about the Nazi past have created very different environments for right-wing political parties and movements in Germany and Austria." In particular, the culture of victimization in Austria have provided a very fertile ground for the resurgence and recent success of the indigenous extreme right: see David Art, *The Politics of the Nazi Past in Germany and Austria* (New York: Cambridge University Press, 2006), p. x.

11 See, among others, Pierre-André Taguieff, "La rhétorique du national-populisme (I)," *Cahiers Bernard Lazare*, 109, 1984, pp. 19–38; Pierre-André Taguieff, "La rhétorique du national-populisme (II)," *Mots*, 9, 1984, pp. 113–39; Pierre-André Taguieff, "La doctrine du national-populisme en France," *Études*, 364, 1986, pp. 27–46.

12 See Pierre-André Taguieff, "Un programme révolutionnaire?" in N. Mayer and P. Perrineau, eds., *Le Front National à découvert* (Paris: Presses de Sciences Po, 1996), p. 196; and Michel Winock, *Nationalisme, antisémitisme et fascisme en France* (Paris: Seuil, 2004), p. 39.

13 See, among many others, Michel Winock, "Populismes Français," *Vingtième "Siècle*, 56, 1997, pp. 77–91. For a critique of this approach see Annie Collovald, *Le "Populisme du FN." Un dangereux contresens* (Broissieux: Éditions du Croquant," 2004); Annie Collovald, "Le 'national-populisme' ou le fascisme disparu," in M. Dobry, ed., *Le mythe de l'allergie française au fascisme* (Paris: Albin Michel, 2003); and, in general, Andrea Mammone, "The Eternal Return? Faux Populism and Contemporarization of Neo-Fascism across Britain, France and Italy," *Journal of Contemporary European Studies*, 17(2), 2009, pp. 171–92.

14 From a transnational standpoint, this statement became a very popular slogan for other parties. Benito Mussolini's granddaughter, Alessandra, a contemporary politician to be mentioned later in the book, said that "we are the new popular, social and national right." Alessandra Mussolini, "Elezioni politiche. Alternativa Sociale ci sarà," *Azione*, February 10, 2006, p. 1.

15 Winock, *Nationalisme*, p. 39.

(*demos plus ethnos*).[16] It is precisely this element referring to the nation, national citizens, and identity that would allow some scholars to classify the FN, and other fellow parties, as national-populist, and France would represent the ideal-type of this party family. In this perspective, the FN should be analyzed as a mixture of Bonapartism or national-popular Caesarism (for example, Peron), reactionary-xenophobic populism (belonging to Enoch Powell among others), and the "populism of politicians." All this also led to the identification of five major (alleged) features characterizing Le Pen's national-populism: (1) the political appeal to the people, (2) the appeal to the whole population (in theory with no class distinction), (3) the direct call to the "authentic" and "honest" people, (4) the call for a purifying "change" (represented by the savior, namely, the party leader), and (5) ethnic discrimination.[17]

Yet these distinctive characteristics of national populism are not a peculiarity of French history. On the contrary, they are shared by much of the extreme-right party family. It is therefore debatable whether one should choose the FN as the perfect type. Moreover, even fascism encompassed many (if not all) of the previous traits. In a similar vein, "national populism" is not even a novel academic concept. In the late 1970s, sociologist Gino Germani, for example, had distinguished different Latin American populisms, the liberal and the national, and this latter "occurred mostly after 1930 in the epoch of mass-mobilization."[18]

In reality, in France, national populism allows the extreme right to appear reasonably different from the controversial Vichy regime and Charles Maurras's Action Française.[19] This national historical interpretation considers the FN mostly as the heir to anti-Dreyfus nationalism, Boulangism, and/or Poujadism (some of which are also retrospectively labeled like national populist). The overriding impression is that the use of this term to describe the extreme right is, first of all, related to the belief that democracy is deeply and irreversibly rooted in postwar France (and Europe) and that the resurgence of fascism is henceforth impossible.[20] Moreover, if France was pure and immune during the turbulent interwar years, "immunity" as such was taken for granted in the post-fascist era. In this way, classifications provide a sort of political

[16] Pierre-André Taguieff, *L'illusione populista. Dall'arcaico al mediatico* (Milan: Mondadori, 2003), p. 136.

[17] Ibid., pp. 141–52.

[18] Gino Germani, *Authoritarianism, Fascism, and National Populism* (New Brunswick, NJ: Transaction Books, 1978), p. 96.

[19] Collovald, *Le Populisme du FN*, p. 35.

[20] Ibid., p. 58.

and democratic legitimization of right-wing extremism.[21] In summary, by playing down the importance and presence of a French fascism and by failing to consider fascism as a wider European and transnational phenomenon, the terms populism and national populism replace fascism/neofascism as the used terminology.

This alleged populism generally became – also in many international studies – the synthesis, the recent label for the extreme right. Remarkably enough, but not surprisingly, it is usually well accepted by the parties it wishes to describe (because it is "une injurie polie," to use Annie Collovald's words). However, as I mentioned previously, populism does not represent a latecomer in the history of political phenomena, and it is not a new historical concept. It is recognized to have deep roots in the "various agrarian movements that arose throughout North America, Russia, and parts of Western Europe in the late nineteenth century. Indeed, American journalists coined the term 'populism' in 1896 to describe the People's party that contested the American election that year."[22] Populist movements also had a great importance in Latin America, where they adopted a more urban nature. This was due to the fact that local populism "was a reaction against the authoritarian nature of the late nineteenth century metropolitan revolution."[23]

The main threat of some of these intellectual abstractions is, paradoxically again, an over-simplification of party philosophy. Populism passes over the authentic strategies adopted by the FN (not to mention all the small parties in Italy that still look at the "positive features" of Mussolini's regime). It does not similarly offer a comprehensive observation of the extreme right as realpolitik. Many of the contemporary populist themes are not also really novel. For example, it is argued that the recent (extreme/

[21] Collovald, "Le national-populisme," pp. 279–80. As suggested, this might in fact lead (1) to the bypassing of the (uncomfortable) burden of the (fascist) past and (2) to different perceptions of some parties which thereby seem less dangerous in people's eyes. In this sense, "national populism" erases from public memory the discredit that comes from being labeled or perceived as fascist or even belonging to the extreme right. Moreover, the national populist category really became a rather "polite insult," although one which then serves to make the extremist ideology even more respectable or acceptable into the political system (and, I wonder, if possibly gives it the opportunity to be placed in a more moderate and genuinely French rightist tradition). See Collovald, *Le Populisme du FN*, p. 53.

[22] Trevor Harrison, T. *Of Passionate Intensity: Right-Wing Populism and the Reform Party of Canada* (Toronto: University of Toronto Press, 1995), p. 6.

[23] Michael L. Conniff, "Introduction: Toward a Comparative Definition of Populism," in M. L. Conniff, ed., *Latin American Populism in Comparative Perspective* (Albuquerque: University of New Mexico Press, 1982), p. 13.

radical right) populism supports moralization against the allegedly corrupted and inefficient political system. This is not an innovative discourse: According to historian Paul Corner, from the start, the same Italian fascism "proclaimed its aim of ... moralising Italian politics. During the regime the cult of the ethical state was the most obvious and continuing expression of this ambition."[24] In the postwar years, the moralization of politics quickly became a tool of the neofascist MSI against mainstream parties. Among the many examples, this was succinctly exposed by a propagandist electoral banner that was published by the party newspaper on July 7, 1983: "A new republic: a promise of renewal, sociality, moralization."

In such a context, national populism was acceptable as only one of the FN's features, not as the prominent or the overarching trait. Moreover, populism may convincingly be simply regarded as a form of political argumentation (and/or action), with parties adopting a very simple and direct communication style. It cannot be considered as a proper ideology; neither can it be particularly applied to all the postwar and recent extreme right nor to the movements, activists, and thinkers described here, as it is an episodic phenomenon, often stemming from the crisis of representative politics and political legitimization, and excessively variegated and eclectic for the purposes of my book.

Some scholars have, in fact, rightly introduced the image of a populism lacking universal key beliefs.[25] This is "invariably remedied with values of other ideologies."[26] We cannot, consequently, stretch this container concept too far. There is a considerable lack of homogeneity in the so-called political group characterized by populist attitudes.[27] It would, in fact, be very complicated to include the FN, the MSI, Silvio Berlusconi, or even leaders such as Tony Blair and George W. Bush, Margaret

[24] Paul Corner, "Everyday Fascism in the 1930s: Centre and Periphery in the Decline of Mussolini's Dictatorship," *Contemporary European History*, 15(2), 2006, pp. 195–96.

[25] Paul Taggart, *Populism* (Buckingham: Open University Press, 2000), pp. 3–4.

[26] Ibid., 2000, p. 115.

[27] Christopher Husbands highlights the fact that "it is not merely that the populist attribution gives to these movements a homogeneity that they do not have but rather it may give them the wrong sort of homogeneity. If some of these movements really are defined ideologically in terms of neoliberalism or libertarianism and others in terms of xenophobia and racism, then it should be recognized that they are different types." Christopher. T. Husbands "How to Tame the Dragon, or What Goes Around Comes Around: A Critical Review of Some Major Contemporary Attempts to Account for Extreme-Right Racist Politics in Western Europe," in M. Schain et al., eds., *Shadows over Europe: The Development and Impact of the Extreme Right in Western Europe* (New York: Palgrave Macmillan 2002), p. 51.

Thatcher, and José Bové, and then Pierre Poujade, Vladimir Zhirinovsky, Ronald Reagan, Pat Buchanan, and Boris Yeltsin, in the same distinctive populist galaxy. Where is the full rationale behind this?

CONTINUITY AND TERMINOLOGY

This "exceptionality" is, however, not confined to the studies on this nebulous national populism. Other, less narrow and nationally focused analyses have excluded the possibility of comparing two of the political movements described here, the FN with the MSI.[28] The main divergences are apparently found in three domains: (1) the different history of parties, (2) their relationship with the political system, and (3) their ideological patterns and cultural references. I will deal shortly with some of these points, but according to these studies, it would be exactly this last point that is most crucial "since the MSI is largely inspired by the fascist tradition and the FN is not."[29] Le Pen's party would be allegedly "more concerned with present day political issues than with a glorious fascist past, which it repudiates even in its French version (Ligues of the 1930s, the Vichy regime)."[30] If, at the beginning of the 1990s, the MSI certainly seemed to be rather different from the FN, this approach ignores the real evolution of the parties, their previous links, the different national socio-political contexts of the 1980s (which allowed the rise of the FN and which are discussed in Chapter 6), the genuine ideological references of the FN, its historical revisionism and heritage, the importance on FN life of other genuinely fascist-like leaders and party officials, the background of some of its members, the foreign influences, and, possibly, the relevance of the mythology of Vichy to that party.

As suggested in the Preface, *Transantional Neofascism* is generally different from many works on the contemporary extreme right in another way too. It also assumes a pattern of "continuity" within the history of right-wing extremism in some European countries. This distances my approach from other existing academic (and disciplinary) tendencies.[31]

[28] Piero Ignazi and Colette Ysmal, "New and Old Extreme Right Parties: The French Front National and the Italian Movimento Sociale," *European Journal of Political Research*, 2 (1), 1992, pp. 101–21. This study is based on an analysis of survey data from middle-level party elites collected at the 1990 FN and MSI national conferences.

[29] Ibid., p. 101. [30] Ibid., p. 110.

[31] In general, classic fascism and the recent extreme right became two very distinct fields of analysis, and "students of contemporary manifestations of right-wing extremism have 'pushed on the accelerator' to escape earlier debates centred on, for example, the fascist

Although it is true that the book essentially devotes only some of its pages to the very recent extreme right, and basically none to "classic" interwar fascism, I still insist on these patterns of historical continuity and on the importance of a long-term historical analysis for a better understanding of recent political processes.[32] This is not really common, as the overall belief is that a new form of extremism, different from its ancestors, developed in recent times. This fundamentally contributed to the ahistorical reading that the extreme-right saga started only in the final stages of the past century when everything seemed a novel story and an unexpected event (and I shall mention how this caused additional problems from a definitional standpoint). Paradoxically, many questions were – and still are in some cases – then left unanswered on the table: May these processes be observed in other times and places? Are modern movements really new? What about the biographies and beliefs of their founders, leaders, and activists? What do we really know about the history of these extreme-right parties and their precursors? How many studies have been based on primary sources and archival documents? What could we also learn from these rightist movements' interconnected histories? What about the extreme-rightist perceptions of interwar (fascist) movements, ideals, and cultures, and some early Cold War thinkers? Would our understanding of the extreme right improve if some analyses were also based on in-depth knowledge of national languages and cultures and political histories of parties, rather than focusing solely on large quantitative data and secondary sources?

In addition, as we have seen, some authors suggest that the ideological and structural differences between "new" radical/extreme right/populism and "old" neo-fascist parties are more important than the similarities. As in the case highlighted earlier, by following this logic, we should not even compare the MSI and the FN, because these parties respectively belonged

credentials of the *Front National* or *Vlaams Belang*." Matthew J. Goodwin, "Grandpa's Fascism and the New Kids on the Block: Contemporary Approaches to the Dark Side of Europe," *Ethnopolitics*, 6(1), 2007, p. 146. Moreover, as I also mentioned, historians have hardly focused on the postwar right-wing extremism.

32 This is what I named the "historical line" that unifies old extremism with its recent permutations ("C'è una linea storica che unisce la destra di oggi e quella di ieri. Si è cercato il nuovo nemico in Islam e immigrazione, adattandosi a un mondo diverso. Caratteristiche principali sono l'odio verso il diverso, il "noi contro loro," la purezza, le tradizioni, la religione, il favorire il cittadino indigeno"). See Andrea Mammone interviewed in Stefano Giantin, "L'Europa ha trascurato la rete estremista interna," *Il Piccolo*, July 27, 2011, p. 7.

to two different types of right-wing extremist movements: the old extreme right and the new one. In this sense, I agree with historian Nigel Copsey and his recent suggestion that the history of this alleged novel party family is, in reality, tied with the history of neofascism (and the use of concepts such as radical right-wing populism shows a "lack of concern for the historical development, traditions, and political cultures" of the postwar extreme right).[33]

Another problem is that some of these classifications and their different criteria (like the fascist legacy, the approach toward the political system, and so on) look at the phenomenon as a fixed entity. They never consider right-wing extremism as a long-term (historical) process, nor do they recognize the pragmatic nature of some movements and leaders. Anna Cento Bull accurately suggests that these old versus new distinctions are sometimes misleading:

> The problem with these taxonomies is that they tend to capture the nature of these parties at a particular moment but do not take into account their development, as they can be highly opportunistic and freely change their policies. ... In short, identifying the ideological core of a party is one thing, accounting for its dynamic trajectory is another, distinguishing between its leadership and rank and file is a third.[34]

Categorizations should then take a certain degree of flexibility and be more fluid. Fascism did not disappear under the ruins of the war and, implicitly, we might even suggest that a different historical periodization might be necessary when empirically discussing the fascist phenomena. When looking at the actual genesis and the outlook of French and Italian movements since the end of the Second World War, they were very often ideologically backward-looking and mostly nostalgic for an old world. In many ways, after 1945, they also represented the rightist answer to the new democratic order. In this sense, these movements were logically neofascist, and they felt like this for an interminable number of years. By borrowing the words of one of the most famous French extreme right-wing intellectuals, Maurice Bardèche (in his own words, "a fascist writer"), the neofascists were so because they

[33] Nigel Copsey, "'Fascism ... but with an open mind.' Reflections on the Contemporary Far Right in (Western) Europe. First Lecture on Fascism – Amsterdam – 25 April 2013," *Fascism. Journal of Comparative Fascist Studies*, 2(1), 2013, p. 12.

[34] Anna Cento Bull, "Neofascism," in R. Bosworth, ed., *The Oxford Handbook of Fascism* (Oxford: Oxford University Press, 2009), p. 602.

first express the refusal of the order that was established in 1945. This refusal is not only to individuals, but to the principles that triumphed the democratic hypocrisy, the lies brought by the mainstream propaganda, the impotent regimes generated by the unnatural coalition between capitalism and Marxism. Although we hope that this refusal will be harder and more importantly, more doctrinally motivated, it is sufficient now that it exists, that it is radical and uncompromising: that is to say that it does not dispute only the new master, but their inspirations and spirit.[35]

As a consequence of all this, and as readers will have already noticed, I use "neofascism" and "extreme right" as overlapping terms.[36] Neofascism seems to me an appropriate terminology in reference to this Franco-Italian political and cultural phenomenon, while extreme right may be considered as an overall all-inclusive term, a kind of container to include the whole political family at the right of the right.[37] Nevertheless, the word "neofascism" more fully describes the background, nature, and ideological references of the bulk of the groups narrated in the following pages. It will therefore not merely be used in reference to movements ideologically tied to Mussolini's fascism, as is the case of the MSI, but also for France, where, as suggested earlier in this Introduction, most academic circles do not even accept the existence of a French fascism due to a myth of national *allergie* to this phenomenon.

This "continuity" and (neo-)fascist label should by no means be surprising. It is highly possible that some fragments of interwar fascism

[35] Maurice Bardèche, *Qu'est-ce que le fascisme?* (Paris: Les Sept Couleurs, 1961), pp. 96–97.

[36] This is at least the case in the context of this monograph. I have, nonetheless, discussed the similar neofascist connotations of the British National Party. See Andrea Mammone, "Il British National Party e l'ideologia neofascista nell'Europa contemporanea," *Studi Storici*, 52(2), 2011, pp. 393–421; but also Andrea Mammone and Timothy Peace, "Cross-national Ideology in Local Elections: The Case of Azione Sociale and the British National Party," in A. Mammone et al., eds., *Mapping the Extreme Right in Contemporary Europe: From Local to Transnational* (New York: Routledge, 2012), pp. 288–302; and Mammone, "The Eternal Return?" This approach inevitably leads me to disagree with a scholar such as James A. Gregor. In his *The Search for Neofascism*, Gregor also considers that there is little space for neofascist right-wing extremism in contemporary Europe: in his view, fascism basically disappeared after 1945. By way of conclusion, he notes that modern parties such as the Front National, and theorists such as Julius Evola (a character to whom readers will encounter in the book), cannot be labeled as neofascists. See James A. Gregor, *The Search for Neofascism: The Use and Abuse of Social Science* (Cambridge: Cambridge University Press, 2006).

[37] To be fair, at the end of the 1980s, Klaus von Beyme had already suggested how "the term right-wing extremism has certain virtues," while radical right had an extensive use in America "and was introduced into other languages through social psychology. The polemical German word *Radikalenerlass* was coined in this tradition." Klaus von Beyme, "Right-wing Extremism in Post-war Europe," in K. von Beyme, ed., *Right-wing Extremism in Western Europe* (London: Frank Cass, 1988), p. 2.

survived after the war and continue to exist in modern society (and I will come back to this). We cannot overlook the fact that some fascist office holders were politically active after the war, and in some European areas extreme-right parties were being organizationally built on significant prewar foundations.[38] These people and organizations worked as a doctrinal and socialization transmission belt across Europe – and surely in France and Italy. However, if someone thinks that modern fascism means exact carbon copies of the interwar blackshirt militias, then one is probably looking in the wrong direction. Precise clones and bio-robotic replicants exist in fiction novels. European neofascism simply reflects the contradictions of its old ancestor, from its pragmatism to the continuous adaptations, and from the revolutionary soul to the more moderate ruling political aspirations.[39] If, in the immediate postwar era, extremist movements were clearly in line with their predecessors, over the years they often tried to adapt to the different sociopolitical contexts. The very latest materializations of the phenomenon could consequently come to represent a sort of evolution and "contemporarization" of what may be called (only in chronological terms) a more traditional extreme right.[40]

CONCEPTUALIZATION AND FASCISM

The previous section also highlighted some of (our) inner propensity in trying to capture the essence of political doctrines and movements. I realize that these are some really troubled waters, and, despite some

[38] David Art similarly highlights how "political parties, voluntary associations, and informal social networks that were originally dominated by collaborators or former fascists after the Second World War persisted in these cases. These organizations possessed some degree of legitimacy in politics and society, and even after the war were not treated as pariahs. These groups adopted other issues in order to recruit new members from a nationalist subculture, thereby adapting to changing conditions in the 1960s and 1970s while retaining their links to the past. This describes the legacy of far right activity in Austria, Flanders, and Italy." In France also, Art continues, "One could discern a nationalist subculture that, while certainly on the defensive in the immediate postwar decades, was large enough to provide resources for the radical right when the time came." Art, *Inside the Radical Right*, p. 40.

[39] On this point see also Bardèche, *Qu'est-ce que le fascisme?* p. 101; but also, on the academic side, Pierre Milza, *Fascisme français. Passé et présent* (Paris: Flammarion, 1987), p. 423.

[40] It seems to me that publications insisting on the populist nature of contemporary parties, and/or on their "newness," do not consider that fascism could have been forced to modernize itself to match the postwar social needs. Other political ideologies have been forced to adapt in politics and society. On this see also Roger Eatwell, "The Rebirth of the 'Extreme Right' in Western Europe," *Parliamentary Affairs*, 53(3), 2000, p. 412.

possible criticism, a further classification is not central to the aims of my book. It is, in fact, not my intention to deal extensively with general discussions on definitions and on the ideological core of all European movements – a debate that has often proved unproductive.[41] Similar, and even more challenging (as full of academic controversies), problems arise for the extreme right's natural ancestor, namely, interwar fascism. I also share some of the concerns related to the conceptual discussion on nationalism, where it is essential

> not to further complicate "vulnerable" concepts, since the existing literature is not just confusing but also convoluted. Both the classification of "types" . . . and a generally recognized consensual definition of the concepts continue to be deeply controversial – no matter how fast the literature grows.[42]

In such a context, I will resist the temptation to strictly define "extremism" and to suggest readers rigorously follow and adapt to my definitional roadmap.

This is also due to the (long) time span that the book covers. Definitions and categorizations would struggle to follow the adaptation or developments in different historical contexts and across decades. Could we take a 100-meter-long picture, from the starter to the finish line, of an athlete running the 100-meter dash? Photos will take little fragments; and in the case of contemporary debates, they would look at the arrival of the athlete (the extreme right today). Static definitions, in fact, often miss the whole picture and, above all, the key book objectives, notably, the transmigration of ideals, people, and actions.

On the other hand, a very concise conceptualization may be useful for some readers, or it may help to identify some of the tangible activists, movements, and ideals that are the object of the historical investigation. If, for example, one looks at fascism, it is clear that it experienced various national permutations and developments, due to the dissimilar local contexts, and the eventual strength of traditional politics and existing

[41] It is by no means my intention to construct an overall categorization. This would be a very complex job that needs a realist higher degree of elasticity. Even recent and large studies, including Art's book, often use broad definitions, which intrinsically offer the chance to include different movements within the same party family. If we look at the spectrum of the contemporary European extreme right, there are many cross-national shared features, but also some variations. Art, for example, recalls their ideological flexibility "while these parties retain their nativist core, they are flexible when it comes to a host of other issues." Art, *Inside the Radical Right*, p. 38 (and p. 12).

[42] Ali Kemal Özcan, "Nationalism: Distilling the *Cultural* and the *Political*," *Nationalism and Ethnic Politics*, 11(2), 2005, p. 163.

parties. According to some influential historical research, there are, furthermore, some differences among the domestic permutations of the fascist phenomenon both in space and in time – in space because fascism was legitimized "not from some universal scripture but from what it considers the most authentic elements of its own community identity," in time "because of the transformations and accommodations demanded of those movements that seek power."[43] I am certainly not arguing that a basic form of fascism never existed. Transnationally, what is interesting to highlight here, and is relevant for the purposes of my book, is that a genuine "fascist wind" blew across interwar European state borders (and probably also outside them). To borrow Finchelstein's transcontinental framing, fascism was a genuine global-transnational doctrine with diverse reformulations, ramifications, and permutations.[44] A web of exchanges, transfers, and adaptations then made this fascist galaxy.

This fascist wind combined a sense of moral and national decadence, nationalism (but also the described "universalism"), the belief in the superiority of a given and pure community/people against all inassimilable "others," a desire for rebirth or regeneration, coupled with a cult of violence, authoritarianism, charismatic leadership, the rejection of parliamentary politics and democratic rules, and – whenever and wherever possible – imperialism. These mobilizing passions, to borrow again Paxton's terms, "are mostly taken for granted and not always overtly argued as intellectual propositions, [and] form the emotional lava that set fascism's foundations."[45] The majority of these traits can be observed, at least in principle or in an incubated form, in a good number of the successful and unsuccessful manifestations of the phenomenon.

Some of these passions or "emotional lava" that framed and shaped the history of interwar fascisms have strongly influenced the discourse of the French and Italian extreme right since 1945 and were (or are) at the heart of its political philosophy. In other words, some of the reformulations and ramifications (in Finchelstein's sense) of the global-transnational fascist doctrine, at least in my case studies, were reproposed – and this

[43] As Paxton pertinently noted, such definitions "frame a static picture of something that is better perceived in movement. … The quest for the perfect definition, by reducing fascism to one ever more finely honed phrase, seems to shut off questions about the origins and course of fascist development rather than open them up. It is like observing … birds mounted in a glass case instead of alive in their habitat." Paxton, "The Five Stages," pp. 3–4.

[44] Finchelstein, *Transatlantic Fascism*, p. 13.

[45] Robert Paxton, *The Anatomy of Fascism* (New York: Vintage, 2005), p. 41.

process was also favored by the mentioned "transmission" of the old extremist personnel in the postwar period. To a certain extent, we can, in fact, observe a sort of adaptation of fascism to the different postwar contexts; this is also another example of what I theorized like the contemporarization of the extreme right. In particular, some fascist themes and strategies were borrowed, or adapted over the years, to what became a very different political and social environment. In some cases, some hardline fascist stances were watered down, and this happened, for example, for some electoral purposes in the 1970s and especially in the 1980s, or were dressed in a pan-national internationalist format (such as in the 1950s with the neofascist international associations) or in other more sophisticated intellectual garbs (like the case of the ND). Ironically, other mobilizing themes were brought to the center of the debate and, henceforth, became more democratically legitimized by some mainstream parties and media (see the debates on ethnicity and about national identity). In other words, neofascism, while maintaining some key characteristics, sometimes tried to change shape. It made adjustments in order to exploit favorable conditions when it was, for example, aiming to gain power or attract voters (like in the early 1970s in Italy and 1980s onwards in France), or when it was in difficulties and attempted to tackle negative conjunctures.

MORE ON ADAPTATION AND CONTEMPORARIZATION

Some ideals and practices of the immediate postwar and modern right-wing extremists therefore belong to a cosmology harking back to the blackshirt years. Ideologically and, again, transnationally, the authentic *neofascist wind* blowing across French and Italian national borders (and often beyond them) is a philosophy and movement that, not unlike fascism, combines a sense of crisis and national decline, a fascination with a glorious past, a (often implicit or covert) process of historical revisionism (mythologizing, rationalization, and justification of Mussolini, Vichy, etc.), a critique of the parliamentary process or, to use Bardèche's words, a suspicion of the "democratic hypocrisy," the need of a strong state, a demand for a stricter "law and order" system, a belief in the (usually white-only) European (also cultural) superiority along with the almost full rejection of an almost inassimilable "other" (which can be the immigrant, but also political opponents such as leftists), a nationalism combined, when possible, with a transnational and international brotherhood that often comes from the existing webs and years of exchanges, the defense of the values of tradition, a justification of violence (this is less evident for the main parties, and it is often implicit or covert, and, sometimes, only verbal or, as in the case of some contemporary groups in some regions of Europe, in the form of vigilante squads against immigrants), and possibly charismatic leadership. Many of these ideological and mobilizing features can be observed with different degrees, and in principle or overtly stated, in most of the movements and people covered in the following pages.

This introductory section is obviously not the place to discuss "ideology" in depth. However, even though the book does not tackle the history of political thought per se, and despite my aversion to constructing catchall categories (which should strictly describe or fit in roughly seventy years of history), it does aim to discuss in slightly more detail some of the earlier mentioned key tools. For example, some important aspects to be considered are the traditional and mystical sides of political ideals. They are often popularized and became fundamental in the establishment of extreme-right collective and individual memories. These memories and beliefs are very often turned backward in the direction of a number of nostalgic and romantic aspects relating to tradition, the greatness of the nation, and/or the unforgettable past. This refers to a supposed golden age that, for French and Italian extremists, includes, as we know, the Duce, the Vichy regime, the interwar leagues, and the RSI. This latter and the "purity" of its ideals have been, for example, an attractive reference point for modern activists and, as readers will notice, also in postwar France. In such a context, revisionism naturally plays a main part in the extreme-right worldview. This was quite expected immediately after the war, and in the Cold War years, but also today we hardly find politicians rejecting their "fathers." Some ideological revisions may occur, for example, in the case of a pan-nationalism, or in electoral strategies, but this does not necessarily mean a revision or a fully critical assessment of the fascist interwar era. Anti-Semitism and negationist attitudes are, in such a context, far from extinct within the discourse of contemporary parties. Positive declarations such as Jean-Marie Le Pen's about the German interwar occupation, the anti-Semitic attacks, and the climate that apparently allowed anti-Jewish racist speeches among FN sympathizers during Marine Le Pen's 2012 presidential campaign, not to mention the continuous exaltation of Il Duce by some politicians in Italy, are clear examples of this approach.[46]

[46] Pierre Birnbaum, "The French Radical Right: From anti-Semitic Zionism to Anti-Semitic Anti-Zionism," *Journal of Israeli History*, 25(1), 2006, pp. 161–74; Olivier Guland, *Le Pen, Mégret et le Juifs. L'obsession du "complot mondialiste"* (Paris: La Découverte,

In any case, in spite of some scholars who seem to have different opinions, both this nationalism and the importance of tradition are very old discourses and therefore cannot be considered as emblematic themes of a "new right." The preservation instinct of virtues of tradition in the extremist vision of the world counterbalanced the dissolution of modern life as well as the waves of modernization that are often considered as something destroying the past and its principles. It is only necessary to read Julius Evola, the MSI pamphlets, and some neofascist weeklies to observe certain disillusionment with the modern world, and the importance of the nation with its virtues – and many similar examples might be drawn for the French case.

All of this is frequently related to specific understandings of history and with a diffuse sense of crisis. Just as interwar fascism exploited suspicions toward a certain type of modernity, the fears of the middle classes that were threatened by the economic crisis, pressure from the rise of socialism, and the growth of capitalist modes of production, contemporary parties have played the card of a somewhat similar generalized perception of decline and threat. To escape from this predicament (and those of contemporary societies), modern neofascism often proposed a backward solution that is often the return (or related) to the past, law and order, and a chauvinism, which also means the defense of the purity of a national (or European) community that has been weakened by both internal (traditional political elites, left-wingers, immigrants), and foreign enemies (the European integration, the United States, Soviet Union and international communism, mass migrations). According to the anthropologist Douglas Holmes, this has also served to politicize a number of latent "integralist sensibilities" that were entrenched in European societies and that, in fact, had a distinctive genus in the intellectual history of the old continent (like in the tradition of the Counter-Enlightenment).[47]

2000); and Jennifer Lipman, "National Front Thugs Mount Anti-Jewish Attack in Paris," *Jewish Chronicle Online*, March 2, 2012, www.thejc.com/news/world-news/64469/national-front-thugs-mount-anti-jewish-attack-paris, accessed March 5, 2012.

[47] Douglas R. Holmes, *Integral Europe: Fast-Capitalism, Multiculturalism, Neofascism* (Princeton: Princeton University Press, 2000), p. 9. Indeed, traditional ultra-right thought predominantly developed in opposition to modernity, as represented by the Enlightenment and the values of French Revolution. This is what Isaiah Berlin termed the Counter-Enlightenment tradition and that was at the core of many of the national permutations of interwar fascism. Traits of this counter-cultural belief were the principles of "self-realization," "aggressive nationalism," rejection of the key Enlightenment ideals, and a "self-identification with … the race." Isaiah Berlin, *Against the Current: Essays in the History of Ideas* (London: Hogarth Press, 1979), pp. 18–19.

Among these integralist sensibilities, I should recall here that there is also the xenophobic discourse – in other words, the purity of one's own community – because readers will find it again in the book. This is based on the belief in the superiority of one's own ethnicity and/or domestic/white European civilization. This naturally leads to prejudice and an exclusionary politics with a tendency to reject all "others," and it transcends Italian and French boundaries. Even when it is, at times, masked with some "cultural-only" and ethno-pluralist connotations (see Chapter 5 on some of this), it is one of the features that transnationally unifies the contemporary extreme right across much of the western globe.[48] It may, nonetheless, cause problems in multicultural societies. Tensions rose, for example, in municipalities such as Toulon, Orange, and Marignane led by the FN in the 1990s, including on the role and place of immigrants in local communities, but also in the fields of culture and public security.[49] In some of these cities, the party had

> encouraged the police to adopt a more authoritarian approach towards immigration and vagrancy. . . . Moreover, it has used its power to disseminate the message that non-white, non-Christian and non-French/European residents are not welcome in the towns which the party controls.[50]

In some ways, this contemporary nationalism clearly resembles fascist xenophobia and its vision of society. Fascism similarly promoted the primacy of the group, but also a feeling of victimization among its members, the belief of a decline and, as Paxton writes, nations "under the corrosive effects ... of alien influences," along with the "need for closer integration of a purer community," and finally the "right of the

[48] Andrea Mammone et al., "Introduction: Mapping the 'Right of the Mainstream Right' in Contemporary Europe," in Mammone et al., eds., *Mapping the Extreme Right*, pp. 5–6. More generally, some recent analyses of successful extremist parties empirically demonstrate that it is precisely the anti-immigration stance that unites all of them. A study of seven parties for example, shows that, of these movements, no one performed well in elections around 2002 without mobilizing immigration as an issue. See Elisabeth Ivarsflaten, "What Unites Right-Wing Populists in Western Europe? Re-examining Grievance Mobilization Models in Seven Successful Cases," *Comparative Political Studies*, (41)1, 2008, pp. 3–23.

[49] See also Cyrille Guiat, (2007), "Le choix du beau et du vrai. La politique culturelle du FN/MNR à Vitrolles: entre néo-classicisme et invention de la tradition, 1997–2002, *e-France*, 1, 2007, pp. 44–68; and John Veugelers, "After Colonialism: Local Politics and Far-Right Affinities in a City of Southern France," in Mammone et al., eds., *Mapping the Extreme Right*, pp. 33–47.

[50] Paul Hainsworth and Paul Mitchell, "France: The Front National from Crossroads to Crossroads?" *Parliamentary Affairs*, 53(3), 2000, p. 450.

chosen people to dominate others."[51] In summary, the anti-egalitarian and authoritarian ideological core of some postwar movements had posed problems to the reborn democracies in the Cold War years and might represent a challenge in the contemporary era.[52] However, we should wonder, again, if, historically, this is a novel situation, or it is simply the repacking of some old extremist themes?

WRITING NEW HISTORIES OF EUROPE

In the sense highlighted earlier, it is clear that "history" matters, and it should be taken seriously. It illuminates the nature of modern political phenomena and assesses the novelty of their ideologies. A historical analysis can really provide a larger frame and place politics more firmly in a proper context. It is true that it has not been common to study postwar right-wing extremism from a historical standpoint (and, as outlined, the ground has been left to other disciplines, mostly focusing on the present years). However, even the most recent manifestations of the extreme right are, "above all," a historical phenomenon, and not a mere bolt from the blue. As I suggest here, they also constitute a genuine cross-national phenomenon, at least as highlighted for France and Italy. In order to achieve a more rounded analysis, it is then necessary to combine the historical dimension with the "transnational lenses of investigation." They allow us to break away from any form of parochialism that might characterize the single-country focus, without falling into the opposing trap of excessively general conceptual models (with inadequate empirical testing). Consequently, these new lenses give us the opportunity to observe, trace, describe, and eventually contextualize the new dimensions

[51] Paxton, *Anatomy of Fascism*, p. 41.

[52] This organicist vision of life, the imagined homogenous community and culture, the division of society into two distinct entities, notably "friends and enemies" or "us and them," may undermine some liberal concepts and the functioning of multi-ethnic communities. Elisabeth Carter summarizes this overall approach on democracy: "Right-wing extremism is defined by two anti-constitutional and anti-democratic elements: 1. a rejection of the fundamental values, procedures and institutions of the democratic constitutional state (a feature that makes right-wing extremism extremist); 2. a rejection of the principle of fundamental human equality (a feature that makes right-wing extremism right wing)." It is not compulsory that a movement should have all these elements to be labeled "extreme right," but Carter argues that the various features of the extreme right are often manifestations of one of the mentioned elements. Elisabeth Carter, *The Extreme Right in Western Europe: Success or Failure?* (Manchester: Manchester University Press, 2005), pp. 17 and 18.

of this phenomenon – ones that are French and Italian, and also genuinely European, full of commonalities, and characterized by exchanges and transfer. This is what creates transnational political webs, spaces, as well as ideologies.

This is also by no means the sole scholarly attempt to reshape and reframe geographical and cultural boundaries. Fortunately enough, the process of European integration, the Europeanization of national politics and societies, and the transnationalization of cultures have become relevant topics for scholars in the humanities and social sciences. The development of a Europeanism, along with the modification of concepts such as space, territory, belonging, and citizenship, has generated much interest and debate in the literature (and, as said, especially in relation to Europe's identity and its public space).[53] In a sense, Europe itself is today a genuine mixture of national and transnational politics. This overall process is leading to a reconsideration of some historical paradigms and, possibly, to fruitful interactions between disciplines.

By the means of my historical methodology, I similarly offer another interpretation of the post-1945 history of Western Europe. Generally speaking, in fact, the history of modern Europe has, instead, "for a long time been treated as little more than the collation of clearly delineated national histories."[54] Essentially, a novel European contemporary history or a common "European view of history" is far from being developed.[55] Even if new studies are challenging old historical interpretations, national-based or, at the best, classic comparative analyses still play a noteworthy role. At times, this also seems a little strange. Well before the twentieth century, "global networks had a deep impact on individual states, as revolutions, cultural movements, social transformations and

[53] See, among the many contributions in this field, the collection of articles edited by Hartmut Kaelble and Luisa Passerini on the rise of a European identity and a public sphere in the past century. According to the editors, the two topics are, in fact, strictly interconnected: "It is impossible to investigate European identity without taking into account the history of the European public sphere, and at the same time European identity as a central issue in any European public sphere." Hartmut Kaelble and Luisa Passerini, "European Public Sphere and European Identity in 20th Century History," *Journal of European Integration History*, 8(2), 2002, p. 5.

[54] Wolfram Kaiser, "Transnational Western Europe since 1945," in W. Kaiser and P. Starie, eds., *Transnational European Union: Towards a Common Political Space* (London: Routledge, 2005), p. 17.

[55] Konrad H. Jarausch and Thomas Lindenberger, "Contours of a Critical History of Contemporary Europe: A Transnational Agenda," in K. H. Jarausch and T. Lindenberger, eds., *Conflicted Memories: Europeanizing Contemporary Histories* (New York: Berghahn Books, 2007), pp. 1–20.

scientific innovation reinforced the interconnectedness of states," as Jan Palmowski put it; and "at the level of the individual actor, too, the growth of print media and communications, as well as the growing ease of travel – hitherto considered to be so essential in shaping the nation – allowed actors to think far beyond the nation."[56]

By overlooking all this, some historical interpretations have, in a number of cases, generated some bizarre readings of specific events and processes, for instance, in the case of the history of nationalism. In the context of a journal edition devoted to political transfer in the long nineteenth century (1789–1914), for example, Henk te Velde highlighted how

> National historians have often written about the special characteristics of one national case (the German Sonderweg, French exceptionalism, etc.) without actually comparing them. The existence of distinguishing national features has often been assumed uncritically. There is, of course, an important tradition of comparative history, but in fact this has often taken separate national cases for granted, because a pure comparison presupposes these separate cases.[57]

He also offered a suitable example to defend his claims:

> [T]he politics of the nineteenth-century Dutch Catholic leader Herman Schaepman … were to a large extent shaped by his knowledge of the German Zentrum party and his visits to German Catholic friends and meetings. … In the 1870s, the German Catholic party was nevertheless the main example that inspired his political work. Schaepman had lived near the German border, he went to Catholic meetings in Germany and he was on friendly terms with the leaders of the German Catholic party. He tried to copy the German Catholic party, and used its success to mobilize his own countrymen. This is not completely unknown, but the traditional historiography has underestimated the importance of this foreign inspiration. His attempts to found a Catholic party were a political transfer, at least partially. This German connection is part of a largely forgotten history of 'métissage' which was ignored because it did not conform to the picture of a clear national identity of politics.[58]

Transnational Neofascism represents another page of this forgotten, underestimated, and *métissage* history. It suggests that politics and culture

[56] Jan Palmowski, "The Europeanization of the Nation-State," *Journal of Contemporary History*, 46(3), 2011, p. 637.

[57] Henk te Velde, "Political Transfer: An Introduction," *European Review of History-Revue européenne d'Histoire*, Special Edition on "Political Transfer," 12(2), 2005, p. 207.

[58] Ibid.

in Europe are more permeable than often thought.[59] On the other hand, it is also true that this transnational frame may present some inner difficulties, and it frequently depends on a scholar's personal background, life in between countries, and a personal knowledge not merely of foreign languages but of different cultures.

In truth, studies on transnationalism very often developed outside the historical discipline and have "emerged as a response to the speed and density of border crossings between nation-states in … spatially fluid times."[60] This is the case with trade, international organizations, and, recently, social movements and transnational protests. However, by looking, from a historical standpoint, at some other European social movements, Padraic Kenney, for instance, raised some points that are, in some ways, similarly discussed for Western European neofascists:

> We know that at certain moments social/political activists become interested in the ideas, the strategies, or the tactics employed elsewhere. What we know less about, especially in any systematic way, is *how* they acquire this information, and in *what* exactly they are interested. Some mechanisms, such as broadcast media or the interventions of political leaders, are more organized, while others are much more informal encounters.[61]

To summarize, there is already, as Kenney suggests, an attempt to offer a non–nation-centered reading of postwar politics, and to deterritorialize some social issues.

[59] See also Krishan Kumar, "The Idea of Europe: Cultural Legacies, Transnational Imaginings, and the Nation-State," in M. Berezin and M. Schain, eds., *Europe without Borders: Remapping Territory, Citizenship, and Identity in a Transnational Age* (Baltimore: Johns Hopkins University Press, 2003), p. 43. Naturally enough, this approach can be extended well outside the European continent. Ian Tyrrell has written an acclaimed transnational history of the United States. His book does not claim that the "history of the United States is the same as that of other countries. … But the perspective is new – the transnational relationships between the United States and comparable countries." Ian Tyrrell, *Transnational Nation: United States History in Global Perspective since 1789* (New York: Palgrave Macmillan, 2007), pp. 2–3.

[60] Brenda S. A. Yeoh et al., "Introduction: Transnationalism and Its Edges," *Ethnic and Racial Studies*, Special Edition on "Transnational Edges," 26(2), 2003, p. 207.

[61] Kenney intriguingly additionally proposes a new typology characterized by six modes of transnational diffusion: "Command (texts or orders by leaders …), Text (the circulation of translated essays …), Legend (in which activists respond to stories of … elsewhere …), Courier (the directed transportation of texts or ideas), Pilgrimage (journeys to a site of renown), and Convocation (international gatherings of activists to exchange ideas)." Padraic Kenney, "Borders Breached: The Transnational in Eastern Europe since Solidarity," *Journal of Modern European History*, 8(2), 2010, p. 183.

This has been more common with works focusing the leftist galaxy and in the case of transnational politics and the European integration.[62] A popular example is, in fact, represented by (mostly political-science–based today) studies on the transnationalization and Europeanization of domestic party politics and the transnational party organizations at the European Union (EU) level.[63] Empirically, the transnational frame has equally been employed quite successfully in historical and anthropological studies on migration and diasporas. These studies on mobility, emigrations, and citizenship also led some scholars to imagine a new "transnational nationalism," usually referring to a deterritorialized "imagined geography" and a number of transnational communities.[64]

Naturally, France played a central role in such a new imagined geographical space. It is for the same concept of *francophonie*, and for the permeable cultural and territorial boundaries of the "francosphere." This was also for its past overseas empire and, later, the relocation of settlers and former "colonized" North Africans on French metropolitan soil. This led to the reconsideration and reshaping of (local) understandings of belonging, identity, and citizenship, along with the formation of cross-national communities in France.[65] Italy is an even more pertinent example of this trans-geographical space and (political) activism (though, for some, it is probably a less evident one). The reasons are its historical patterns of emigration, the mobility of labor forces, and the building of Italian communities abroad (the various "Little Italies").[66] In this sense, Italy may appear a transnational entity itself, and it has been properly defined as an "emigrant nation."[67] However, this story does not end with

[62] See, for example, Gerd-Rainer Horn, *Western European Liberation Theology: The First Wave (1924–1959)* (Oxford: Oxford University Press, 2008); Gerd-Rainer Horn, *European Socialists Respond to Fascism: Ideology, Activism and Contingency in the 1930s* (New York: Oxford University Press, 1996); and Wolfram Kaiser, *Christian Democracy and the Origins of European Union* (Cambridge: Cambridge University Press, 2007).

[63] On the concept, and use, of Europeanization – including among historians – see Palmowski, "The Europeanization," especially pp. 635–41.

[64] See Riva Kastoryano, "Vers un nationalisme transnational. Redéfinir la nation, le nationalisme et le territoire," *Revue Française de Science Politique*, 56(4), 2006, pp. 533–53.

[65] See, for example, Paul A. Silverstein, *Algeria in France: Transpolitics, Race, and Nation* (Bloomington: Indiana University Press, 2004).

[66] See, among others, Donna R. Gabaccia and Fraser M. Ottanelli, eds., *Italian Workers of the World: Labor Migration and the Formation of Multiethnic States* (Urbana: University of Illinois Press, 2001).

[67] Mark I. Choate, *Emigrant Nation: The Making of Italy Abroad* (Cambridge, MA: Harvard University Press, 2008).

workers and nostalgic migrants. Politics matters, and, for example, for the interwar years, we know how fascism had an "universalist" aspiration, links with movements across the globe, and attempted to influence the various Italian communities (for instance, through the *fasci all'estero*) as well foreign policies and public opinions, including France (through local extremists, and propaganda).[68]

GOING TRANSNATIONAL

All of the earlier mentioned discussion shows that the transnational frame can be very eclectic. It is the same word "transnational" that suffers from ongoing overuse, and the term is employed in different ways.[69] In reality, it is probably even impossible to describe a unique methodology used by transnational historians. According to Patricia Clavin, transnational history is "motivated by the desire to highlight the importance of connections and transfers across boundaries at the sub- or supra-state level, the composition of categories, and the character and exploitation of boundaries."[70] Pierre-Yves Saunier correspondingly raised this flexibility of the transnational framework that developed as

> not being too preoccupied with the definition of epistemological, methodological or writing canons, those usual guns of academic wars. A versatile and enthusiastic attitude developed instead, which has made the transnational approach attractive

[68] Other political cultures had similar transnational connotation. A further, and possibly little known, example is Italian anarchism. Studies reveal its networks across Europe and the Atlantic Ocean, along with some neglected forms of mobilization and organization. Anarchism moved from one place to another, and played an important role at the transnational level – exactly like other types of activism and politics have done across France and Italy or at a supranational dimension. See Davide Turcato, "Italian Anarchism as a Transnational Movement, 1885–1915," *International Review of Social History*, 52(3), 2007, pp. 407–44.

[69] Kenney, "Borders Breached," p. 182.

[70] Patricia Clavin, "Time, Manner, Place: Writing Modern European History in Global, Transnational and International Contexts," *European History Quarterly*, 40(4), 2010, p. 625. However, I only partially agree with Clavin when she argues that "although transnational history traverses the fields of institutional history (international organizations, supranational political entities), cultural history (cultural and intellectual transfers) and economic history (exchanges of goods and people), it is largely social history. It is about the people who forge these connections, thereby constitutes a means through which social history can be refashioned" (pp. 628–29). It is very true that transnational history is about "people," and activists are a significant part of the interconnected story narrated on these pages. People may, in fact, be involved in larger political organizations, or specific groups, sharing the same political ideals, and being influenced accordingly. In this sense, transnational history is also political history.

for researchers and students as it opened stimulating vistas and perspectives. The exciting feeling of free experimentation many researchers have felt has been the most formidable by-product of this 'no logo' status.[71]

Transnational Neofascism is placed in this variegated, and often very pragmatic, methodological field, and, as suggested in the previous section, it aims to add another dimension to the study of political movements and cultures. This is a framework that looks at the neofascists' exchanges, their awareness of and borrowing from foreign fellows, and the circulation of non-national models. This cannot be traced through some classic historical prisms, and this is why transnational history is so central and can bring something really new to our understanding of nationalist phenomena. Conversely the basic comparative study encompasses an asymmetrical dimension that hardly matches the subtleties of a wider project encompassing both a horizontal (cross-country) and a vertical dimension (cross-time). This is obvious when comparative history uses a single (best) case to test the other(s). The former is often employed like a "mirror" (or as a sort of best model), while the others are compared to it: The focus is frequently on differences. This may be very useful if one wants to compare the success of a party in a country with the failure of a similar movement in another nation (the rise of fascism may be a good example, as would be the electoral successes of the FN described in the final chapter). In such a case, the structural differences and the different national contexts or institutional frames and electoral systems may certainly be highlighted.

Transnational history, on the other hand, points toward other significant features, including movement through time and space.[72] This is what *Transnational Fascism* is mostly about: forgotten people crossing borders, and neglected cultural transfer. Through these analytical lenses, readers will notice the creation of this interconnected neofascist web, or, better still, a neofascist honeycomb structure across France and Italy. As helpfully introduced by Clavin, earlier a "honeycomb" allows us to imagine a variegated and interrelated framework with movements of activists, strategies, and imaginaries within and across it. Exactly like

[71] Pierre-Yves Saunier, "Learning by Doing: Notes about the Making of the *Palgrave Dictionary of Transnational History*," *Journal of Modern European History*, 6(2), 2008, p. 168. On the transnational historical method, see also Akira Iriye and Pierre-Yves Saunier, eds., *The Palgrave Dictionary of Transnational History* (Basingstoke: Palgrave Macmillan, 2009).

[72] See David Thelen, "The Nation and Beyond: Transnational Perspectives on United States History," *Journal of American History*, 86(3), 1999, pp. 965–75.

what happened in the long postwar history of the extreme right in France and Italy, a honeycomb "also contains hollowed-out spaces where organisations, individuals and ideas can wither away to be replaced by new groups, people and innovations."[73]

"Going transnational" also has the advantage that borders can be used in a very eclectic way, even if this does not mean that, in all cases, we have to demolish the entire national frame.[74] In fact, to quote Saunier again, "It is on and in countries that flows originate and end, and it is according to national bearings that we label goods, people, ideas, and funds which are on the move."[75] We can – at least in theory – thereby consider each case study as a single unit, but always also as a component of a larger whole.[76] This "larger whole" also means that the intention of this book was not to use a microscope for every single leaf of the main "trees" – namely, the very important FN and MSI – but to look at the whole forest of right-wing extremism. This forest contained doctrines, movements, and people interacting constantly and extensively with each other, and this happened immediately after the war with the resurgence of fascist groupings during the Cold War years with an attempt to reorganize forces, tackle the decolonization issue, and react to the left during the 1960s and 1970s, but also with the unification of forces for the first European parliament election, and from the 1980s onwards with neofascist movements countering together the society of immigration and globalization, and, today, the economic downturn and the EU austerity plans.

OUTLINE

The structure of the book mirrors its methodological framework. It generally adopts a chronological historical narrative, although the discussion does not exactly cover the whole story of neofascism, since I do not want to provide another narrative history of the extreme right. Sometimes there is also overlap in the historical periods covered by some chapters. When this occurs, it is because a specific theme in those pages allows the

[73] Patricia Clavin, "Defining Transnationalism," *Contemporary European History*, 14(4), 2005, p. 421.

[74] I use here Saunier's expression. See Pierre-Yves Saunier, "Going Transnational? News from Down Under," *History. Transnational*, January 13, 2006, http://geschichte-transnational.clio-online.net/forum/type=artikel&id=680, accessed October 25, 2007.

[75] Saunier, "Learning by Doing," p. 169.

[76] On this, see generally Padraic Kenney and Gerd-Rainer Horn, "Introduction: Approaches to the Transnational," in G.-R. Horn and P. Kenney, eds., *Transnational Moments of Change. Europe 1945, 1968, 1989* (Lanham, MD: Rowman and Littlefield 2004).

showing of the transnational stance in a more proficient way. The monograph is therefore fully placed into a transnational narrative and on a cross-national roadmap. The story, as well as the observer's attention, recurrently jumps from one case to another: from Rome to Paris, from a movement to a thinker, from an activist to an organization, and from an event in France to a newspaper article in Italy.

In particular, Chapter 1 shows that fascism, in both France and Italy, did not disappear under the ruins of regimes, collaboration, and defeat. The discussion reveals the common ambivalence of national public memories and mainstream politics that favored the rebirth, or the enduring presence, of the former wartime enemies in the postwar societies. I will show the resurgence of a backward-looking and nostalgic extreme right, initially in the shape of nebulous associations and semiclandestine groupings, and, later, in a more respectable parliamentary guise, along with their first transnational contacts.

Chapter 2 reveals an almost hidden story, notably, the attempts of some French and Italian right-wing extremists to revitalize fascist ideology, roughly from the early 1950s, through two interconnected pathways: a radicalization (via rejection of the democratic system) and a deterritorialization (in the sense of converting narrow fascist nationalism into pan-European nationalism). It describes these projects, including the influence of thinkers like Evola and Bardèche. These pages also trace how the immediate outcome of this deterritorialized fascism was the formation of some international associations in which Frenchmen and Italians played a central role. Following from this, the chapter ends with an analysis of other activists, journals, and movements that promoted a genuine postwar Eurofascist doctrine (up to the 1960s).

Chapter 3 analyzes the extreme right within the context of French decolonization. It is shown that the Algerian war of independence played a key role for right-wing extremism in France. The reception of these French events and politics in neofascist Italy is also highlighted. I describe how international events like decolonization, and France's involvement in it, were treated, borrowed, and reinterpreted by Italian neofascists. Attention is paid to the Italian "fascination" with General Charles de Gaulle, French settlers, and rebellious paratroops defending French Algeria. The chapter also provides an overview of extreme-right forces up until the year 1968.

Chapter 4 represents another intriguing, and largely forgotten, story in traditional history books. It describes neofascism in and around the radical leftist year of 1968 and the student revolts. It emphasizes the importance (and legacy) of this rebellious era in the readings and policies of transnational neofascists. It first illustrates the reaction of the MSI with the building of a political front, gathering other rightist forces. The chapter then highlights another of the never-ending patterns of right-wing cross-fertilization across the Alps. It is the identical reaction to 1968 in France, with a movement, the FN, heavily inspired by the Italian MSI.

Chapter 5 looks at the rise of extremist cultural activism. Moving away from pure party politics, it underlines the crucial importance of 1968 in the development of extreme-right intellectual strategies in both countries. It points out the similar reactions to the hegemony of the left over popular and youth culture. It begins by describing the cultural project led by the MSI and some rightist publishing houses to make the heirs of Mussolini's fascism more acceptable. It is, nonetheless, argued that this cultural reaction was also especially developed outside political parties, and an example discussed here will be the French ND, for its importance in rebranding classic extreme-right themes, for the influence in Italy, and for the borrowing and reformulation of the discourses of Italian thinkers.

Chapter 6 reflects the theme of transnationalism and focuses on what clearly unifies the political extreme right in France and Italy since the 1970s to the present day, though it does mostly overlook phenomena such as the the Italian Lega Nord (Northern League, LN) that cannot be included in a long-term neofascist tradition.[77] It analyzes the enduring importance of neofascist Italy for its contemporary French counterparts – including the changing (French) "allies" of the MSI and the Euroright project with French and Spanish forces. It also describes the favorable conditions for the FN, which became the most successful example of Western European right-wing extremism. It will be demonstrated how the MSI tried, sometimes controversially, to borrow from, and was attracted by, the FN and Jean-Marie Le Pen. It additionally suggests that the FN political discourse (in particular, the anti-immigrant, "national

[77] Careful readers will surely notice that the book in fact briefly mentions the transnational interactions of one of the most successful Europe's parties of the latest generation, notably, the Lega Nord, which was led by the charismatic leader Umberto Bossi. Some scholars consider it to be a member of the new (populist) right along with the French FN. The choice not to include it may generate some (partially understandable) criticism. However, this party is a relatively recent organization, although it has an evident extreme-right platform, and there are links with right-wing France. It does not, nonetheless, really come from the "genuine" neofascit pedigree that this monograph covers for the long postwar decades.

preference," rhetoric) strongly influences the most recent neofascist movements in Italy. It also mentions the activism of some of these Italian groups and how they became attractive for French activists usually placed outside the FN. Similarly the chapter highlights the first links that Marine Le Pen, since she became party leader, formed with her Italian counterparts.

The Afterword summarizes some of the key findings and also tries to imagine a tentative research agenda. It also briefly reflects upon the present political, social, and economic situation in Europe and its ongoing influence on the neofascist environment. It discusses how austerity politics, the anti-EU stances, and the anti-bank rhetoric are having an impact on the extreme-right policies and international networks. Further mention is then made of some recent attempts of reorganization across national borders, although these pages also describe how Marine Le Pen became very appealing among Italian extremists and some mainstream right-wing politicians.

1

Nations and Fascisms

The aftermath of the Second World War was very traumatic for the entire old European continent. It left a heritage of sufferance and ruins: "Europe ... offered a prospect of utter misery and desolation. ... Everyone and everything – with the notable exception of the well-fed Allied occupation forces – seems worn out, without resources, exhausted."[1] There was, however, some scope for hope. A general, and at least initial, feeling was that common people sought radical change, a deep renewal of the existing society along the lines promoted by the liberation forces. Both the French Fourth Republic and the young Italian state were in a confused, but intense, phase of material reconstruction. If there was a generic perception, it was that this was certainly not the momentum of the followers and sons of the various (big and little) European dictators and fascist chiefs. This was the victory of anti-fascist forces and the Allies. French and Italian communists appeared to seize the moment for a second time: "the years 1943–7 were an exceptional moment of European history – the moment of anti-fascist unity – which contained radical opportunities in some ways comparable to those in 1917–18."[2]

Life in the immediate postwar period was obviously problematic for the heirs of the fascist right. Collaborationists, Vichy officers, and RSI soldiers were, in a good number of cases, viewed, at the best, with suspicion from the population. They were associated with direct

[1] Tony Judt, *Postwar: A History of Europe Since 1945* (London: Pimlico, 2007), p. 13.

[2] Geoff Eley, "When Europe Was New: Liberation and the Making of the Post-war Era," in M. Reina and G. Schaffer, eds., *The Lasting War: Society and Identity in Britain, France and Germany After 1945* (Basingstoke: Palgrave Macmillan, 2008), p. 20.

involvement in national dictatorship, violence against civilians, the discrediting of their leaders, and the hardships of war. Conversely, fascists and collaborationists perceived themselves as victims of a national betrayal; they were, very often, unable to understand a different world that seemingly rejected them. In their view, those newly founded democracies were unwelcomed entities, if not genuine military occupations. Writing in 1954, a neofascist source visualized both France and Italy under a "foreign regime."[3]

Yet, fascist ideals had not disappeared completely and were, in many ways, still perceptible under the war ruins. Paradoxically, they benefited from a somewhat favorable (and bizarre, in some cases) sociopolitical context – mainly developed by mainstream political forces, state apparatuses, and a certain acquiescence of nations that wanted to "punish" and, at the same time, were willing to "forget" (also because there were most urgent pragmatic issues to deal with). Another "encouraging" role was also played by some diplomatic agencies and the U.S. secret services that were often interested in promoting an anti-communist environment across Western Europe, also involving some of their former (fascist) enemies. Along these lines, this chapter reveals a rather common ambivalence of public memories and state policies across France and Italy and, particularly, those similarities that led to a policy of "amnesia" – and was, at least partially, shared with other European and liberated lands where, as mentioned, nationalistic forces were needed to strengthen a specific western influence. This would raise some light on the role of moderate politics in the rise of the extreme right along with political tolerance promoted by governments and some international actors. This ambivalence, probably often unintentionally, de facto backed the rebuilding of a nostalgic extremism. Readers will then briefly observe the actual process of reconstruction of these neighboring fascisms (and, when possible, their initial transborder links). In hindsight, in Italy this phenomenon appears more evident than in its French equivalent. This was because of its historical background: the importance of Benito Mussolini, the dictatorial experience, together with the presence of a predominant fascist party and its influence on people and popular culture. The Italian case was therefore structurally quite different, at least up until the war armistice of September 8, 1943. Public opinion was, in fact, shaped and manipulated by fascist propaganda and

[3] "Purtroppo la Francia mancava," p. 4.

education, repression, and social control.[4] As a result, many enthusiastic devotees of Mussolini were very active even after the defeat (and, as we will see, also benefited from the help of some mainstream, religious, and aristocratic circles).[5] French fascists could not counterbalance any similar legacy, including in reference to Vichy. In France the humiliation of the German occupation, the collaboration, and the failure of a unique and well-structured French fascism meant that the extreme right was almost crushed after 1945. Some right-leaning and nationalist "deeds" had, nonetheless, survived, and, as I shall discuss, fascists were trying to prepare a comeback.

In sum, the Italian phenomenon soon materialized into a structured party, while immediate postwar French right-wing extremism was much more *groupusculaire* and, almost intrinsically, *protestataire*. It is also worth mentioning that these were not isolated examples. The extreme right began to develop from the ashes of the past in other Western European countries and was always influenced by both the interwar dictatorial or fascist-like experiences and the current political climate.[6]

[4] See, generally, Paul Corner, "Consenso e coercizione. L'opinione popolare nella Germania Nazista e nell'Italia fascista," *Contemporanea*, 6(3), 2003, pp. 425–45; Paul Corner, *The Fascist Party and Popular Opinion in Mussolini's Italy* (Oxford: Oxford University Press, 2012); and also Richard J. Bosworth, "War, Totalitarianism and 'Deep Belief' in Fascist Italy, 1935–43," *European History Quarterly*, 34(4), 2004, pp. 475–505.

[5] To be fair, the situation in Italy was historically slightly more complex than in France. If a certain French neofascism quickly rose after World War II, and openly proclaimed its Pétainist or fascist ideals, its Italian permutation, at least as a psychological state, was, in my reading, developed from 1943 onwards with the difficulties of fascists after the "withdrawal" of Mussolini in July (by the Grand Council of Fascism) and then the armistice, as well as the decision of some Italians to support the Duce's last adventure with the RSI. This historical transition was to strongly influence the MSI. For an overview of this process (and, generally, of the birth of the MSI), see Andrea Mammone, "Gli orfani del Duce. Fascisti dal 1943 al 1946," *Italia contemporanea*, 239–40(2), 2005, pp. 249–74.

[6] In Great Britain, for example, Oswald Mosley was especially active. His Union Movement acted as a transmission belt between pre- and postwar fascism (and, as in Italy, imprisonment camps played a major role in the formation of new extremist leaders and in the rise of a native neofascism). See Richard Thurlow, "The Guardian of the 'Sacred Flame': The Failed Political Resurrection of Sir Oswald Mosley after 1945," *Journal of Contemporary History*, 33(2), 1998, p. 241. On the persistent fascist roots of the extreme right in Great Britain after the war, and its direct ties with the nascent fascism of the 1920s, see also Nicholas Hillman, "'Tell Me Chum, in Case I Got It Wrong. What Was It We Were Fighting during the War?' The Re-emergence of British Fascism, 1945–58," *Contemporary British History*, 15(4), 2001, pp. 1–34; and, more generally, Graham Macklin, *Very Deeply Dyed in Black: Sir Oswald Mosley and the Postwar Reconstruction of British Fascism* (London: I. B. Tauris, 2007).

In this sense, history and the role of some historical memories played a central role.

NEOFASCISM AND MEMORIES: SOME INITIAL REFLECTIONS

After their liberation from fascism, France and Italy seemed to repudiate their most recent past. Some former *fascisti* and *vichystes* were sent to jail and were (at least partially) purged from public administration. Some of them lost their public respectability or were executed for their previous anti-Semitic, Mussolinian and pro-Vichy. Even intellectuals (and, in some cases, probably even more than others) were forced into the struggle for a democratic national identity that allegedly had to exclude or eliminate old collaborationists and the traitors of the fatherland. The case of Robert Brasillach, an editor of the weekly fascist-supporting and, later, deliberately collaborationist *Je suis partout*, was a rather emblematic one in liberated Paris. As I mentioned earlier, he was, in fact, executed for treason in February 1945.[7] Yet the historical picture was not as optimistic as it appeared, and right-wing extremism was, in some ways, alive.

A brief consideration of what can be termed the transnational ambivalence of domestic memories is also now needed. We are dealing with two countries that were, on the one hand, controversially trying to exclude former internal enemies from any leading position and, on the other hand, unable to deal properly – and, at times, fairly – with their own histories. In doing so, the door was left open for the resurgence of fascist values. The lack of an Italian and French Nuremberg, of a serious collective discussion, including public opinion, gave neofascists the opportunity to profess the same backward-looking ideals, even if they were delegitimized by the previous undemocratic regimes and movements.

The lack of a serious reflection on the state (administrative) apparatuses, the "difficulties" of some French intellectuals and scholars, for example, in admitting a fascist or racist past, along with the silences on the role played by some religious circles – all contributed to the aftermath of this latent rehabilitation of former enemies. Not many mainstream agencies and institutions seemed prepared, or willing, to cope with events.

7 For a study of this trial, see Alice Kaplan, *The Collaboration: The Trial and Execution of Robert Brasillach* (Chicago: University of Chicago Press, 2000). For a short account of the intellectual climate surrounding Brasillach's case, see also Imogen Long, "L'Épuration: The Intervention of Simone de Beauvoir," in J. Wardhaugh, ed., *Paris and the Right in the Twentieth Century* (Cambridge: Cambridge Scholars Press, 2007), pp. 193–210.

The Catholic Church was, for example, indeed probably lacking such moral recognition, which could have helped in those tough times. On the contrary, it promoted more than an "act of forgiveness" and avoided any investigation into a past made up of an (often underground) resistance to fascisms, and also of a number of shades of gray. The Vatican had maintained a notable silence on its links with Mussolini and other nationalist regimes. Part of the French clergy was similarly discredited, as it was sympathetic to some of the Vichy policies.

In sum, Mussolini's years in power, and France of the period 1940–44 (but also the previous presence of fascist personages and leagues), had to be removed from history. This was what the liberal philosopher Benedetto Croce called a "parenthesis" in Italian political history, and what André Mornet, a prosecutor at Pétain's trial, simply called the years to "erase" in French history. Many foremost politicians in these nations similarly followed such an approach. An interrelation of factors made it possible that an ambivalent present era in France and Italy consisted of persistent, although often hidden, connections with the past.

In the first years after the war, France promoted, moreover, an image of a nation with no blame for wartime violence or the deportations of Jews (while, very paradoxically, Italy is presently failing to face its interwar fascist years). The heirs of the glorious French Revolution had been saddled with the status of an invaded state, and political forces shared this view. This process had some unexpected outcomes in the years and decades to come, influencing, for example, the integration of ethnic minorities, colonial policies, and international relations.[8]

Yet this is not even the end of the story. It is highly possible that this activity of selective removal, or dismissal, and a subsequent building of official memorial narratives later allowed extreme-right groups like the Front National to creep into the contradictions of this reading of national history – by presenting, for instance, different images of Nazi collaborators and Vichy, and minimizing their betrayal of the nation. In this historical interpretation, war collaborators became "soldiers not mercenaries, patriots not men who had sold themselves out," and specifically, "Vichy collaborators [were] patriots who had tried to serve France by protecting her from Germany through negotiation rather than

[8] Andrew Knapp, "Introduction: France's 'Long' Liberation, 1944–47," in A. Knapp, ed., *The Uncertain Foundation: France at the Liberation, 1944–47* (Basingstoke: Palgrave Macmillan, 2007), pp. 18–19.

confrontation."[9] All this is, however, less unexpected if we think that it was only the 1973 French translation of Robert Paxton's *Vichy France: Old Guard and New Order*, that offered a more realistic picture of Pétain's National Revolution.[10] Before this, the intellectual mantra was that, almost like the described neofascist perspective, Vichy was a means to "protect" France.[11]

A very similar case occurred in Italy, although, ironically, it experienced a palpable fascist dictatorship. The overall and widespread belief of the *Italiani brava gente* (Italians good people), a country of harmless fascist followers or its opposite, notably a nation of anti-fascists, had the same negative outcomes as in France: Fascist Italy's anti-Semitism was ignored. With the passing of the years, the works of revisionist historians, or of the so-called anti–anti-fascist scholars (including Renzo De Felice), along with the attitude of a number of contemporary political actors, made the unthinkable possible. In other words, *fascismo* became sort of neutral phenomenon, even revalued in some cases. As in France with the FN, if this immediately looks like a posthumous victory for neofascism, it has in reality a more subtle and pragmatic side. It led to an environment that, after the war, favored the birth of the strongest European extreme-right party, the MSI, and that, as Chapter 6 will show, in contemporary times makes it normal to have the granddaughter of the Duce, Alessandra Mussolini, becoming a national politician, leading a neofascist electoral coalition, and then supporting the center-right (she is, in fact, an MP, very active in Silvo Berlusconi's party and well accepted by the media).[12]

Writing today, it is evident how mainstream politics worked to avoid any serious debate regarding recent history. French and Italian societies had not sought to come to terms with their past. In Italy, for instance, the

[9] Philippe Buton, "Occupation, Liberation, Purges: The Changing Landscape of French Memory," in Knapp, ed., *The Uncertain Foundation*, p. 241.

[10] See Robert Paxton, *Vichy France: Old Guard and New Order, 1940–1944* (New York: Knopf, 1972). For a brief overview of the controversies following Paxton's book, see Moshik Temkin, "'Avec un certain malaise': The Paxtonian Trauma in France, 1973–74," *Journal of Contemporary History*, 38(2), 2003, pp. 291–306.

[11] The first influential work of this kind was produced by a writer: Robert Aron (in collaboration with Georgette Elgey), *Historie de Vichy, 1940–1944* (Paris: Fayard, 1954).

[12] On interwar fascism, the rewriting of Italian history and its more recent outcomes, see Andrea Mammone, "A Daily Revision of the Past." On Alessandra Mussolini and some of her political activity, see Chapter 6 and also Mammone and Peace, "Cross-national Ideology in Local Elections," especially pp. 288–90, and pp. 299–300.

clash between fascism and anti-fascism was polarized and became the mythology that allowed the legitimization of political forces that sought to lead governments and the parliamentary opposition. This also allowed the bizarre presence of the MSI, which, in some cases, existed also to legitimize parties that fought against fascism and thereby were eventually ready to challenge the presence of these activists. It is, indeed, worth remembering that the neofascist MSI was in an "illegal" position within the political system. According to the Italian constitution, it is, in fact, forbidden to reorganize, in any form, a fascist-like party or to exalt fascist ideals.

There is, in sum, a strong suspicion that all these reborn fascisms were, to some degree, and at least on Italian soil, deliberately left politically unsuppressed (by the state and some of the U.S. secret services) to face the menace of the Partito Comunista Italiano (Italian Communist Party, PCI) and, as noted earlier, for the mutual legitimization of anti-fascist political forces.[13] It is also worth pointing out how a political tolerance is always, and naturally, central in the flourishing of extremist movements. In their study of the emergence of a Euro-American radical right in recent decades, Jeffrey Kaplan and Leonard Weinberg, for example, explain that

> a relatively permissive political environment (one with abundant opportunities for direct action and a high threshold for repression) ... along with the presence of energetic and skillful (at organizing and gaining attention) movement entrepreneurs seem to have been essential ingredients. In their absence it seems unlikely that these Euro-American movements would have emerged.[14]

Moving back to the years immediately after the war and to the question of historical memory, and looking on another level, Italy often has been presented, depending on the circumstances, as either a population of conscious or unconscious followers of the Duce, or, as said, as a mass of people belonging to the heroic anti-fascist Resistance. In a very similar vein, both Charles de Gaulle and the French communists constructed an image of a glorious France as a united nation of anti-Nazi activists (including the ideal of the *Résistancialisme*), often overlooking Marshal Pétain's regime and the collaboration with National Socialism. This unshakable myth of the French Resistance included the presence of intact democratic values, the moral transparency of liberation forces,

[13] On this, see also Fabio Gentile, "Fra vissuto e scelta politica. I fascisti napoletani da Salò al Movimento sociale italiano 1943–1948," *Italia contemporanea*, 237(1), 2004, pp. 599 and 602.

[14] Kaplan and Weinberg, *The Emergence of a Euro-American Radical Right*, p. 15.

and a strong democratic and republican idealism, as well as a novel politics well represented by the new governments.[15]

In France and Italy selective memory and this peculiar historical writing became, at the same time, both "official" and "artificial." They were artificial in the sense that this twisted some historical events. In some ways, one could observe here a sort of dualism: (constructed) memory versus (more realistic) history. In retrospect, this was what happened in these neighboring nations: It was not always genuine "history," it was official memory to be narrated.

Given this, national public memories were always immaculately preserved; the guilt was viewed as rather abstract and eventually collective, if not minimized completely, or it was blamed on a nebulous or easy scapegoat (usually the "bad German"). And the reality of the past, as it could have strongly influenced the political present, the actual reconstruction of countries and, probably, their (aimed for) international role and acceptance as well, was quickly cast into oblivion.

CONTINUITIES, PURGES, AND SUPPORT

It was natural, though, that a genuine break with the past was beyond any expectation in the aftermath of the war. French politicians' intentions to forget Vichy and go back to 1940 as well as avoid contemporary accusations of Pétainism proved to be a rather difficult task. It became hard, for example, to stay away from some of Petain's legislation.[16] There was therefore the necessity to show some democratic credentials and the "democratic immunity" of French politics in the interwar years. Vichy was, to borrow Croce's expression, a parenthesis, and "this legal fiction became the foundation of a heroic reinterpretation of the Dark Years."[17] This need for a unified democratic momentum (with roots not only in the Resistance, but also in the pre-liberation era) led to watered-down criticism of this (precarious) pre-Vichy system and, at the same time, mitigated some of de Gaulle's planned reforms. On the other

[15] See also Henry Rousso, *The Vichy Syndrome: History and Memory in France Since 1944* (Cambridge, Mass.: Harvard University Press, 1991), p. 19. To be sure, this new politics never started, or at least not as desired or claimed.

[16] Paxton, *Vichy France* p. 331.

[17] Julian Jackson, *France: The Dark Years, 1940–1944* (Oxford: Oxford University Press, 2001), p. 1. See also Jon Cowans, "French Public Opinion and the Founding of the Fourth Republic," *French Historical Studies*, 17(1), 1991, p. 66.

hand, in a way, this belief in turning back the historical clock was successful. The new Fourth Republic, with the strong power granted to its parliaments, political scandals, and high level of government turnover, pragmatically showed some continuity with the prewar Third Republic, while Vichy had certainly not disappeared from the country's political, cultural, and administrative landscape.

Likewise, some political observers of the time wondered if fascism in Italy had really ended with Mussolini. Anti-fascist leader Ferruccio Parri, former head of government (June–December 1945), admitted that "in spite of the Liberation, Italy had not really changed, it was still, largely, the same fascist country of the previous twenty years."[18] Another influential political character, Don Luigi Sturzo, the father of Christian Democracy in Italy, discussed a perpetual fascism. Although Sturzo's tone and argument was slightly exaggerated in this case, it showed some truth regarding the endurance of fascism. It was, in his view, endemic and linked with some habits and sociopolitical attitudes:

> Mussolini's Fascism – that of the black shirts, of banners bearing the skull and bones emblem, of the so-called Roman salute, of parades, punitive expeditions with muskets, clubs and castor oil, of the East African Empire and the Albanian Kingdom – may be called dead, even buried. But the Fascism that ante-dates Mussolini, the Fascism of all times and all countries – that brand of Fascism never dies. It adapts itself, instead, to all climates and all temperatures; it dresses according to the fashion, disguises itself and hides. That brand of Fascism has not died because it is deathless. … If real Fascism, the Mussolinian brand, has fallen, totalitarianism survives its unhappy "literary" author [Mussolini], because at bottom it lived before him. Napoleon Bonaparte gave a first sample of it to the modern world.[19]

Fascists survived in all parties, Don Sturzo continued, and the "ninety per cent of them were [previously] deceived or attracted by the environing atmosphere (as many were in foreign countries outside Italy) … It is their mentality, their spirit, their education that must be changed."[20]

The fact that many had no obvious charges to be prosecuted for was quite central. It is also related to a problem that arose immediately after

[18] Quoted in Nicola Tranfaglia, *Come Nasce la Repubblica. La mafia, il Vaticano e il neofascismo nei documenti americani e italiani 1943–1947* (Milan: Bompiani, 2004), p. XXII.

[19] Luigi Sturzo, "Has Fascism Ended with Mussolini?" *Review of Politics*, 7(3), 1945, pp. 306 and 310.

[20] Ibid., p. 311.

democratic governments took power in many Western European nations: What to do with former "national" enemies? The relative acquiescence of the state apparatuses and the failure of any meaningful postwar purge further allowed this historical continuity with the interwar years in France and Italy. In the latter even before the end of the war, the Allies seemed to back the Kingdom of the South (based in southern Italy) and then the socialist and anti-fascist leader Ivanoe Bonomi's government in their attempts to implement some purges. However, as the nation was becoming liberated, some leading politicians and the U.S. forces basically stopped supporting any radical purge.[21] In fact, as part of a drive for reconciliation, and the need of forces to reconstruct the country, in 1946, the Minister for Justice, the well-known communist politician Palmiro Togliatti, granted amnesty to many political prisoners. What is important to remember here is that the amnesty also represented the result of unclear and unofficial agreements among the representatives of clandestine fascist networks and the leaders of mainstream politics, in order to obtain the former's votes in the June 1946 referendum on the institutional system (and this was a key political moment as the referendum later rejected monarchy and implanted a genuine republican order). In some ways, votes were being exchanged for "freedom." The 1948 law readmitting former fascist bureaucrats to their posts in public administration was another step toward this rehabilitation process: All this, along with the mentioned hidden discussions with prominent outlawed fascists, gave them an (un)official political legitimization.

In France the postwar purges caused division between the party of *75000 fusillés*, namely, the Parti Communiste Français (French Communist Party, PCF) and General de Gaulle. French communists, on the one hand, aimed, through the (intended) purges and the selection of new administrators and officers more sympathetic to their cause, to have an influence on both local and central institutions.[22] Instead, the latter worked to limit the effectiveness of the overall *épuration*. De Gaulle probably thought that, in order to relaunch the international image of the country, a damaged page had to be turned. Traitors were eventually better to be condemned through a perennial oblivion.[23] In domestic

[21] Tranfaglia, *Come Nasce la Repubblica*, p. XIX.

[22] David Drake, *Intellectuals and Politics in Post-War France* (Basingstoke: Palgrave, 2002), pp. 12–13.

[23] Buton, "Occupation, Liberation, Purges," p. 235.

politics, national harmony was possible only by playing down some of the hates and resentments stemming from occupation and wartime. As we know, in the Gaullist credo, the French people had instead heroically reacted to, resisted, and – with the help of the Allied troops – overthrown the Nazi occupation. It was now time to rally forces and simply work together.[24]

Naturally, extreme right-wing forces strongly and openly criticized the purge. Writing roughly a decade later on the French situation of the "great purge" of 1944–45, Italian neofascist Emilio Canevari argued that this excessive punishment reversed "all moral and disciplinary values, as they were cheekily negating the rule of law. This is because the hierarchic obedience to the legal authorities is considered like a treason, while the [anti-fascist] rebellion is awarded like patriotism." Canavari, in the middle of the Algerian crisis that was intensely influencing life in France, concluded that, within this context of vanished national moral values, the consequences were to be expected: Colonized Africans could only feel "scorn" for a country like France (the colonizer) that "sentenced" its real patriots.[25]

The outcome of this overall process was also that many of the state personnel were carried over into the new institutional systems. The survival of the public administration here represents, in fact, one of the main examples. This led to the presence of bureaucrats who carried out their professional activities with the same fascist mentality – especially, and more evidently, in postwar Italy. In fact, in Italy, to justify this, a peculiar approach also developed: the "neutrality" of bureaucracy, its difference with politics and distance from the fascist regime while carrying out its administrative duties.[26] Rather than replacing the administrative sector, it became easier, or strategically relevant, to keep it, and eventually to use it. This continuity of the public administration was noticeable at least up to

[24] See also Oliver Wieviorka, "Replacement or Renewal? The French Political Élite at the Liberation," in Knapp, ed., *The Uncertain Foundation*, p. 80.

[25] Emilio Canevari, "La crisi algerina," *Meridiano d'Italia*, 13(37), June 3, 1958, p. 3. Ironically, in the article de Gaulle is accused for the implementation of the purges. A very similar accusation is also made in another neofascist journal such as *La Sfida*, where the decision not to release Pétain from prison was, moreover, considered to be the "first mistake" of de Gaulle's political career. Umberto Giusti, "Bivio De Gaulle," *La Sfida*, I(2), October 16, 1948, p. 3.

[26] On this concept of "neutrality," see also Christopher Duggan, "Italy in the Cold War Years and the Legacy of Fascism," in C. Duggan and C. Wagstaff, eds., *Italy in the Cold War: Politics, Culture and Society, 1948–1958* (Oxford: Berg, 1995), p. 3.

the 1960s, while in France all parties, as under Vichy, preferred to control many state agencies rather than revolutionize the sector.[27]

The judiciary was another of the most significant bodies involved in this process of continuity with the past. Particularly in Italy, some existing state agencies were reactionary and even anti–anti-fascists. This also helps to explain the decision not to fully punish fascists made by a number of judicial courts. Unsurprisingly, early students of Italian neofascism, such as Franco Ferraresi, could notice that in 1960, "out of the 64 first-class prefects, 62 had served under Fascism. So have all 241 deputy prefects, the 135 *Questori* (provincial chiefs of the state police), and the 139 deputy chiefs. . . . These are clear indicators of the failure of the attempt to purge the apparatuses, a matter deserving attention not only for its importance at the time but for the effects it had on the future of the radical Right."[28] This weakened people's perceptions of a real rupture with previous authoritarianisms. This trend was replicated in France, where the High Court of Justice imposed light sentences on many officials of the Vichy regime (which, as we know, were quickly followed by an amnesty). Many other people also escaped purges, and France, compared to some other nations, had only a small portion of the population convicted. While many Nazi collaborationists (and intellectuals) were punished, Vichy officials were even elected to parliament, and others became government ministers.

Amnesty legislation was, in fact, voted by the national democratic parliaments in the spirit of the need to move on, to put Mussolini and Pétain to one side, to foster political reconciliation, and to concentrate on the economic and social demands of reconstruction and modernization. What is more, even if the extreme right showed much hostility toward de Gaulle, some Gaullists – as was the case for Italian mainstream politics with many fascists – tried to rehabilitate former Vichyistes, probably in order to attract voters in an anti-leftist perspective. Colonel Rémy, a close associate of de Gaulle, wrote in such hectic years that the "France of June

[27] See Claudio Pavone, *Alle origini della repubblica. Scritti su fascismo, anti-fascismo e continuità dello Stato* (Turin: Bollati Boringhieri, 1995), p. 70 onwards, and Paxton, *Vichy France*, p. 335.

[28] Franco Ferraresi, *Threats to Democracy: The Radical Right in Italy After the War* (Princeton: Princeton University Press, 1996), p. 18. It is also symptomatic that the first four chiefs of Rome's police (the *questori*) were all former inspectors of the fascist secret police (usually simply known as OVRA): on this, see Tranfaglia, *Come Nasce la Repubblica*, p. XXIII.

1940 needed, at the same time, Marshal Pétain and General de Gaulle."[29] As already suggested, this was almost an overall Western European tendency and attitude, including in the newly born Federal Republic of Germany (1949), where a stable democracy was also, and at least initially, to be built with only a very limited public discussion about interwar Nazism. Indeed, David Art, for example, rightly reminds us how

> one of the first priorities of Konrad Adenauer's government was to gain amnesties for the 'victims' of denazification. With the support of all political parties, Adenauer passed a series of amnesty laws that essentially overturned denazification and led to the reintegration of former Nazis into the professions and the government. ... Political discourse about the Nazi past reflected these policies of amnesty and integration. Politicians from all political parties, when they spoke about the Nazi past at all, used [a number of] general strategies to distance Germans from the crimes of the recent past.[30]

Another point has to be made clear. Former fascists enjoyed the support of some Catholic circles. In almost all Europe some of them were outlawed. In Italy, immediately after April 25, 1945 (notably, the liberation of the country), the Ministero dell'Interno (Home Office) warned the local police authorities about the risk that people who were wanted in relation to their connections with the dictatorship were trying to reach the Italian center-south and islands, or the "safer" South America and Franco's Spain.[31] In Europe, Spain was, in fact, a promised land for fascists. Italians already had a special tie with the country since the Spanish Civil War, and this network was reinforced in the era of the RSI. This favored a strong extreme right-wing web between the two nations and also reinforced the impression that Spain was a substantial transnational landmark for European neofascist activity in the Cold War years.[32] It was therefore apparent that fascists were not on their own after their

[29] Quoted in René Rémond, *La droite en France. Vol. II: 1940–Juin 1968* (Aubier: Paris, 1980), p. 257.

[30] Art, *The Politics*, p. 53.

[31] On this, see the various police reports in Archivio Centrale di Stato (hereafter ACS), Ministero dell'Interno (MI), Direzione Generale di Pubblica Sicurezza (DGPS), Divisione Servizi Informativi Speciali (SIS), Sezione II, 1944–47, B. 29 ("Ricerca fascisti latitanti, fascisti da identificare"), B. 31 ("Fascisti del Nord rifugiatisi al Sud"), and B. 39 ("Fascisti all'estero"); and the short journalistic report on former fascist party secretary Carlo Scorza's flight from northern Italy: F.R., "Se lo sono lasciato scappare. Era Scorza," *Milano-Sera*, December 17, 1945, p. 1.

[32] See Matteo Albanese and Pablo Del Hierro, "A Transnational Network: The Contact between Fascist Elements in Spain and Italy, 1943–1968," *Politics, Religion & Identity*, 15(1), 2014, pp. 82–102.

military defeats. It is well known that some people in the Vatican and in the religious establishment, at times with the help of the International Red Cross and other international humanitarian institutions, facilitated some escape routes (often to Latin America) for about five thousand Nazi-fascists, including Frenchmen.[33] In Italy, the Church, in some cases, provided outlawed fascists with new passports, and moral and economic assistance. For example, the collaborationist Marcel Déat, sentenced by a French court, was hidden with the help of the Vatican and a local religious order and lived with a new identity in northern Italy.

Some Italian prelates worked side by side with semiclandestine fascist-supporting networks or even played a key role in the creation of such organizations. This is, for example, the case of the Movimento Italiano Femminile "Fede e Famiglia" (Italian Female Movement "Faith and Family"), founded by Princess Maria Pignatelli di Cerchiara, with the help of Monsignor Silverio Mattei in the Vatican State.[34] (Even Pope Pius XII gave militants a special hearing in 1950.) It brought together a group of women often related to the fascist regime and from the *aristocrazia nera* ("black aristocracy," which were, and are, Italian aristocrats with extreme-right sympathies) and that supported fascist veterans and their families. This association, which later joined the MSI, apparently received some funding from the Italian government and certainly helped fascists and war collaborators to leave the country. It also had some foreign branches and links with fascist figures in Europe and the American continent.[35]

The legacy of prewar fascisms was then perceptible in everyday life, with former Italian fascists or Vichy officers and soldiers returning, after only a few years (or even months in some cases), to a normal existence, in many cases as if nothing had happened, in other cases by risking their lives due to the awkward aftermath of the war and the violence inflicted on partisans and civilians. The presence of those fascists strongly influenced the sociopolitical systems and climate of

33 In general, some were very active in rescuing and evacuating fascists through organizations like ODESSA (Organization of Former SS Members), which, as suggested, usually used Italy and Spain.

34 Useful information on this women's movement is found in Federica Bertagna, *La patria di riserva. L'emigrazione fascista in Argentina* (Rome: Donzelli, 2006), pp. 103–36; Andrea Mammone, "The Black-shirt Resistance: Clandestine Fascism in Italy, 1943–1950," *The Italianist*, 27(2), 2007, pp. 293–95; and at the Fondo Movimento Italiano Femminile at the Archivio di Stato di Cosenza, Italy.

35 See Albanese and Del Hierro, "A Transnational Network."

the late 1940s, 1950s, and even the 1960s (in the latter case with subversion and potential takeovers, and a revival of anti-fascism). As we know, the amnesty legislations, with their parliamentary legitimization and the "political reconciliation" rhetoric, contributed to this overall picture and gave the impression that a good number of extremist elements were not as politically marginalized as one might have assumed.

The evidence of the will of the political system to leave the door at least semiopen to some fascists, and the resurgence of fascism unchecked, was also made noticeable by other facts: for example, by the immediate and "undisturbed" birth, as I shall show, of pro-Vichy associations in France and a prominent neofascist party in Italy, and by a myriad of pamphlets whose main goal was to denounce the purge as the "revenge of the winners."[36] It is precisely this, along with the rapid national amnesias, that

explains why former Vichy ministers were quick to try to rehabilitate Marshall Pétain through reviews and associations which persisted in denouncing the Resistance and *épuration* as periods of summary justice which, they claimed, were as criminal as the Nazi Occupation. The subsequent emergence of the myth of the "épuration crimes," which is a form of historical revisionism, is one of the bases of contemporary extreme right thought.[37]

NOSTALGIA IN EXTREME-RIGHT FRANCE

This resurgence worked in fact very quickly. Indeed, right-wing extremism also reappeared in the immediate postwar years in France in the form of minuscule clandestine or semi-clandestine periodicals, associations, and movements, more or less, as we will see shortly, like in Italy before the founding of the MSI.[38] Some French right-wingers were in the

[36] Henry Rousso, "La Seconde Guerre mondiale dans la mémoire des droites françaises," in J.-F. Sirinelli, ed., *Histoire des droites en France. 2. Cultures* (Paris: Gallimard, 1992), p. 559.

[37] Jean-Yves Camus, "Nostalgia and Political Impotence: Neo-Nazi and Extreme Right Movements in France, 1944–64," in E. J. Arnold, ed., *The Development of the Radical Right in France: From Boulanger to Le Pen* (New York: St. Martin's Press, 2000), pp. 199–200.

[38] According to Pierre Milza, "d'abord essentiellement peuplées de nostalgiques de la collaboration et de rescapés des procès de l'épuration, les formations groupusculaires qui se sont alors constituées ont peu à peu attiré dans leur rangs de jeunes éléments en quête d'un instrument efficace de lutte contre le communisme et d'un monde éloigné des valeurs et du confort « bourgeois ," ainsi que des mécontents et des laissés-pour-compte de la société néo-capitaliste," Milza, *Fascisme Français*, p. 276.

neo-Nazis' international network, with a few French-based movements such as the Front Noir International (International Black Front) and the Secours Noir International (International Black Rescue).[39] From the ruins of the interwar years, other groups, such as the Parti Républicain de la Réconciliation Française (Republican Party of the French Reconciliation), also appeared after 1945; it was founded by former followers of Colonel La Roque's Parti Social Français (French Social Party).

On the other hand, extremist publications also flourished in this period: *Questions Actuelles*, which later became *Écrits de Paris, La Fronde* (which gave way to *Rivarol*), *Aspects de la France*, *Paroles Françaises* (the official journal of the *Parti Républicain de la Liberté*), *Les Documents Nationaux*, *La Sentinelle*, *Le Nouveau Prométhée*, *Le Drapeau Noir*, and *Le Combattant Européen*. A movement that survived was the well-known Action Française, which continued to publish *Aspects de France* and seemed to have an influence on the editorial line of *Rivarol* and *Écrits de Paris*.[40]

Given the background of their collaborators, it was anticipated that many of these publications also turned out to be anti-communist, racist, and anti-Semitic pamphlets. Through the propaganda promoted by this politicized press, these were generally the mobilizing themes of this novel French neofascism, along with a combination of anti-Gaullism, some anti-parliamentarian stances, and the rehabilitation of collaboration.[41] Some of those groups were keen to develop transnational links. *La Sentinelle*, for instance, aimed to support the alliance of postwar European fascists and featured articles from Karl Heinz Priester (a former Nazi youth member and SS soldier), who was also a promoter of neofascist international fronts.[42]

A number of these periodicals were started or directed by René Binet, a soldier in the French-manned *Charlemagne* fascist division. He established political movements and promoted a doctrine that was looking at

[39] See also the previously mentioned fleeing and the escape channels through southern European countries.

[40] Ariane Chebel d'Appollonia, *L'extrême-droite en France. De Maurras à Le Pen* (Brussels: Editions Complexe, 1988), pp. 280–81.

[41] According to early scholar of French right-wing extremism Joseph Algazy, in the neofascist press, we can, in fact, observe that "la lutte sans merci contre le communisme … continua d'être leur principal thème, mais il ne fut cependant pas question de renoncer au thème raciste …, l'ennemi juif garda toute sa place aux côtés de l'ennemi bolchevique." For this reason, "ils consacrèrent," Algazy writes, "une part importante de leur efforts de propagande à expliquer les raisons de leur engagement récent dans le camp nazi." Joseph Algazy, *La tentation néo-fasciste en France de 1944 à 1965* (Paris: Fayard, 1984), p. 63.

[42] Ibid., pp. 77 and 80.

the most xenophobic and anti-capitalist ideological wings of interwar fascism. Binet, specifically, formed the Parti Républican d'Union Populaire (Republican Party of Popular Union) in 1946 and, two years later, the Mouvement Socialiste d'Unité Française (Socialist Movement for French Unity), which published *L'Unité*. Readers will similarly encounter Binet again in the next chapter when the neofascist attempts to create a Europe-wide extremism will be described. Indeed, he represents an interesting early example of a pannational activist who supported a genuine pan-Europe (in his case, also grounded in the superiority of its white civilization). For instance, in March 1951, *La Sentinelle* was completely devoted to a single article written by Binet. In this essay, the French neofascist analyzed developments in France and Europe since World War II, criticized democracy and parliamentarism as well as Soviet and U.S. imperialisms, and rejected this first "Europe de Strasbourg," while calling for the union of the "National Workers' States of Europe."[43]

Binet was read in Italy also for his virulent pro-Nazi stances and overtly xenophobic approach. The neofascist journal *Cantiere* reported in 1951 that this politician offered the most "accurate" doctrine: This was a philosophy criticizing democracy and capitalism because they were used by "an inferior and non-white race, the Judaic race" to subjugate the Aryan populations.[44] The year before, Binet had published a volume that, in fact, was to influence some future extremist literature, entitled *Théorie du racisme* (Theory of Racism).[45]

As is evident, this was an extreme right directly rooted within interwar fascism, collaboration, or the Vichy *filière*, one that never discarded those past experiences. In other words, activists followed a line of continuity with their own (recent) political trajectories. The next section will reveal that this was precisely also the case with the MSI: It naturally associated itself with the interwar fascist experience, and members never felt obliged to look more critically at Italy's past. On the contrary, the MSI attempted to safeguard all the ideals that the RSI had reproposed for

43 Quoted in ibid., p. 80.

44 Quoted in Gianni Scipione Rossi, *La destra e gli ebrei. Una storia italiana* (Soveria Mannelli: Rubbettino, 2005), p. 203

45 In his own words: "depuis quelques années, un drapeau a été levé sur le monde. Ce n'est pas celui d'une nation, ce n'est pas celui d'un parti, mais c'est celui d'une nouvelle sorte d'hommes armés d'une connaissance nouvelle et qui appartiennent à toutes les nations blanches: ces hommes sont les racistes." René Binet, *Théorie du racisme* (Paris: Éditions des Vikings, 1950), p. 3. He later published *Socialisme national contre marxisme* (1953) and *Contribution à une éthique raciste* (1975).

the political present and, more importantly, also for posterity. While Italians exalted the mystical figure of Benito Mussolini, a reasonable number of French neofascists generally backed and venerated the memory of Philippe Pétain – which "gave rise to [a] cult like that of the decapitated king."[46] They continuously demanded the liberation of Pétain and tried to defend the image of the *Maréchal*.

In such a context, the Association pour Défendre la Mémoire du Maréchal Pétain (Association to Defend the Memory of Marshal Pétain), with its monthly *Le Maréchal*, was established in 1951 to the honor the hero of the National Revolution (and was, incredibly, never banned by the government). This probably represented the major pro-Pétain group. Other similar associations and magazines were the Association National Pétain-Verdun (National Association Pétain-Verdun), the Association pour la Défense du Maréchal Pétain (Association for the Defense of Marshal Pétain), *L'Espoir*, *Paroles du Maréchal*, *L'Appel de Doudaumont*, and *La Voix de l'île d'Yeu*.[47] In a somewhat similar vein, the profascist Association des Amis de Robert Brasillach (Robert Brasillach's Friends Association) was founded in 1948. Since 1951, it has published *Les Cahiers des Amis de Robert Brasillach*.

The Vichy leader was, nonetheless, also honored and defended by the neofascist press in Italy, where he was also portrayed as an immortal figure. The *Meridiano d'Italia* reported that "France will cry for him." The Marshal was consequently described as "a man who sacrificed his life ... and fame in order to shield his country with his name and his prestige."[48] On May 3, 1951, another caption from *La Rivolta Ideale* reflected a feeling shared across geographical boundaries: "it seems impossible to serve a country without becoming, sooner or later, its victim."[49] Both magazines, which were quite influential and central in the founding of the MSI, criticized those French who put Pétain in jail, while, in their view, he had only worked for the sake of his fatherland. In this reading of historical events, when France was surrendering to the Nazi invaders, while General Charles de Gaulle played the effortless, and "ingrate," card of the "rebellion," Pétain incarnated deep virtues like "patience" and "courage."[50] As we can see, there is a direct association

46 Rémond, *La droite en France*, p. 257.

47 Fiammetta Venner, *Extrême France. Les mouvements frontistes, nationaux-radicaux, royalistes, catholiques traditionalistes et provie* (Paris: Grasset, 2006), p. 86.

48 "Pétain immortale," *Meridiano d'Italia*, VI(17), April 29, 1951, p. 3.

49 Carlo Delcroix, "Pétain e la Francia," *La Rivolta Ideale*, 6(18), May 3, 1951, p. 1.

50 Ibid.

and similarity between Pétain and Mussolini: The Italian dictator was equally considered by local neofascists as a man who made a supreme sacrifice by creating the RSI (as Vichy was for Pétain) to protect Italy and to avoid a "Germanization" of the nation following a colonization like in Poland. It was in this nostalgic and revisionist context that both Italy and France saw some other neofascist-supporting groups, such as the Movimento Italiano Femminile and the various "Comités de défense des épurés," developing in the early Cold War years.[51] Along with a latent rehabilitation of past regimes and the attempt to reorganize extreme right-wing forces, these associations were, in fact, generally concerned with providing spiritual, economic, and legal assistance to veterans and prisoners.

Moreover, just as the MSI obviously criticized the anti-fascist *Resistenza* myth, the French extreme right-wing groups virulently opposed the winning *Résistance*. The strategy was to rehabilitate the experience of Vichy, with its radical and racist philosophy. As Rémond put it, in France, this *vichyste* and somewhat minority extreme right was excessively "doctrinarian, [and] trapped in anger, to establish a [genuine] political force."[52] It is, nonetheless, not only the fact of being nostalgic and ideological that prevented them from creeping into the political system. The problem harks back to the interwar years and, as mentioned, the incapacity of extremists to gather forces under the same movement led by a strong leader. This was then simply the continuation and outcome of an historical trend made by divisions and weaknesses (and some unfavorable external conditions). What is clear is instead that, as with its Italian counterpart, the refusal to surrender represented their revenge against an inexplicable post-Pétain society. Some genuine extremist features were hence reborn, and the present was built on a strong nostalgic ideal.

AN OATH OF FASCIST ALLEGIANCE: THE BIRTH OF THE MSI

If "pulverization" and "groupuscules" were words in reference to the French nostalgic right, the situation for its Italian analogous backward-looking counterpart was richer and more successful in these early years. The first appearance of *neofascismo* took the shape of clandestine

[51] Mammone, "The Black-shirt Resistance," pp. 293–95; and Algazy, *La tentation néo-fasciste*, pp. 71–72.

[52] Rémond, *La droite en France*, p. 258.

and subversive fascist activity.[53] This was a phenomenon that ran parallel – and sometimes in conjunction – with legal extreme-right activity since 1943 and up until the beginning of the 1950s. It is usually known as *fascismo clandestino* (clandestine fascism) and represented an initial reaction against the fact that Benito Mussolini's ideals were completely disappearing from democratic Italy. This led to the activists "distancing" themselves from Italy, to which, in their eyes, it was possible to counter only the fascist iconographic symbol of Mussolini and the uncontaminated and mystical values embodied within the Salò Republic. In any case, due to the absence of favorable conditions, clandestine fascists ended up merely attacking leftist headquarters and distributing illegal propaganda (but without any considerable results).[54] They carried out some spectacular actions, such as the theft of the Duce's corpse from a cemetery near Milan in April 1946, which was organized by Domenico Leccisi's illegal Partito Fascista Democratico (Democratic Fascist Party).[55]

Setting aside the clandestine activity, the first legal activism of Italian fascists in politics consisted of an attempted "entrism" within existing small parties, often with the aim of radicalizing their policies. Guglielmo Giannini's Uomo Qualunque (Party of the Common Man, UQ) turned out to be the most emblematic example. This movement was officially formed on February 18, 1946.[56] According to the different terminology used, the UQ represented the official "Italian Foreign Legion," a "Trojan horse,"[57] or the political "umbrella" for fascists.[58] All these definitions were usually well accepted by Giannini.[59] The UQ actually had strong financial support from the same economic and social sectors that

[53] On this phenomenon, see Mammone, "The Black-shirt Resistance," pp. 282–303; and a classic study like Giuseppe Conti, "La RSI e l'attività del fascismo clandestino nell'Italia liberata dal settembre 1943 all'aprile 1945," *Storia contemporanea*, 10, 1979, pp. 941–1018.

[54] A key group was the Fasci d'Azione Rivoluzionaria (Revolutionary Action Fasci), which tried to set up a proper subversive and anti-democratic network.

[55] See the reports by the Milan Prefecture (e.g., No. 036174, 15/02/1947) and the Ministero dell'Interno (e.g., No. 224/81156, 26/08/1946) in ACS, MI, DGPS, SIS, Sezione II, 1944–47, B. 37. Interestingly, Mussolini's corpse was moved to a monastery and hidden by two priests.

[56] On the birth of the UQ, see generally the party periodical, *L'Uomo qualunque*, and, in particular, issue (8) published on February 20, 1946 (p. 1); and, above all, Sandro Setta, *L'Uomo Qualunque 1944–1948* (Rome: Laterza, 2000).

[57] Mario Tedeschi, *Fascisti dopo Mussolini* (Rome: Settimo Sigillo, 1996; 1st ed. 1950), pp. 91 and 135.

[58] Sandro Setta, personal communication with the author (May 2004).

[59] Sandro Setta, *La Destra nell'Italia del dopoguerra* (Rome: Laterza, 2001), p. 106.

promoted the success of Mussolini's initial fascism just a few decades previously. It was a political force with that "anti-politics" connotation that had arguably characterized part of the Italian bourgeoisie. Its ideological and electoral program was consequently

> a demagogic collection of populist measures, such as protection for the ordinary taxpayer from the rapacious state. On this largely negative platform, the Party of the Common Man attracted considerable support during 1946—twenty percent of the vote in Rome and Naples, and more in alliance with other parties elsewhere in the south. Yet the party's days were numbered: it had little sense of internal coherence, and more importantly the Christian Democrats feared that it could undermine their moves to build support in the south.[60]

The UQ offered, nonetheless, a voice to those common citizens "who had been extraneous to the feverish events" that had characterized that historical era and, at the same time, gave some fascists the legal opportunity to express their discontent regarding mainstream politics and the society of post-1945.[61] The movement served as a "resonance chamber" for the activism of some of them, as well as a launching pad for their future political careers.[62] This is confirmed by the fact that U.S. secret agents also monitored this movement because they seemed very interested in the links between the UQ and the extreme-right world. In a report of April 1947, an American agent pointed out how Giannini had meetings with outlawed fascists, and that some of them believed they could make use of the UQ, while others even perceived him as a (in retrospect, an unlikely) leader for clandestine fascism.[63]

In any case, this underground fascist presence was a problem that could not be avoided by the democratic system. It references the previously mentioned question of what to do with former national enemies; in Italy the route seemed to be an attempt to reintegrate a good number of them in politics and society. As suggested earlier, the first secret contacts between victorious democratic forces and clandestine fascists started with

60 Eatwell, *Fascism*, pp. 248–49.

61 See Maurizio Ridolfi, *Interessi e passioni. Storia dei partiti italiani tra l'Europa e il Mediterraneo* (Milan: Bruno Mondadori, 1999), p. 411.

62 It is worth remembering that many of the UQ's voters were later to support the MSI. On this, see the opinion of the first-rank neofascist Giorgio Pini in "Verbale della riunione del Comitato centrale del Msi," July 20, 1947, p. 2, in Archivio Fondazione Ugo Spirito (hereafter AFUS), Fondo Mario Cassiano (hereafter FMC), II, II, 2, B. 14, sottofascicolo 4.

63 Some of this material is available at the National Archives and Records Administration, NARA, at College Park, Maryland. I am here referring to some U.S. files that are published in Tranfaglia, *Come Nasce la Repubblica*, pp. 72–76; see especially footnote 65.

the agreements on amnesty and the referendum on Italy's institutional frame. These accords clearly became a symbol of the legitimization of neofascists as suitable political actors and, subsequently, "a sort of approval to come into [political] action."[64]

This was therefore the right time to found a neofascist party simultaneously representing an alleged (and controversial) adaptation of fascists to the postwar (democratic) parliamentary life as well as a revaluation of their (fascist and nostalgic) ideals.[65] Many small parties and groupings like, among others, the Movimento Unità Sociale (Social Unity Movement) came into being in this period.[66] They were all proudly willing to show an oath of allegiance toward the Duce. For this latter reason, parties' membership was usually forbidden to politicians who contributed to the decadence of the fascist regime, betrayed Mussolini, or accepted the 1943 war armistice, or were perceived as political careerists. In 1972, a French neofascist intellectual, François Duprat, a historian, anti-Zionist, revisionist, and contributor to neo-Nazi and fascist periodicals (including *Revue d'histore du fascisme*, *Défense de l'Occident*, *Rivarol*, *Combat Européen,* and *Cahiers Européens*), who will be encountered again in the book, praised this strategy, which led to the actual creation of the MSI. He wrote how "the 'hierarchs' from the ... fascist regime were not included in the ranks of the new party (a man like Scorza, former secretary of the Fascist National Party, ... never joined the MSI)." Given this, the Italian party "immediately took an extremely combative connotation."[67] This banning of not loyal politicians eventually provoked an interest across Franco-Italian borders and was partially reproposed, as we shall see in Chapter 4, with the establishment of the FN in the early 1970s.

64 Piero Ignazi, *Il polo escluso. Profilo storico del Movimento Sociale Italiano* (Bologna: Il Mulino, 1998), p. 24.

65 It must be acknowledged that, at least according to some internal neofascist sources and for some activists, the MSI seemed only to "accept" democracy at a later stage. See, among others, the anti-system position of a leading politician like Roberto Mieville, in Roberto Mieville, "Dichiarazione nazionale repubblicana," *Mozione presentata al Comitato Centrale del Msi*, July 20, 1947, in AFUS, FMC, II, II, 2, B. 14, sottofascicolo 4.

66 See the "Atto costitutivo del Movimento unità sociale, 1946," and the "Atto di deposito," Repertorio 6916, Racc. No. 3557, both in AFUS, FMC, Serie II, Sottoserie II, 2, B. 14, sottofascicolo 1.

67 François Duprat, *L'Ascension du M.S.I (Movimento Sociale Italiano)* (Paris: Les Sept Couleurs, 1972), p. 37. We will also notice how Duprat was involved with a number extreme-right movements in postwar France and emerged as the main theoretician of revolutionary nationalism, influenced by the doctrines of Julius Evola and Leon Degrelle.

In Italy, extreme right-wing periodicals such as *Rataplan*, *Manifesto*, *Orizzonti d'Italia*, *Il Verdone*, *Rosso e Nero*, *Fracassa*, and, especially, Giovanni Tonelli's *Rivolta ideale* were also created and were very active in the establishing of a unique neofascist front.[68] As a direct consequence of this intellectual and political ferment, the Movimento Sociale Italiano was finally formed on December 26, 1946, in Arturo Michelini's office in Rome.[69] This latter was a former minor leader in the Roman Fascist Federation during the regime and had excellent relationships with the Roman bourgeoisie and the Vatican. Roughly fifteen former fascists contributed to the foundation of the MSI; among them were Giorgo Almirante and Michelini, Pino Romualdi, Biagio Pace, Giorgio Pini, and the mentioned Tonelli. The young Almirante became the first party secretary.[70] He was a journalist with a fascist pedigree who had worked in the cabinet of the RSI Minister of Popular Culture and on various fascist periodicals, such as *La Difesa della Razza*.

According to an internal neofascist source, this "legal" postwar extreme right came out

> with an enormous desire for revenge, inevitably "against" not only the other [political] side, but also against a destiny that ... appeared to be unfair. ... This psychological element gave us [fascists] not only a polemical position toward antifascism but also represented an act of defiance toward the old fascist ruling class.[71]

There was a strong will for revenge and to reproduce a collective history and identity.[72] This was fairly normal in an adverse political and social environment. The party accordingly presented itself as the voice of the prison survivors, war veterans, anti-Marxist workers, political refugees, exiles, and outcasts. From such a perspective, it was willing to represent

[68] See, for example, the neofascist appeal to unify forces in *Rataplan* on November 11, 1946, p. 1. On the other hand, *Rivolta ideale* promoted the establishment of one of the first movements named Fronte dell'italiano (Front of the Italian). It is worth mentioning that, as Ugo Di Meglio, "Il ruolo della stampa nella nascita del MSI," *Rivista di Studi Corporativi*, 5–6, 1981, pp. 219–36, shows, the role of the extremist press was fundamental in the birth of Italian neofascism.

[69] Mario Caciagli, "The Movimento Sociale Italiano-Destra Nazionale and Neo-Fascism in Italy," in K. Von Beyme, ed., *Right-Wing Extremism in Western Europe* (London: Frank Cass, 1988), p. 23.

[70] Almirante was also "a forceful and theatrical speaker (his father had been an actor). ... In many ways, he led the party into an open defense of both fascist ideology and style." Eatwell, *Fascism*, p. 249.

[71] Bruno Cacciola, *Appunti per una storia del M.S.I.* (Rome: Fuan, 1990), p. 9.

[72] MSI, *Appello agli Italiani*, 1946.

the true voice of the fatherland.[73] The early political philosophy of most supporters was unsurprisingly rooted in the Salò Republic, on this pure version of fascism, with its anti-capitalist and more proletarian doctrine. This was perceived as a sort of golden age and a "revolutionary" belief. In line with this, and as *La Rivolta Ideale* summed up in August 1947, they were fascists "but the ones who fought to grant social and trade unionist legislation." The RSI's ideals were therefore casting a long light on these postwar fascists.[74]

The cult of the RSI, and the identification between the established movement and this political experience, was, in this first stage, then natural. Moreover, as mentioned earlier, if one keeps in mind that neofascism, at least as a state of mind, had its roots on September 8, 1943 (as said, Italy's armistice), and that the birth of the party in December 1946 was only a consequence of previous ferments born out and forged in these years, the experience of the RSI, and the immediate postwar era, it was understandable that neofascists never felt obliged to look more critically at the fascist past. Revision or rejection of fascism was evidently impossible, politically useless, with activists eventually joining the Democrazia Cristiana (Christian Democrats, DC) and other conservative parties.[75]

The reference to interwar fascism was marked in many other ways. The party symbol, a tricolor flame above a bier, first drawn by Almirante and inspired by the emblem of a combatants' association, was, in fact, directly connected to the RSI.[76] The flame also symbolized the capacity to radiate the Duce's ideals toward the future. The name of the party is tied up with the spiritual leader. As Cesco Giulio Baghino, later editor of the party newspaper *Secolo d'Italia*, observed, "the militants soon started to read these initials [MSI] as 'Mussolini Sei Immortale' [Mussolini, you are immortal]."[77]

[73] AFUS, FMC, II, II, 2, B. 14. "Movimento Sociale Italiano. Notiziario settimanale" (probably February 1947), p. 2.

[74] Ferraresi, *Threats to Democracy*, p. 36.

[75] Giampaolo Pansa and Marco Tarchi interviewed by Simonetta Fiori in "Salò: Quell'Italia lontana e tragica che rivive nella memoria divisa," *La Repubblica*, November 13, 2002, p. 39

[76] See also Simonetta Fiori, "La Fiamma, un simbolo ereditato dal MSI," *La Repubblica*, November 26, 2003, p. 39.

[77] Neofascist Cesco Giulio Baghino quoted in Luciano Lanna and Filippo Rossi, *Fascisti immaginari. Tutto quello che c'è da sapere sulla destra* (Florence: Vallecchi, 2003), p. 325; see also Alessandro Caprettini, *La nuova destra. E quindi uscimmo a riveder le stelle* ... (Palermo: Arbor, 1995), p. 19.

The incessant references to Mussolini, and the emotional charm of the Salò Republic, were apparently decontextualized from the political reality of a post-liberation democratic Europe.[78] The fascist experience and the Duce became, nonetheless, central in the construction, delineation, and defense of the distinctive identity of the *missini* (as the MSI members have been called). Fascist salutes were a feature of their meetings (an example is the MSI rally in Rome in 1952 pictured on the front cover of the book). "Memory" was, in this sense, essential in the building of any collective (party) and individual (activists') identity.[79]

In sum, these early neofascists reproposed, immediately after the founding of their movement, the immortal values of fascism that they had mostly experienced under Salò. In the eyes of rightists, the RSI represented one of Mussolini's signs of love. The Duce had not deserted Italy and had not betrayed it and his followers. It was Italy that had, rather, betrayed them, but with the making of the MSI they were being faithful to his memory and everything he stood for.[80] The postwar fascists had finally sworn an oath of allegiance to their beloved Duce, exactly as other like-minded people across Europe were doing after the defeat of World War II.

THE MULTIFACETED EXTREME RIGHT GOES TO PARLIAMENT

The MSI, in this first political phase, was searching to find a distinctive position in the political system. Although all symbolism related to Benito Mussolini was the unifying magma for members, the party was hoping to propose a common political strategy, even if it was experiencing disagreements between its revolutionary soul and the most conservative stances.

78 Luciano Lucci Chiarissi, *Esame di coscienza di un fascista* (Rome: IRSE, 1978), p. 108.

79 As it has been noted, in general terms, "the cult of Mussolini was something apart, and people occasionally spoke of the possibility of the continuation of a Mussolinismo even after the fall of Fascism." Corner, "Everyday Fascism," p. 218.

80 I do not share historian Giuseppe Parlato's version (although in the context of a well-researched book) of the MSI as a "non-nostalgic" political actor but as an almost exclusive product of a mixture of the Cold War, agreements with mainstream politics, links with international agencies, post-fascism, and anti-communism. Parlato reverses the reading of neofascism as a fascist backward-looking phenomenon and gives the impression of a movement well placed in the context of the Cold War and with a certain freedom of political action. Nonetheless, his analysis clashes with MSI identity, and doctrinal fascist references, and with the fact that the party was in reality excluded from governmental circles and relegated to the margines of the political system. Moreover, the help of the secret services, its anti-communist stance, and its fascist and nostalgic political philosophy are not mutually exclusive. See Giuseppe Parlato, *Fascisti senza Mussolini. Le origini del neofascismo in Italia, 1943–1948* (Bologna: Il Mulino, 2006).

This probably also reflected the classic syncretism of interwar fascism and the tension between its diverse currents.

As mentioned, the genesis of the MSI tells us that many original founders were RSI veterans rooted in the most revolutionary (at times known like "leftist" and "social") features of fascism and in its anti-bourgeois credo. They believed in a corporative system, a fascist-type socialization that saw the participation of workers in the profit and management of businesses. In addition, many were anti-monarchist and anti-clerical (for both the king's and church's "betrayals" of Mussolini).[81] This was known as the "northern wind" (as the RSI was located in northern Italy). This also shaped the party's platform for the first parliamentary elections in 1948. In such a context, some activists even hoped for a vague leftist repositioning of the MSI and generally tried to attract the working-class electorate (and this would have been paradoxical considering that the real left-wing forces, namely, the communists and socialists, had fought against fascism).[82]

At the elections the party presented this anti-bourgeois platform, including redistribution of wealth, and labor participation in the economic system. The electoral result was, nonetheless, rather surprising for this "northern" anti-capitalist line. The wind was, in fact, only blowing from the south. The seven elected MPs (Luigi Filosa, Enrico Franza, Arturo, Roberto Mieville, Guido Russo Perez, Gianni Roberti, and Almirante and Michelini) all gained their votes in the center-south Italy. In other words, it became clear that Rome and its region (Lazio), along with the southern end of the peninsula, represented the electoral base of the party. One reason was that these geographical areas had not experienced the radicalism of the RSI. In contrast, they had a more nostalgic, "paternalistic," and clerical image of the fascist regime. They were mostly related to the history of the *Ventennio*, to the most conservative sides of the twenty-year dictatorship. RSI themes here were fairly distant from the local political background and unattractive for voters.

Indeed, despite the RSI-inspired leadership, in the meantime, a powerful "national-conservative" or "moderate" wing had already quickly

[81] See also Ferraresi, *Threats to Democracy*, p. 23.

[82] For an example of this, see Carlo Costamagna, "Discorso agli operai," *L'Ordine Sociale*, March 20, 1948, pp. 1–2. On this bizarre neofascist identity and positioning in the political system (that is to say, "right or left?"), see Marco Tarchi, "L'impossibile identità. Il neofascismo tra destra e sinistra," *Trasgressioni*, 4(2), 1989, pp. 3–26.

emerged in the party.[83] This included people like Augusto de Marsanich and Michelini, who fundamentally contributed to the resurgence of the whole right-wing extremist politics. Along with these big currents, there was also a "spiritual" wing within the MSI, which was mainly generated from the experience of outlawed or more rebellious fascists and was especially inspired by the doctrine of another key character to be discussed in the following chapter, Julius Evola. The party henceforth turned into a sort of multifaced political force. In the north, it advocated activism, a "national state of labor," and anti-capitalism, and, unofficially, even supported the clandestine groups. In the south, it often backed the status quo and the usual conservative and rightist themes, a politics of dialogue, and the will to collaborate with other right-wing parties.[84] This would have certainly influenced the MSI's future political agenda and the internal ideological tensions, including the disagreements in relation to foreign policy. However, the immediate result of this clash between different party positions was that De Marsanich replaced Almirante as party secretary in 1950. In some ways, a more moderate line prevailed. As described in an article published in French neofascist periodical *Défense de l'Occident* (a journal that will be also mentioned later), this was also made, in an ideal world, with the hope of creating the conditions for an official agreement to join a conservative Christian Democrat–led administration and, consequently, to mild anti-fascist policies.[85] This shift in political strategy meant, nonetheless, gaining thirty-eight parliamentary seats in the 1953 general election.

If Italian neofascism already had its proper and structured permutation with the MSI within the MSI, the first serious attempt to create a parliamentary force in France naturally stemmed from a similar nostalgic milieu and was represented by Jacques Isorni's Union des Nationaux Indépendants et Républicains (Union of Independent and Republican Nationalists, UNIR) with its publication *Unir*. Isorni was Marshal Pétain's lawyer, and his party was consequently backed by the pro-Pétain associations and groupings like the the Association des Intellectuels Indépendants (Association of Independent Intellectuals) and the mentioned Association pour Défendre la Mémoire du Maréchal Pétain, by figures such as Binet, the brothers

[83] We need to keep in mind that this was only the more moderate wing of an extreme-right party. The MSI was certainly not a moderate right-wing movement.

[84] See also Ignazi, *Il polo escluso*, p. 62.

[85] Fabio Lonciari, "La signification des élections italiennes," *Défense de l'Occident*, June 6, 1953, pp. 13–16.

Pierre and Jacques Sidos, Roger de Saivre (founder in the late 1920s of the university phalanges of the fascist league Jeunesses Patriotes), Admiral Jean Decoix (ex-Vichy), Georges Loustaunau-Lacau, Paul Estèbe, and a former Vichy minister such as Jacques Le Roy Ladurie and much of the neofascist press such as *Le Nouveau Prométhée*.

UNIR promoted the rehabilitation of Pétain, a political amnesty, and the defense of colonialism, and it contested the 1951 legislative elections. Although its electoral campaign was disturbed by some communist protesters, young extreme-right students led by Jean-Marie Le Pen confronted their opponents on the streets and, apparently, similarly tried to disrupt their electoral meetings.[86] Four deputies were elected, but they later joined the conservative party Centre National des Indépendants (National Center of Independents). The extreme right was then deprived of any institutional representation, although, according to James Shields, the main importance of this "presence in the 1951 campaign was that it marked the first – and last – attempt to gain electoral legitimacy on an openly pro-Pétainist platform."[87]

More impressively, French right-wing extremism seemed to see a light at the end of this political marginalization (and before returning to the margins of the political system for a number of years) from the time when a new, controversial, movement developed in Midi-Pyrénées. Pierre Poujade, a Guglielmo Giannini–like politician, in fact led a short-lived movement of opposition to the national tax system and government inspectors.[88] Poujade was a local Gaullist politician and small businessman from Saint-Céré in the Lot, which was precisely the place where this sort of fiscal rebellion started. He grew out of an interwar extremist milieu (including Action Française) and joined Jacques Doriot's Parti Populaire Français and Vichy France. Ideologically, he positioned himself within a genuine French tradition with references to the values of family and work and the virtues of the nation.[89]

[86] On this point, see also François Duprat, *Les mouvements d'extrême-droite en France depuis 1944* (Paris: Editions Albatros, 1972), p. 47, and Shields, *The Extreme Right*, p. 63.

[87] Shields, *The Extreme Right*, p. 63.

[88] Even if in a very different context, the contemporary LN has also played the card of opposition to the central tax system (identified with the "voracious Rome" and its parliamentary elites), which, as they claim, take all the wealth produced by the more economically productive northern regions.

[89] To introduce himself, it is also known that Poujade was keen of quoting writer Frédéric Mistral's poem: "J'aime mon village plus que ton village, J'aime ma province plus que ta

Poujade benefited from a number of favorable factors and the immediate postwar political and socioeconomic conditions. France, in the early 1950s, in spite of the waves of modernization, was, in some ways, a rural country with a large number of self-employed artisans and shopkeepers. The process of rapid industrialization, and social, fiscal, and economic state legislation, provoked, however, discontent and disillusion within some sectors of the population, and the result was a spontaneous artisans' and shopkeepers' anti-tax revolt. It was this fight against the strict *contrôle fiscal* that drove Poujade's protest movement in this allegedly "apolitical" first stage.[90] In this phase, Poujadists endorsed a strong activism, called for tax strikes, criticized the banking system, and promoted a rebellion against big business, intellectuals, and traditional politicians.[91]

In November 1953 Poujade and his comrades launched the Union de Défense des Commerçants et Artisans (Union for the Defense of Shopkeepers and Artisans, UDCA). This was considered to be a reaction to a profound national crisis, the cry of the poor and underdeveloped France, which was excluded from the rapid changes taking place. Conceived of as a protest movement, UDCA quickly radicalized its political propositions and its anti-system character and embraced a somewhat rightist platform. On a more political side, its march toward France's institutions started with the creation of the party Union et Fraternité Française (French Union and Fraternity) to contest the general elections on January 2, 1956. The electoral result was incredible: 11.6 percent of votes and fifty-two seats in parliament, and with the ability to launch the young Le Pen within the French political arena. Nonetheless, internal divisions and different views of the party's aims, along with the lack of a precise political strategy and the return of de Gaulle to power, provoked the rapid implosion of Poujadism and its failure. Poujadism represented, nonetheless, a UQ-type movement and a container for some of the nostalgic extreme right. It became a Trojan horse by which French neofascists integrated themselves back into official politics.[92]

province, J'aime la France par-dessus tout." This is also quoted in Dominique Borne, *Petits-bourgeois en révolte? Le mouvement Poujade* (Paris: Flammarion, 1977), p. 41.

90 Ibid., p. 57.

91 James G. Shields, "The Poujadist Movement: A Faux 'Fascism,'" *Modern & Contemporary France*, 8(1), 2000, p. 21.

92 Neofascists naturally shaped some of the UDCA policies. Yet it is beyond my aims to discuss the controversies that have since arisen about the nature of the Poujadist phenomenon, mainly regarding whether it should be perceived as something essentially fascist. It was not fascist, at least not if we bear in mind the German and Italian historical

Fascinatingly, an Italian section of Poujadism, a (very) nebulous and obscure Italian Poujadist League, was established. Vittorio Ambrosini, a peculiar and bizarre political character who jumped from one ideology (and side) to another, was its animator. He was a Roman lawyer and former member of the Italian army elite troops named the Arditi (The Daring Ones). Ambrosini also founded the Poujadist "International of the Middle Class," an almost unknown association that had apparently some links with German and French right-wing extremists like Otto Strasser and Frédérick Becker.[93]

In sum, the links among public memory, mainstream politics, and the rebirth of the extreme right in France and Italy were more evident than it may appear. The door was hence left open for a common return of nostalgic and undemocratic stances in these anti-fascist countries. Indeed, "nostalgia" became the watchword for this right-wing extremism reborn from the ruins of the war. Periodicals, parties, and associations reappeared in a very different world. Their doctrinal references were, nonetheless, turned in the direction of the past. These years are hardly considered central in the developments of the extreme-right politics. On the contrary, they left a mark on the identity and worldviews of many neofascist sympathizers and represent a heritage created by feelings of revenge and suspicion regarding the democratic order and the winning anti-fascist and leftist forces. These are also the years of the first cross-national exchanges and international networks.

In such a context, the Cold War had clearly started to influence Europe and national political systems, and the French and Italian extreme right

forms of the phenomenon. I suspect, however, that it may be included in a broad family of "anti-system" extreme right parties. Second, starting from the first congress in Algiers in November 1954, the UDCA began a process of radicalization following its choice to become a proper political actor. It also developed an anti-parliamentary position. As Poujade wrote in the periodical *Fraternité Française*, "Et vous, parlementaires, qui à la lecture de cet éditorial, allez peut-être ricaner, il y en a en général autant à votre service. Le Peuple de France en a assez des compromissions, des scandales, des trahisons et des abandons. Il en a assez de voir danser 'le rigodon sur son ventre' par une maffia apatride de trafiquants ou de pédérastes. Retenez bien ce que je vous dis, tout ce qui devra être le sera en temps utile. Personne ne m'empêchera de gueuler la vérité et, le jour du grand règlement de comptes, il y en aura pour tous." Pierre Poujade, "Faure, c'en est assez !," *Fraternité Française,* September 10, 1955, p. 2. See also Stanley Hoffman, *Le mouvement Poujade* (Paris: Armand Colin, 1956), p. 142. The movement also showed some anti-Semitism (especially toward politician Pierre Mendès-France). On this, see, for example, Pierre Poujade, *J'ai choisi le combat* (Saint-Céré: Société Générales des Editions et des Publications, 1955), p. 231.

[93] Kurt P. Tauber, "German Nationalists and European Union," *Political Science Quarterly*, 74(4), 1959, p. 579.

could not escape from this. Some activists therefore turned their attention to the defense of their nation against local and international communism, and others aimed to achieve deals with the mainstream conservative forces. However, some thinkers radicalized their ideological positions by promoting different visions of postwar fascism and, also, by looking through and beyond the rather narrow state geographical borders. Some of them challenged the pillars of postwar democracy, although many others related this to the elaboration a new spatial dimension (and possibly to that fascist-like "universalism" and internationalism developed in the interwar years). "Europe" and pan-nationalism became, in fact, the mantra to update the extreme-right doctrine.

2

Regenerating Right-Wing Extremism

The end of the 1940s saw the beginning of the "European dream," with the establishment of the Council of Europe and, in 1950, the European Convention on Human Rights. This period also experienced other further steps in the direction of a fruitful, and peaceful, integration of Western Europe's lands and people – including the Treaty of Paris and the subsequent European Coal and Steel Community. France, West Germany, Italy, the Netherlands, Luxembourg, and Belgium basically agreed to work on the building of a common economic market and a future federation of European states.

In the same period, Per Engdahl, an obscure Swedish fascist, thundered: "The [European integration] of Strasbourg represents a development phase that is already outdated."[1] If Europe was to be reborn – and in a postwar fascistic guise – Engdahl argued, it would have to be under a corporatist and organic system, the only one eventually also able to guarantee the proper functioning of a market.[2]

After the defeat of fascism in wartime, and the discrediting of its nationalism and imperialism, at first glance this could simply look like a delirious claim made by a nostalgic fascist ideologue. Yet, if this was indeed a kind of delirium, it was a collective one for like-minded right-wing extremists. The French writer Bardèche similarly argued: "To the 'fiscally' voracious Europe of Strasbourg we oppose the fundamental notion of an

[1] Per Engdahl, "Nouvelles européennes, Nouvelles politiques. Une déclaration du bureau de liaison du Mouvement Sociale Européen," *Défense de l'Occident*, 1, 1953, p. 27.

[2] Per Engdahl, "Le Marché Commune et l'avenir," *Défense de l'Occident*, 59, 1953, p. 35.

independent Europe."[3] The Italian scholar Ernesto Massi also reinforced this approach: "In Europe we need an economy based on a corporatist basis and according to the European viewpoint rather than the American or British one."[4]

Massi and the others were, as suggested, not alone: They gathered in Rome and Malmö in the early 1950s, along with a diverse group of other fellow ideologues and neofascist leaders, all "spiritually" still waving fascist flags and dressing in old blackshirts. They aimed at both responding to the mainstream integration of Europe and developing their own pan-national stance. This naturally went with some clashes, given the ultra-nationalist stances of some extremists. However, and as I mentioned earlier, the same interwar fascism embodied a universal dimension, and a shared ideological agenda was promoted, and spread, by some fascists across European borders as a way to internationalize their doctrine and beliefs. After 1945 international politics and relations mattered again. In fact, it is evident (as also discussed in the previous chapter) that the political climate of the immediate postwar era had a strong impact on the extreme right – and this was not only due to the launching of a supranational European community. The struggle for hegemony between the United States and the Soviet Union also had repercussions almost everywhere, including in national elections.

The heirs of fascism could not fully support the hated United States, the war victors – or to use a colorful neofascist expression, the "invaders" – and the Americanization of European societies. Although we noted that the extreme right experienced, at least in Italy, a certain acquiescence from the U.S. forces because of its anti-communist connotation, and that, in some cases, was even favored by Washington's secret agents, American cultural and political interference was still at the core of many neofascist preoccupations. However, at the same time, activists generally had a similar, if not even stronger, rejection of Russia's communism. "Neofascism is essentially anti-communist," Bardèche wrote,

> it considers communist parties as Soviet imperialism's expeditionary corps in different nations. It demands that these political-strategic movements should be regarded for what they are [in reality], that they should not be treated like

[3] Maurice Bardèche, "Pour un 'Mouvement Populaire Européen' au service de l'indépendance nationale et européenne," *Défense de l'Occident*, 1, 1953, p. 5.

[4] Ernesto Massi, "Une Politique Sociale Européenne," *Défense de l'Occident*, 14, June 1954, p. 30.

ordinary parties ... but they must be put out from pursuing their need of dissociation and of treason.[5]

Neofascism stood for an authentic national independence. According to the Italian neofascist press, for example, both France and Italy were experiencing a fairly common destiny of suffering, where "the regime in charge can be pertinently defined ... as a regime led by foreigners [*regime dello straniero*]." Hopefully, once people got rid of these foreign invaders, these fraternal nations would have finally found their real objective: "the Catholic and national Italy and the national and Catholic France would have been able ... to meet again."[6]

In this reading of events, governmental decisions were influenced by international powers and equilibrium and were not based on national interests and citizens' will: "Restoring the sovereignty of our nations," Bardèche suggested, "is one of most serious concerns that the postwar disorders has left us." In this sense, the demand for free nations was the only bona fide "politics of liberation" (as compared to the perceived "anti-fascist invasion").[7]

If this was the general approach of the Western European extreme right, its strongest representative at that point, the MSI, experienced some internal disagreements in foreign policy in relation to the international positioning of the country (with some members even supporting the policy of recognizing, via an anti-communist perspective, the Atlantic alliance with the former enemies).[8] Yet other rightist currents (some even structured within the MSI) openly adopted an outspoken pro-internationalist stance. Rather than pursuing moderation, thinkers such as the Italian baron and philosopher Julius Evola encouraged radicalization. The ideological core

[5] Bardèche, *Qu'est-ce que le fascisme?* p. 103.

[6] "Purtroppo la Francia mancava," p. 4.

[7] Bardèche, *Qu'est-ce que le fascisme?* p. 109.

[8] Almirante, the "spiritual" fringe (Enzo Erra), and the "leftist" *missini* (Ernesto Massi, Giorgio Pini) in some ways all virulently criticized the acceptance of a policy that was distant from a third way neofascism. The acceptance, even if it was never fully shared by everyone, of NATO then took place at the end of the 1950s. This *Atlantismo* was seen as an endeavor to move from the internal dualism "fascism versus anti-fascism" to the international clash of "communism versus anti-communism." In this imagined world, the MSI could have potentially played a stable anti-communist political role. On the foreign policy of the party, see Pietro Neglie, "Il Movimento sociale italiano fra terzaforzismo e atlantismo," *Storia contemporanea*, 25(6), 1994, pp. 1167–95; Roberto Chiarini, "'Sacro egoismo' e 'missione civilizzatrice.' La politica estera del Msi dalla fondazione alla metà degli anni Cinquanta," *Storia contemporanea*, 21(3), 1990, pp. 541–60; and Stefano Finotti, "Difesa occidentale e Patto Atlantico: la scelta internazionale del Msi," *Storia delle Relazioni Internazionali*, 2(1), 1988, pp. 94–124.

of this was a rejection of the existing order and a regeneration of activism. The same narrow and nostalgic nationalist-only fascism had to be revised. Along with his Francophone counterparts (mostly Bardèche), Evola played the card of a fascist ideology that was not to found in its usual past materialization: If it was to be depicted at all, fascism was to be pure, an aspiration, crossing borders, and, consequently, de-territorialized and independent from the existing world powers.

Regenerating fascist doctrine was vital to make post-1945 right-wing extremism acceptable. A solution was, indeed, to reshape its territorial connotations, expunging it from aggressive expansionism and nationalism. In sum, fascism could really only be a spiritual, universal, or "pan-European" philosophy – probably as the interwar fascist streams had intended. The strategy to avoid stigmatization, as imagined by some French and Italian extremists, was designed to look at the non-national dimension and use the European continent (in the sense of "Western Europe," although at other times even as a whole "Eurafrica" and "Eurasia") as the new spatial dimension. This was, in some ways, natural, as it was entrenched in a common (European) fascist brotherhood developed in the previous years. This led to the creation of neofascist international organizations and the development of a "Nation-Europe" imaginary. This also generated a good number of French and Italian groups (and publications) spreading this pan-national extremism. This will be, for example, the cases (here described) of Filippo Anfuso, Adriano Romualdi, and *Europe-Action*.

Neofascists in both France and Italy, as this chapter will reveal, usually worked hand-in-hand to elaborate this ideal further and pursue the consequential pan-European (political) projects at least up until the early 1960s (and then again in the late 1970s and also today). At other times, they acted in parallel to develop this new Europeanism, but always, and "transnationally," looking at each other as they perceived the other to belong to the same (fascist) entity.

THE BLACK BARON: JULIUS EVOLA

Immediately after the war, a number of Italian fascists, especially the ones who were young to have fought under the Salò Republic and to have lost the Second World War, joined the MSI. Some of them, nonetheless, experienced a contraposition with part of the (usually older) activists grounded in the experience of slightly less radical features of the twenty-year fascist regime (the *Ventennio*). The most rebellious ones specifically formed an organizational strand called the Figli del Sole (Sun's Sons) but were also known as the "spiritualists." Along with Evola, they looked abroad to find their sources of doctrinal inspiration: Thinkers such as Bardèche and Brasillach and the French fascist writer and war collaborator Pierre Drieu la Rochelle became their champions for a borderless nationalism.[9]

These radical fringes of the right-wing extremist youth in Italy had first gathered around the periodical *La Sfida* and since 1950 also in the review *Imperium*, directed by Enzo Erra, which benefited from the activism of people such as Pino Rauti, Paolo Andriani, Fausto Gianfranceschi, and Giano Accame (and some collaborators of this latter journal seemed to have joined some fascist clandestine activity). They were opposing the other youth publication *Architrave*, which was close to Roberto Mieville and the official line of the MSI.

La Sfida and *Imperium* promoted a somewhat spiritual politics. It was, in some ways, an ascetic activism that would have led to the production of a revolutionary policy. This would have also avoided, at least in their views, a sure failure in the fight against the "complete and formidable doctrinal system" that was characterizing and defending both "the liberal and the communist world."[10] This was, above all, a right-leaning elitist doctrine. To use Erra's own words, "only the best people" had the right to lead and command and to impose their will (but also to comprehend the needs of a nation). The building of a "new aristocracy" was henceforth the necessity, as it was the "rejection of the whole democratic structure and conception of the state."[11] All this was placed in a spatial framework that also made use of references to the "universality of Rome," the importance of a supreme overall empire, the need to spread these policies worldwide, and the leading role of Italy in a federated Europe.[12]

Imperium's doctrinal elaboration was naturally strongly influenced by Evola. It was, in fact, the encounter with books like *Rivolta contro il condo moderno* (Revolt against the Modern World), first published in 1934, that changed the lives and doctrinal outlook of this rebellious

[9] See also Loredana Guerrieri, "... *Essere fascisti in democrazia" Destra ed estrema destra in Italia (1956–1969)* (Ph.D. dissertation, Università degli Studi di Macerata, 2007), p. 32.

[10] "Questa Rivista," *Imperium*, 1, May 1950, p. 4.

[11] Enzo Erra, "Liberazione radicale," *Imperium*, 1, May 1950, p. 4.

[12] Fernando Stasi, "L'Universalità," *Imperium*, 1, May 1950, p. 18.

youth.[13] This comes as a surprise if we consider that Evola had no great fondness for the MSI and was against the "leftism" of some of its party circles. Yet at the same time, Evola firmly believed in the capacities of these young neofascists, who probably represented his imagined "new men" (this was probably a fascist concept borrowed from the interwar years).[14] He especially gave them the opportunity to bypass a traditional Italian-only nationalist rhetoric linked to Il Duce, and thereby let them explore another theoretical universe made up of references to Indo-Aryanism, esotericism, paganism, oriental doctrines, and spiritual racism, but also to thinkers such as Drieu la Rochelle, Brasillach, René Guénon, Leon Degrelle, Ananda Coomaraswamy, Mircea Eliade, Carl Schmitt, Ernst Jünger, Corneliu Codreanu and the Iron Guard, Mircea Eliade, and Oswald Spengler (and with some of them, like Guénon and Codreanu, Evola maintained a friendship). This opened up new perspectives and expanded the pan-national dimensions of Italian neofascism. In so doing, Evola, the anti-modern philosopher of the "world of tradition," a man who came up against the principles promoted by an interwar clerical fascism, became the spiritual guide of some generations of, not just Italian, but genuinely European extreme-right activists. Intriguingly, some of the contemporary extremists currently criticizing the power of banks, financial institutions, and economic globalization mention, at times, this old fascist intellectual as a reference point in their challenge to a perceived markets-led world.

Evola's political philosophy was, in fact, grounded in the values of concepts such as tradition, idealism, spiritualism, counter-revolution, and hierarchy. This was a truly aristocratic and elitist doctrine (as also materialized with *La Sfida* and *Imperium*) that was, in turn, also inspired by oriental doctrines, together with Guénon and the organic, anti-egalitarian, and rightist-nationalist environment of the German *Konservative Revolution* (Conservative Revolution) movement that had developed after the First World War.

[13] I use here the English translation, Julius Evola, *Revolt against the Modern World* (Rochester, VT: Inner Traditions, 1995).

[14] Evola's influence cannot be limited to this youth current of the MSI. It was widespread in different party circles. According to scholar Giovanni Tassani: "egli esercita un fascino culturale più vasto che lo rende ambito alle principali testate di destra, di cui sarà più o meno occasionale collaboratore, da 'Il Meridano d'Italia' . . . a 'Il Nazionale'" Giovanni Tassani, "Le culture della destra italiana tra dopoguerra e centrosinistra. Gentilianesimo, collaboratore ed evolismo a confronto e in concorrenza," *Nuova Storia Contemporanea*, 7(2), 2003, p. 141.

Evola's aim was to promote a small elite of pure and uncontaminated "warriors." It was clear in his own mind that his ideology was not for wider public consumption. As already suggested, this elitist thinker wanted especially "to lay down a 'testimony' written for those who are 'different' – *l'uomo differenziato* – those who are of the type that does not belong to this time."[15] Evola, in *Cavalcare la Tigre* (Riding the Tiger), was notably outspoken on this point: His doctrine was not for the everyday man, it was theorized for those who intimately did not belong to the modern world, but who were, instead, convinced that they belonged to a "race" different from their contemporaries. In such a vein, Evola called for an abstract and "distant" political engagement against the hedonistic contemporary period: This was summarized with the concept of *apolitia* (or *apoliteia*), and it embodied an inner distance for the society of the time.[16] This mankind had to find origins into the world of tradition, and this tradition, according to Evola, was a concept close to Guénon's interpretations of the crisis of the modern world.[17]

All this supported the image of an organic and hierarchal community, as opposed to the existing nation-state. The popular legitimization that arises from below (*demos*, voters), and that characterizes the democratic system, was, in Evola's opinion, an expression of "ideological perversion" and "political regression."[18] The outcome of his doctrine was the rejection of the postwar order, and of the decadence caused by democracy and egalitarianism. This was also tied up with a call for the acceptance of the divine nature of power and authority – as in the Middle Ages or the Roman Empire – that were perceived either in terms of Regnum (Kingdom) or Imperium (Empire).[19] The baron highlighted the need to return to the respect of discipline, honor, and obedience, and emphasized the

[15] H. T. Hansen, "A Short Introduction to Julius Evola," in Evola, *Revolt*, p. xiii. H. T. Hansen should be the pseudonym for Hans Thomas Hakl, an Austrian essayist who translated many Evola's writings into German.

[16] For the terminology used, I borrow the title of this collection of essays: Julius Evola (edited by Riccardo Paradisi), *Apolitia. Scritti sugli "orientamenti esistenziali" 1934–1973* (Rome: Controcorrente, 2004).

[17] Julius Evola, *Cavalcare la Tigre. Orientamenti esistenziali per un'epoca della dissoluzione* (Rome: Edizioni Mediterranee, 1995, originally published in 1961), p. 19.

[18] Evola, *Revolt*, p. 24.

[19] This would have also avoided a "revolution from below" led by socialist forces. See Julius Evola "Idee sulla destra," in Julius Evola (edited by Alessandro Barbera), *Idee per una Destra* (Rome: Fondazione Julius Evola, 1997), p. 28. The periodical *Carattere* first published this essay in 1957. On this idea of a "decadent democracy" see also Julius Evola, *Gli uomini e le rovine* (Rome: Volpe, 1972, first published in 1953), but also Evola, *Revolt*, pp. 7–15 and 24–28.

virtues of uncontaminated fascist, timeless, and spaceless activists imbued with a legionary spirit (at times shaped, for example, via the mythology of samurais).[20] However, this theorization also influenced, to some extent, a revolutionary subversive activism assaulting the democratic order.

All this was coupled with contemptuous criticism of existing political philosophies – especially those generated by the Enlightenment and the French Revolution. They were, in essence, the different faces of the same tradition, and they intrinsically correlated with each other: "Liberalism, then democracy, then socialism, then radicalism and finally communism and bolshevism," Evola writes, "historically appeared like degrees of the same evil, each of them preparing the following one in a whole downfall process."[21] His critique of the United States especially strong, including its lifestyles and free-market thinking; neither did he accepted American individualist connotations and what he saw as the "irritability" of its related ideological liberalism.[22] Such views were embodied in the title of an essay that Evola published in French: "Le Libéralisme grand route de la décadence" (Liberalism, Main Road of Decadence).[23] The problem, as he put it, was the "illusion" that democracy and liberalism were the "antithesis" of communism and they had the power to stem the rise of progressive forces.[24] Given this, Europe was (allegedly) at risk of being caught in the grip of the Soviet and American powers.[25]

A "UNIVERSAL" NEOFASCISM

In an often hectic immediate postwar era characterized for fascists by feelings of isolation and defeat (and, with only few exceptions, lack of intellectual elaboration), Evola turned out to be a source for young activists. This was, in fact, the time of new winning forces, along with the growing popularity of anti-fascism. In such a context, Evola

[20] The "legionary spirit" was the attitude of those who had chosen "the hardest lifestyle" and were fighting, even if they knew that the battle was lost. Ferraresi, *Threats to Democracy*, p. 20.

[21] Julius Evola, *Orientamenti* (Rome: Settimo Sigillo, 2002, first published in 1950, and revised in 1971), pp. 25–26.

[22] Julius Evola, "I due volti del liberalismo," in Evola, *Idee*, p. 32. The essay was first published on October 1968, by *Il Borghese*. On this Americanism considered as, in some ways, more dangerous than communism, see also Evola, *Orientamenti*, p. 30.

[23] Julius Evola, "Le Libéralisme grand route de la décadence," *Défense de l'Occident*, 102, 1972, pp. 23–37.

[24] Evola, *Orientamenti*, p. 27.

[25] Ibid., p. 29.

became "decisive in transforming ghettoization into a badge of honor, marginalization into a proud boast (the damnation of the modern world), and victimization into the superiority complex of the 'differentiated man.'"[26] As mentioned before, he firmly advised his disciples (although he was publically rather reluctant to create his own "school" or to be considered as a *maestro*) to distance themselves from the materialist perversion of liberalism and communism as well as the immoral modern society.

The only possible opposition to this modern decadence was to bypass the conformist, bourgeois, and nationalist vision of the contemporary political and cultural right.[27] The key was a radical reinterpretation of right-wing politics, along with the founding of an independent Europe. This latter was perceived to be a real third force grounded in the tradition, and also anti-Marxist, anti-democratic, and racially defined. This was later summarized in a short script published by the British rightist periodical *Scorpion* in 1986 (and titled "United Europe: The Spiritual Prerequisite"):

> The condition of a truly *European* entity must be the binding force of an idea and tradition which Europe is irrevocably linked. Some argue that the nation state ... is a model for the merging European nation. ... This view is inadequate. The birth of the European nations was largely the work of dynasties representing a tradition of loyalty to a particular crown. ... The concept of nationhood is [similarly] inappropriate. The notion of European unity is spiritual and supranational. ... The European *Imperium* will belong to a higher order than the parts which compose it, and to be European should be conceived as being something qualitatively different from being Italian ..., Scottish or Hungarian, something which appeals to a different aspect of our character.[28]

Evola also in other writings placed specific importance on this pan-Europe, which, in his understanding, was shaped in the interwar years:

> These Waffen-SS ... generated what has been called the "first European army." ... Perspectives changed in this period. People stopped to identify Aryanism with Germanism. The intention was not to fight for a National Socialism unilaterally racist and for a "Pan-Germanism," but for a superior idea, for Europe and a European "New Order."[29]

[26] Ferraresi, *Threats to Democracy*, p. 191. [27] Evola "Idee sulla destra," p. 26.

[28] Evola's essay is a short adaptation from *Gli uomini e le rovine*, and republished in Roger Griffin, *Fascism* (Oxford: Oxford University Press, 1995), p. 343.

[29] Julius Evola, *Il fascismo visto dalla destra. Note sul Terzo Reich*, 3rd ed. (Rome: Giovanni Volpe Editore, 1974), pp. 216–17.

Evola, above all, offered neofascists a nonterritorial nationalism, or, better, a nationalism expunged by all territorial fanaticisms and factionalisms.[30] "National" was, in this reading, a byword for "universal," as the actual "apex of traditional civilizations consisted in the principle of universalism."[31] The Italian baron proposed to abandon any sentimental perception of the nation (*patria*, motherland). The new dimension was to be found in supranational units, whereby the unifying issue was the supremacy of the "Ideal" – it was in this that right-leaning sympathizers worldwide had to recognize their real fatherland, not in existing and material countries and shared mother tongues.[32]

Stemming from this "spiritual-intellectual" current, an extreme right-wing group that rapidly achieved renown from the 1950s was Ordine Nuovo (New Order, ON), which published a journal of the same title, *Ordine Nuovo*. Its leading figure was Pino Rauti, a first-rank representative of Italian neofascism. This rightist think tank was, at the beginning, an organic unit within the MSI. It came into being with the name Centro Studi Ordine Nuovo (Study Center New Order), later becoming an independent movement in 1956. ON's political propositions became excessively radical for the official policy of the MSI. Indeed, it rejected the working of the parliamentary and democratic system, along with all mainstream political philosophies, and turned out to be a training ground for the most extreme and extra-parliamentary neofascist activist streams.[33] Rauti believed that the MSI strategy of a potential collaboration with the center-right in an anti-communist front was doomed to failure.[34] Nor could ON accept to any further degree the pragmatic, conservative, and nostalgic qualities of the party led, at the time, by Michelini. ON's main project was instead to become a proper study center for the elaboration of neofascist thinking. This was carried out under the influence of Evola's writings, including *Cavalcare la Tigre*, a

30 Evola, *Gli uomini*, p. 242. 31 Evola, *Revolt*, p. 338.

32 Evola, *Orientamenti*, pp. 41–42.

33 For a brief account on the evolution of this movement, see Petra Rosenbaum, *Il nuovo fascismo, da Salò ad Almirante* (Milan: Feltrinelli, 1975), pp. 79–81. Chapter 3 mentions how ON was also inspired by the French decolonization.

34 Interestingly, before leaving the MSI, Rauti pointed toward what he saw as the "problem at the heart of the MSI" – in other words, did the party want to become one of the usual democratic parties, or was it willing to serve as "a tool of the National Revolution"? Quoted in Roberto Chiarini and Paolo Corsini, *Da Salò a Piazza della Loggia. Blocco d'ordine, neofascismo, radicalismo di destra a Brescia (1945–1974)* (Milan: Franco Angeli, 1983), p. 187.

book that called for the concept of *apolitia* – where political action was taken over by an ascetic engagement and spiritualist self. This was unsurprising, because of the background of sympathizers, many of whom had links with *Imperium*. Evola regularly contributed to the review *Ordine Nuovo*, attempting to shift, once more, Italian extremist culture from old fascists like the interwar philosopher, promoter of the Manifesto of the Fascist Intellectuals, and Mussolini's Education Minister, Giovanni Gentile (with, for example, his concept of an "ethical state"), to organicism, tradition, elitism, radicalism, spiritualism – all placed in a wider European, and fascist, framework.[35]

Although Evola's work was a strong reference point, ON's "bibliography" also contained Guénon, Spengler, Eliade, and, of course, all the mythology borrowed from National Socialism.[36] In line with this, ON theorized an Evolian vision of society and political militancy. It was fascist-like movement, anti-Semite (and, consequently, virulently anti-egalitarian), culturally intransigent, and politically revolutionary. It also supported a xenophobic symbology, calling for a unified fascist Europe.[37]

ON had a relevant international network. In 1958 it created a special section of the study center dealing with foreign relations and exchanges and published a journal named *Ordine Nuovo Europeo*. This publication had articles in a variety of languages and aimed to design and spread an imagined "Fatherland Europe" that, as we shall see, became a key objective for many European neofascists.[38] The common denominator was a fraternal European nationalism, which was also theorized and spread through other ON bulletins such as *Noi Europa* and *Europa Korrespondenz*. The group also had links with a number of foreign secret services (especially the ones in not fully democratic countries such as Spain, Greece, South Africa, Portugal, and Rhodesia) and transnational groupings and structures (including some with almost subversive aims) like the former French army officer Yves Guérin-Sérac's Ordre et Tradition

[35] See also Guerrieri, *Essere fascisti*, p. 47; and Francesco Cassata, *A destra del fascismo. Profilo politico di Julius Evola* (Turin: Bollati Boringhieri, 2003), pp. 340–42.

[36] See also AFUS, Fondo Movimento Sociale Italiano (hereafter FMSI), Serie 1 "Istituto di Studi Corporativi (Isc)," Sottoserie, 1 "Documentazione Storica MSI," UA 8 "Ordine Nuovo."

[37] On this neofascist belief on the "damages" that egalitarianism would have caused to the political and constitutional structure of the nation-states, see Pino Rauti, *Le idee che mossero il mondo* (Rome: Edizioni Europa, 1976), pp. 295–96.

[38] Guerrieri, *Essere fascisti*, p. 91.

(Order and Tradition) and his Lisbon-based Aginter Press.[39] Moreover, ON's activities were also regularly covered in publications abroad. For example, in 1965, the neofascist press in France, including *Europe Action* (a journal and movement to be discussed in the following pages), praised some of the ON political projects, as they would have generated "a new tool of political action that leaves in its wake the vagaries and old formulas of the 'archeological right.'" In doing so, in French eyes, ON would have become the "elite group" of the "permanent guard" of the revolution.[40] France was an obvious ally for Rauti's group. Political circles close to ON, including the periodical *Riscossa*, considered French publications such as *Rivarol* and *Écrits de Paris* and their editorialists (labeled like the heirs of the "great war collaborators") as chiefly contributing to the establishment of a novel European culture, which would have also led the continent.[41]

These links with France were facilitated by, and benefited from, the existing Evolian web. Evola's works had been, in fact, permeating into France since the interwar period, and he maintained a close camaraderie with Guénon, as both had criticized the modern western world. After the Second World War, Evola kept strong ties with the anti-modernist extremist writer Pierre Pascal and had many of his writings translated into French. In the 1950s his influence in France was spread through the networks of the most radical and revolutionary neofascist fringes, and later by personalities such as Giorgio Locchi and Antonio Lombardi, who were, subsequently, to influence the Nouvelle Droite.[42] Furthermore, the Italian philosopher intermittently collaborated with fascist and neofascist periodicals such as *Contre-Révolution*, *Études traditionnelles*, *Cahiers de l'herméneutique*, *Études et recherches*, *Écrits de Paris*, and, later, with *Défense de l'Occident*. In this last publication, Evola was intensely and

[39] See also Franco Ferraresi, "The Radical Right in Postwar Italy," *Politics and Society*, 16(1), 1988, p. 82; and Alessandro Silj, *Malpaese. Criminalità, corruzione, e politica nell'Italia della prima Repubblica. 1943–1994* (Rome: Donzelli Editore, 1994), pp. 79–80. It is worth mentioning that Guérin-Sérac was one of the founders of the Organisation Armée Secrète and had, over the years, some direct links with many Italian neofascists, including Rauti, Stefano delle Chiaie, and Guido Giannettini (see Chapter 3).

[40] Europe-Action, "Un entretien exclusif avec l'un des dirigeants du Centre Italien 'Ordine Nuovo,'" *Europe Action Hebdomadaire*, 108, February 1966, p. 6.

[41] Quoted in Chiarini and Corsini, *Da Salò*, p. 254.

[42] See Pierre Milza, "Julius Evola et la 'Nouvelle Droite' française," in E. Decleva and P. Milza, eds., *Italia e Francia: i nazionalismi a confronto* (Milan: Franco Angeli, 1993), pp. 318–19.

outspokenly taken as a key European *maîtres à penser*, and his doctrine was regularly discussed by French writers.[43]

MAURICE BARDÈCHE, A FASCIST EUROPEAN WRITER

The reference to *Défense de l'Occident* helps us to turn our attention, on the other side of the Alps, to its editor, Maurice Bardèche, who was notably one of the promoters of right-wing extremism in the postwar world. Bardèche, who married the sister of the controversial writer Robert Brasillach, was an intellectual who had no hesitation in defining himself as a "fascist writer" and influenced by José Antonio Primo de Rivera (the founder of the Spanish Falange in the 1930s – in his view, the only "true Spanish fascist"), Evola, Drieu la Rochelle, Brasillach, and the most revolutionary versions of Benito Mussolini's enterprise.[44] Bardèche also wrote an influential manuscript, *Qu'est-ce que le fascisme?* (What Is Fascism?), published in the early 1960s – a study that, when it was translated into Italian, became a cult book for local neofascists.[45]

From an ideological standpoint, he had an anti-modern and anti-capitalist vision of *fascismo* that was well represented by the epopee and intimate spirit of the March on Rome (including the *squadristi*) and Salò.[46] Therefore, for Bardèche, as with people like Evola, fascism was something different from the stereotypical images referring to Mussolini in power:

> Fascism is not about the hierarchs [the fascist party officials], the arms raised upward [the Roman salute] and the betrayal of the moment [in July1943]. In that small lakefront republic [the RSI on Lake Garda] it was even the opposite of all this; that republic where Mussolini tried to go back, though by then it was too late, to the spirit of the March on Rome, and to find again the fascism of the origins in the middle of his early comrades.[47]

[43] See, for example, François Huyghe, "Julius Evola et l''Etat organique,'" *Défense de l'Occident*, 112, 1973, pp. 8–15; Philippe Baillet, "L'œuvre d'Evola (I)," *Défense de l'Occident*, 129, 1975, pp. 67–88; and Philippe Baillet, "L'œuvre d'Evola (II)," *Défense de l'Occident*, 130, 1975, pp. 29–57.

[44] Bardèche, *Qu'est-ce que le fascisme?* pp. 9 and 61.

[45] See Maurice Bardèche, *Che cosa è il fascismo?* (Rome: Volpe, 1963).

[46] Bardèche, *Qu'est-ce que le fascisme?* p. 20.

[47] Maurice Bardèche, "Reflexions sur le fascisme," *Défense de l'Occident*, 46, 1957, p. 5.

Fascist political doctrine had, nonetheless, to be isolated from its most famous historical manifestations, trying to save at least the "beauty of the ideal" and its other most intangible features.[48] In this way,

> the fascist writer wanted to give fascist ideology all its strength again. By distinguishing ideology from its deviances, he wants to reach the 'fascist dream.' In his perspective, the 'fascist contract' represents much more than an ideological engagement. It reveals … a global perception of the warrior, of the fighter.[49]

Given this, Bardèche was rightly portrayed as a significant fascist Trojan horse in the post-1945 world, one also able to describe fascism in many different and colorful ways.[50]

All this came with a virulent historical revisionism. He lamented the tragic consequences (for France) of the German defeat of May 8, 1945, and, also, through essays published in different languages (including in Italian), minimizing the fascist policies.[51] This led to a sentence for apology, and he spent a few weeks in prison. In this case, the fascist writer was strongly defended by the neofascist press in Italy, which described his imprisonment as like a "sadness." The *Meridiano d'Italia* considered his writing on Nuremberg as probably the "most lucid and brave manuscript published in Europe after the so-called 'liberation.'" This was a book for

[48] As Bardèche later summed up: "Je ne récuse pas *tout* ce que fut le national-socialisme allemand ni le fascisme mussolinien. J'essai de dégager ce que Stendhal eût appelé le *beau idéal* du fascisme, en éliminant des éléments qui sont, les uns, des variantes nationales, les autres, des circuits qu'une conception doctrinale du fascisme ne retient pas comme indispensables." Maurice Bardèche, "Réponse sur le Fascisme," *Défense de l'Occident*, 22, 1962, p. 31.

[49] Valerie Igounet, *Histoire du négationnisme en France* (Paris: Seuil, 2000), p. 58.

[50] As suggested by Ian Barnes, Bardèche, in fact, "clothes fascism with various virtues and qualities: the spectacle of joyfulness, health and happiness. His fascism also incorporates images of chivalry, the exaltation of brave and loyal heroes, the development of straightforward and humane relationships, and the vision of a hierarchical but harmonious society. Such colourful and dreamlike visions arguably have provided a fertile nursery ground for other fascists throughout the 1960s, 1970s and 1980s. … This poetic aspect of Bardèche makes him one of the most potentially dangerous neo-fascist philosophers since 1945." Ian Barnes, "A Fascist Trojan Horse: Maurice Bardèche, Fascism and Authoritarian Socialism," *Patterns of Prejudice*, 37(2), 2003, p. 194.

[51] This postwar French writer equally defended collaborationists and virulently criticized all anti-fascist Resistance's values. See, for example, Maurice Bardèche, "Norimberga II ovvero di falsi monetari," *Meridiano d'Italia*, VI(12), March 25, 1951, p. 3; Maurice Bardèche, "8 Mai 1945," *Défense de l'Occident*, 24, 1955, pp. 11–15; Maurice Bardèche, *Lettre à François Mauriac* (Paris: La Pensée Libre, 1947); and Maurice Bardèche, *Nuremberg ou la terre promise* (Paris: Les Sept Couleurs, 1948). For a brief account of his views see also Deborah E. Lipstadt, *Denying the Holocaust. The Growing Assault on Truth and Memory* (New York: Penguin, 1994), pp. 50–52.

future generations, and the only guilt of Bardèche was that he was not defending an ideology, but simply "the fundamental values of our civilization."[52]

Bardèche was not only a mere fascist writer and theoretician; he was also a man full of political activism. He was the animator of many extremist circles, which represented the training ground for a generation of neofascists such as François Duprat and Alain de Benoist, and he had an impact well beyond France. For example, he influenced the Belgian Jean Thiriart and his Jeune Europe (Young Europe), which was an authentic transnational movement with ramifications in both France and Italy. In 1952, Bardèche founded and directed (up to 1982) the earlier mentioned *Défense de l'Occident*. Some "supporting committees" were immediately formed to back the journal and included foremost right-wing figures including the lawyer Jean-Louis Tixier-Vignancour (who was involved in the Vichy government and very active in postwar French right-leaning politics). Supporters were also provided with a booklet entitled *Principes d'action pour politique européenne* (Principles of Action for a European Politics), informing such sympathizers about the ideology of the journal and of one of the international neofascist fronts to be shortly described.

Once (correctly) considered the most important and influential extreme-right publication in postwar France, *Défense de l'Occident* additionally became a "crossroad" for French and foreign activists, as well as a focal point for the promotion of the non-French permutations of the fascist and neofascist phenomenon.[53] A section of the journal was named "Nouvelles Européennes, Nouvelles Politiques" (European News, Political News). Considerable exposure was given, obviously, to Italian politics – especially to Mussolini's fascism, Evola, and the MSI. MSI newspaper editor Filippo Anfuso, along with Giorgio Almirante, Ernesto Massi, and Evola, among others, contributed to this publication with essays, and this fascination with Italy (and also with the other main former fascist nation, Germany) was more than evident from the very first issue of the journal.[54]

52 "Da Guareschi a Bardèche," *Meridiano d'Italia*, 9(27), July 11, 1954, p. 3.

53 Jean-Yves Camus and René Monzat, *Les Droites nationales et radicales en France* (Lyon: Presses Universitaires de Lyon, 1992). On the internationalism promoted by the journal, see, among the many examples, the special edition on "the unknown fascisms" published in April 1969 (issue no. 81), and featuring articles on fascism across the world. This latter was also translated in Italian firstly by Edizioni del Borghese.

54 A good example of this is the article "Nouvelle d'Allemagne et d'Italie," *Défense de l'Occident*, 1, 1952, pp. 21–24.

All this was in line with Bardèche's political projects and his Europe-wide (and, in many ways, "borderless") fascism. His fascism was a synthesis (at times also slightly controversial) of socialism and nationalism, a movement and ideal capable of defending a specific European civilization and identity. The French fascist writer turned out to be, with a few others, the European hub for a number of extremist attempts to challenge the existing global order and the supposed feeble parliamentary systems, and also to create a right-wing international entity. Bardèche, in fact, supported a European order based on a truly neofascist worldview. This was to be a united Europe with a mission of the defense of the western world. This would have, first, assumed the habit of a confederation of nation-states, while later becoming a true federal state.[55] The key doctrinal point for the French ideologue was that a European community was certainly "indispensable," and nations were containers that were no more in line with the modern world. In this sense, old nationalisms had to modernize.[56] In sum, a reborn fascism had to take a pan-European connotation and became, in this way, less perceptible in people's eyes.[57]

This vision was naturally far from the mainstream version of the European integration and the existing balance of powers in international politics.[58] These neofascists believed that Europe had a future exclusively as a bastion against capitalism and Marxism and equally distant from the U.S. and Soviet superpowers.[59] This European community was willing to become a "healthy political force," as Bardèche suggested, and it had to "remove" all communists and crypto-communists from its own politics and structure.[60] The United States was apparently seen as little less dangerous, even if Bardèche similarly warned his fellow readers against American policy, because their market-led ideology would have been, in longer terms, negative for the continent.[61]

[55] Maurice Bardèche, "Pourquoi nous combattons," *Défense de l'Occident*, 4, 1953, p. 4.
[56] On this point, see, for example, Maurice Bardèche, "Notre Europe," *Défense de l'Occident*, 20, 1955, p. 3.
[57] Tamir Bar-On, "Fascism to the Nouvelle Droite: The Dream of Pan-European Empire," *Journal of Contemporary European Studies*, 16(3), 2008, pp. 335–36.
[58] Maurice Bardèche, "La Communauté européenne," in *Vingt-cinq ans contre l'imposture: Positions, Propositions, Extraits, Fragments de Défense de l'Occident. 1952–1977*, Special Edition of *Défense de l'Occident*, 153–54, 1977–78, p. 12. This essay was originally published in December 1953.
[59] Bardèche, *Qu'est-ce que le fascisme?* pp. 105–13.
[60] Bardèche, "Pourquoi," p. 5; and Maurice Bardèche, "L'Europe réelle," *Défense de l'Occident*, 116, 1974, p. 10.
[61] Maurice Bardèche, "L'amitié américaine," *Défense de l'Occident*, 88, 1970, p. 5.

In such a novel context, from Bardèche's perspective, as with other likeminded activists, the interwar version of fascist nationalism had to be genuinely updated to match the consequences of the defeat and the postwar environment. Indeed, a supranational community was the sole entity able to guarantee the independence of countries. For this reason, Bardèche explicitly wrote that "the mission of fascism became through necessity a European-wide one because only the European community brings meaning to our desire for national independence."[62]

The belief was that a "European national ideal" was due to develop, and this was linked to the making of a "moral elite" of citizens. This select vanguard of humankind had to show a virile and healthy conception of life, along with such unavoidable qualities as abnegation.[63] The similarities with, and the influence of, Evola are more than clear. In an Evolian perspective, they were the western counterparts of modern samurais; as warrior priests, they represented "another race which was born among us ... ; a *State within the State*."[64] These ideals were based on an elitist anti-egalitarian stance.[65] But, most pragmatically, this elite would have later established an "authentic European socialism."[66]

Other movements and thinkers would have subsequently developed many of Bardèche's themes over the years. The intellectual elaborations of ideologues such as Evola and Bardèche had, nonetheless, an immediate impact: They allowed the formation of a very fertile ideological ground made of allusions to universal ideals, spiritualism, and references across state borders, that all combined powerfully to contribute to the development of some genuine neofascist international associations and promote Europe like a forceful and appealing landscape.

BLACK INTERNATIONALS: "WE FOUGHT FOR EUROPE"

"Europe" became, in this case, a transposition of national identity, something rooted in a common and specific cultural (and often also ethnic) differentialism. As we know, this was an almost sentimental Europe that the French fascist writer built together with other postwar fascists such as

[62] Bardèche, "Reflexions," p. 9. [63] Bardèche, "La Communauté européenne," p. 14.
[64] Maurice Bardèche, "Les sept samurais," *Défense de l'Occident*, 3, 1960, p. 6.
[65] Like Evola, the French writer also believed in the values of the hierarchic feudal system. This was, in fact, a system promoting the inequality between "races, humans, and souls." See Bardèche, "Reflexions," p. 9.
[66] Ibid., p. 13.

Massi. As Bardèche wrote, "'What we do over there it is a bit of pure poetry,' the likable Ernesto Massi sighed one day, with a typical Italian irony, when he saw us building our Europe in the clouds."[67]

Massi was a university professor of economic geography. In the interwar years, he coedited, under the sponsorship of Fascism's Minister of Education Giuseppe Bottai, the journal *Geopolitica*. In the immediate postwar era, he was the founder of the study center Nazione Sociale (Social Nation), and he later chaired the Istituto di Studi Corporativi (Institute of Corporative Studies), playing some roles in the MSI.[68] Massi was close to (and also influential on) activists such as Bardèche for his "socialism." This was a fascistic form of socialism associated in interwar Italy with the so-called *sinistra fascista* (left fascism), and grounded in the Risorgimento's mythology of Italian patriots such as Carlo Pisacane, Giuseppe Mazzini, and Giuseppe Garibaldi, but also in some of the artistic vanguards, and the revolutionary syndicalism inspired by the French philosopher and thinker Georges Sorel. Sympathizers of this *sinistra fascista* were also involved in the MSI (and, for example, in publications like *Nazionalismo Sociale*, which will be discussed later). These *fascisti di sinistra* (left-wing fascists) embraced corporatism and socialization and envisioned a third way. It was exactly that supposedly novel "social and economic conception," the organic social nationalism or European socialism, that informed many of Massi's, Engdahl's and Bardèche's works.[69] What is important to note here is that this ideologue was very active, along with Bardèche, in promoting a pan-European vision of extremism, and this "corporatist" base strongly influenced the doctrine of the 1950s fascist-type internationals.

Indeed, as Massi pointed out, one of the features of the early Cold War years was actually the proliferation of internationals. These organizations were not "super-parties or international parties" because national autonomy was preserved. They acted like transnational hubs and places of encounters (and collaboration) for likeminded people and ideals.[70] This had to be also the time for postwar fascist internationals – those

[67] Maurice Bardèche, "Autocritique," *Défense de l'Occident*, 62, 1959, p. 3.

[68] It is worth mentioning that Massi left the MSI in the late 1950s.

[69] For an example see Ernesto Massi, "Per una politica sociale ed economica al servizio dell'unità europea," in Ernesto Massi, *Nazione Sociale. Scritti Politici, 1948–1976* (Rome: ISC, 1990), pp. 269–75 (originally published in *Nazione Sociale*, November 1953).

[70] Ernesto Massi, "La funzione delle 'Internazionali,'" in ibid., p. 204 (originally published in *Nazione Sociale*, October 1952).

based on a European (rightist) socialism, or better, on a corporatist-like "social nationalism."[71]

This new Eurofascist dogma was initially discussed in the English-speaking extreme-right world. Sir Oswald Mosley called for "Europe a Nation" and Francis Parker Yockey for an "Imperium," and they sought to bypass fascist ultra-nationalism.[72] Intriguingly, even a non-European like the American-born Yockey, who wrote in 1948 *Imperium: The Philosophy of History and Politics*, an influential book for many postwar fascists across the western globe, was one of the most fervent promoters (also through his small British-based European Liberation Front) of a united and independent Europe.[73] As a great admirer of and expert on the old continent, he traveled extensively across European lands and was hosted in Italy by the MSI and Maria Pignatelli di Cerchiara (in this last case, for a whole month, to help in the organization of one of the MIF conferences, the earlier mentioned neofascist female association). Yockey was, in many ways, a precursor of many of the thinkers whom readers will find in this and in some other chapters.

He was influential among neofascists attracted by the renewed image of a pan-Europe – where this latter was a space for fascistic encounters and a place where one could redeploy the previous nation-based ideologies. Many of them were also very interested in moving away from the image of fascists as solely physical street fighters: If another revolution was about to happen, it had to be based on a legitimate doctrinal elaboration – as it was, for example, in the case of Evola's writings. In fact, it was evident to some of them that fascist nationalism could be revitalized and regenerated only through a deterritorialization followed by a reterritorialization at a pan-European, and basically supra-national, level.

The MSI, the most organized and successful European neofascist movement of the time, was about to play a central in role in these attempts to refresh fascism through the construction of a black international. However, French neofascists also made their own strong contribution to this

[71] Ibid., p. 208.

[72] Kevin Coogan, "Lost Imperium: The European Liberation Front (1949–54)," *Patterns of Prejudice*, 36(3), 2002, p. 11. Yockey and Mosley soon disagreed because of the former's belief that the main enemy for Europe was his motherland America (and only secondly Russia). This was also certainly far from the pragmatic approach of a number of neofascist movements that in the Cold War, in some ways, supported the U.S. in an anti-communist perspective.

[73] On Yockey, see Kevin Coogan, *Dreamer of the Day: Francis Parker Yockey and the Postwar Fascist International* (New York: Autonomedia, 1999).

strategy. Immediately after the war they were, as mentioned, in a number of international right-leaning fronts and supporting organizations. In 1947, in an interview with an Italian newspaper, the French fascist collaborationist Marcel Déat – who was shielded in northern Italy – shouted an unambiguous and premonitory battle cry: "Let Italians know, those Italians who share our ideals, that we are coming back very soon. The construction of a fascist international is not a secret."[74]

This was not an unknown project then, and its promoters worked fast. Binet and Bardèche, together with the MSI, Karl Heinz Priester, Per Engdahl, and other prominent fascists like Mosley, all promoted the 1950 conference in Rome for the establishment of a proper international network, which was mainly organized by the MSI. A second conference was then held in the quieter, and more "tolerable" (for former fascists), Swedish city of Malmö in 1951.[75] It led to the Mouvement Social Européen (European Social Movement, MSE), which was also known as the Malmö International and chaired by Engdahl. In this way, the old continent officially became the new battlefield for a never-disappeared fascist brotherhood: "nous combattions pour l'Europe" (we fought for Europe), as one of the pro-Europeanist ideologues, Massi, put it at a meeting of the MSE held in Holzminden (Germany) in October 1953. He also referred to the "European spirit" emerging from the interwar fascist comradeship. [76]

This international association was organized in national sections, allowing a dual membership with existing parties. This was because, in the intentions of the founders, the MSE would have not replaced the single national movements, but, rather, aimed to act as their representative at the European level.[77] Ideologically, their overall political agenda developed that popular image of a third-way Europe (a "young" and "social" Europe) grounded in fascist corporatism, different workers' and industrial arrangements, and anti-liberalism.[78]

[74] Quoted in Algazy, *La tentation néo-fasciste*, p. 76.

[75] See also Angelo Del Boca and Mario Giovana, *Fascism Today: A World Survey* (London: Heinemann, 1970), pp. 83–84.

[76] Massi, "Une Politique Sociale Européenne," p. 30. This essay was a reproduction of Massi's intervention at this conference organized by the MSE's European Studies Commission. It was also republished in Ernesto Massi, "Per una politica sociale ed economica al servizio dell'unità europea," in Massi, *Nazione Sociale*, pp. 268–79.

[77] "Qu'est-ce que le M.S.E.?" *Défense de l'Occident*, 13, 1954, p. 37.

[78] The reorganization of the European labor and economy was a recurrent preoccupation emerging from the writings of the MSE ideologues. See, for example, Per Engdahl,

The MSE was also more than this collection of ideals. Setting aside an apology for interwar authoritarianism and the rehabilitation of dictatorial regimes, this international front backed a hierarchical restructuring of Europe, and a Europe to be liberated from the two blocks of U.S. capitalism and Soviet communism. Moreover, and in line with some of the neofascist doctrines of the time, it carried on a strident critique of parliamentary democracy. As reported during the Malmö conference:

> Democracy which is currently supreme in the European countries is incompetent to rally those material and moral forces which could make Europe a third factor in the development of world politics. The goal of the Congress is a united and independent Europe. But this goal presupposes that each country will have carried out its social and national revolution.[79]

Although the MSI's influence was manifest in the choice of name, MSE, it was *Défense de l'Occident* that turned out to be the vector, at least in Francophone countries, for the diffusion of their policies. [80] Its first issue, in December 1952, included a brochure with the MSE manifesto ("Principes d'action pour politique européenne"), and, over the years, it hosted articles from Engdahl and other activists of this association. In practice, it acted as a platform where the most up-to-date Eurofascist doctrine was elaborated and discussed.

Another international extreme right-wing organization developed in the same period. It mainly generated from some doctrinal disagreements in the MSE and, specifically, on the necessity to have a racially pure fascist continent. Binet, in fact, left the MSE a short time after its foundation, and he played a key role in the founding of the Nouvel Ordre Européen (New European Order, NOE) in late September 1951.[81] This movement later published the Belgium-based review *Europe Réelle*. It also established a European Liaison Center and organized some international

"Le Marché Commune et l'avenir," *Défense de l'Occident*, 58, 1959, pp. 30–36; and Massi, "Per una politica sociale," pp. 272–77.

[79] Quoted in Tauber, "German Nationalists," p. 571.

[80] As Duprat noted a few years later, the MSI was by far the most important movement, although this would have also (probably) led to an imbalance in the organization. Duprat, *Les Mouvements*, p. 48.

[81] In reference to the split in the MSE, Duprat argued that Binet was in reality driven by a strong desire to take power and overthrow Bardèche from the French section of the MSE (and also to replace him in the European executive board). This was probably true. However, I tend to agree with the general belief that there was mostly an ideological policy referring to ethnic relations behind the NOE. See, respectively, Duprat, *Les Mouvements*, pp. 51–52, and Stephen Dorril, *Blackshirt: Sir Oswald Mosley and British Fascism* (London: Penguin/Viking, 2007), p. 596.

meetings and conferences. Many groups and leaders were invited to the largest one in December 1953, including the MSI representative Tullio Abelli.[82] A main concern of this group, which still formally exists, was the preservation of white civilization. Consequently, along with the usual anti-communism and anti-capitalism, it was strongly inspired by a blend of social Darwinism and anti-Semitism. For example, Turin's neofascist journal *I Quaderni Neri* published a document produced in one of the NOE conferences in the early 1960s, which argued that Jews "shall obey the law of the country" where they live or they would be forced "to leave it."[83]

A network of French neofascists backed the NOE. This included Binet's groups and publications and had among its sympathizers the Phalange Française (French Phalange), led by Charles Luca, an activist who shared Binet's politics toward postwar Europe (and dreamed of a new "fascist century").[84] (To show the usual high degree of transnationality that pervaded the extreme right in those Cold War years, it is important to note that Luca's young Phalangistes participated in summer camps organized by various European neofascist groups, including in Italy).[85] Another quite active group was the Fédération d'Action Nationale et Européenne (Federation of National and European Action, FANE), which published *Notre Europe*. The editor, and leader of the movement, was Marc Frédriksen. The FANE quickly became one of the chief representatives of the NOE in France, and, according to some commentators, it was even built locally by the French NOE supporters, along with the Comité de soutien à l'Europe Réelle (Supporting Committee for the Real Europe), to avoid the dispersion of their members.[86] *Notre Europe* had, quite regularly (and predictably), a section of the journal devoted to the latest developments from Italy, especially the most radical fringes of Italian neofascism. At the turn of the 1960s, its main contact in Italy became ON. *Notre Europe* indeed promoted Rauti's

[82] On this meeting, held at Lorrach in Germany, see Tauber, "German Nationalists," pp. 573–74.

[83] Quoted in Gianni Scipione Rossi, *La destra e gli ebrei. Una storia italiana* (Soveria Mannelli: Rubbettino, 2005), p. 82, note 63.

[84] Luca quoted in Chebel d'Appollonia, *L'extrême-droite en France*, p. 285.

[85] ACS, MI, DGPS, SIS, Ufficio Affari Riservati (hereafter UAR), 1957–60, B. 108 ("Mouvement Populaire Français"); and also Algazy, *La tentation néo-fasciste*, p. 304.

[86] On the creation of the FANE and the influence of the NOE, see Joseph Algazy, *L'extrême-droite en France de 1965 à 1984* (Paris: L'Harmattan, 1989), pp. 41–44.

related publications in France, and, in 1967, it proudly declared that it had received the first issue of ON's periodical *Noi Europa*.[87]

This proximity is because of the "national-revolutionary" denominator of such movements (and where national-revolutionary ideology is intended also that doctrinal blend that included, among others, third-wayism, a sort of anti-capitalism and anti-Americanization, although some of this is also in line with the *sinistra fascista* tradition). ON was, in fact, the group closer to the NOE in Italy: The European unification and Euro-nationalism were themes that ON reelaborated and reproposed to its national public. This happened in particular through its journal *Nuovo Ordine Europeo*, which played a strong role in promoting the NOE doctrine, and became a hub for analogous foreign movements linked to Binet's organization.[88]

All these earlier mentioned mentioned organizations and internationals were also, in a meaningful sense, cross-national examples of some of the blackshirted Europeans who did not want to surrender to democracy, and hoped to promote more favorable readings of past authoritarian experiences. In essence, they borrowed from the universalist tendencies of the various European fascisms and from a specific "pan-European romanticism."[89] However, at a deeper level, the importance of this postwar Eurofascist doctrine is that it contributed to an environment that fascinated and influenced extremist thinking well beyond the 1950s and 1960s. On the other hand, their immediate outcome was the development of a myriad of publications and groupings across state borders that were clearly considering Europe as their political-ideological landscape.

AN ITALIAN ACTION FOR EUROPE

These Europeanist tendencies were, as we know, well developed within the extreme-right environment in Italy. As mentioned previously, in 1958, ON published a bulletin called *Nuovo Ordine Europeo* that had articles published in different languages, and that aimed at both acting as a transnational web and promoting this right-wing "Nation Europe." However, this wider attraction for Europe had been in place in Italy at least since

87 See Notre Europe, "Nouvelles d'Italie," *Notre Europe*, 5, June 19, 1967, p. 4.

88 Guerrieri, *Essere fascisti*, p. 94.

89 As discussed earlier in the book, a nationalist and romantic pan-European imaginary attracted some conservative revolutionary circles, and this ideal later rematerialized in fascism. It has then been reproposed after the war in the German and international fascist organizations. See Tauber, "German Nationalists," p. 565.

the beginning of the 1950s, with the publication of the influential journal *Europa Nazione*, founded by Filippo Anfuso. Since that point, the fascination with Europe had quickly pervaded the cosmology of local neofascists.[90] Anfuso was a Sicilian journalist and writer, the last of Mussolini's ambassadors to Berlin, who became an MSI member of parliament in 1953. He was also the editor of the party newspaper, *Il Secolo d'Italia*.

In the first editorial, Anfuso suggested that this concept of a Europe-Nation meant "a free and united Europe. ... A continent that had to follow the dream of many young Europeans who died for it: the dream of a greater Europe."[91] Although *Europa Nazione* lasted two issues (this might have been for financial reasons), its influence and legacy were notably strong in the following years. For example, the Associazione Studentesca di Azione Nazionale-Giovane Italia (Student Association of National Action–Young Italy) and the Fronte Universitario d'Azione Nazionale (University Front of National Action, FUAN) – with which readers will become familiar when I turn the discussion to 1968 – were the MSI's youth and student organizations (even if they experienced a good degree of autonomy), which had, at least in their initial phases, an evident European nationalist and revolutionary connotation. Europe was, in their vision, also perceived as a "battlefield" between communism and the Christian (or western) tradition.[92] According to some Italian neofascist sources, it was common for young MSI followers of the 1950s and 1960s to sing a slogan borrowed from Anfuso's milieu: "Europe/nation/ tradition."[93]

The case of *Nazionalismo Sociale*, a journal led by Edmondo Cione and based in Naples, is another example of how this European myth was spread well beyond Evola or the MSE. Cione, a RSI character, had been a student of the famous liberal intellectual Benedetto Croce, and for a certain period he was one of the few "real" intellectuals close to the

90 Guerrieri, *Essere fascisti*, p. 94. For a neofascist assessment of Anfuso and his doctrine, see Pino Romualdi, *Filippo Anfuso e l'idea d'Europa-nazione: Discorso commemorativo nel 20. anniversario della scomparsa* (Palermo: I.S.S.P.E., 1984).

91 Quoted in Lanna and Rossi, *Fascisti immaginari*, p. 159.

92 Ignazi, *Il polo escluso*, pp. 116–21.

93 Incidentally, almost twenty years later in an article entitled "Objectif: Europe-nation," a paper close to the French Mouvement Jeune Révolution (Young Revolution Movement) offered to its readers some very similar themes related to a European nationalism and pan-Europeanism, and even relaunched this type of neofascist slogans: "France! Europe! Revolution!" See Algazy, *L'extrême-droite*, p. 86.

MSI. Fascinatingly, in April 1958 his journal changed the title to *Europa Sociale*, followed by a subtitle of *Per un'Europa Unita* (For a United Europe). In one of the last issues before this change, Cione made this doctrinal development of the journal clear; it was, of course, in line with its previous ideological stances, yet another political phase was (allegedly) approaching. In such a context, he argued, Italy would be better to avoid any form of "nationalist isolationism." The country, instead, had to become the promoter of a "continental union."[94] This was not just propaganda. The dream, as for many other neofascists of this period, was, in his words, of a "forthcoming unification of the continent" in the guise of a "Social Europe."[95]

Nevertheless, it has been correctly suggested that Adriano Romualdi should be considered the thinker of this Italian neofascist Europeanism, although this might be slightly reductive for one of the ideologues of postwar (Italian) right-wing extremism who served as a model and source for his young fellows. Indeed, his written works are probably still, along with Evola's, among the most republished texts by the neofascist presses. This young neofascist was the son of Pino Romualdi, one of the founders of the MSI. He studied at the University of Rome, graduating under the supervision of historian Renzo de Felice.

Romualdi proved to be a chief interpreter of Evola's thought, but he was also one of the few admirers of the Italian baron who was able to elaborate his own distinctive doctrine.[96] The two men greatly admired each other, and this shows the great respect that this young man had among the "fathers" of postwar fascism.[97] Romualdi was certainly not a melancholic Mussolinian in the same way that many of the MSI followers appeared to be. He spatially grounded his doctrinal elaboration well beyond the boundaries of a localist *fascismo*. Indeed, he was fluent in German, was an expert on the wider Germanic world, and an admirer of both the Konservative Revolution and Indo-European culture. He also had a high consideration for France, which, if compared with what he perceived as the petty bourgeois Italian extreme right, was a country

[94] Nazionalismo Sociale, "Necessità dell'unione europea," *Nazionalismo Sociale*, 8(2), February 25–March 25, 1958, p. 2.

[95] S.A., "Europa Sociale," *Nazionalismo Sociale*, 8(1), January 25–February 25, 1958, p. 17.

[96] Romualdi wrote a somewhat authorized biography of Evola, entitled *Julius Evola: l'uomo e l'opera* (Rome: Volpe, 1966).

[97] Evola wrote a piece, "Per Adriano Romualdi," firstly published in Pino Romualdi's journal *L'Italiano*, to honor him when he passed away.

experiencing a genuine rightist activism and a growing number of like-minded publications.[98] His doctrinal elaboration borrowed concepts from the 1930s writings of the journalist, writer, and intellectual Thierry Maulnier (also a former collaborator of Action Française) and Drieu La Rochelle (whom he considered a proper "prophet") and promoted a less traditional nationalism.[99] For this reason, Romualdi similarly considered Brasillach a "poet" of fascism, a man gifted enough to catch the non-national essence of such ideology.[100]

The main goals of Romualdi were to contemporize Italian fascism and update the mythology of postwar right-wing extremism by making it less wistful than this latter used to be.[101] This was probably a massive undertaking, one that could not be fully accomplished. Yet he still worked to place the Italian variation of this extremism into a larger European context, as well as reactualize some of its inner Mussolinian references. Fascism, in Romualdi's view, had to be interpreted and updated by looking not at the nostalgic and conservative readings, nor even at the Italian blackshirts' permutation (the famous *camicie nere*). Fascism was, instead, that movement as radically imagined by precursors like Evola and Drieu La Rochelle.[102] The essence of extreme-right culture had, consequently, to be found in the heroic and warrior myths, and in the actions and sacrifice of the interwar fascist fighters, and in the international battalions that joined them. These latter organizations were embodying what Evola used to call the legionary spirit. This allowed Romualdi to theorize National Socialism as a nationalist as well as a European phenomenon.

In practice, this vision of a united Europe, which Romualdi perceived as being like the motherland of the "Aryan race," and therefore as a mono-cultural, white, and anti-Jewish entity, had to be shaped as a reminiscence of the Nazi New Order. Intrinsically, as Romualdi believed, this unification of the continent would have forcibly led to a resurgence of a

98 Adriano Romualdi, *Su Evola*, quoted in Francesco Germinario, *Estranei alla Democrazia. Negazionismo e antisemitismo nella destra radicale italiana* (Pisa: BFS Edizioni, 2001), p. 39.
99 Ibid., p. 51.
100 Romualdi wrote the Preface ("Brasillach, poeta del fascismo") for the Italian version of Brasillach's book *Lettre à un soldat de la classe 60*.
101 Germinario, *Estranei alla Democrazia*, p. 35.
102 See Romualdi's Introduction to Mario Prisco et al., *Drieu La Rochelle: Il mito dell'Europa* (Rome: Edizioni del Solstizio, 1965); and Rossi, *La destra*, pp. 169 and 174–75.

non-narrowly patriotic fascism.[103] In some ways, when discussing the themes of Europe and nationalism, the young Romualdi was rather close to the existing neofascist Europeanist and pan-national doctrines that were attracting some of the extremist imaginations of the time across the western side of the old continent. In his last book, on the right and the predicaments of nationalism, he openly proclaimed his view that the only perspective for neofascists was a "Nation Europe." There was, in his reading, the need for rightist nationalism to adapt to the spatial dimension of the modern world, and then to fully become a European nationalism.[104] This reorganization of "space" would, in fact, be forged through a novel Europeanism.

EUROPE-ACTION IN FRANCE

Such a fruitful pan-European environment was to influence the imaginary of many French extremists. Some students, including François d'Orcival (later similarly active in other groups, and a recognized journalist), established the Fédération des Étudiants Nationalistes (Federation of Nationalist Students, FEN) in 1960, a movement based on an anti-democratic and pro–French Algeria platform. Through its main publication, the *Cahiers universitaires*, the FEN promoted a less French-focused nationalism. In 1963, it also contributed, along with Jeune Nation (and I shall mention in the next chapter the link between these movements), to the development of another relevant group, Europe-Action (Europe Action, EA), which became the foremost example of such neofascist internationalism. It can be also considered as one of the intellectual grounds for the postwar French extreme right and gathered some of the Nouvelle Droite's people, including de Benoist and Pierre Vial.

This was an elitist journal-movement, led by Dominique Venner and, as mentioned, became a source of attraction for the different generations of neofascists. Indeed, it had a great importance in the future developments of the cultural streams of right-wing extremism and set about the regeneration of traditional fascist thinking roughly along the MSE's lines. EA, also with the help of a mentor such as Bardèche, criticized what it saw as the worrying lack of an accurate intellectual elaboration that characterized the extreme right, including its traditional fascist interwar

[103] This point is also raised by Nicola Rao, *La Fiamma e la Celtica* (Milan: Sperling & Kupfer Editori, 2007), p. 116.

[104] Lanna and Rossi, *Fascisti immaginari*, p. 160.

version.[105] To counterbalance this, the EA tried – as Evola also suggested – emphasizing ideals (from pan-nationalism to European white civilization) rather than pure action.

Although the key doctrinal references were the usual milestones of French rightist nationalism, notably figures like, among others, Drieu La Rochelle (but also Sorel), what is interesting here to note is the attempt to promote a genuine pan-European nationalism.[106] The first issue of the journal, dated January 1963, proudly stated that there were some people who were building a novel white and immigrant-free Europe with a new fate: "They are not preparing the latest war, but [they prepare] future events. They are revolutionaries, they are Nationalists, they are the Europeans."[107]

EA was, nevertheless, not the sole publication of this kind during the 1950s and 1960s. We have mentioned some of the others, and, similarly, in the 1970s, the label, prefix, and suffix "Europe" (like "European") was frequently present in the names of right-leaning groups or publications – including Marc Frédriksen's *Notre Europe*, and Alain Renault's *Cahiers Européens-Hebdo*. We also find parties such as the Mouvement Populaire Français (French Popular Movement, MPF), a group led by Charles Luca, that at its first congress in 1958 proudly announced that an "international fascism" was born.[108] Luca claimed that Italians, Belgians, Englishmen, and activists from other nations were all joining this international fascism.[109] According to an Italian state source, foreign extremists were invited to this event (but a representative from the MSI, Ampelio Spadoni, was unable to attend because he did not obtain a passport from the Italian authorities).[110] Luca's aim was, in fact, to create an international network

105 According to Shields, "Italian Fascism has relied too heavily on the strong leader, while National Socialism had, despite its 'inspired intuitions,' succumbed to its inherent flaws, notably its excessive reliance on the Führer-Prinzip, its 'narrow, vengeful, aggressive nationalism,' and its 'romanticised (unscientific) racism.' In this attempt to diagnose the failings of fascism in practice, the better to rescue an improved conception of fascism in theory, the influence of Bardèche was clear. ... Bardèche himself set the tone in the first issue of the journal, declaring: 'Our ideas have a bright future, provided we learn to defend them a little less badly.'" Shields, *The Extreme Right*, pp. 120–21.

106 Europe-Action, "Les précurseurs," Special Edition: "Qu'est-ce que le Nationalisme," *Europe Action*, 5, May 1963, pp. 10–17.

107 Europe-Action, "Les Européens," *Europe Action*, 1, January 1963, p. 8.

108 Bibliothèque de Documentation Internationale Contemporaine (hereafter BDIC), Fonds Jacques Delarue (hereafter FJD), Jacques Delarue (hereafter JD), "Documents internes aux groupes d'extrême-droite," Poster 1.

109 Ibid., Poster 2.

110 ACS, MI, DGPS, SIS, UAR, 1957–60, B. 108 ("Mouvement Populaire Français – Primo Congresso").

ready to work for the "unity of Europe" and that involved ON from Italy.[111] This project, up to the dissolution of the MPF, was rooted in this overall politically independent Europe.[112]

The EA's direct emanation was, however, the Mouvement Nationaliste du Progrès (Nationalist Movement for Progress, MNP). The bulk of MNP propaganda was basically focused on two themes: pan-nationalism and racism. As for other similar movements, they were fully wielding the European flag, and the main goal was to achieve a "nationalist Europe and the defense of the white man and western culture, which are threatened by the black people and communism."[113] The constitutive congress of the movement, in 1966, was attended by some noteworthy Italian rightists who had links with EA, including Pino Rauti and the ON's members Paolo Andriani, Romano Costellacci, and Antonio Lombardo, and journalists Armando Mortella (from the press agency Agenzia Notizie Latine) and Giorgio Locchi (from Rome's newspaper *Il Tempo*).[114] It is evident that if Europe was the imagined and appealing center of gravity for these pan-national Frenchmen, Italy was, as we have seen, their pragmatic transnational ally.

LINKS IN ITALY

Over the years, the EA proved to be often active in promoting various policies and discussions. It encouraged, for example, a lively debate on the need for an "organic economy." This was a theme that, across the Alps, was similarly pursued by a young journalist and university student who was probably unknown to the public, the already mentioned Antonio Lombardo (who later became a political scientist and was close to the Christian Democrats).[115] He was, incidentally, also a member of the national bureau of Ordine Nuovo.[116] Lombardo was the director of ON's publication *Nazione-Europa*. He animated, in the Sicilian city of Catania, an obscure Centro Europeo di Studio per una Economia Organica

[111] Algazy, *La tentation néo-fasciste*, pp. 304–05.

[112] On this last point see also Shields, *The Extreme Right*, p. 59.

[113] Quoted in Algazy, *L'extrême-droite*, p. 31.

[114] BDIC, FJD, JD, "Activité des Mouvements en France. Leurs liaisons internationales," Annexe No. 2, 1966.

[115] On this see Rossi, *La destra*, pp. 237–38, note 58.

[116] Antonio Lombardo, Le Haut-Adige Tyrolien et l'Europe," *Europe Action*, 47, November 1966, pp. 24–25.

(European Study Center for an Organic Economy) and was the founder of the Seminario Studi sul Realismo Biologico (Study Seminar on the Biological Realism). This Italian center was probably formed by ON through a collaboration with the EA and the FEN. It was, in fact, apparently planned to coordinate its activities with a similar French study center called the Centre d'Études pour une Economie Organique (Study Center for an Organic Economy). This ON enterprise was also supposed to publish a bulletin that had to be founded by neofascists from France, Portugal (Jovem Europa), and Spain (Circulos Doctrinales Josè Antonio).[117]

Lombardo quickly became an expert on French politics and promoted Francophone fascists in Italy as well as their Italian fellows in France, also functioning, meanwhile, as a somewhat official correspondent of EA in Italy. Some reports confirm that both the FEN and Europe-Action had, actually, noteworthy links with Italy, including ON, the editor Giovanni Volpe, Alessandro Gemma, and the publishing house Centro Editoriale Nazionale. They also suggest that Lombardo was a key element in such exchanges and a very dynamic connection in Italy.[118] Moreover, he built, with the support of ON (and possibly of Adriano Romualdi), the Centro Nazione Europa (Center Nation Europe) in 1966.[119] It also seems that Alain de Benoist was about to collaborate with this center.[120] The creation of the Centro Nazione Europa confirmed how popular the international stances and transnational dimension of Western European neofascism were. It also had links with the German Federal Republic (and it is worth remembering that German extremists were gaining some seats in regional elections in those years) and was planning to organize in 1968 an international meeting inviting notable politicians such as Oswald Mosley and Aldof von Thadden.[121] They wanted, in fact, to attract youth activists with the aim to build a national, and revolutionary, front in Europe.[122]

117 ACS, MI, DGPS, SIS, UAR, 1957–60, B. 108. See also Albanese and Del Hierro, "A Transnational Network," p. 15.

118 BDIC, FJD, JD, "Activité des Mouvements en France. Leurs liaisons internationales," Annexe No. 3, 1966.

119 The first provisional quarter was hosted in the Catania's local branch of the RSI combatants and veterans' national association. It apparently was then based in Rome. ACS, MI, DGPS, SIS, UAR, 1957–60, B. 108 ("Centro Studi Nazione Europa").

120 ACS, MI, DGPS, SIS, UAR, 1957–60, B. 108 ("Neonazismo in Italia").

121 ACS, MI, DGPS, SIS, Ufficio di Gabinetto (hereafter UG), 1967–70, B. 31 ("Costituzione del Centro Nazione Europa").

122 See ibid., and ACS, MI, DGPS, SIS, UAR, 1957–60, B. 108 ("Centro Studi Nazione Europa").

Neofascist Italy was therefore showing a strong activism and was very attractive abroad. In a journal issue of *Europe Action* dated November 1963, for example, leaders discussed the role and scopes of their rightist *Opposition Nationale* (which is how the ultra-rightist opposition was generally named by its protagonists) and the electoral and political strategies to be developed. Once more, the best examples were to be found on Italian soil.[123] EA's articles discussed the history and evolution of the MSI, its internal diversity as well as its "unitary" project, the documents and themes produced in the party congresses, and the importance of a revolutionary current such as Ordine Nuovo. The MSI was indeed perceived as the greatest movement belonging to the post-1945 European fascism.[124]

Furthermore, EA also looked with a proven curiosity at the youth wing of the Italian party (and followed some of its meetings). The Italian young people were highly praised for their dynamism and activism, courage, rigorous approach to political activism, and contraposition to communists.[125] In February 1963, for example, the journal followed the work of the MSI youth organization's conference, and it admired the fact that the "best" young people from the French movements were represented. However, as already suggested, it was not only the MSI environment that was to be scrutinized: A special place in the hearts of EA's writers and followers was taken by ON (in contraposition, in some occasions, with the excessively "bureaucratic" MSI). In November 1965, EA even approached Giulio Maceratini and Ezio Spaziani-Testa, from the ON in Rome, to put together some common publications.[126] In line with this, during an interview with Lombardo, a great emphasis was therefore given to the process of converting ON into an independent political movement fully autonomous from the MSI.[127]

This was in line with some of the described attempts at the regeneration of fascism in postwar Western Europe, and also the various

[123] Europe-Action, "L'opposition nationale et la succession," *Europe Action*, 11, November 1963, p. 7.

[124] Laroche, "Le M.S.I.," p. 20.

[125] "Les jeunes du M.S.I. sont en effet connus pour la rigueur et l'efficacité de leur action. Ils ont d'ailleurs coutume de tenir leur Congrès particulier dans les villes les plus communistes d'Italie afin que les nouveaux militants puissent faire leurs preuves." Europe-Action, "L'Europe en action," *Europe Action*, 3, March 1963, p. 74.

[126] BDIC, FJD, JD, "Situation des mouvements d'extrême-droite en France," March 29, 1968. It is understood that this attempt was not successful.

[127] See, for instance, Europe-Action, "Un entretien exclusif," pp. 5–6.

endeavors to give it an authentic international dimension. It is clear how French and Italian ideologues, alone and in combination, worked hard to offer an alternative to anti-fascist democracies. In this sense, a genuine radicalization (the rejection of the parliamentary system) and a pan-nationalization (the Europeanization) of neofascist doctrine would have, potentially, served to reach this aim and, hopefully, to gain prominence. This ambitious enterprise was theoretically prepared and led by a number of theorists and activists across Europe. These ideological elaborations, although far from being fully cohesive and successful, had repercussions, contributing to the establishment of an environment that promoted collaboration among extremist parties (including today at the European Union parliament level, along with the many international gatherings and pan-national European associations).

Likewise, it was international politics, and specifically European decolonization, that, roughly in those same years, gave the extreme right an opportunity to come to the fore again and cross state borders. There was an Algerian "connection" linking different movements as well as France and Italy. Algeria, French decolonization, and the "nationalist" activities of the French settlers and the rebellious paratroops, with their passions and national and international tensions, came to represent some key episodes that, in turn, influenced the universe and fantasy of neofascism well beyond France. This is what the next chapter will address.

3

The Algerian Years

In general terms, and bearing in mind some different national settings, we must also observe how, from the 1950s onwards, France and Italy faced a period of economic growth and modernization. The two nations seemed predominantly preoccupied with national reconstruction and regaining international prestige. It was not, in other words, only the mainstream process of European integration that characterized international politics and eventually mobilized postwar fascists. In such a busy historical phase, and setting aside the fascist pan-Europeanism and the international cooperation described in the previous pages, one might assume that merely a very few other transnational links may be discerned between the extreme right across the Alps during this period. The more evident cross-national reaction against communist radicalism (as I shall reveal in the following chapter) seemed to appear in 1968, following the establishing of a leftist trans-border movement. However, this represents one side of the neofascist chronicle of the time. Other international developments had an influence on the neofascist agenda of these years.

At a deeper level, this period, in fact, saw the beginnings of decolonization as a matter of intense debate. It was a considerable shock for many Europeans. As Tony Judt gracefully pointed out,

> At the close of the Second World War, the people of Western Europe … continued to rule much of the non-European world. This unseemly paradox, whose implications were not lost on indigenous elites in the European colonies, had perverse consequences. To many in Britain, France or the Netherlands, their countries' colonies and imperial holdings in Africa, Asia, the Middle East and the Americas were balm for the suffering and humiliations of the war in

Europe; they had demonstrated their material value in that war as vital national resources.[1]

The combination of decolonization, regime collapse, and mass immigration were, in reality, exclusive to nations like France and not immediately available as mobilizing themes in the Italian political context. The loss of colonies had, in fact, an immediate influence even on the imagination of youths in the later events of *Mai 1968*, especially on their perception of violence during the students' and workers' rebellion, and the politicization of some of its leaders. Although a colonial territory, Algeria was perceived as part of the nation, and this was the way a million French settlers (the *Pieds Noirs*) were considering it. For France, the Algerian decolonization exerted, in sum, a huge impact on political and social life (and it is presently debated in reference to public and collective memories).[2]

Yet it is also especially interesting here to highlight how transnationalism (and the transnational historical framework) may manifest itself in many different ways. One of them is the treatment of, and response to, foreign events, and, specifically, how they are borrowed and interpreted by national actors. Readers will, for example, discover a fascination for General de Gaulle, who was perceived by some Italians as a kind of dictator or fascist leader and by others as a genuine nationalist character. This went along with the Italian neofascists' defense of French Algeria as a bastion of European civilization, an admiration for the movements fighting to retain it, and the captivating mythology of one of the most updated examples of Julius Evola's imagined warriors, notably, the French paratroopers defending European colonization.[3]

Some of the "perverse consequences" mentioned in the previous quotation by Judt, and referring to the Europeans controlling overseas colonies, were very true for neofascist forces. Losing the non-European territories represented, in their estimation, a defeat for the "superiority" of white civilization and a challenge to the heartiness and prestige of their European nations. In essence, there is no doubt that this played a relevant

[1] Judt, *Postwar*, p. 278.
[2] See generally Kristin Ross, *May '68 and Its Afterlives* (Chicago: University of Chicago Press, 2002); and Peter Dunwoodie, "Postface: History, Memory and Identity – Today's Crisis, Yesterday's Issue," *French History*, 20(3), 2006, pp. 318–32.
[3] As Alain de Benoist proudly spelt out, some youth groups in Italy, in fact, adopted the Celtic cross as their symbol only because contemporary French nationalists employed it. Laroche, "Le M.S.I.," p. 27.

role for right-wing extremists and represented a powerful mobilization flag.

The memory of French Algeria has been, in fact, perpetuated and manipulated by extreme-right activists and parties over the years, right up until the present day.[4] The French rightist periodical *Rivarol*, for example, in 2007 still looked with suspicion at any agreement with Algeria and demanded an official investigation into the French citizens who disappeared during the Algerian War. This memory was revitalized by the Front National's propaganda campaigns against non-European immigration. "The old debate on the possible integration of a foreign, and Muslim, population ... has been re-proposed in a metropolitan setting," as historian Guy Pervillé has written. Fearing the threat of a contemporary *France Islamique*, the extreme right endorses the view that it is impossible to integrate the immigrant Muslim population into a European country.[5] There are naturally some links and affinities between this colonial (and anti-Muslim) culture and right-wing extremism. There are places where former settlers established a specific environment that affected local politics up to the present. This is, for example, clearly the case with Toulon in southern France. Roughly 20,000 former French settlers from Algeria went to live in this town after 1962, and in 1995 it was the largest European city since 1945 to elect as its mayor a politician from the extreme right.[6]

ACTIVISM IN THE 1950S

The Cold War years of the 1950s allowed for a spurious collaboration, and even a precarious overlapping convergence of interests, between some more rightist Christian Democrats and the MSI, mostly in the name of anti-communism. This gave neofascists the necessary optimism to envisage a light out of the political corner in which they had been pushed in a nation legally based on an anti-fascist statute. Michelini, one of the founders of the MSI, was the party secretary in 1958 and was hoping to insert the MSI into the political system. This aimed at participation in governmental coalitions led by mainstream right, as well as acceptance in other

[4] See, for example, Jean-Paul Angelelli, "France-Algérie: Chirac pressé de conclure," *Rivarol*, February 2, 2007, p. 9.

[5] They possibly make an exception for those French Muslims who fought for French Algeria. Guy Pervillé, "L'Algérie dans la mémoire des droites," in J.-F. Sirinelli, ed., *Histoire des droites en France. 2. Cultures* (Paris: Gallimard, 1992), pp. 651–52.

[6] See Veugelers, "After Colonialism," pp. 33–47.

respectable circles. As suggested, there had been some informal support for the DC governments and various arrangements at regional and local levels. It is worth mentioning that some neofascists did, nonetheless, not share this line: The most revolutionary currents were overtly antagonistic to that democratic system in which Michelini wanted to play a role of some significance.

This latter was instead convinced of a possible opening up of the political system in favor of the MSI. His vision was backed by some of the most anti-leftist sectors of the DC and possibly by some in the Vatican.[7] This was especially true for those among the mainstream political (and cultural) right who were not really sympathetic to both anti-fascism and partitocracy and believed that an agreement with the MSI would restore the pre-fascist (liberal) regime.[8] Despite the 1958 general election result, which represented a defeat for the MSI (it dropped to about the 4.6 percent of the vote), the party maintained this rapprochement in line with Michelini's vision. Indeed, this policy became the central strategy for the MSI up until the early 1970s, which aimed at the establishment of a catch-all right-wing party (this will be discussed in Chapter 4 where I also highlight its transnational implications).

The Cold War also marked the beginning of the French decolonization that ended only with the Évian agreement of March 1962 and the Algerian independence. On the whole, this was an extremely turbulent time for the French state, with the revival of a rightist radicalism and the founding (in early 1961) of the group Organisation Armée Secrète (Secret Armed Organization, OAS). The late 1950s became, in addition, highly significant due to the delicate transition from the Fourth to the Fifth Republic (in 1958). These facts are not merely relevant in themselves, but also because, retrospectively, the Algerian War provided one of the first overt political expressions of anti-Arab racism.[9]

Neofascism tried to use all this for mobilization. Even if the "global movement which opposed Algerian independence and supported the 'Putsch of the Generals' did not belong to the extreme right," French movements were actually able to "orchestrate the Algerian conflict, which took on a particular meaning in their overall view of the world. It was

[7] See also Eatwell, *Fascism*, p. 251.

[8] See Giuliano Carocci, *Destra e sinistra nella storia d'Italia* (Rome: Laterza, 2002), p. 170.

[9] There had been an anti-Arab press campaign in Paris in the late 1940s. See Jim House, *Antiracism and Antiracist Discourse in France from 1900 to the Present Day* (Ph.D. dissertation, University of Leeds, 1997), pp. 225–30.

seen as the struggle of the free world against Soviet-backed third world subversion."[10] The defense of colonialism, and the political and social troubles, were all well exploited (although often historically decontextualized) by right extremists. Leaders like Tixier-Vignancour, for example, defended the OAS but believed that it had "nothing to do with Fascism." Others such as Bardèche similarly thought that the OAS was not fascist, but he also suggested that "there [were] among its supporters a number of people who [were] Fascists by temperament, who [dreamed of] a regime closely resembling Fascism. In a certain sense they [were] Fascists without knowing it."[11]

French Algeria became, in other words, the pivotal issue for the ancestors of the FN. It created, among other factors, the conditions for another regeneration of extremism. These events offered – along with the Europeanist stances previously described – a novel spatial, and geopolitical dimension to local nationalism. This was also the opinion of neofascist intellectuals of the time. François Duprat wrote in his *Les Mouvements d'Extrême Droite* that the Algerian revolts of the 1950s favored the birth of a climate where everything seemed possible: from a military putsch to a fascist takeover. This was, in sum, a period of (often unachieved and pretentious) hopes. As Duprat envisaged:

> The time of the long punishment of the purge seems to have reached an end. The extreme right activists, with a revived and enthusiastic approach, will now launch an assault on the [democratic] regime. . . . This is the time of the resurrection of the Opposition Nationale.[12]

French neofascists played the Algeria card to reinvigorate activism, and they aimed to make a spectacular comeback in the political system. The right to resistance for local settlers, and to maintain the colonies in North Africa, the prestige of the army – all were constantly defended, as well as strong criticisms voiced of de Gaulle's lack of support for the rebels and his "compromise" with the democratic institutions.[13] This became very common in the extreme-right press.[14] The periodical *Défense de*

[10] Camus, "Nostalgia and Political Impotence," p. 209.
[11] Both quoted in Del Boca and Giovana, *Fascism Today*, p. 197.
[12] Duprat, *Les Mouvements*, p. 60.
[13] ACS, MI, DGPS, SIS, UAR, 1957–60, B. 108 ("Mouvement Populaire Français – Primo Congresso").
[14] It is clear that de Gaulle was very pragmatic and had little sympathy for this insurrectionary politics. His primary aim was to restore and maintain order. See also Judt, *Postwar*, p. 287.

l'Occident played, once again, a relevant role. In April 1956, for example, in a column entitled "Le drame Algérien" (The Algerian Drama), Bardèche denounced how the current governments were unable to keep the empire and its colonies and to use military force. The solution, he claimed, was to change the regime and its political elites, and, consequently, to implement an effective politics proficient enough to stop the "decadence" of the country.[15] A few months later, the French writer backed the local resistance:

> This abandoned Algeria ... can remain French only through the actions of the resistance. This is the only way that the Frenchmen of Algeria have to keep it, their property, and, perhaps, their own existence.[16]

This strategy seemed to become reality when the Fourth Republic fell due to the demonstrations in Algiers held on May 13, 1958, against the Algerian Front de Libération Nationale (National Liberation Front, FLN). This challenge to the institutional system also represented a collective revenge mixing different people, political interests, and ideological values.[17] The so-called Algiers Putsch was led by people such as one of the future OAS founders, Pierre Lagaillarde, and by General Raoul Salan, and supported by the interwar anti-fascist character (and scholar) and former Minister Jacques Soustelle, together with General Jacques Massu. It led to the constitution of a Comité de Salut Public (Committee of Public Safety), chaired by Massu. However, events took a different path than the one envisaged by the extreme right. Rather than having the rightist coup d'état of which they originally dreamed, the president of the French Republic, René Coty, asked de Gaulle to lead the government, and, on June 1, the General was granted full powers to resolve the political and military crisis. With the September referendum on the new constitution, and the consequent creation of the Fifth Republic, another Gaullist era officially began, and de Gaulle was elected president of France in December 1958.

Yet the Algerian issue was far from resolved, and the empire was showing deep signs of strain. Starting on January 24, 1960, France faced the famous *semaine des barricades* (barricades week) in Algiers. This was led by the famed "Ultras" of French Algeria, who were mostly students and settlers. The situation became even worse a year later with the

[15] Maurice Bardèche, "Le drame Algérien," *Défense de l'Occident*, 32, 1956, p. 3.
[16] Maurice Bardèche, "La politique de la violence," *Défense de l'Occident*, 34, 1956, p. 9.
[17] Pervillé, "L'Algérie," pp. 639–40.

referendum on the independence of Algeria (approved both in France and in its main overseas colony) and the failed takeover in Algiers, which was organized by some retired generals, including Salan, to overthrow President de Gaulle. This in turn was followed by a number of other events, including the anti-OAS demonstration in Paris on February 8, 1962.[18] This period was, therefore, intense, and, needless to say, it left a mark on extreme-right activists and politics.

THE FRENCH EXTREME RIGHT AT THE TIME OF ALGERIA

The most remarkable and forceful French extreme right-wing movement of the time was probably Jeune Nation (Young Nation, JN). Brothers Jacques and Pierre Sidos had started this neofascist, national-revolutionary, and violent group in late 1949. It was characterized by significant street activism and inspired by national and foreign models, such as the right-wing nationalist writer and politician Maurice Barrès (also close to the Italian Gabriele D'Annunzio and, for some, one of the early French fascists), Drieu la Rochelle, Robert Brasillach, and Primo de Rivera.[19] JN attracted a few thousand supporters, including many young students, although in its initial phases, the movement generated very little interest, and membership grew only with the recruitment of veterans from the Indochina War.[20] By 1952, it published a monthly magazine, the *Peuple de France et d'Outre-mer*, replaced in July 1958 by another journal, simply called *Jeune Nation*.[21] In this period, the movement also tried to create links with fellow fascists based abroad. Pierre Sidos, for example, visited fellow extremists in London in the 1950s.[22]

JN was very active in the Algerian crisis in France and in Algiers and in OAS subversive actions. Indeed, many of its clandestine pamphlets regularly reported the need for a *grande France* on both sides of the Mediterranean, together with a call for nationalist rebellions and respect for the

[18] On this, see generally Jim House and Nigel MacMaster, *Paris 1961: Algerians, State Terror, and Memory* (Oxford: Oxford University Press, 2006).

[19] See Robert Blanc, "Les Maîtres du Nationalisme," *Jeune Nation*, 17, May 1959, pp. 13–16; and Jacques Plancard D'Assac, "Doctrines du Nationalisme. La réponse de José Antonio Primo de Rivera," *Jeune Nation*, 3, August 1958, pp. 6–7.

[20] See also Duprat, *Les Mouvements*, p. 56.

[21] During 1958–1959, JN was also dissolved and reformed many times and under different names.

[22] Macklin, *Very Deeply Dyed in Black*, p. 137.

OAS. A number of its members, including Dominique Venner and Pierre Sidos, were arrested. Predictably, the failure of OAS provoked a collapse of JN's ability to mobilize.

In doctrinal terms, however, JN was less nostalgic and *vichyiste* than other contemporary groups that were more interested in defending the memory of Pétain. Apart from the usual anti-communism, it had a more radical perspective by promoting anti-Semitism and generally xenophobic nationalism.[23] Its ideological and practical syntheses of fascist corporatism, anti-capitalism, and nationalization of industries, together with anti-parliamentarianism and anti-democratic subversion, exemplified the group's intention to build a strong crypto-fascist state. As described in *Jeune Nation*: "The goal of the Nationalist State is to gather and organize in the same *faisceau* all Nation's activities and forces. The Nationalist State is authoritarian . . .; it is hierarchical."[24]

Certainly, these were not unusual themes, but they were re-proposed in a context that, as we have seen, was promoting some authoritarian aspirations. This was an environment that was, in many ways, also markedly similar to that which Evola and ON had foreseen in Italy. Indeed, some of JN's policies, especially its corporatist syndicalism, were in line with some of the *fascisti di sinistra*. JN's originality was, however, probably in the use of violence and street activism – along with the previously mentioned lower degree of nostalgia for Vichy. This was a strategy of revolutionary action – an action that, in their understanding, was "the only hope for nationalism."[25] This doctrine was proclaimed to irremediably change the *République* and suppress the various parties, along with all "electoral practices."[26] This would also have halted France's "decadence" and restored the country's old vitality (in opposition to the perceived

[23] Symptomatic is an article published in defense of South African apartheid, in which racist segregation was perceived as something natural and (allegedly) foreseen in the Bible and in the Old Testament. Pierre Hofstetter, "Quand les blancs se défendent," *Jeune Nation*, 7, October 1958, p. 5. On the importance of a white European colonialism, see also the essay by the French interwar fascist Jean Malardier, "Le 'Fardeau de l'homme blanc' et le Nationalisme," *Jeune Nation*, 17, May 1959, pp. 7–9.

[24] Jeune Nation, "Ce que veulent les Nationalistes Français," *Jeune Nation*, 12, December 1958, p. 7.

[25] Hubert Saint-Julien, "Notre espérance est révolutionnaire," *Jeune Nation*, 1, July 1958, p. 4.

[26] Jeune Nation, "Ce que veulent," pp. 6–7. For an ideological and programmatic manifesto, see also Dominique Venner, "Jalons de route," *Jeune Nation*, 18, June-July 1959, pp. 3–5.

"tiring" years of parliamentarianism).[27] "Democracy" and "decadence," for JN supporters, were, hence, indissolubly linked to each other. In this sense, they could claim that "fighting against [France's] decadence means fighting against the [democratic] regime."[28]

Aside from this radicalism and hardline political stance, JN was able to generate not merely aggressive nationalist and violent movements (like Occident, which will be discussed in the book along with other groups mentioned in these pages), but also to strongly influence groupings, such as EA, which were clearly more interested in producing an Evolian-like intellectual elaboration, rather than direct and pragmatic political action.[29] Moreover, Sidos's movement was important for its attempt to unify different extreme-right currents. It became the point of attraction for the many right-wing leaders, intellectuals, and activists of this period and beyond, such as François Duprat (future Occident, Ordre Nouveau, and FN), Alain Robert (Occident, Ordre Nouveau, FN, and Parti des Forces Nouvelles), Pierre Vial (GRECE and Nouvelle Droite), and Jean-Gilles Malliarakis (Occident, Mouvement Nationaliste Révolutionnaire, and Troisième Voie).[30] Dominique Venner (EA, GRECE) and Jean-Louis Tixier-Vignancour were also in JN. In sum, as with the Italian fellow movement ON (whose milieu also influenced hardliners and intellectuals, along with young neofascists who joined the Italian permutation of the ND), JN turned out to be another valuable ideological and political training ground for neofascism.

Apart from JN, and setting aside the neofascist pro-Europeanist constellation as discussed in the previous chapter, other movements came into being. In reference to the EA, I had previously briefly mentioned the establishment in 1960 of the FEN by some students. The ideological manifesto of this youth organization (the Manifeste de la Classe 60) clearly showed their doctrinal attitudes: anti-democratic, anti-communist, for law and order, and racist. In sum, both the FEN and JN gave voice and offered an open platform to "an elitist, racist, authoritarian ideology that had been kept largely underground since the Liberation."[31] Probably more intriguing, was, nonetheless, FEN's work for a doctrinal

[27] Pierre Sidos, "Ce ne sont ni les électeurs ni les élus qui sauveront LA FRANCE: Il faut une revolution," *Jeune Nation*, 10, November 1958, p. 3.

[28] Saint-Julien, "Notre espérance," p. 4.

[29] Anne-Marie Duranton-Crabol, *Le Temps de l'OAS* (Brussels: Éditions Complexe, 1995), p. 252.

[30] See also Camus, "Nostalgia and Political Impotence," p. 206.

[31] Shields, *The Extreme Right*, p. 98.

reelaboration of some of the more narrow aspects of French nationalism. The support of French Algeria was, in fact, considered to be part of a global fight against communists. It was the continuation of the interwar fascist contraposition to European socialism and communism.[32]

A well-known group of the time was also the Front National des Combatants (War Combatants National Front), instituted in 1957. It had, among its leaders, Jean-Marie Le Pen and was formed by other future first-rank activists of the FN. They edited the periodical *L'Unité*. Another prominent extremist, and ultra-Catholic, group led by Robert Martel was named the Mouvement Populaire du 13 Mai (Popular Movement of May 13), better known as MP 13 (May 13, 1958, became, for some, a symbolic date because it coincided with the revolt for Algeria). It was also involved against de Gaulle's policy on Algeria and in attacks against the local Muslim population.[33]

"Non à De Gaulle!" was similarly shouted by the neofascist and racist MPF (mentioned in the previous chapter). The heir of Charles Luca's Phalange Française, it was founded on June 16, 1958, and dissolved in 1960. It turned into a purely fascist group, proudly claiming that *Le Fascisme passera!* As already highlighted, it longed for the development of an international fascism.[34] However, the MPF also put its colonial policy in line with the Phalange, a movement that had been claiming that "France's renunciation of Algeria would mean the ruin of the white race [and] a defeat for European civilization, the end of Eurafrica and, beyond that, the end of European mutual understanding."[35]

In 1958, yet another group, the Front National Français (French National Front), came into being through the efforts of future OAS leaders Jean-Jacques Susini and Joseph Ortiz, aimed at developing a parallel military organization. It was very active on the *barricades* of January 1960. In the same year, a further movement also appeared in metropolitan France, the Front National pour l'Algérie Française (National Front for the French Algeria). Tixier-Vignancour and Le Pen, among others, signed its manifesto.[36]

[32] See also ibid. [33] Chebel d'Appollonia, *L'extrême droite en France*, p. 302.
[34] BDIC, FJD, JD, "Documents internes aux groupes d'extrême-droite," Poster 2.
[35] Quoted in Tauber, "German Nationalists," p. 580.
[36] Jean-Pierre Rioux, "Des clandestines aux activistes (1945–1965)," in M. Winock, ed., *Histoire de l'extrême droite en France* (Paris: Seuil, 1993), p. 237.

The extreme-right milieu was then in a state of ferment. The growing economic changes and the potent environment generated by the loss of the colonial empire were all favorable factors in helping neofascism to survive and mobilize some people's preoccupations and fears.[37] Nonetheless, while the decline of the Gaullist Rassemblement du Peuple Français (Rally of the French People) after 1953 was one of the factors that also made room for the emergence of Poujadism, the rise of Gaullism – as a majority party tending to monopolize the right-of-center political space – pushed neofascism again toward the fringe of the political system (and we can also note a similar case in Italy with the presence of the influential Christian Democrats). General de Gaulle was, in all cases, at the core of domestic politics. His fame quickly crossed geographical boundaries and attracted the interest of some Italian neofascists.

IMPORTING "NATIONALIST" DE GAULLE TO ITALY?

The charismatic, nationalist, and anti-communist features of Gaullism became rather appealing for some of the French extremist electorate and, at times, for a number of foreign neofascists. Italy could not escape this trend, and de Gaulle enjoyed a considerable pattern of popularity in the peninsula, among MSI activists as well, and, in general, the party often had a fascination with strong foreign leaders perceived to be global promoters of right-wing, conservative, anti-leftist, traditional, and nationalist stances (this is the case, for example, of Margaret Thatcher and Ronald Reagan). As Filippo Anfuso reported in the official party newspaper, *Il Secolo d'Italia*, General de Gaulle's *prise de pouvoir* in 1958, together with his "control" over the litigious party system and the overall anti-Marxist approach, represented, from the MSI's perspective, a worthwhile authoritarian-type milestone in contemporary Europe.[38]

In particular, as *Europe Action* observed after a few years, the events of May 1958 had a strong impact on the imaginary of the neofascist elites in Italy.[39] Indeed, for the first anniversary of de Gaulle's (latest) leadership of French government, Anfuso, in an enthusiastic article on this key Gaullist year, reinforced this point: What mainly generated interest

[37] Milza, *Fascisme Français*, p. 277.

[38] Filippo Anfuso, "Dittatore o meno," *Il Secolo d'Italia*, January 10, 1959, p. 1. On the approach toward de Gaulle see also Roberto Chiarini, "La fortuna del gollismo in Italia," in E. Decleva and P. Milza, eds., *Italia e Francia: I nazionalismi a confronto* (Milan: Franco Angeli, 1993), pp. 268–300.

[39] Laroche, "Le M.S.I.," p. 25.

around the May 13 coup d'état was not the demise of the Fourth Republic, and the dreamed-for (but in reality misunderstood) conversion of de Gaulle to fascism. What Italian neofascists were really impressed by was his nationalist belief in "a European continent regenerated by the cult of the Fatherlands." This Gaullist nationalist project had to be defended especially against those that "in the name of democracy, gave more than half of Europe in the hands of communists."[40]

Setting aside the evident strong charisma of such a "nationalist" politician, this transnational fascination with the French leader was also probably promoted, according to the neofascist press in France, through the contacts that a number of members of the Gaullist Rassemblement du Peuple Français had previously maintained up to 1955 with the MSI. This generated among some Italian neofascists a twisted reading of events: basically, that de Gaulle's taking of power was the sign of a nationalist revolution.[41]

The high-profile image of this political leader had, in fact, exerted an impact on many sectors of the Italian extreme right. As early as 1948, the hardline Evolian youth journal *La Sfida* (even if it was against the post-war purges previously made by the General) showed some attraction to his nationalism and apparent disapproval of the party system. They interpreted this as an attack on the whole democracy. What is more, the policies and decisions taken by de Gaulle and his party (and, at times, also by other foreign nationalist leaders) had, for *La Sfida*, a Europe-wide significance.[42] For this reason the journal wondered if he wanted to create "a personal dictatorship or a new [revolutionary] system that could serve as a model for other countries." A dictatorship, for the journal, would not have resolved existing problems, while the hoped-for revolution would have developed a novel political phase in France and Europe.[43]

Later, in 1966, even a periodical such as *L'Orologio* reproposed some of the Gaullist themes in Italy and backed his seeming opposition to

[40] Filippo Anfuso, "Un anno di De Gaulle," *Il Secolo d'Italia*, May 13, 1959, p. 1.

[41] Laroche, "Le M.S.I.," pp. 25–26.

[42] In the same years, *La Sfida* showed, at times, an admiration for Oswald Mosley, for his anti-Americanism, pro-colonization, and pan-European stances. See "Young Italy looks to Union Movement," *Union*, 50, Januray 29, 1949, p. 3.

[43] According to neofascist journalist Umberto Giusti, "De Gaulle è quindi a un bivio tra la reazione e la Rivoluzione. Speriamo, per la Francia e per l'Europa, che egli sappia scegliere bene. E scegliere anche presto perché i Boulanger non restano nella storia che per far ridere." See Giusti, "Bivio De Gaulle," pp. 3–4.

NATO.[44] This "heretic," although noteworthy, publication was directed by former clandestine fascist Luciano Lucci Chiarissi and exemplified another representative of that *fascisti di sinistra* tradition. It was in line with the doctrine of the famous corporatist philosopher Ugo Spirito and Massi's *Nazione Sociale*. The outspoken aim was to update and modernize the fascist presence in contemporary society, and to work against American imperialism and capitalism. Given this ideological basis, any challenge to the Atlantic alliance was more than welcomed.[45]

Dissenting voices over de Gaulle and what he possibly represented especially started in the critical phases of the Algeria crisis. The right-leaning periodical *Il Borghese* was rather skeptical about this admiration toward the French politician. *Il Borghese* had a strong interest in French affairs. It frequently ran a weekly column called "Diario di Parigi" (Paris Diary), which focused on French and Francophone culture and politics. This paper was founded by writer Leo Longanesi and directed, at the time, by Mario Tedeschi, a journalist writing for *Roma Fascista* in the interwar years and, like Chiarissi, also an immediate postwar clandestine fascist. (Tedeschi will be involved in designing political and cultural strategies for the MSI in the 1970s.) From the pages of *Il Borghese*, Eggardo Beltrametti, a journalist that will be mentioned again here, published an article in April 1958, and warned, for example, against the appointment of the General as prime minister. Beltrametti showed a deep knowledge of French issues and was aware of developments of, and opinions expressed in, many rightist publications on the other side of the Alps, including *Rivarol*. De Gaulle was portrayed as the man who signed the Franco-Soviet alliance in December 1944 and had accepted international communism. He also promised "a mythological independence to all African populations," and, the journalist continued, was missing "any political logic and prudence." He was (apparently) pleased to erase Italy from some of its territories in the bordering French southern region of Provence. Moreover, Beltrametti was suspicious that de Gaulle's government was (allegedly) backed by center-left socialist Pierre Mendès-France, with no opposition from communist forces. This would have led to a "dictatorship" of the anti-fascist

44 Lanna and Rossi, *Fascisti immaginari*, p. 179.

45 On the doctrinal and political agenda of *L'Orologio*, see also Luciano Lucci Chiarissi, "Editoriale," *L'Orologio*, 1, June 1963, pp. 1–2.

Resistance forces (and this was not acceptable for political movements that were subjected to the anti-fascist liberations).[46]

Along the same lines, Emilio Canevari, from the pages of the *Meridiano d'Italia*, almost derided the French if they were really about to give de Gaulle the chance to create a (supposed) dictatorship. They forgot, complained Canevari, that in 1940–44 de Gaulle was "in service of England, and he had been the symbol of division and hate for his own people."[47] In 1951, Canevari had already expressed a degree of mistrust in regard to de Gaulle. He warned against the opinion, developed in some Italian circles, that the General was linked to fascism, and, consequently, that once in power he would have had a sympathetic approach to nationalist activities and tendencies in Italy (like in the case of the MSI).[48] Almost the same readings led *Europe Action*, in 1963, to argue that, in a moment of profound democratic and political crisis for the French nation, some Italian neofascists twisted de Gaulle's takeover, which they considered a nationalist, even fascist, revolution.

Significantly, years before, Beltrametti had the same feelings and promoted the rejection of the General for more genuine nationalist ideals. He referred to the Algerian quest for independence and compared it with Italy and the MSI's own politics: What should Italians do if, in an Algeria-style uprising, the Italians of the bordering South Tyrol would rebel to join Austria? Would Italian nationalists have lost their territory, even if populations were joining the democratic and peaceful Austria? The dramatic difference, in the Algerian case, was, for him, that the French citizens of Algeria would then have lived, at best, in a despotic nation. Further, the loss of North Africa would have simply favored the Soviet Union and the local communist movements.[49] This was, for neofascists, somewhat in line with what happened in Indochina (and it seemed common for the Italian rightist press to blame French politics for the "dangerous spread" of communism in Southeast Asia). Indeed, almost all Italian neofascists had supported France in the fight against the Indochinese communists, and their aspirations were frustrated.[50] The foreseeable outcome of de Gaulle's new leadership was clear: the abandoning of Algeria and its

[46] Eggardo Beltrametti, "Il pericolo De Gaulle," *Il Borghese*, 16, April 24, 1958, p. 723.

[47] Canevari, "La crisi algerina," p. 3

[48] Emilio Canevari, "Diffidare di De Gaulle," *La Rivolta Ideale*, VI(28), July 12, 1951, p. 2.

[49] Beltrametti, "Il pericolo De Gaulle," p. 723.

[50] According to *Nazionalismo Sociale*, for instance, France's biggest failure in Indochina was that it did not give local nationalism the opportunity to grow up. The population did not have any help from France. For this reason, Indochina looked at the support given by Chinese and Russian communists. See Luigi Villari, "La marea rivoluzionaria nel medio e

independence. This would, Beltrametti reasoned, have provoked the reflux in France of many settlers, and disappointed soldiers "who, once again, fought, like in Indochina, for nothing. … Along with the forces of the political right …, they would represent a revolutionary source …, one that de Gaulle will be unable to control, as they will consider him the responsible of humiliations and renunciations." "The behavior of some Italian nationalists is bizarre," Beltrametti concluded, "they should, theoretically, show solidarity with French nationalists [the *Pieds-Noirs* and the supporters of French Algeria]."[51] Even Italian right-wing extremists, in sum, could not get away from this battle on French decolonization.

DEFENDING FRENCH ALGERIA?

Decolonization and the associated political emergency rapidly became part of Italian neofascist discourse. They generally used this as pretexts to criticize the alleged precarious foundations of all postwar democracies, the corruption of the "regime of parties," and the weak western defense against totalitarian communism.[52] Similar to their French extremist compatriots, they also believed that this was a fight of the free western world against Soviet expansionism. For this reason, their press drew strong parallels between the social and political situation of contemporary France and the Italy of the early 1920s that had allowed the rise of Mussolini's fascism.[53]

Some initial divisions, in reality, arose over the Algerian issue. On the one hand, since the beginning, the official line of the MSI seemed to support French colonial policy in North Africa, although there were some dissident voices. On the other hand, a pro-Arab stance was alive within the Italian extreme-right constellation due to the anti-Semitism and anti-Zionism found in some circles. All this was strengthened by the support given by some Arab nationalists to Italian fascism during the war. Moreover, Italian fascism, and, specifically, governor of Libya Italo Balbo, had been able to build up some good contacts and relations with parts of the Islamic world in Africa.[54] However, this backing of Arab nationalism was

estremo oriente," *Nazionalismo Sociale*, 4(2), February 15–March 15, 1954, pp. 7–8 and 19–21.

51 Beltrametti, "Il pericolo De Gaulle," p. 723.

52 Filippo Ansufo, "Il Generale fascista e antifascista," *Il Secolo d'Italia*, June 4, 1958, p. 1.

53 Filippo Anfuso, "Lezione francese?," *Il Secolo d'Italia*, November 28, 1958, p. 1.

54 Rossi, *La destra*, pp. 73–74.

also because of another, simple, reason: A number of neofascists did not like the victorious nations in World War II and the existing colonial powers – including Great Britain and France. This had much to do with Italy's having experienced the loss of some of its colonial territories. It was both a form of jealousy and revenge. If, for example, Italy lost Libya, France could consequently lose its beloved Algeria.

According to Edmondo Cione's *Europa Sociale*, Africa had started a "liberation march" that could hardly be stopped and that was also (in ideological terms) bound up with international politics. The Arab struggles for liberation were to be placed in the middle of the Cold War contrapositions between east and west. Moreover, the interests of big capital and farmers who had invested in Africa, it was claimed, excessively influenced the western countries. For this reason, they struggled to find the right solution for the African continent.[55] Massi similarly pointed out the fact that, currently, "Africa was knocking at the doors of History," and the "African populations have realized that colonial governments have deprived them of one of the key elements of their rebirth: their own history."[56] Africa's emancipation was henceforth an "irreversible historical fact" and settlers, including the Italian ones, did not really represent Europe.[57] The solution was to be found in a common, noncolonialist, European policy based on corporatism. Indeed, in Massi's reading, this specific Italian fascist policy did not strive for Europeanization, "but for the evolution and development of the native society."[58]

As we have just seen, extreme-right propaganda also put forward another argument to dismiss France's colonial power: Problems in Africa were additionally linked with the fact that the "usual" colonizers only had a pragmatic approach and material interests in the continent. They simply wanted to exploit the resources of the land and the energy sources.[59] In the neofascist viewpoint (as Massi equally suggested), Italy was different:

> All this would have never happened . . . if the Italian flag , Italian settlers, the Italian population and government were still in Cyrenaica, in Bengasi, in Tripolitania, at the borders of Egypt and Tunisia. Fifty million people have been driven

[55] Europa Sociale, "Le soluzioni di ricambio," *Europa Sociale*, 8(12), December 20, 1958–January 20, 1959, pp. 1–2.

[56] Ernesto Massi, *L'Europa e la crisi africana* (Milan: Istituto Editoriale Sociale, 1960), p. 3.

[57] Ibid., p. 4. [58] Ibid., pp. 14–15.

[59] A.B., "L'Europa si difende a Tunisi," *Meridiano d'Italia*, 13(4), March 4, 1958, p. 28.

out from Africa and the Mediterranean coasts by the French and the British. This was a territory civilized by people [the Italians] who do not look for oil, [were] pleased to make the land better and give justice to the natives. This should not be forgotten.[60]

However, the growing prominence of the FLN, which the extreme-right viewed as a genuine Marxist faction and even as a Soviet Trojan horse, within the independence movement effectively shuffled the cards for Italians and led some to seriously reconsider their nostalgic pro-Arabism. Indeed, the very last thing they wanted was to promote any form of Moscow-type expansion.[61] For this reason, de Gaulle and mainstream French politics deserved heavy criticism for their policy on Algeria and the local French nationalists.

Rightist forces henceforth robustly supported European colonialism and the fight for French Algeria (even if some minor divisions remained between pro-Arab anti-French stances and pro–*Pieds Noirs* anti-communism). Since 1958, in the middle of the Algerian drama, the MSI newspaper had sent two journalists to Paris, Gaspare Barbiellini Amidei and Franz Maria D'Asaro, to follow the hectic events.[62] In 1961 the MSI MP Giulio Caradonna visited Algiers to support the struggle of local settlers, where, according to his own account, he was warmly welcomed in the most working-class neighborhoods of the city.[63]

The interest in this international event was therefore very strong. By discussing the students barricaded in Algiers University on January 24, 1960, at the start of the famous *semaine*, *Il Secolo d'Italia* remembered how these young people, by refusing to accept and in rebellion against the government's dismissal of French Algeria, were simply committed to serving a superior national ideal. Their fight would have also stopped Marxist imperialism, and they would have deserved, if not a full political support, at least an emotional solidarity from Italian neofascists.[64] As the *Meridiano d'Italia* argued, it was then natural to accuse de Gaulle of the repression of true nationalists and for the mortification of France's grandeur.[65]

[60] Ibid., p. 29.

[61] Pragmatically, as was noted by the MSI press – which also interviewed Bardèche on the topic – it was true that even former Vichy soldiers joined the detested de Gaulle, when this was crucial, in a common anti-communist perspective. See, for example, Franz Maria D'Asaro, "In piedi la Francia contro i comunisti. Intervista a Maurice Bardèche," *Il Secolo d'Italia*, June 7, 1958, p. 2.

[62] Rossi, *La destra*, p. 81. [63] Ibid., p. 84.

[64] Filippo Anfuso, "Sangue all'università," *Il Secolo d'Italia*, January 26, 1960, p. 1.

[65] Cesare Pozzo, "De Gaulle nei guai," *Meridiano d'Italia*, 16(14), April 27, 1961, p. 5.

In some strands of Italian neofascism, there was also the fear that granting equal rights to Algerians would have sent many Muslim deputies in the French Assembly.[66] This, in turn, would have contributed to the decadence of western values, whose superiority was challenged by some non-European, and non-Christian, traditions.[67] This trepidation about other cultures was part of a policy promoting the supremacy of the European civilization.[68] Arabs, according to some Italian propaganda, were also known for their not properly civilized approach.[69] Given this stereotyping, it is unsurprising that, after the second Evian conference, Tedeschi warned against the enthusiasm of those in Italy who, despite belonging to the "white race" and being born in Europe, had shown counter-racism and considered the "defeat" of France as the victory of the civil(ized) world. Tedeschi, with evident disdain, labeled these people "negri *ad honorem*."[70]

The support for French Algeria went beyond the MSI and the other main extreme-right environment. Interesting is, for example, Giovane Nazione (Young Nation). This was essentially a youth and student movement and was also tied up with Ordine Nuovo. Intriguingly, it became the main Italian representative of the mentioned transnational movement, Jeune Europe. Indeed, after 1963, the Italian group changed its name to Giovane Europa.[71] It also published the journals *Giovane Nazione* and *Europa Combattente*. The former, based in Milan, according to *Europe Action*, showed a strong dynamism and promoted the fight for French Algeria.[72]

On April 24, 1960, Giovane Nazione distributed in Milan some propaganda material supporting the *Pieds Noirs*, which was followed by a conference on "Europa, Francia e Italia" (Europe, France, and Italy).

66 Emilio Canevari, "L'Italia è inerme," *Meridiano d'Italia*, June 10, 1958, p. 3.

67 See, for example, Ezio M. Gray, "Da Algeri all'Avana: destituito l'Occidente," *Il Secolo d'Italia*, October 23, 1962, p. 1.

68 Nicola Rao, *Neofascisti! La Destra italiana da Salò a Fiuggi nel ricordo dei protagonisti* (Rome: Settimo Sigillo, 1999), p. 91.

69 Cesare Pozzo, "La mano pesante di De Gaulle contro un milione di 'Piedi Neri,'" *Meridiano d'Italia*, XVII(15), April 19, 1962, p. 4.

70 Mario Tedeschi, "Algeria, ultima Europa," *Il Borghese*, 20, March 22, 1962, p. 443.

71 Along with Giovane Nazione, apparently seven other groups related with Jeune Europe were active in Italy. See Ugo Maria Tassinari, *Naufraghi. Da Mussolini alla Mussolini: 60 anni di storia della destra radicale* (Naples: Immaginapoli, 2007), p. 35, footnote 17. On this Italian Jeune Europe see Orazio Ferrara, *Il mito negato. Da Giovane Europa ad Avanguardia di Popolo. La destra eretica negli anni Settanta* (Sarno: Centro Studi I Diòscuri, 1996).

72 Europe-Action, "L'Europe," p. 71.

A leaflet contained this unambiguous statement: "We are with the "Ultras" in their desperate but not useless fight. ... They do not defend any specific material interest, but they are the heroic defenders of the European Civilization." It ended with a peremptory *Viva l'Algeria Francese! Viva il governo rivoluzionario di Algeri!*[73]

THE AUTHORITARIAN AND SUBVERSIVE TEMPTATION

It was also some of the Italian cultural and intellectual neofascist right, along with activists fascinated by coups d'état, that supported the armed resistance of *Pieds Noirs* in French Algeria and an eventual independent state.[74] Some attempted to create a web of international connections. What was happening in Algeria was perceived as an opportunity for the entire universe of the European extreme right. Accroding to Rauti, the whole authoritarian, revolutionary, and subversive "temptation" that pervaded the Italian, and wider European, extreme-right world (especially, although not exclusively, the extra-parliamentarian one) stemmed precisely from the example of the OAS.[75] This was often seen as one of the main examples of a reborn fascism.

In 1963, Clemente Graziani, one of the leaders of the ON (who later lived in, and escaped to, Britain, France, and South America, among other places), published a pamphlet on the revolutionary and subversive war. Graziani basically argued that this was needed to stop international communism's imperialist projects in many areas of the globe. To this end, he claimed, all moral and humanitarian principles had to be suspended. To react to Russian expansionist plans, he argued, all forms of actions were allowed. The OAS, to Graziani, represented one of the most successful and noteworthy examples of this guerrilla-type warfare, and Graziani apparently became an Italian member of the French organization.[76] The uprising of Algiers in May 1958, with the reaction of French

[73] Giovane Nazione, *Consuntivo di un anno di attività 1960–61*, Milan, 1961, p. 8, in AFUS, FMSI, Serie 2 "Carte raccolte da Mario Cassiano, 1946–1963," UA 56 "Attività del Partito 1961."

[74] Rossi, *La destra*, pp. 78–79.

[75] Pino Rauti quoted in Rao, *Neofascisti*, p. 99.

[76] Clemente Graziani, "La guerra rivoluzionaria," *Quaderni di Ordine Nuovo*, 1, April 1963, p. 15. Tedeschi had highlighted, although with less radicalism, this point: "L'OAS combatte contro questa resa a discrezione con i metodi imposti dalla moderna guerriglia; e del resto, quando un milione e mezzo di uomini sanno che entro breve tempo dovranno scegliere tra l'abbandonare la loro terra e il farsi scannare dai seguaci di Ben Bella, nessuno ha il diritto di impiantare discussioni sui metodi usati per legittima difesa." Tedeschi, "Algeria," p. 444.

settlers, students, and sectors of the army (especially paratroops) to defend the colony, was, in fact, a good example of this unconventional war.[77] According to the neofascist press in Italy, these "insubordinate" generals were, in fact, the expression of a military school of thought. (This revolutionary strategy was, in reality, popular in certain French military circles, and well before this radical theorization offered by Graziani.) Following this doctrine, the army should act like the parties in the existing monoparty regimes of the communist world, and they should place themselves above the (elected) executive powers and guarantee the "continuity" of the French nation.[78]

Many activists were consequently fascinated by the French paratroopers and the activity of the OAS. Their military and resistant saga and actions were immediately mythologized. The magazine *Il Borghese* noted that, in a rather decadent western society, the paratroops in Algeria represented one of the best role models for European civilization. It was therefore paradoxical to criticize their anti-democratic actions because it was the same, old, eighteenth-century democracy that was fully outdated. They were among the few examples of human beings believing in something, in "a superior ideal."[79] The *Meridiano d'Italia* also held contacts with the OAS. As journalist Cesare Pozzo pointed out, "terrorism has not been invented by the OAS ..., and there are now in Algeria also some other types of terrorism that do not belong to the OAS."[80]

This attraction to, and admiration of, the OAS, rebellious paratroopers, and ultra-nationalist generals was especially strong among Italian extreme-right hardliners. Stefano Delle Chiaie, for example, leader of the extra-parliamentary group Avanguardia Nazionale (National Vanguard), admitted that they were supporting the "national-revolutionary" wing of the OAS.[81] Similar to JN (which was mentioned in some of the previous pages), this was a violent movement, promoting street activism and attracting a few thousand members.[82] It stemmed from the ON current and was strongly fascinated by German National Socialism.

[77] On this French military doctrine, see Giorgio Galli, *I colonnelli della guerra rivoluzionaria* (Bologna: Il Mulino, 1962), especially pp. 9–12.

[78] Pozzo, "De Gaulle nei guai," p. 5.

[79] "La rivolta di Algeri," *Il Borghese*, 17, April 27, 1961, p. 648.

[80] Pozzo, "La mano pesante di De Gaulle," p. 4.

[81] Rao, *Neofascisti*, p. 93.

[82] Avanguardia Nazionale was established on April 25, 1960. The choice of April 25 was an obvious provocation as it is the anniversary of the liberation from fascism. ON and Avanguardia Nazionale, in many ways, became the bridge between the old fascists and

However, it was also the MSI that (at least unofficially) maintained links with the OAS world. Some of this network was built at a personal and uncoordinated level. Before the establishment of this organization, for example, the *Secolo d'Italia* editor-in-chief, Filippo Anfuso, in 1960, first visited Soustelle and other likeminded politicians in Paris and then went to Madrid to meet Lagaillarde.[83] More generally, according to some newspapers' enquiries, the party had ties with extremists in Belgium, France, and Spain that were supporting the anti-decolonization struggles in some African countries.[84] The extreme-right press in France noted how Italian neofascists also had an OAS-supporting organization under the cover of the newly formed group Formazione Nazionale Giovanile (Young National Movement), created to endorse a French Algeria policy and possibly shield some of its clandestine members.[85] Indeed, it might be possible that "agents and leaders of the French and Belgian OAS found hospitality and freedom of movement in Italy, or that neo-Fascist organizations like *Giovane Italia* [the youth wing of the MSI] could make them known by taking them all around Italy, or, like the *Fronte Nazionale Giovanile*, borrow emblems and operational schemes from them."[86]

Another group promoting the OAS was the previously mentioned Giovane Nazione. It organized a European conference of movements associated with Jeune Europe, which took place in Bologna in 1963 (Antonio Lombardo covered it for *I Quaderni Neri*).[87] Thiriart chaired the conference, and Oswald Mosley contributed (Thiriart also built the OAS-Belgique to support the original OAS members with funding and other material help).[88] Giovane Nazione suggested that rebellions and revolutionary insurrections were spreading and that it was time for the emergence of a European-wide nationalism.[89] This mythicization of the OAS and its subversive strategy was certainly favored by the existing Evolian ideological environment. Rebels were generally seen by those who subscribed to this philosophy as the contemporary symbolic expression of the fascist new man, and as bastions of a pure European identity.

the RSI veterans and these postwar neofascist subversives. For a brief overview on this group, see Rosenbaum, *Il nuovo fascismo*, pp. 81–82.

[83] Laroche, "Le M.S.I.," p. 26. [84] Del Boca and Giovana, *Fascism Today*, p. 158.

[85] Laroche, "Le M.S.I.," pp. 25–26.

[86] Del Boca and Giovana, *Fascism Today*, p. 157. Duranton-Crabol also argues that it was especially the revolutionary wings of the MSI that were involved in this network. Duranton-Crabol, *Le Temps de l'OAS*, p. 112.

[87] Rossi, *La destra*, pp. 237–38, note 58.

[88] Duranton-Crabol, *Le Temps de l'OAS*, pp. 111–14. [89] Dorril, *Blackshirt*, p. 619.

They were the heirs of the elite warriors which, as mentioned, included examples from the Romanian Iron Squad to the fascist unit Decima Mas.

Another Italian who was very active in OAS-supporting networks was the journalist Guido Giannettini – who was, in fact, arrested in Spain with Lagaillarde in 1961. Giannettini wrote, among others, for the MSI's *Il Secolo d'Italia* and *L'Italiano*, which was directed by Pino Romualdi. He also seemed rather close to some Italian secret agencies and high military circles. In 1963, for example, he authored with Rauti a book on the armed forces.[90] He featured in the 1965 conference on "La Guerra Rivoluzionaria" (The Revolutionary War), organized by the Istituto Alberto Pollio, chaired by the president of Milan's Court of Appeal and by a general of the Italian army.[91]

State and military authorities, together with neofascists such as Giannettini, Rauti, Giorgio Pisanò, and Giano Accame, as well as journalists such as Beltrametti and Enrico de Boccard (who often wrote articles on Algeria and the OAS) and various university students led by Delle Chiaie, all contributed to or attended this conference. The Istituto Pollio's workshop can be rightly considered as one of the main ideological bases of neofascist subversion in Italy and will be mentioned in the following chapter. Among the points of discussion was the need for anti-Marxist counter-mobilization and the French counter-revolutionary war in Algeria.[92]

NEOFASCISM BEFORE 1968

This was also a period of the resurgence of militant anti-fascism. A powerful extreme left additionally began to influence the youth and culture. In the long term, this renewed leftism, combined with a strong revolutionary desire to change the world, culminated in a cross-national movement of revolts simply known as 1968, and marginalized the extreme right during this decade and forced it to update its strategies (this is also discussed in Chapter 4).

This was undoubtedly the case with Italy, but was also true for France, especially from spring 1961 to spring 1962. In fact, we observe an

[90] See Guido Giannettini and Pino Rauti, *Le mani rosse sulle forze armate* (Rome: Savelli, 1975).

[91] On the conference, see Aa.Vv., *La guerra rivoluzionaria. Atti del Primo Convegno organizzato dall'Istituto Pollio* (Rome: Volpe, 1965).

[92] Chiarini and Corsini, *Da Salò*, pp. 247–48.

increased cooperation between socialists and communists in the context of OAS attacks and the perceived complicity of state agencies that failed to repress them. They also shared a belief that de Gaulle was ambivalent about the OAS campaigns. From December 1961, the political left rallied against police repression. Moreover, it is worth remembering the parliamentary marginalization of the Poujadists and their portrayal by the PCF as "fascists."[93]

Given this overall anti-fascist reawakening, we can better comprehend the anti-fascist protests for Fernando Tambroni's one-party DC cabinet in Italy in 1960. The DC, in fact, experienced difficulties in receiving the necessary parliamentary votes for the new government. The result was that Tambroni officially received the external support of MSI parliamentarians. For the first time in postwar Italy a government-to-be needed the votes, at least formally, of the neofascists, and polemics stirred up the heady political climate. It is, however, true that, as mentioned earlier in this chapter, the MSI party leader Michelini was, in fact, trying to approach mainstream politics with a slightly more conservative strategy. Some political collaboration had existed at various levels (for example, in 1947, the votes of the MSI local councilors were needed to elect DC mayor of Rome Salvatore Rebecchini).

However, the rightist government led by Tambroni granted permission for the celebration of the 6th MSI Congress in Genoa (in early July 1960). This northwestern city, located in Liguria, had been the site of a steadfastly anti-fascist resistance during the war, and the memory of that historical moment was strong. The PCI and trade unions perceived this as insulting to the values of anti-fascism. A few days before the congress, demonstrations took place in Genoa and other cities. This resulted in stone-throwing and riots against the police. The troubles led the government to ban the congress from Genoa. Following from this, the DC government itself resigned and was replaced by another cabinet, with the informal support of the Partito Socialista Italiano (Italian Socialist Party, PSI).

This demonstrated that it was not possible, in 1960s Italian politics, to give neofascists any official space in a governmental coalition. This also showed that the DC was hoping to enlarge its political and social base through means of center-left orientated executives, with the official participation (which, in fact, did happen in 1963) of moderate leftist forces

[93] House and MacMaster, *Paris 1961*, pp. 242–52.

such as the PSI. For this reason, they were due to exclude the extreme right even from local arrangements, and from this point onward, the fortunes of the MSI were shaped by a marginalization that, with some very few exceptions, ran until the 1990s.

As with the MSI in Italy, this period also turned out to be a difficult historical phase for right-leaning France (the matter of decolonization was very close). The only considerable effort, after JN and, partially, EA, to unify the forces was Jean-Louis Tixier-Vignancour's candidature at the 1965 presidential election. Naturally, the defending lawyer for the OAS leaders saw his anti-Gaullist electoral enterprise supported by former French Algerian activists and by a network of so-called Comités TV (TV Committees). At the time, a good part of the French right-leaning press, as always, looked at the MSI as the main political model: It was actually the best-structured party in Western Europe and an "interesting unitary experience" in a quarrelling extreme-right world.[94] There were then some great expectations for this candidate leading the *Opposition Nationale*, with the hope that he could replicate the strategy of the Italian party. This would have made domestic neofascism compacted and relevant in the political system.[95]

Yet the modest result gained in the election (about 5.27 percent), as well as Tixier-Vignancour's support for the socialist François Mitterrand in the second round, did not allow any further and direct development of an all-encompassing extremist movement. Failure in elections, and disillusionment with the political abilities of Tixier-Vignancour, led to a fracture within the Comités TV. The somewhat positive outcome for the extreme right was that this election showed the activity of the young Jean-Marie Le Pen as an electoral campaign manager.[96] More generally, even if French neofascism was, in these years, unable to promote a common agenda (as the existence of a number of some small groups proved), this political activism was useful for the creation of the FN in the 1970s.

The would-be leader, followed by the majority of campaigners, founded, for example, the Alliance Républicaine pour les Libertés et Progrès (Republican Alliance for Freedoms and Progress, ARLP), which

[94] Europe-Action, "L'opposition nationale," p. 7.

[95] See Dominique Venner, "L'Opposition nationale," *Europe Action*, 35, November 1965, p. 3.

[96] See also Paul Hainsworth, "The Extreme Right in Post-War France: The Emergence and Success of the Front National," in P. Hainsworth, ed., *The Extreme Right in Europe and the USA* (London: Pinter, 1992), p. 33.

also had a youth wing. A group stemming from such an environment (in particular, from the OAS Métro-Jeunes), and initially close to the ARLP, was the Mouvement Jeune Révolution (Young Revolution Movement), which published *Jeune Révolution*. Established in 1966, it had among its founders the future FN key activist Jean-Pierre Stirbois. One of its members, Joël Freymond, editor of *L'Élite européenne*, became the correspondent in France of the MSI journal *L'Italiano*.[97]

On the other hand, a minority of TV supporters, along with the bulk of the EA, FEN, and the Fédération des Étudiants Réfugiés (Federation of Refugees Students), instituted the MNP. In practice, the FEN became the student section of this new party and was de facto merged into it.[98] The MNP was another pro-European nationalist movement with some foreign associations, and the French press highlighted the promising fact that Rome's newspaper *Il Tempo* devoted a page and a half to the birth of this party.[99] In order to contest the elections, the MNP and the EA's galaxy built another umbrella organization, the Rassemblement Européen de la Liberté (European Rally of Liberty, REL). The REL claimed to be "the youngest French movement," with the youngest candidates.[100] Similarly, its founders aimed at the liberation of European nations from communism, the political unity of Europe (in the guise of a federal state respecting national traditions), and the banning of North African immigration.[101] The French extreme right-wing field was, in sum, once again divided into some opposing, and often competing, movements. The consequence was that neither the ARLP nor the REL received any considerable attention from public opinion and the electorate. The 1967 legislative elections, predictably, turned into a glaring defeat for them.

As was the case for Tixier-Vignancour in 1965, the defeat in the 1963 legislative Italian election, roughly equally, gave rise to local discontent toward the strategy of the MSI. In the 7th Congress, a party

97 Charpier, *Génération Occident*, p. 208.

98 BDIC, FJD, JD, "Activité des Mouvements en France. Leurs liaisons internationales," Annexe No. 2, 1966, p. 5.

99 Europe-Action, "Mouvement Nationaliste pour le Progrès," *Europe Action Hebdomadaire*, 107, February 1966, p. 1.

100 Marcel Billard et al., "Avec vous," *REL. Numéro spécial d'Europe-Action*, January 1967, p. 14.

101 Marcel Billard et al., "Un programme sans compromissions," *REL. Numéro spécial d'Europe-Action*, January 1967, pp. 10–13.

stream called Rinnovamento (Renewal), which was composed of, among others, Giorgio Almirante, Ezio Maria Gray, Giovanni Maria Angioy, and Luciano Leccisi, virulently contested the political line of gradual insertion into the democratic system. This group pushed for a sustained action targeting the public and a more anti-system opposition in parliament and criticized the (perceived) existing communist-friendly democratic regime.[102] Even if the congress in June 1965 saw an alignment of Almirante (but not of the whole Rinnovamento) to preserve party unity, the disillusionment following the failure of this more moderate strategy revitalized activism, especially the youth elements. This latter looked abroad to, for example, the OAS, Franco's Spain, and the Greek Colonels and sought to promote and intensify mobilization and anti-left action.[103] In such a context, the MSI lost its full hegemony over neofascism and the youth generation. Many young MSI supporters became disenchanted by some of their leaders' arrangements with Michelini. Apart from ON and Avanguardia Nazionale, other youth groups, such as Giovane Nazione/Europa, were formed in response.

This was, in sum, the fragmented extreme right that approached the famous 1968. Indeed, it was only in the aftermath of this year that an unexpected awakening for this blackshirted archipelago could be observed. The year 1968 served as a transnational mobilizing passion, as the following chapters will recount, in politics and culture, with an extreme-right reaction to the left. The MSI would, in fact, carry on the strategy of insertion into mainstream political circles and tried to gather all forces around the party. This project represented the example and inspirational role model to be followed by French neofascism and served as the main basis for the establishment of the FN. In the cultural field, in many ways, it was France that, instead, offered an attractive intellectual elaboration for Italian activists.

The year 1968 was therefore "prepared" by the activism of the previous decades. A number of personalities, organizations, and developments exerted their influence: the works of Evola and Bardèche, the attempts to build international associations, the activities of groups such as EA and intellectuals like Massi and Anfuso, the fight against the spread of international communism, and the presence of a strong party such as the MSI,

[102] See especially Giovanni Maria Angoy and Primo Siena, quoted in Adalberto Baldoni, *La Destra in Italia. 1945–1969* (Rome: Editoriale Pantheon, 2000), pp. 566 and 577.

[103] On this, see also Caciagli, "The Movimento Sociale Italiano," pp. 23–24.

are all relevant components in this story. Added to this, since the 1950s, the fascination with a nationalist leader like President de Gaulle, decolonization, the need for a European nationalism, the defense of Europe's civilization – all further combined to promote domestic nationalist milieus that were certainly more open to look across state borders and borrow from foreign models.

4

1968 and the Response of Political Fronts

The year 1968 was exciting and significant from an international perspective. Gerd-Rainer Horn noted that "whether understood as that single year or as a metaphor for the larger mobilization cycle of 1965–1967 to 1975–1977, [it] is one of those 'moments of madness,' like 1848, that has left an indelible imprint on – and changed the direction of – the modern societies we live in."[1] Indeed, even if the importance of 1968 has to be contextualized in the longer process of change that affected the western world over a decade, and keeping in mind some national differences, this overall period 1958–79 was generally characterized by deep transformations. This is the era of new cultural, political, social, and economic ferments, modernization, and strong growth.[2]

France and Italy shared many traits in this historical phase. Politics had to cope with unpredictable street protests, a lively presence of Marxist culture, and the emergence of alternative cultures and lifestyles. Among all the western countries, these two nations faced the most intense student protests that were combined with the attempted alliance with workers' strikes. This mixture of the students-workers' union with strong Marxist elements was missing in some other nations "where there was not the full

[1] Gerd-Rainer Horn, "The Working-Class Dimension of 1968," in Horn and Kenney, eds., *Transnational Moments*, p. 95.

[2] Mathias Bernard, for example, suggests that the same history of France from 1958 to 1981 is indissolubly linked with the history of modernity from its "débuts à son reflux." Mathias Bernard, *La France de mai 1958 a mai 1981. La grande mutation* (Paris: Seuil, 2003), p. 205.

reconsideration of the basis of society, and the carrying on of any ideology of reversal of the 'capitalist and bourgeois' system."[3]

All this would have a great impact upon the extreme right. After the passions of Algeria, right-leaning movements had fallen into the middle of the earthquake of 1968 and its surrounding environment. As the following discussion will reveal, this mutinous moment in Western European history was of crucial importance to the development of political, electoral, and cultural strategies in the extreme right in France and Italy. Rather than dreaming, as in the 1950s, of the promotion of international networks, and now without the distraction of decolonization, it was, however, another international event itself, namely, 1968, that served to change the cards on the table for the neofascists. In fact, activists realized that, in such a context, the focus had to be on the events of those years and their eventual legacies. The leftist tide associated with 1968 was perceived, in many ways, as a key struggle.

Europe, in fact, saw the rise of "youth" as a political force, alternative ideals, some post-materialist desires, and, especially, the explosion of radical leftism. This left-wing momentum could have destroyed neofascism. In this sense, 1968 represents another genuine transnational moment.[4] This did not lead to an allegedly new extreme right (which, for some scholars, was to be developed only during the 1980s and the 1990s). In other words, there was not a moment of a full transition between an old political neofascism and a novel party. Rather, 1968 was relevant due to the fact that it led movements to develop new policies made of unified fronts and renewed activism. French and Italian neofascists were worried with the hegemony of the left and Marxism over popular and youth culture. The strategy was to reunite diverse factions, adopt counter-revolutionary stances in politics, develop bastions against communism, gain respectability in mainstream circles, and revitalize cultures. They really felt a strong need for unity and attempted to act as the guardian of the social order and the status quo. For this reason, as we shall see, the MSI tried to overlook neofascist students' participation in the barricades and faculty occupations. The following pages especially reveal the vitality of the MSI with its electoral success and the project to enlarge its political base with the inclusion of other rightist forces, and its

[3] Sommier, *La violence politique*, p. 21.

[4] In general, on the cross-national dimension of 1968, see Gerd-Rainer Horn, *The Spirit of '68: Rebellion in Western Europe and North America, 1956–1976* (Oxford: Oxford University Press, 2007).

influence on the French press and Ordre Nouveau (New Order) in the establishment of the Front National.

At first glance, the neofascist political and cultural reactions to 1968 seem to diverge. The year led the political extreme right to adopt conservative counter-revolutionary positions and a national front strategy to reunite the various groups. On the other hand, culturally, it is possible to observe some (at least apparent) innovations resulting from the ferments of post-1968 society. This latter pattern, as I shall describe in the coming chapter, was especially related to the rise of the Nouvelle Droite, and partially to the MSI's national right cultural project (actually under the leadership of the nonfascist and ex-Marxist philosopher Armando Plebe), as well as a certain cultural activism mainly developed outside the Italian party.

Yet the reality was noticeably different. Innovative themes and discourses were certainly used, but there had not always been a genuine break with the past, and, in some cases, all this was made for opportunistic and electoral reasons. The ideological inspirations usually remained fascist and neofascist thinkers. The post-1968 political extreme right and its cultural counterpart held a common objective, which was to make neofascism more acceptable, including in parliament, culture, and society, and to influence mass media discourse. There was then a similar reaction, in different fields, to the ongoing changing world, although it is also reasonable to assume that there were clashes, as will be mentioned, on what to borrow from and how to use 1968 and the youth revolt.

However, what is also fascinating to discover is effectively another forgotten story – the importance of 1968 in the transnational policies of neofascism which led to very similar responses to it in France and Italy.

ON THE SIGNIFICANCE OF 1968

The year 1968 is commonly associated with social revolt and opposition. René Rémond argues that 1968 was one of the principal crises in France's contemporary history and that it took a three-dimensional shape: a crisis of the political system, a crisis within "society," and a deeper crisis of (French) civilization.[5] According to Henri Mendras:

[5] René Rémond, *The Right Wing in France: From 1815 to de Gaulle* (Philadelphia: University of Pennsylvania Press, 1971), p. 395.

only a fundamental transformation of society could explain why such a movement emerged in France. The awareness and violent expression of this transformation gave the May 1968 movement its particular character. Both ideology and symbolism contain their own dynamism which can slow down or accelerate movements within society; they became the central moving forces of the May 1968 social uprising.[6]

The famous May 1968 is, as a result, regarded as the most potentially revolutionary revolt, with a political system near total collapse, numerous university and factory occupations, and the "largest strike movement in French history."[7] In Italy, the legacy of 1968 was, in some ways, probably even more radical. As we know, the nation had experienced a tradition of neofascist clandestine activity immediately after the war.[8] By this time, an aggressive extra-parliamentary policy was also developed. The peninsula faced the risk of a takeover, which was characterized by subversion from both the extreme left and right. The MSI pursued a dual strategy of street action and defense of the existing system, advocating reaction and activism. Its more radical fringes also developed links with some sectors of the secret services and foreign dictatorships and seemed to tolerate a gray zone between the party and revolution. In this sense, it was discredited.[9]

In general, for the whole extreme-right galaxy the end of the 1960s constituted, on the one hand, not easy years. On the other hand, however, they were also moments of cultural, doctrinal, and political elaboration and saw repeated attempts to unify forces. As described at the end of the preceding chapter, neofascism was essentially isolated. Nonetheless, the left-leaning tide of 1968, with its mythology and subversive slogans, was to exert a politically regenerating effect on neofascism.

If we look at its appeal in the wider universe of the youths of the period, even if it was a complicated situation for the political extreme right, it did not benefit from *Mai 68* and the period of 1967–69 in Italy. Its

[6] Henri Mendras (with Alistair Cole), *Social Change in Modern France. Towards a Cultural Anthropology of the Fifth Republic* (Cambridge: Cambridge University Press, 1991), p. 9.

[7] See also Julian Jackson, "The Mystery of May 1968," *French Historical Studies*, 33(4), 2010, p. 626.

[8] See Chapter 1 and Mammone, "The Black-shirt Resistance."

[9] For a discussion in English see Leonard Weinberg and William Lee Eubank, "Neo-Fascist and Far Left Terrorists in Italy: Some Bibliographical Observations," *British Journal of Political Science*, 18(4), 1988, pp. 531–49; Ferraresi, "The Radical Right," pp. 87–94; and Anna Cento Bull and Philip Cooke, *Ending Terrorism in Italy* (London: Routledge, 2013).

place in 1968 became that of the guardian of social order, the bastions of an ultra-conservative counter-revolution and, when it was possible, it moved closer to the traditional powers in society and the mainstream right. Moreover, in Italy – where the role of neofascism was more significant than in France (it is worth remembering that the MSI dated back to 1946) and where it was fairly well represented at local and national levels – it suffered from initial divisions and contrapositions between the party line and younger activists, its backward-looking core and the most subversive fringes, and the national-conservative elements usually stemming from the years of the fascist *Ventennio* and the anti-capitalist and revolutionary groups linked with the RSI.[10]

However, in retrospect, what might have been the real involvement of the extreme right in the revolt of 1968? What did this year signify for right-wing extremism? Teodoro Buontempo, a leader of youth *missini* of the time in Rome, and then active for a number of years in neofascist parties, considers the year 1968 to be "a great missed occasion, maybe the biggest in our history."[11] Similarly, Philippe Ariès, historian and former member of Action Française, sees a parallel between leftist themes and the extremist royalist discourse: "What a surprise. Under the flood of speeches and graffiti, we found the familiar themes of our reactionary youth. Suspicion of the centralizing state, attachment to real freedoms and to small intermediate communities, to the region and its language."[12]

In Italy, this debate on the extreme right and 1968 has recently been quite lively – and this was especially because of the fortieth anniversary of this famous event and mainly due to the presence in government of the successors of the MSI. Adriano Scianca, from the pages of the *Secolo d'Italia* in a long article entitled "Frodo, gli Who e il '68 tradito" ("Frodo, the Who and the betrayed 1968"), published on November 21, 2006, argued for "another" 1968 experienced by the western world, a non-leftist one. Although this represents a slightly peculiar, and post-ideological, interpretation of events (as a mere generational conflict, and partially used to legitimize some contemporary right-wing political cultures that had to probably appear more modern and updated), it also reinforced the impression that the *missini* initially in the student revolt were not decontextualized.

10 See also Marco Tarchi, *Esuli in patria. I fascisti nell'Italia repubblicana* (Parma: Guanda, 1995), pp. 56–57.
11 Teodoro Buontempo quoted in Rao, *Neofascisti!*, p. 125.
12 Philippe Ariès, *Un historien du dimanche* (Paris: Seuil, 1980), p. 184, also quoted in Richard Vinen, *France, 1934–1970* (London: Macmillan, 1996), p. 189.

They were allegedly rather well placed in the (then) ésprit du temps. This attempt to generate a different type of debate on 1968 and its legacy, was, in fact, reproposed by the then Alleanza Nazionale's leader, the well-known Gianfranco Fini, and his think tank Fondazione Farefuturo, in a special edition ("Quel che resta del Sessantotto") of *Charta Minuta*, published in January 2008, and also in an interview with the *Corriere della Sera*, where he also talked about 1968 as a lost chance for the political right.[13]

The bulk of the neofascist intelligentsia, along with the political elites, nonetheless rejected 1968 and its values. In the same January issue of *Charta Minuta*, Gianni Scipione Rossi, in another essay ("Il Sessantotto che non c'era"), warned against this neofascist nostalgia and reminded readers that the leftist values were fundamentally different from the extreme-right world, while in those years the MSI worked, proficiently in his view, for the stability of the democratic system. In this sense, it also may appear today that valid participation by neofascists in this leftist historical moment was difficult and, perhaps, improbable. In general, the ideals of 1968 and its libertarian aspects were very far from rightist philosophy. The myths to follow were those of Allen Ginsberg, Greenwich Village, Jean-Paul Sartre, Herbert Marcuse, Mao, and Che Guevara. In contrast, extreme right-wing watchwords became "tradition," "reaction," and "order," and this, as the next sections will delineate, became evident in their approach toward the youth uprising and their own neofascist students' participation in the protests.

Indeed, the MSI's more traditional approach did not mean that it overlooked all youth demands. The party was glad to support its most loyal young supporters including in their efforts to create international and anti-communist networks. In November 1969, for example, the MSI's official youth organized, in collaboration with their Portuguese fellows, a European conference in Rome along with representatives from

[13] See Andrea Garibaldi, "Fini e il '68: la destra perse un'occasione," in the *Corriere della Sera* on February 3, 2008, p. 5. Andrea Hajek suggests that this journal edition tried to connect 1968 to "the cultural products that were imported from the United States: the poetry of the beat generation, American music, fashion, etc. The picture on the front cover of the magazine, which shows a girl wearing a mini-skirt, illustrates this. The statement that 1968, initially, wasn't political in nature, but existential and generational, undoes 1968 of its ideological 'burden' and negates its left-wing connotations in order to fit it into a right-wing memory as well." Andrea Hajek, "*E se il '68 fosse (anche) di destra? Media and Identity Formation: Rereading the Protest Movement of 1968 from the Right*," ASMI Conference, 2008, p. 3.

other countries, including Per Engdahl for the MSE and Jean-François Galvaire from what they labeled a "French anti-communist front" (and, most importantly, a member of Ordre Nouveau, and then FN). The event was attended by roughly forty people, and apparently a thousand activists followed the final public speech in a cinema. The project was to build a common ideological and organizational platform of European youth, defend (European) civilization, and react against the left.[14] For other young neofascists, nonetheless, the story with 1968 was at least slightly different.

ITALIAN NEOFASCISTS: ORDER AND DISORDER

At the time of the revolts, the MSI youth organizations were the Raggruppamento Giovanile Studenti e Lavoratori (Students and Workers' Youth Group), led by Massimo Anderson, and, especially focused on the educational sector, the Associazione Studentesca di Azione Nazionale-Giovane Italia, directed by Pietro Cerullo for high-school students, and, in the university milieu, Cesare Mantovani's FUAN. The national leaders were linked to the party line and apparatus, while the local neofascists were undoubtedly closer to the peripheral structures than to the national organizations. Among the local associations, the FUAN-Caravella – established in 1950 – was particularly dynamic in the first phase of 1968, mainly at the University of Rome *La Sapienza*, where neofascists were numerous. However, the FUAN also joined the occupations of universities in Naples and Modena, among others.[15] The chronicle of the events in Rome is, nonetheless, perhaps the most interesting.

The Caravella initially took part in the protests together with the hated left-wingers, developing similar themes and declarations.[16] To a certain extent, neofascists had the imperceptible feeling of fighting for a common cause. However, the reality was that leftists and rightists acted in parallel to one another. This early collaboration was unofficial and contingent. This was, in fact, a moment when young people, no matter what their ideological beliefs, thought that the sociopolitical status quo might and

[14] ACS, MI, DGPS, SIS, UG, 1967–70, B. 31 ("Raggruppamento giovanile del M.S.I.").

[15] One should consider that the presence of MSI activists was, in general, rather marginal in the student movement.

[16] Arianna Streccioni, *A destra della destra. Dentro e fuori l'MSI, dai FAR a Terza Posizione* (Rome: Settimo Sigillo, 2000), pp. 100–01.

should be altered. Indeed, although there were some exceptions, it seems that neofascist participation in 1968 did not take, at least initially, a strong ideological stand. In the majority of cases, it was mostly a campaign limited to student, and more generally youth, demands. However, as Marcello Veneziani, a distinguished rightist intellectual in contemporary Italy, argued, it was also evident that some students believed that 1968 would serve to modernize the MSI.[17]

The apogee of this improbable unity between the younger generations of both left and right was represented by the demonstration at Valle Giulia, in Rome, in front of the Faculty of Architecture, on March 1, 1968. This demonstration symbolized the starting point of the Italian events of 1968, even if students had previously occupied some other departments. At the end of February, the dean of *La Sapienza*, Agostino D'Avack, invalidated all examinations held during the occupations and sent in the police force to remove students occupying university premises. The student response was unanimous: a demonstration of nearly three thousand people against the authorities. This represented the first victory of the student movement, involving neofascists (including Stefano Delle Chiaie's group Avanguardia Nazionale) and communists together, and led to the occupation of other academic faculties.[18] FUAN-Caravella and other extreme-right students held the Law Department, while leftists occupied the Literature Faculty.

At this point, the MSI's primary aim became that of breaking this alleged union between young neofascists and the left.[19] In so doing, the party radicalized its anti-left standpoint and consequently showed its more conservative face. Michelini, the leader, had made the position of mainstream neofascism inconvertibly clear: Citizens had to side with movements like the MSI "for a national and social order" and to prevent the country becoming a communist landscape.[20]

[17] Marcello Veneziani, *68 pensieri sul '68. Un trentennio di Sessantottite visto da destra* (Florence: Loggia De' Lanzi, 1998), p. 37.

[18] Nicola Rao records that students were (apparently) even led in the riots by neofascists and especially by Avanguardia Nazionale. Rao, *La Fiamma*, p. 126.

[19] Marco De Troia, *Fronte della Gioventù. Una militanza difficile tra partito e società civile* (Rome: Settimo Sigillo, 2001), p. 19; and Giuseppe Pensabene, "La sovversione allarga la sua macchia d'olio," *Il Secolo d'Italia*, March 9, 1968, p. 3.

[20] Arturo Michelini, "Per non svegliarsi in un Italia comunista," *Politica*, 1(1), 1968, p. 23, in AFUS, FMC, Serie 2 "Attività nel Movimento sociale italiano, 1930–1990," Sottoserie 2 "Propaganda e documentazione," UA 51 "Materiale di propaganda a stampa, 1948–1980."

Paradoxically, and linked with this overall strategy of "order," the MSI, by means of *Il Secolo d'Italia*, ignored the participation of its own members in the 1968 revolt, and strongly attacked the demands of the younger generation. For example, on February 25, in reference to the student occupations, *Il Secolo d'Italia*'s headline was "A pantomime that has already lasted too long."[21] The day after the Valle Giulia demonstration, the MSI press, overlooking the presence of its activists, identified the street brawls as a plan of the communist party, and the front-page of the newspaper claimed that "The PCI sparked off the revolt."[22]

From such a perspective, we can easily understand why the attempts to promote an agreement between some young *missini* and the MSI failed, or why the party decided to retain its intransigent anti-communist policy. The point of irreversible clash arose due to the imminent national student demonstration of March 16. On this turbulent day, the MSI organized a semiofficial rally to *La Sapienza*. The party wanted to restore order, even if some of their members were actually involved in the disorder. The MSI group, which consisted of more than three hundred activists, was made up of, among others, the Volontari Nazionali (National Volunteers), the national youth leaders Mantovani, Anderson, Cerullo, and Sandro Tribuzi, and the parliamentary deputies Giorgio Almirante and Giulio Caradonna. This last named was escorted by members of the Rome Boxing Academy. These people attacked the Literature Faculty occupied by left-wing students. At this point, many neofascist students joined the MSI faction. In the meantime, the MSI group had to shelter in the Law Department and was attacked by the leftist protesters.

The outcome of the riots was one hundred and fifty people injured, including fifty-two right-wing extremists. The defeat of the MSI commandos appeared unquestionable, but *Il Secolo d'Italia* claimed that the *gioventù nazionale* (the extreme-right "national youth") had broken the communist control over the universities.[23] According to the MSI propaganda, the PCI had, in fact, planned to exploit the student demonstration and protests for a "Bolshevik conquest of the Italian universities."[24] The party could then claim to be one of the "guardians" of the democratic system.

[21] "Una carnevalata che è durata anche troppo," *Il Secolo d'Italia*, February 25, 1968, p. 1.

[22] "Il PCI scatena la piazza," *Il Secolo d'Italia,* March 2, 1968, p. 1.

[23] "Dura lezione ai sovversivi durante tre ore di scontri," *Il Secolo d'Italia*, March 17, 1968, p. 1.

[24] "Basta con gli stracci rossi. Il tricolore all'università," *Il Secolo d'Italia*, March 17, 1968, p. 1.

Another kind of MSI victory was, on the other hand, obvious. These events caused a fracture among students, and they preserved the traditional divisions in the political spectrum. Different views arose in the youth association, and it is known that after 1968 many sympathizers left the MSI because of its ultra-conservative policy. The organizations in Rome, in fact, tried to have an active participation in the revolt.[25] For this reason, for example, some dissidents of FUAN-Caravella later founded the Nuova Caravella (New Caravella). However, March 16 marked, above all, the conclusion of neofascist participation in 1968, along with the loss of influence for the MSI in the university milieu.

MSI students were isolated, and their own leaders marginalized them, and this act that would leave a real mark on these activists.[26] In essence, they were almost left alone. Adriano Romualdi, Mario Tedeschi, and other prominent neofascist intellectuals, such as Maurice Bardèche and Julius Evola, virulently criticized the revolt of 1968. The latter, for example, accused Marcuse's sociology of being "banal" and based on "crude Freudianism."[27] The images of Paris's *Mai 1968* gave rise to a range of concerns. Italian neofascists feared an imminent propagation of similar events in their own country. In the second half of May, the rightist Rome newspaper *Il Tempo* promoted the Comitato dei Padri (Fathers Committee) to restore some "irreplaceable moral values," which were inevitably challenged by the forces of 1968. Similarly, *Il Borghese* tried to mobilize its readers toward anti-communist unity in order to avoid a French-inspired rebellion.[28]

It was therefore evident that there was not great sympathy for these neofascist students. The only rightist extremists supporting their demands were the intellectual Giano Accame, Luciano Leccisi with his journal *L'Orologio*, the young MSI official Adalberto Baldoni with his weekly *La Sfida*, and other publications such as *Corrispondenza Repubblicana* and *Controcorrente* (supported and published by the Federazione Nazionale Combattenti della Repubblica Sociale Italiana, which gathered some

[25] Adalberto Baldoni, *Il Crollo dei Miti. Utopie, Ideologie, Estremismi* (Rome: Settimo Sigillo, 1996), pp. 36–37.

[26] Marco Tarchi, *Cinquant'anni di nostalgia. La destra italiana dopo il fascismo* (Milan: Rizzoli, 1995), p. 108. Along with the missing party support, rebellious neofascists also lacked charismatic and appealing leaders.

[27] Julius Evola, "La vera 'contestazione' è a Destra: L'uomo di vetta" (interview with Gianfranco de Turris), *Il Conciliatore*, 1, January 15, 1970, pp. 16–19.

[28] See Alessandro Gasparetti, *La destra e il '68* (Rome: Settimo Sigillo, 2007), pp. 157–59.

RSI veterans). Romolo Giuliana and the Futurist artist Principio Federico Altomonte were leading these last two publications.[29] *Corrispondenza Repubblicana* published, for example, some interesting material related to the student revolt. In April 1968, on its pages appeared an "introductory statement" produced by the Caravella in the Economics Department at *La Sapienza*. This discussed the state of the university and the overall parliamentary system. On July 5, in an article entitled "De Gaulle and the Student 'Revolution,'" the journal analyzed the events of May in Paris. It also announced the creation of the Movimento Studentesco e Operaio "Avanguardia Europea" (Students and Workers Movement "European Vanguard"), which published *Creatività*. This publication, in the first issue dated October 1968, contained what they called the "Sorbonne Charta." In reality, this document was a translation, although not an entirely accurate one, of *Nous sommes en marche* ("We Are on the March"), the manifesto of the radical worker and student group Comité d'Action Censier (Censier Action Committee).[30]

The magazine *L'Orologio* similarly offered help to neofascists involved in the events of 1968. It set up a number of supporting groups (the Gruppi dell'Orologio) in some occupied university faculties because, as reported in the journal, "the battle" had to "go on."[31] This is, perhaps, unsurprising, given the *fascisti di sinistra* tradition of *L'Orologio*. In line with this, it published documents and notes from occupied universities worldwide, and, through Antonio Lombardo from Paris, it also featured articles on the French strikes and demonstrations.[32]

In sum, if there was no direct sustain from the MSI, this latter position was nonetheless also understandable, as it was linked to the electoral fear of losing loyal voters. However, this also meant that, to a certain extent, the MSI was unable to take advantage of the difficulties experienced by the ruling parties. In such a context, the May 1968 elections represented a

[29] Lanna and Rossi, *Fascisti immaginari*, p. 180.

[30] On the *Thèses* of "Nous sommes en marche" see also Boris Gobille, "La vocation d'hétérodoxie," in D. Damamme et al., eds., *Mai-June 68* (Paris: Éditions de l'Atelier, 2008), pp. 281–82. For a collection of French students' texts and scripts, including some of the mentioned documentation, see also Centre de regroupement des informations universitaires, ed., *Quelle Université? Quelle Société? Textes réunis par le Centre de Regroupement des Informations Universitaires* (Paris: Seuil, 1968). On Censier, see Ross, *May '68*, pp. 83 and 107–8.

[31] Romano Neri, "Dagli atenei la rivolta al sistema," *L'Orologio*, 5, March 15, 1968, p. 10.

[32] See Luciano Lanna, "La lunga marcia della destra maggioritaria," *Il Secolo d'Italia*, February 26, 2008, http://robertoalfattiappetiti.blogspot.com/2008/02/la-lunga-marcia-della-destra.html, accessed October 31, 2010.

defeat for the party (4.5 percent of the vote in the Chamber of Deputies, 4.8 percent in the Senate). Rather than the growth of the PCI, it is worth highlighting the rise of the DC, which won about 40 percent of the vote. This retrospectively shows that, in a moment of national downturn, right-wing voters preferred to support a more stable and moderate party. This tendency was repeated a month later in the French elections with the victory of Gaullism.

LIBÉRONS LA SORBONNE!

The French academic year 1967–68 began with struggles between left-wing students and the ultra-right Fédération Nationale des Étudiants de France (National Federation of France's Students). This did not, however, signify that neofascism was acting like a genuinely unified front. Although the extreme-right environment had been in a state of ferment due to the issue of Algerian decolonization, we know that movements were facing some disagreements and, indeed, were unable to elaborate a common strategy. They experienced such enormous difficulties that, according to many of their own sources, even their future "looked fairly compromised."[33] The absence of a long-established party, and its structured youth organization, additionally meant that there was less intense involvement in the events of 1968 than might have been expected (at least if compared with Italy). For this reason, it was also difficult for activists to respond effectively to the events of *Mai 1968* and oppose the more combative, and ideologically appealing, leftist groups. As Duprat sarcastically put it in that same year: "By repeating the gigantic mistakes of their predecessors of the Croix de Feu in 1936, instead of fighting against the leftists, they will organize parades in the 'Beaux Quartier,' which anger their activists, and provoke clashes between 'hardliner' and 'soft' movements."[34]

In general, the French neofascist fascination with 1968 was limited. Enthusiasm for these events was usually lacking. It was a moment of structural crisis of the democratic system, and some were essentially caught in the dilemma of either joining the hated Gaullist regime to destroy the left-wing opponents or backing these latter to subvert the republic.

[33] François Duprat, *Les journées de Mai 68. Les dessous d'une révolution* (Paris: Nouvelles Éditions Latines, 1968), p. 157.

[34] Ibid.

In the end, only a very few of them actually joined the leftists on the barricades.[35] However, some right-leaning extremists saw the protests

> as motivated by straightforward, and justified, demands of bourgeois children for better campus facilities and job opportunities. This was the view expressed by the former Pétainist Bernard Fay in the conservative journal *Écrits de Paris*. Others sympathized with the more radical student demands. The New Left . . . bore some resemblance to the old Maurrassian right. Both condemned centralization, materialism, and both were at odds with the Communist party.[36]

A movement called Occident was the one to show more interest in the events of 1968. It was directly generated by the activism of Pierre Sidos and the FEN's *filière* in 1964 (after some disagreement with EA), and, in fact, it borrowed the JN's symbol, the Celtic cross. The group was rooted in the student milieu, with members such as Alain Robert, Alain Madelin, and François Duprat, and it was known for its street fighting. It also published *Occident-Université*. Half of its supporters were based in Paris, but it had a presence in other university cities, such as Rennes, Bordeaux, and Montpellier.[37]

According to Paris's Prefecture's police, Occident's ideology was based apparently on a fascist one. It combined the cult of the leader, exaltation of physical strength (including military paratrooper training), anti-Semitism, and strong support and appreciation for nature and youth, along with virulent criticism of the parliamentary democratic system.[38] Occident was also one of the few right-wing extremist factions that at least tried to exploit some anti-system aspects of the revolt. In some cases, its activists mixed with leftists on the *barricades* and distributed their political leaflets and brochures, such as "Pour une Jeune Nation – Occident" (For a Young Nation – Occident).[39] In some ways, they paid honor to the rebellious youth. Its revolt represented the healthy "vital impetus" of western civilization.[40] Occident's reflections on the crisis sought, on the other hand, to put the blame – as was happening in neofascist Italy – for its genesis and development on a "minority portion leftist agitators," as well as Gaullist philosophy and on the structure of French society itself.[41]

35 Jean-Christian Petitfils, *L'extrême droite en France: De Maurras à Le Pen* (Paris: Presses Universitaires de France, 1983), p. 99.

36 Vinen, *France*, p. 189.

37 Shields, *The Extreme Right*, p. 139.

38 BDIC, FJD, JD, Préfecture de Police, "Le Mouvement 'Occident,'" I. "'L'ideal' des militants d'Occident," August 1968, pp. 2–3.

39 BDIC, FJD, JD, Préfecture de Police, "Le Mouvement 'Occident,'" III. "Les prises de positions du mouvement Occident face à la crise de mai," August 1968, p. 8.

40 BDIC, FJD, JD, "Pour une Jeune Nation – Occident," 1968, p. 6.

41 Ibid., p. 9.

The problem was that the European extreme right, including Occident, was not "particularly open to new counter-cultural trends ... since these developments were increasingly associated with 'pacifist' hippies and the 'anti-national' New Left."[42] Overall, a more appropriate "Libérons la Sorbonne" (Let's liberate the Sorbonne!) became, therefore, one of the main slogans for Occident. The reality was that, as for the MSI in Italy, the domestic neofascists were taken aback by the events of 1968. There were divergent strategies toward students and the ruling powers.[43] There was even, at times, a generational divide, with some young rightist extremists challenging an old world. Nonetheless, fundamentally, just as a young intellectual such as Adriano Romualdi in Italy had questioned the "authenticity" of the rebellion and showed a revulsion for hippies with their long hair, riches, and fondness for bolsheviks, Bardèche equally questioned this "revolutionary comedy" played out by a part of the younger generation.[44] He argued that these youths fully enjoyed all the fruits of the consumer society that they had just "apparently" rejected.[45] Nothing was then "spontaneous" about the *Quartier Latin* uprising.[46] The student revolution that was being imagined at Nanterre University, on the outskirts of Paris, was basically only a "laboratory" for subversion. This dual belief in the power of violence and in the future role of the univeristy led Nanterre to create that strange chimera of "student power."[47]

In such a context, the Gaullist regime, with its call for "order against anarchy," became very attractive even for Poujade and Tixier-Vignancour. Gaullism turned out to be, in anti-communist and counter-revolutionary terms, a flag of convenience for forces willing to protect the social and political order. Moreover, the government also granted a political amnesty, and this helped to overcome some of the divisions between the mainstream right and some extreme-right activists. The OAS's leaders, most notably General Salan, and other leading French Algeria Ultras were released from prison. Others came back from exile,

[42] Jeffrey M. Bale, "'National Revolutionary' Groupuscules and the Resurgence of 'Left-Wing' Fascism: The Case of France's Nouvelle Résistance," *Patterns of Prejudice*, 36(3), 2002, p. 29.

[43] Duprat, *Les Mouvements*, pp. 158–59.

[44] Adriano Romualdi, "Contestazione controluce," *Ordine Nuovo*, I (1), 1970, pp. 22–24; and Maurice Bardèche, "Post-Face," in Duprat, *Les journées de Mai 68*, pp. 181 and 199.

[45] Bardèche, "Post-Face," p. 199. [46] Ibid., p. 182.

[47] Maurice Bardèche, "Introduction," in Duprat, *Les journées de Mai 68*, p. 14.

such as George Bidault.[48] Predictably, groups formerly in the struggle to retain *Algérie Française* welcomed these events.

On May 30 the massive Gaullist demonstration on the Avenue des Champs-Elysées in Paris marked the high point of unity among the different streams of rightist France. All the opponents of communism seemed to be rallied around Charles de Gaulle. Many Occident activists marched with their Celtic crosses alongside conservatives, and the neofascist press in Italy, impressed by de Gaulle's mobilization, reestablished its fascination with the General.[49]

Yet old resentments did not disappear, and, even if de Gaulle had granted an amnesty to the OAS, not all supporters of Vichy offered amnesty to the political leader.[50] Since the loss of Algeria, the feeling among many in the extreme right was one of renewed disagreement with de Gaulle and everything he did. Moreover, in the Fourth Republic, he managed to attract, in the anti-communist Cold War years, almost all the nationalist vote. This left neofascism without one of its mobilizing passions and marginalized a political galaxy that was unable to offer a viable alternative to his nationalist appeal and leadership.[51]

This is one of the reasons that explain why Poujade and Tixier-Vignancour's support for the regime produced further fractures. Their strategy was unable to provide a political voice and representation to all extreme right-wingers. Periodicals such as *Minute* and *Rivarol* were still overtly anti-Gaullist, while famous neofascist figures, such as Isorni, would even have preferred a socialist government to a Gaullist cabinet.[52]

Meanwhile, the parliamentary elections of June 1968 led to the impressive and triumphant victory of Gaullism. The two Gaullist movements, the Union pour la Défense de la République (Union for the Defense of the Republic) and the Républicains Indépendants (Independent Republicans), received more than 40 percent of the vote. The final result of 1968 for neofascism was roughly a mere 0.13 percent of the vote.[53]

[48] De Gaulle pardoned people like Salan less because he wished to unify the far and moderate right than because it was part of the bargain he reached when he flew in secret to West Germany on May 29, 1968, to discuss with General Massu his willingness to deploy in France the troops stationed in Germany. Massu agreed to do this, if needed, to buttress the Gaullist regime. The condition was that his old putschist and OAS friends were liberated. De Gaulle agreed, and former members of the OAS were indeed pardoned on June 7, 1968, and released.

[49] Gasperetti, *La destra*, p. 155.

[50] Rémond, *The Right Wing in France*, p. 413.

[51] Vinen, *France*, pp. 173–74; Rioux, "Des clandestines aux activistes," p. 239.

[52] Vinen, *France*, p. 190.

[53] Duprat, *Les journées de Mai 68*, p. 161.

Nevertheless, the times were edging toward a new page in the history of right-wing extremism. As indicated, it did not generally follow people in the streets, nor did it begin a process of ideological modernization. Instead, it defended the status quo in the name of an anti-left counter-revolution. In politics, this reaction, along with the fear of being overcome by Marxist values, promoted a highly significant development: the creation of a unified party in Italy first, and then on French soil.

THE MSI-DESTRA NAZIONALE

In Italy 1969 represented another turbulent year. After the student rebellions, widespread worker unrest affected the nation, leading to the famous Autunno Caldo (Hot Autumn) and trade union demands. The year also opened with Giorgio Almirante advancing his claim to the party leadership. The more moderate elements within the party were worried about a radicalization because his political background seemed really close to the RSI experience.[54] On the other hand, they were aware that unless it gained power, Almirante's group might leave the party. This fear of a split and the need to show an image of unity backed the acceptance of Almirante as general secretary in June 1969, and, following the internal division of 1968, under the new leader the party structure was strongly centralized and peripheral organizations were kept on a tight rein.

Nevertheless, the new political program was roughly syncretic, often demagogic, and excessively ambitious. The MSI, in a celebratory euphoria, claimed it was developing a novel image of a nontotalitarian, pro-European, and socially progressive movement.[55] In reality, Almirante's general approach was that of defending public order by presenting the MSI to Italian society as a bastion of public security against the revolutionaries.[56]

[54] See also Ignazi, *Il polo escluso*, p. 136.

[55] The party moved to the Destra Nazionale, following those programmatic lines. The mixture between nationalism and Europeanism – which, as we have seen, was not novel for neofascism, and which will also influence some other party strategies in the 1970s, as I shall show in Chapter 6 – is also present in Giorgio Almirante, "La Destra vince. La DC spalle al muro" (interview with Mario Tedeschi), *Italia Tricolore*, 3, 1971, p. 11.

[56] For a neofascist account of the communist riots, see, for example, AFUS, FMSI, Serie 3 "Carte raccolte da Giorgio Bacchi," UA 59 "Relazioni delle federazioni provinciali, 1971 – 1972," "MSI – Federazione Provinciale di Ancona," "Relazione sulla violenza di sinistra in Ancona," No. 00567/GV/za, January 12, 1972. This is a quite controversial point considering that, especially in the early stages, street fighting was mostly associated with the extreme right.

This was conceptualized with the famous, and controversial, theory of the "Piazza di Destra" (Right-wing Town Square), where activists were encouraged to stand up to and confront leftist demonstrations and riots.[57]

This was to lead the MSI in a supposedly new direction, although one that did not lose sight of the past. Almirante summed up this policy with the enigmatic phrase "Nostalgia dell'Avvenire" (Back to the Future).[58] To be sure, this recently appointed leader continued the strategy of gradual insertion into the political system and agreements with other rightist parliamentary forces. There was, indeed, a compelling need to enlarge the electoral base after the failure of the 1968 elections. The Ninth MSI Congress, held in Rome in November 1970, renewed this policy through the proposed creation of a Fronte Articolato Anticomunista (Articulated Anti-Communist Front), open to all anti-leftist forces. The party similarly emphasized its counter-revolutionary core and was determined to take advantage of the conservative-bourgeois fears of social disorder and alternative cultures.[59]

This overall political line was intended to woo moderate voters. It was designed to establish a more appealing "National Right," a federation of authentic rightist forces, with the MSI acting as a magnet. The aim, as reported a few years later in the neofascist *Défense de l'Occident* in an article that was a tribute to the Italian party, entitled "Leçon de la campagne italienne" (Lesson from the Italian [Political and Electoral] Campaign), was to promote a *politique d'ouverture*, attract non-fascist personalities, and moderate language and style, in order to be accepted as a national-conservative party. However, as was argued on the French

[57] Ferraresi translated this as "right-wing street fighters." However, the core of the concept is the same: "The ability of this ... party, if need be, to call its militants into the streets ... was all the more reassuring to conservative frightened by generalized social unrest." Ferraresi, "The Radical Right," p. 88.

[58] Eatwell, *Fascism*, p. 260. A useful discussion on the party propaganda related to this Nostalgia dell'Avvenire is in Luciano Cheles, "'Nostalgia dell'Avvenire.' The New Propaganda of the MSI between Tradition and Innovation," in L. Cheles et al., eds., *Neo-Fascism in Europe* (London: Longman, 1991), pp. 43–65.

[59] The overall approach of the conservatives to 1968 was, in fact, rather critical: "to right-wing politicians ... the sixties was a time of decadence and loss of discipline." Arthur Marwick, "Six Novels of the Sixties — Three French, Three Italian," *Journal of Contemporary History*, 28(4), 1993, p. 565. Margaret Thatcher would have, for example, eventually "blamed the 1960s for 'the block mentality: tower blocks, trade union block votes, block schools' and the insidious cult of 'breaking the rules.'" David Edgar, "Much like the 1950s," *London Review of Books*, 29(11), June 2007, p. 21.

side, neofascist leaders had to take a tight control of this process to prevent any "liberal" drift.[60]

In doing so, the party probably wished to force the mainstream right to accept its presence in a governmental coalition and subsequently influence domestic politics. Ideally, this process would have led to the hegemony of the MSI over the whole right-wing spectrum, undermining the strength of the powerful DC. To this end, the party held some demonstrations in the country, looking not only to co-opt non-nostalgic forces and potential electors, but also with the aim of overcoming existing and spontaneous movements stemming from people's disaffection toward mainstream parties, and from fears of a Marxist revolution (see, for example, the 1971 "Silent Majority" movement in Milan). This was, in other words, the ambitious project of the Destra Nazionale (National Right, DN), which had to be perceived as something different from the old MSI. The only way to do this was to merge completely the neofascist identity – and party – into the new structure. The MSI could, as a result, have claimed to be an innovative force, rooted in the rightist tradition, but able to understand the predicaments of contemporary politics and society (and against the other parties apparently interested in holding power).

The focal aim of the MSI was to water down, in some ways, the more fascistic ideological connotations and, consequently, to rally an alleged anti-communist strength of public opinion. To achieve this, it discouraged among activists the use of the Roman salute and the wearing of blackshirts, and the party propaganda was, at least partially, renewed.[61] In such a vein, the party strengthened its essentially "unconditional anti-communism."[62] Linked to this, and while maintaining its fascist core, DN also sought to move away from the classic dichotomy of "fascism versus anti-fascism." As Almirante wrote in Bardèche's *Défense de l'Occident* in 1971, the real fight (and alternative) was between freedom and communism, and the MSI stood for the former.[63]

[60] Pascal Yague, "Leçon de la campagne italienne," *Défense de l'Occident*, 139, 1976, p. 11.

[61] Luciano Cheles, "Il '68 nella propaganda figurativa del Movimento Sociale Italiano," in S. Casilio and L. Guerrieri, eds., *Il '68 diffuso. Contestazione e linguaggi in movimento* (Bologna: Clueb, 2009), pp. 153–54.

[62] Aldo De Quarto, "La Constituante de la Droite en Italie," *Défense de l'Occident*, 173, 1976, p. 53.

[63] "Notre alternative ... est la liberté contre le communisme. ... Les deux termes de l'alternative ne sont pas aujourd'hui fascisme et antifascisme, mais communisme et liberté." Giorgio Almirante, "Position actuelle du M.S.I.," *Défense de l'Occident*, 95, 1971, p. 67.

Most fascinatingly, the MSI also abandoned conventional disagreements with the monarchist fringes that harked back to King Vittorio Emanuele III's "rejection" of Benito Mussolini and the armistice of 1943.[64] The *missini* in this case highlighted the apparent shared beliefs, such as anti-collectivism, cult of the nation and state, and authority, with Alfredo Covelli's monarchist party, the Partito Democratico Italiano di Unità Monarchica (Italian Democratic Party of Monarchist Unity).[65]

The DN project – which officially saw the light of day with the change of the party name only a year later – was also carefully considered in some conservative and bourgeois circles and attracted "members of the bureaucracy and the aristocracy."[66] Various personalities, including the philosopher Armando Plebe, the former mayor of Naples and industrialist Achille Lauro, the editor of *Il Borghese* Mario Tedeschi, the writer Giovanni Altieri, and two Christian Democrat MPs, Agostino Greggi and Filippo Murdaca, joined the Destra Nazionale party.[67] High army officer and ex-chief of NATO naval troops in the Mediterranean area, Admiral Gino Birindelli, also officially became member of the DN venture (after this, *Défense de l'Occident* republished one of his essays on Mediterranean geo-politics previously published by the Italian journal *Intervento* in November 1972).[68] The subsequent electoral result of 8.7 percent in the April 13, 1972, legislative election was their best ever.[69] Approximately three million Italians voted for the Movimento Sociale Italiano-Destra Nazionale (MSI-DN). Although the result fell short of their expectations (roughly 15 percent of the vote), the party impressively gained eighty-two MPs.

All in all, this electoral achievement was even more significant as the process of party doctrinal change had hitherto hardly started. The MSI-

64 On the legacy of the armistice for Italian neofascists, see Mammone, "Gli orfani del duce," pp. 250–59.

65 Gianni Roberti, *L'opposizione di destra in Italia, 1946–1979* (Naples: Gallina, 1988), p. 239.

66 Caciagli, "The Movimento Sociale Italiano-Destra Nazionale," p. 24.

67 See, for instance, Senator Filippo Murdaca's letter to Almirante expressing his accession to the Destra Nazionale project and in its anti-communist and national struggle, in Biblioteca U. Balestrazzi (Parma), Archivio '68, Busta 3, "Il linguaggio dei volantini," *Fascicolo* 2, http://biblioteche2.comune.parma.it/BibParma/Archivio68/index.htm, accessed May 4, 2007.

68 See Admiral Gino Birindelli, "Une stratégie nouvelle pour le Méditerranée," *Défense de l'Occident*, 108, 1973, pp. 23–37.

69 The MSI's success after 1968 was not an isolated case. In Germany, the failure of the Great Coalition led to the rise of the fascist National Democratic Party in local elections, and contributed to its best ever result (4.3 percent of the vote) in the 1969 federal election.

DN was still thought of only as an electoral tool by many of its members. Rather than an authentic renewal of the MSI, Almirante was interested in broadening its electoral base and regenerating fascist identity. Indeed, this led some of Rauti's radical ON to rejoin the MSI. To put it differently, Almirante had been trying to redesign the external cultural-ideological facade by using a new, and often moderate, style of communication. At that time, the leadership was adopting a twofold strategy of street activism while maintaining a respectable parliamentary appearance. This became known as "manganello e doppio petto" (bludgeon and double-breasted suit).

It is also worth noting that some external events sped up (and even forced) the apparent modernization of the MSI. First, neofascists were involved in the revolt of the southern city of Reggio Calabria. The town was affected in 1970–71 by a wave of riots, due to the decision not to grant it the status of regional capital of the newly instituted region of Calabria. The party had opposed the division in different regions, in the name of the supreme unity of the state. They also felt it was a device to allow left-wing parties to gain control of many regional governments and achieve more power.[70] However, paradoxically, the MSI, the party *of* the state, was leading, through the local leader Ciccio Franco, the demonstrators of Reggio Calabria *against* the central state.[71] They backed a "southern" protectionism for the economically disadvantaged south of Italy and its exploited farmers and demagogically attacked the rich northern Italian regions, the center-left governments, and media such as the *Corriere della Sera* and *Il Giorno*, perceived as being close to the private sector and central state interests.[72] Reggio Calabria's revolt strengthened the party's electoral clout

[70] The MSI MP Ernesto De Marzio claimed that the new regionalist "fragmentation" was to be the "communist way to gain power." Ernesto De Marzio, "La battaglia del M.S.I. contro la disgregazione della Nazione," in AFUS, FMC, Serie 2 "Attività nel Movimento sociale italiano, 1930–1990," Sottoserie 2 "Propaganda e documentazione," UA 51 "Materiale di propaganda a stampa, 1948–1980."

[71] As one can observe in Giuseppe Niccolai, "Reggio Calabria," *Il Machiavelli*, 17(7), 1970, p. 1, neofascists strongly criticized the government's intervention in the revolt (especially after the arrest of Franco). Interestingly, in 2006, under the local mayor, Giuseppe Scopelliti, a former representative of the MSI (then of Alleanza Nazionale and also member of Silvio Berlusconi's party and Calabria's regional governor), a theater in Reggio Calabria was renamed the "Ciccio Franco Arena."

[72] AFUS, FMSI, Serie 1 "Istituto di Studi Corporativi (Isc)," Sottoserie 1 "Documentazione Storica MSI," UA 13, "X Congresso nazionale, Roma 18–21 gennaio 1973," "Dalla Calabria tradita la protesta del Mezzogiorno," p. 128

in the southern regions but led also to further criticisms of the MSI's approach to democracy. Second, after the 1972 election, Almirante was formally accused of attempting to resurrect a fascist party (which is forbidden by the Italian law), and the MSI was forced quickly to moderate its external image.

The MSI Congress, held in Rome on January 18–21, 1973, provided the perfect opportunity to increase its respectability, as well as to counter accusations of persistent fascist roots. A new central committee was elected, with Almirante as senior secretary and the "non-fascists" Covelli and Birindelli as presidents, and the party took the official denomination of Movimento Sociale Italiano-Destra Nazionale, a project that had aroused great interest in European extreme-right circles since 1972.[73] *Rivarol*, the French neofascist periodical, for example, published a long and positive essay based on the official birth of the DN, where it was claimed the entire French press, after a period of "oblivion" for Italian neofascism, had looked again at Almirante and the MSI. This happened immediately after the 1972 electoral breakthrough, the foundation of the MSI-DN, and the gain in the Sicilian elections of June 1973 (about 11 percent of the vote). From this moment onward, the journal proudly reported that "the name of Almirante became synonymous, in the French press, of MSI and Italian neofascim."[74]

FOR A NEW ORDER

With the end of de Gaulle's presidency after the referendum of April 1969 on Senate powers and regional reform, the domestic extreme right was divested of one of its main mobilization themes. Moreover, after the dissolution of Occident in winter 1968, banned for public order reasons, French neofascists were once more scattered into a nebulous universe of Lilliputian groups. However, after 1968, at least the fear of left wing hegemony and the youth revolt still provided the perfect opportunity for some reorganization. This attempt to renew activism basically showed that there was generally the perception that a form of political right had to survive beyond the traditional conservative forces. Many French extremists were, in fact, looking critically at the moderate right's performance

[73] See Ado Marchigiani, "Chronique italienne: 10e Congrès du M.S.I.: la Droite nationale est née," *Rivarol*, 1151, February 1, 1973, p. 11.

[74] Pascal Yague, "L'Italie 'rouge et noire,'" *Défense de l'Occident*, 122–23, 1974, p. 29.

during the 1968, and its leaders were seen as "incapable of representing the concerns of the traditional right, the 'true' right."[75]

One of these "true" right-wing movements was Jeune Europe, a group that also had links with Thiriart's (Belgian and pan-European) networks and that, like Occident, had similarly criticized Zionism and liberal capitalism. According to the journalist Charpier, it immediately looked at the MSI for political and material help. Indeed, activist Nicolas Tandler had contacts with the young MSI leader Gianfranco Fini.[76] Nevertheless, among these groups, it was the Groupe Union Droit (Union Law Group, GUD), generated by Occident, Alain Robert, and Gérard Longuet, which was, at least locally, one of the most active movements. In ideological terms, its manifesto was revolutionary, corporatist, and anti-communist. Its aim was to gather all anti-Marxist students around a minimal program and, in their own words, "to fight against communism and its leftist drive . . ., to fight for a selective and . . . educative university. This is GUD's objective since the turbulence of May 1968."[77]

It was influential in the University of Paris II Panthéon-Assas. The hope was to transform Assas into a national fascist bastion for the movement. As a GUD slogan put it: "Let make our example to be followed: Let create two, three, a hundred Assas!"[78] However, this group also had a certain strength at Saint-Etienne University, where it had five members elected as student representatives in 1971. In the same year, at Toulouse, it also gained a score of 35 percent of the vote in the faculties of law, political science, and economics.[79]

The GUD, along with other former Occident activists, injected some vigor into neofascism through the creation of Ordre Nouveau during the spring of 1969. Foremost figures of the movement were Jean-François Galvaire, Alain Robert, François Brigneau, and François Duprat, and the latter quickly became the leading ideologue. Roughly five thousand young people represented its total strength. They were mostly students based in Paris, Marseilles, Lyons, and Nice. Ordre Nouveau turned out to be an

[75] Edward G. DeClair, *Politics on the Fringe: The People, Policies, and Organization of the French National Front* (Durham: Duke University Press, 1999), p. 34.

[76] Charpier, *Génération Occident*, p. 212.

[77] Le Rat Noir, "Editorial," *GUD-OCCIDENTE-UNIVERSITE*, 1, December 1972, p. 1. The GUD later changed its name to Groupe d'Union et de Défense.

[78] Ibid.

[79] François Solchaga, "Nouvelles du 'Front,'" *Rivarol*, 1092, December 16, 1971, p. 7; and François Solchaga, "Nouvelles du 'Front,'" *Rivarol*, 1094, December 30, 1971, p. 6.

umbrella organization, keeping together different extremist currents, including Roger Holeindre's South Vietnam support network. It also published the periodical *Pour un Ordre Nouveau*. Ideologically the party was situated in the revolutionary nationalist fringe of the neofascist tradition. It was an anti-capitalist and anti-Marxist movement, attacking liberalism. Like a number of parties across Western Europe, it also promoted an archetypical European third way. The party manifesto called for the defense of national traditions, a strong state, and a presidential regime. It also tried to exploit the apocalyptic belief in a new wave of North African immigrants assaulting national borders and starting to counter-colonize metropolitan France.[80]

In spite of some internal disagreement, the party decided to contest elections, starting with the 1971 Paris City Council. The example to be imitated was obviously that of the MSI (from whom it received some noteworthy material and financial help).[81] As they suggested: "We want to acquire a dimension beyond that of a sect or a minor group. ... We want to build a large party, like the Italian MSI, which we have set up as a model for ourselves."[82]

Indeed, Italian neofascism was really a source of inspiration and attraction for these Frenchmen. *Rivarol* had a weekly column, *Chronique italienne* (News from Italy), which followed all the events concerning the MSI. *Rivarol* had a strong and historical admiration for Italian neofascists. In 1954 *Union*, the journal of Oswald Mosley's Union Movement, had, for example, praised the French bulletin for their "interesting and informative articles" on the MSI, which was, in their view, almost misrepresented (and probably overlooked) by the traditional British media.[83] However, it was really the whole of right-wing France that was following Italy (and contributing to its international reputation). Later, in 1972, some members of Ordre Nouveau, in fact, went so far as to organize a demonstration in Paris to congratulate the MSI-DN on their results in the

[80] On this see "Les dangers de l'immigration sauvage," *Rivarol*, 1134, October 5, 1972, p. 2.

[81] Jean-Christophe Cambadélis and Eric Osmond, *La France blafarde. Une histoire politique de l'extrême droite* (Paris: Plon, 1998), p. 79. According to Shields, the MSI "was thought to have provided financial support and which made some of its poster designs available for use by the new French movement." Although the extreme-right network was much more articulated, Shields also rightly suggests that the links between the parties "were fostered largely through the [MSI]'s youth wing, the Fronte della Gioventù," which was formed in 1972. Shields, *The Extreme Right*, pp. 161 and 346 (note 91).

[82] *Pour un Ordre Nouveau*, 1972, quoted in DeClair, *Politics on the Fringe*, pp. 30–31.

[83] Jeffrey Hamm, "M.S.I and European Union," *Union*, 301, February 13, 1954, p. 2.

Italian elections.[84] This fascination with the Destra Nazionale was rather widespread among other local extreme-right forces. When discussing Ordre Nouveau's congress leading to the establishment of a new party – as I shall show shortly – some from the GUD wrote that this latter had the duty to gather all the different, defeated, and quarrelling currents of the "Droite Nationale" and to realize all the long-term objectives of this "Front" by creating a structurally unified large "Parti de la Droite Nationale."[85]

Moreover, there was in the extreme-right world a deeply held belief that the sociopolitical situation of these European lands had similar dynamics.[86] Affinities with Italy's neofascist environment were consequently natural. The "Ordre Nouveau" label was a literal translation of "Ordine Nuovo," and the French side immediately had trans-border contacts with the Italians (setting aside the financial support from the MSI). Galvaire, in November 1969, participated in the European meeting organized in Rome by the MSI for the youth national-revolutionary movements. The party also invited notable Italian leaders to France. Almirante, for instance, was an acclaimed special guest at the first party conference in Paris on February 14, 1970, while, on May 13, Massimo Anderson was the MSI representative at a Paris meeting, where he was also enthusiastically greeted by all the participants.[87]

Moreover, just as the MSI had combined some hardline street activism with a respectable electoral strategy, so the Ordre Nouveau hoped to pursue a similar line of attack. This tactic was made abundantly clear by Duprat in a meeting at the Maison de la Mutualité in Paris. He took the Italian MSI's electoral strength and the "bludgeon and double-breasted suit" philosophy as the key examples to follow, and it is probably no coincidence that his pamphlet *L'Ascension du M.S.I.* (The Rise of the MSI) was published exactly in 1972. Accordingly, the party would continue to face leftists in the streets but would also, and above all, contest "elections by presenting political solutions."[88] It therefore used a dual style of communication. It denied the use of any physical fight for political

[84] There were also a few street clashes with leftist students. François Solchaga, "Nouvelles du 'Front,'" *Rivarol*, 1114, May 18, 1972, p. 4.

[85] "Le Front National contre E. Faure," *GUD-OCCIDENTE-UNIVERSITE*, 1, December 1972, p. 4.

[86] Antoine Parrot, "Le 22 mars d'Ordre Nouveau," *Rivarol*, March 30, 1972, p. 5.

[87] BDIC, FJD, JD, de Police, "Relance de l'extrême-droite pro-fasciste en France," pp. 3–4. See also ACS, MI, DGPS, SIS, UG, 1967–70, B. 31 ("Raggruppamento giovanile del M.S.I.").

[88] Duprat quoted in Parrot, "Le 22 mars," p. 5.

ends and, indeed, condemned this. Yet the reality was that some of its sympathizers were often directly implicated in riots with the police and leftist organizations.[89]

The inconsistent results of the 1971 elections led to the second phase in extreme-right political tactics. This was the building of a mass party controlled by the same revolutionary nationalists, a would-be Front National pour un Ordre Nouveau (National Front for a New Order), gathering all forces in order to contest the forthcoming legislative elections. As *Rivarol* put it: "The struggle for the 1973 elections has just begun!"[90]

ESTABLISHING THE FRONT NATIONAL: "WITH US, BEFORE IT IS TOO LATE!"

Some party strategists also (and rightly) began to feel that the image of their movement was probably radical for the moderate electorate. In such a context, Brigneau and Maurice Gaït organized in Paris in December 1971 a dinner debate with 150 in attendance (including Jean-Marie Le Pen, Roland Gaucher, Abbé Serralta, Colonel Romains-Defossés, and other representatives of the *Opposition Nationale*). They discussed the strategy for a common political action, based on two dimensions. The first one was a "moral and material support for the national campaigns led by Ordre Nouveau, spearhead of the [neo-fascist militant] opposition, within a spirit of unity." The second was instead the "constitution of a national front gathering together all our political family in order to lead a

[89] See, for instance, the riots at the Lycée Montaigne (Paris) between *gauchistes* and Ordre Nouveau students in 1971, and the ones against the Trotskyite *Ligue Communiste* in Toulon in December 1972. The extreme-right publications often wrote about joint action between the *Ligue Communiste* (in the name of the "lutte antifasciste") and the Maoists (in the name of the "Cause du Peuple") against the weakest and more isolated neofascist "groupes nationaux." But, according to the press, the response was usually "rapide, grace à la mise en pratique du [neofascist] front unique sur le terrain." See François Solchaga, "Nouvelles du 'Front,'" *Rivarol*, 1090, December 2, 1971, p. 6. It is also worth remembering that Ordre Nouveau's anti-system values continued to play an important role after the party's decision to contest elections. On this see also Renaud Dély, *Histoire secrète du Front National* (Paris: Grasset, 1999), p. 54.

[90] Solchaga, "Nouvelles," 1094, p. 6. On this national front in the light of coming elections, see also François Solchaga, "Nouvelles du 'Front,'" *Rivarol*, 1115, May 25, 1972, p. 5.

combat assuring the national opposition's insertion within the country's political life, at the moment of the 1973 legislative elections."[91]

This unitary national front (a term that was already in use since the end of 1971) quickly became a priority, and many other meetings and *dîner-débats* in cities such as Bordeaux and Toulouse, among others, were organized.[92] In this heady atmosphere, right-wing periodicals greatly encouraged this policy. *Rivarol* had a weekly column, *Nouvelles du "Front"* (News from the "Front"), which was usually written by the "François Solchaga" (a pseudonym used by Duprat). This publication was strongly engaged in this "permanent campaign" to unify the party family and asked its readers to work hard for it (we know that the extreme-right press was equally fundamental for the initial developments of neofascism in Italy).[93]

As was the case for the MSI-DN, the establishment of a party capable of acting as a federator for the different extremist ideological currents (and a magnet for ex-OAS supporters, monarchists, ultra-conservatives, Catholic fundamentalists, and former Vichy collaborationists) was very relevant – and especially with a huge threat coming from the left-wing side, as, in 1972, the socialists and the PCF were elaborating a common program to achieve political power.[94] The French extreme-right line was that of creating, first, a structure that would foster the reception of activists

[91] François Solchaga, "Nouvelles du 'Front,'" *Rivarol*, 1093, December 23, 1971, p. 4.

[92] Solchaga, "Nouvelles," 1094, p. 6; Solchaga, "Nouvelles," 1104, p. 7. In the same period, the press also highlighted a (alleged) progression of neofascist trade unionism and specifically of the Union Générale des Travailleurs (Workers General Union). See François Solchaga, "Nouvelles du 'Front,'" *Rivarol*, 1112, May 4, 1972, p. 4.

[93] On the role of the neofascist press in Italy, see Chapter 1, and Di Meglio, "Il ruolo della stampa."

[94] As a member of the FN put it: "For a very long time, the French Communist and Socialist Parties had remained divided . . ., they each followed their own path, and then one fine day in 1972 they created a common program. . . . And it was in the face of this danger and the inability of the mainstream right to face these dangers, to contain these dangers, that the National Front was created"; quoted in DeClair, *Politics on the Fringe*, p. 35. Another more "institutional" event should be also taken in mind. The Ordre Nouveau's tactic of creating a bigger party, and an extreme-right federation, might be, at least partially, perceived as "a first response to the Fifth Republic whose two-round majority system creates – at the very least – a party-political imperative which forces groups, nebulous movements and smaller parties to federate into more mainstream political parties." Catherine Fieschi, *Fascism, Populism and the French Fifth Republic: In the Shadow of Democracy* (Manchester: Manchester University Press, 2004), pp. 159–60.

as they moved on a sort of dual track (a double party membership).[95] During the June 1972 congress, the foundations of the party were, in any case, well laid.[96]

Ordre Nouveau decided to exclude from the new movement some influential, but controversial, *notables* such as Tixier-Vignancour. We have seen that the establishment of the MSI demonstrated a similar trend. Party membership was forbidden to fascist politicians who had contributed to the decline of Mussolini's regime or accepted the 1943 armistice, or to political "careerists."[97] However, just as the support of the MSI was former *fascisti*, many old French fascists and collaborators, including people from the Vichy Regime, rallied around the neofascist front. By way of example, this was the case with Brigneau, a follower of Marcel Déat and volunteer with the Vichy militia, Pierre Bousquet, of the former Parti Franciste and member of the Charlemagne Division, Victor Barthélémy, the general secretary of Jacques Doriot's interwar party, and future FN politician Roland Gaucher

In France, the main challenge was, nonetheless, also that of keeping together two competing, and broad in some ways, extremist cultures, the *nationalistes* and the *nationaux*. The *nationaux* were mostly currents stemming from French Algeria groups, Poujadists, and supporters of Tixier-Vignancour and were more favorable toward the parliamentary strategy. The *nationalistes* were, on the other hand, those nostalgic for Action Française, close to Ordre Nouveau and Occident, and rooted in national-revolutionary activism – people such as Robert Gauchon and groups like Jeune Nation.

Nevertheless, little time was wasted, and the Front National was formed on October 5, 1972, during a meeting at the Salle des Horticulteurs in Paris. A week before its founding, thousands of leaflets with a tricolor flame and the slogan "Front National – Avec nous avant qu'il ne soit trop tard" (National Front – With Us, before It Is Too Late) were distributed across France.[98]

95 The diverse streams would have completely merged, although Ordre Nouveau initially called for a unity which had to respect the political and ideological autonomy of single groups forming the "national opposition." François Solchaga, "Nouvelles du 'Front,'" *Rivarol*, 1135, October 12, 1972, p. 6.

96 On this congress see "Conseil national d''Ordre Nouveau,'" *Rivarol*, 1134, October 5, 1972, p. 4.

97 See also Mammone, "Gli orfani del duce," p. 272.

98 See, "Conseil national d''Ordre Nouveau,'" p. 4. "Front National Avec nous, avant qu'il ne soit trop tard" was an Ordre Nouveau's slogan. See François Solchaga, "Nouvelles du 'Front,'" *Rivarol*, 1104, March 9, 1972, p. 7.

FIGURE 1: FN meeting in Paris, 1972. Courtesy of © Marc Simon/Apis/Sygma/Corbis.

Le Pen was chosen as party leader. The movement, in fact, needed someone capable of carving out a niche in the mass media and public opinion, and some of the young leaders of Ordre Nouveau probably did not have the political stature for such position. James Shields suggests how Le Pen benefited from a number of favorable factors:

> aged 44, he was a former parliamentary deputy, a veteran of Indo-China and Algeria, a well-known militant nationalist and an able speaker. He was also, within the personnel of the extreme right, a relative moderate who could aspire to some degree of political respectability. The factor playing most strongly in Le Pen's favour was, however, a negative one: he was not associated closely enough with any single faction to preclude the unifying leadership which the new movement required.[99]

The composition of the party's first Political Bureau may be also considered as a compromise between the different French extreme-right streams (and this, as at least partially suggested, included wider and further "parliamentary" currents, more "revolutionaries" stances, Maurrasian, and pan-Europeans).[100] It was made up of Le Pen as party president, Brigneau as

[99] Shields, *The Extreme Right*, p. 170. [100] See also ibid.

vice-president, and Robert as general secretary (as noted before, from Ordre Nouveau), while *lepeniste* and *national*, as well as a former OAS member, Holeindre, was nominated deputy general secretary. As with the early MSI, with the competition between the revolutionary and more conservative forms of Italian fascism, compromises between some diverse traditions similarly took place in the elaboration of the first FN political program, and this was characterized by certain ambiguities.[101]

The FN really had the ambition of developing into a mass party. It presented itself as an all-inclusive "social, popular and national right."[102] Its early political discourse focused prominently on some usual themes, such as the defense of colonialism, anti-Gaullism, immigration control, and the need for a proportional electoral system. Like the MSI-DN, it favored a strong presidential regime and the respect of traditional values (for example, the defense of the family) – all in the name of the moral and social regeneration of France.[103] In another analogy with the Italian case, the overall mobilizing strategy was resoundingly anti-communist.

The appeal of the neofascist MSI-DN (and in part of the British-based extreme-right National Front) was extremely strong for the French party.[104] Indeed, it adopted a tricolor flame as the emblem of the movement, similar to that of the MSI, replacing the green of the Italian flag with the more consonant French blue. This overall influence was pretty natural (as we have noted in these pages). When remembering events of the 1972 October meeting leading to the establishing of Le Pen's party, Duprat admitted this fascination with Italy very candidly:

> The meeting ended with a call for the creation of the "Front National." Ordre Nouveau lobbied for the adoption of this acronym because it was well used [by activists], and also because 80,000 posters bearing the Tricolour Flame (copied

101 Jim Wolfreys specifically defines the first FN program as a "compromise between [the] revolutionary nationalist element and the ... conservatism of other members." Jim Wolfreys, "An Iron Hand in a Velvet Glove: The Programme of the French Front National," *Parliamentary Affairs*, 46(3), 1993, p. 416.

102 "Jean-Marie Le Pen chez les Intellectuels indépendants," *Rivarol*, 1149, January 18, 1973, p. 4.

103 The only, initial, innovation in comparison with other groups, and probably under the influence of Le Pen, was a call for a reduction of the state's presence in the economy and for the defense of private property and free enterprise. See Scrutator, "Le Front National," *Rivarol*, 1150, January 25, 1973, pp. 6–7.

104 For a positive account referring to the policies of the British National Front, see, for example, "La percée du 'National Front,'" *Rivarol*, 1333, July 29, 1976, p. 8.

from the Movimento Sociale Italiano) were printed. This badge of the Flame showed that the new [French] Front wants to follow the same tactic as the "Destra Nazionale" – which is used, successfully, ... by Almirante's MSI. This latter is a movement which fully supports the Ordre Nouveau since its establishment, and that today has praised the French nationalists for their use of the same Destra Nazionale's strategy, in its newspaper *Il Secolo d'Italia*.[105]

It is evident, then, that neofascist France and Italy shared a lot in the late 1960s and early 1970s – isolation, reaction, and similar political, social, and ideological trends. After 1968, these European neofascisms were, indeed, affected by the same fears and preoccupations, as well as by an unusual dynamism in politics, activism, and, as the following pages will demonstrate, even culture.

[105] François Duprat, *Droite Nationale en France: de 1971 à 1975* (Paris: Éditions de l'Homme Libre, 2002), p. 27. This edition has a preface written by Jean-Marie Le Pen.

5

Culture after 1968

The previous pages described how the MSI-DN as a model for an overall political strategy was extremely appealing for French neofascists. This MSI project, in fact, seemed electorally successful and able to overcome fragmentation among groups. However, the *destra nazionale*, very ambitiously, was also a cultural venture willing to display the renewed image of the sons of the Mussolinian right. Indeed, an interesting part of this transnational narrative is linked with another right-wing reaction to 1968. This was a response engendered as a cultural refusal, although also borrowing, at times, some of the deeds and mobilizing themes of 1968.

This appropriation of 1968 was easier for the neofascist youth (such as the Fronte della Gioventù) and the heterodox and nonconformist intellectuals. However, in some ways, the MSI propaganda also took some of the lexicon, and iconography, of the rebellious year.[1] This was also for opportunistic reasons. According to MSI leader Almirante, communists had won the "war of words."[2] In such a context, the same *fascismo* had to be portrayed with a fresh and modernized visage – and especially if the right wanted to succeed in elections. Activists were advised to avoid all grotesque, anachronistic, and "stupidly nostalgic" representations of the interwar fascist phenomenon, even if this did not happen very often.[3] In other words, the leftist revolt pushed the extreme right on a corner and made it, with its call to order and tradition, even less interesting to youths

[1] See Cheles, "Il '68 nella propaganda," pp. 154 and 158. [2] Ibid., p. 160.

[3] Almirante quoted in Luciano Cheles, "Le 'new look' du néo-fascisme italien," *Mots*, Special Edition on "Droite, nouvelle droite, extrême droite. Discours et idéologie en France et en Italie," 12, 1986, p. 29.

than before. At the same time, it, nonetheless, promoted some ferment within the rightist side the cultural-political spectrum. In Italy, more pragmatically, and given the presence of a strong party such as the MSI, the main goal was to break Marxist cultural hegemony and alternative lifestyles, and to legitimize neofascism in the public eye, high society, and mainstream culture. The DN's task may, therefore, surely be ascribed along these lines.

In reality, as we will notice, the genuine 1970s regeneration of postwar fascism and the policy of insertion in mainstream circles were better carried out by other individuals mainly outside the parties. Some Italian publishers, with nationalist, ultra-conservative, and extreme right-wing sympathies, in fact, contributed to the launch of a more intellectual right-leaning enterprise. This approach was especially obvious through the establishment or rebranding of periodicals and associations, together with the translation of overseas conservative and fascistic authors, publication of book series, and the organization of study centers, seminars, and international conferences. All this activity, along with the electoral strength of the MSI-DN, made Italy again seem like a golden land to foreign like-minded activists. This was predictable in the case of France, where, as Chapter 6 will describe, even after the creation of the FN in 1972, the domestic extreme right was not really unified. In 1977, the neofascist ideologue Bardèche referred to the predicament of French right-wing extremism as being something "neither capable of generating realistic political programs calculated to mobilize the popular imagination, nor forceful enough to confront reality."

Nevertheless, this situation was about to change at the turn of the decade. Two years later, "Bardèche recognizes that Alain de Benoist of the New Right has proposed how the Right can leave the ideological ghetto it has inhabited since 1945."[4] In retrospect, this was correct. Indeed, a productive intellectual fringe like de Benoist's Nouvelle Droite promoted another reading of postwar fascism and, most importantly, was to influence part of the mainstream political discourse. It was also an evident example of transnationalism, a honeycomb structure where extreme-right ideals circulate within, across, and beyond geographical boundaries. In Italy, for example, it was persuasive among some young fringes, and intellectuals. However, theoretically, it was deeply indebted to the philosophy of Julius Evola and also aimed to develop a rightist

[4] Ian Barnes, "Intellectual Processes on the French Far Right," *Patterns of Prejudice*, 16(1), 1982, p. 3.

version of the famous Italian Marxist thinker Antonio Gramsci's distinguished concept of "hegemony." A cross-fertilization was then, once more, inevitable. The difference between these neighboring nations was that, while the MSI finally rejected all possible ideological modifications, the FN later enjoyed a favorable sociopolitical environment stimulated by the ND, and even reinterpreted and reshaped some of de Benoist's ideals.

In truth, and setting aside the intellectual activism developed in these years, some of the post-1968 right-wing cultural innovations were less innovative than they might appear. The following sections will, for example, highlight that the DN was ineffective in altering the fascist philosophies of the Italian party. Similarly, many of the ND themes were not something unprecedented in the history of the extreme right in modern Europe. However, the ND and, more generally, the 1970s rightist culture, represented a type of bridge that led the extreme right to try to adapt to some developments. These leftist years around 1968 were not the sole preoccupations that influenced the right-leaning strategies of the time. By the mid-1970s, the wind of economic prosperity had begun to slacken under the impact of the 1973 oil crisis. The resulting economic emergency, which affected the whole industrialized world, slowed the process of change. Nevertheless, this ushered in another process of transformation, leading to a novel phase of modernity. It is a moment that marks the passage, for many western countries, from class conflict and industrial capitalism to a different post-industrial society.

Consequently, for neofascism, there was a paramount need to offer more updated solutions for a world that was rapidly changing. As a neofascist observer put it: "The right must therefore face the modern-day conditions, by using contemporary tools and solutions which are adapted to the present time."[5] This overall process led to the theoretical reelaboration of some old right-wing themes, and, especially in the case of the ND, made a number of fascistic stances and nationalistic literatures, more acceptable.

CULTURE IN EXTREME-RIGHT ITALY

Culture really mattered for the post-1968 Italian extreme right. This was especially because the intellectual battle, and consequently the political-electoral one as well, seemed to be in the hands of the left and of its

[5] Marchigiani, "10e Congrès du M.S.I.," p. 11.

youth-appealing gurus. The Destra Nazionale represented, politically and also culturally, the key response to the events and changes brought by the late 1960s onward and constituted an example of the neofascist search for some public forms of legitimization.

Did this really happen? Not always, and not everywhere. The outcome of this process was controversial for the extreme right. To some extent, its approach generally represented more a closure to both that social transformation and new international western society. In the medium to long term, this would contribute to the decline of the MSI and the loss of leadership over much of its fellow Western European movements. This closure was hardly surprising if we consider that this was tied up with much of the MSI's thinking and with an archetypical right-wing anti-modern worldview.[6] In this sense, the DN project also symbolized the expression of a cultural counter-revolt against the libertarian principles of the modern world. On the other hand, the DN at least denoted a partial attempt to produce a livelier cultural environment after years of isolation.

The attempt to update party doctrine and to slowly move into mainstream culture was entrusted to figures such as the philosopher Armando Plebe.[7] Plebe, a university professor of the history of philosophy, was a Marxist who converted to a fervent anti-communist. Almirante quickly offered him the chance to become the symbol responsible, in some ways, for the MSI's cultural sector. Indeed, and setting aside party secretary Almirante's efforts, the DN doctrine was also elaborated through the pamphlet on the right (*Il libretto della Destra*) published by Plebe in 1972. He represented, together with the monarchists and others, the moderate external image of the MSI – at a time when the party was often accused by its critics of encouraging the resurgence of fascism.

All in all, Plebe turned out to be organizer of cultural activities through conferences, seminars, and the establishment of journals, where he also tried to involve some famous conservative and rightist intellectuals from around the globe. Under his leadership much effort was focused on this intellectual world. DN felt it was vital to help intellectuals to modify their leftist positions, and to bring to an end the Marxist monopoly over the cultural industry, which, in Plebe's vision, forced intellectuals to be

6 The introductory pages of this book have already mentioned this opposition to modernity and the values of the Enlightenment. On this point, see also Holmes, *Integral Europe*, p. 4.

7 See Armando Plebe, *Il libretto della Destra* (Rome: Il Borghese, 1972). This was basically Plebe's overview of his vision of the right. Another publication of the time was Mario Tedeschi, *Destra Nazionale. Sintesi di una politica nuova* (Rome: Il Borghese, 1972).

"financially dependent" on the communists. According to this view, the intelligentsia had "no freedom of expression." As long as this was so, their cultural activity could only be justified if its products supported the culture of the political left. Plebe argued that a novel right-leaning culture was emerging. This was a "people's culture" and was clearly opposed to what he saw as the elitist communist ideology. It was also a "new literature" that was willing to be "ironic," "dissident," and "critical" in reference to the official powers.[8]

In line with his recent doctrinal conversion, Armando Plebe was energetic in promoting a non-Marxist culture. Alain de Benoist, Fausto Gianfranceschi, and Claudio Quarantotto became members of his international association for the advancement of western culture. He also formed the journal *La Destra*, directed by Quarantotto, with an editorial board that included Ernst Jünger, Michel de Saint Pierre, Thomas Molnar, Giuseppe Prezzolini, and Mircea Eliade. The establishment of this publication also aroused interest among French neofascists. *Rivarol* considered the journal, along with similar periodicals such as *Defense de l'Occident* and the German monthly magazine *Criticon*, as representing the best examples of a moral and intellectual (European) renaissance that was (supposedly) growing.[9] Simultaneously, within other MSI circles, some research centers and journals such as the *Rivista Italiana di Studi Corporativi* and *Linea* were built to spread neofascism within the world of youth, society, and the mass media.

Despite his activism, Plebe was, in reality, unable to produce an innovative philosophy based on any substantial theoretical bases. The new doctrine was merely a set of "anti-" definitions and values. The right represented a mere opposition to the left, and DN's culture came down to a series of noncommittal and "conventional clichés."[10] The general political programs were economically corporatist, in favor of public security and order, against the class struggle, and, in the words of the French neofascist press, in opposition to communism.[11] What is more, the DN project was perceived differently among Italian extremists. For some it was excessively moderate, while for others it was simply a tactical tool

[8] Plebe, *Il libretto della Destra*, pp. 80–94.
[9] Marchigiani, "10e Congrès du M.S.I.," p. 11.
[10] Piero Ignazi, "La cultura politica del Movimento Sociale Italiano," *Rivista Italiana di Scienza Politica*, 19(3), 1989, p. 441.
[11] C.N., "Chronique italienne: 'La Destra,'" *Rivarol*, 1098, January 27, 1972, p. 13.

and a transitory political line. Being considered as an "external non-fascist," Plebe was, moreover, categorically and virulently disapproved of, and opposed by, those who saw themselves as the true fascists, and by many hardline thinkers such as Adriano Romualdi, along with the followers of ON.[12]

Destra Nazionale turned out to be a loose coalition masquerading as a new party. It was then soaked in the neofascist tradition and was simply a linear continuation of the MSI. Any difference lay in borrowing some conservative figures and, possibly, in the use of a more sophisticated style of communication, trying to avoid all nostalgic references to the fascist past and formally accepting democracy and liberal values. Senior party strategists believed that the MSI could still become a noticeable electoral force and influence political life with no serious revision of its past and doctrinal modernization. They felt there was no need to cut ties with street fights but simply show a more respectable face. In this sense, DN seems to have been no more than a new mask worn by Mussolini's successors. It was unable to promote a change in mentality. It was, as suggested, an attempt to legitimize the MSI and to make neofascism more acceptable, if not welcome, in mainstream envirnoments. The year 1972 was therefore the moment of the best-ever electoral result and, simultaneously, also the beginning of a slow decline. The party, despite its achievements at the ballot box, was indeed once again excluded from the coalition government, and it pursued – even if not unanimously – a policy of radical parliamentary opposition.

The extreme right's revived interest in culture was not exclusively due to the endeavors of official parties and their linked intellectuals (and readers will find a somewhat similar stance when we turn back to the French case). The rightist publishing industry was pretty dynamic during this period. Publishers such as Rusconi Editore, Edizioni del Borghese, and Edizioni Giovanni Volpe promoted the "other" cultural reaction to the leftist hegemony. The last publishing house was, for example, quite relevant in the spreading of right-leaning culture. Its owner and editor, Giovanni Volpe, was the son of Gioacchino Volpe, a notable historian who played an important role under the fascist regime and also led the Fondazione Gioacchino Volpe, which promoted conferences and seminars on political and historical topics. Volpe became the founder of

[12] See, among others, Adriano Romualdi, *Una cultura per l'Europa* (Rome: Settimo Sigillo, 1986), pp. 87–89.

two distinguished journals, *Intervento* and *La Torre*.[13] His eponymous publishing company attracted right-wing intellectuals and published essays and books by theorists such as Oswald Spengler, Julius Evola, Ernst Jünger, Pierre Drieu La Rochelle, Abel Bonnard, Paul Sérant, Gabriel Marcel, Maurice Bardèche, and Charles Maurras. In addition, it published some revisionist works such as the translated version (*I volontari europei delle Waffen SS*) of one of the books produced by French fascist and collaborator Marc Augier.[14] This was published with a preface from Adriano Romualdi that represented an apologetic homage to the German interwar fascism.[15]

The Edizioni del Borghese, alongside the daily paper *Il Borghese* and the journal *La Destra*, similarly tried to revitalize and spread non-leftist cultures. It published works by Mario Tedeschi, Plebe, and Giuseppe Prezzolini's important *Intervista sulla Destra* (Interview on the Right). Rusconi Editore was similarly promoting an anti-materialist culture by publishing, among others, Guenon, Joseph de Maistre, and Eliade. However, even here, the common ground for all these non-communist, conservative, fascist, and traditionalist intellectuals was the reaction against historical materialism and libertarian values. In sum, Volpe and others represented a remarkable melting pot for the cultural and political non-mainstream right in Italy. They helped to expand the international doctrinal references of domestic neofascists but failed to produce any coherent alternative philosophy – and this was, once more, hardly astonishingly, given the doctrinal orthodoxy and the anti-intellectualism of many neofascist circles. As usual, pivotal importance was on the negative features of certain concepts. For this reason, this process, more than an up-to-date project for society, merely attempted sketchily to oppose communism and the leftist lifestyle, as well as to prevent the convergence between Marxist and Catholic cultures (a number of Catholics, in fact, moved to the left in the 1960s).[16]

13 On Volpe's activity, see Francesco Germinario, "Giovanni Volpe e 'Intervento': Storia di una rivista di cultura della destra (1972–1984)," *Studi Piacentini*, 30, 2001, pp. 77–114.

14 Marc Augier used, as usual, his *nom de plume* "Saint-Loup:" Saint-Loup, *I volontari europei delle Waffen SS* (Rome: Edizioni Giovanni Volpe, 1967).

15 Furio Jesi, *Cultura di destra* (Milan: Garzanti, 1979), p. 68.

16 See also Francesco Germinario, *Da Salò al governo. Immaginario e cultura politica della destra italiana* (Turin: Bollati Boringhieri, 2005), pp. 69–72. In the summer 1968, Pope Paul VI's enunciation of the *Humanae Vitae* represented a clear shift of the Catholic Church toward a more conservative brand of politics. This development offers some interesting parallels with the way the right – both secular and religious – has responded to 1968.

THE NOUVELLE DROITE

In retrospect, the FN represented the most interesting political outcome of French extremist activism of this era, but, as highlighted earlier, it was "left to others like Alain de Benoist who remained outside the [party] during the 1970s, to undertake the doctrinal renewal which the Front and the movement as a whole needed if it was to succeed."[17] De Benoist, still a very prolific writer, was born in 1943 in the French department of Indre-et-Loire and studied at the Sorbonne in Paris. As we have noted, he was backing some neofascist movements and featured articles for a number of their publications. However, he came to the fore mainly due to his collaboration with the widely read weekly *Le Figaro Magazine*, and because, in 1978, the Académie Française awarded him with the Grand Prix de l'Essai (for his book *Vu de droite*).[18] He quickly became the *maître à penser* of the think tank Groupement de Recherche et d'Études pour la Civilisation Européenne (Research and Study Grouping for European Civilization, GRECE), later known as Nouvelle Droite.

GRECE was founded in 1968, but only formally established in January 1969, while the ND achieved prominence at the end of the 1970s when it controlled the editorial line of *Le Figaro Dimanche* and of *Le Figaro Magazine*.[19] The ND benefited from the activism of a group of young "thinking" activists such as Yvan Blot, de Benoist, Jean-Yves Le Gallou, Guillaume Faye, Jean-Claude Valla, and Pierre Vial. They drew inspiration from a variety of sources. While they borrowed old concepts and themes from Barrès, the mythology of early revolutionary fascism and the RSI, together with Guénon, Brasillach, Drieu La Rochelle, Bardèche, Georges Valois, Evola, and the German Konservative Revolution (in

[17] Peter Fysh and Jim Wolfreys, *The Politics of Racism in France* (London: Palgrave, 2003), p. 112. For a matter of coherence, I mainly try to consider here the ND's performance up until the 1980s.

[18] See Alan de Benoist, *Vu de droite. Anthologie critique des idées contemporaines* (Paris: Copernic, 1977)

[19] As Louis Pauwels, the editor of *Le Figaro Magazine*, once affirmed, "mes positions sont celles de ce que l'on pourrait appeler la 'nouvelle droite' et qui n'a rien à voir avec la droite bourgeoise, conservatrice et réactionnaire." Quoted in Thierry Pfister, "La nouvelle droite s'installe," *Le Monde*, June 22, 1979, p. 1. On Pauwels's discourse see Natalie Krikorian, "Européanisme, nationalisme, libéralisme dans les éditoriaux de Louis Pauwels (*Figaro-Magazine*, 1977–1984)," *Mots*, Special Edition on "Droite, nouvelle droite, extrême droite. Discours et idéologie en France et en Italie," 12, 1986, pp. 171–88. This late 1970s exposure provoked a media campaign against the ND and, to a certain extent, stopped its wider spreading and influence.

particular Armir Mohler and Arthur Moeller van den Bruck), the most recent roots of GRECE/ND were to be found in the 1950s JN, and then the FEN and the journal-movement *Europe Action*.[20] The EA leader Venner had also an echo in Italy in these years, where the circles close to the ND highly praised the translations in his books *Baltikum* and *Il sole dei vinti* ("an essential contribution to the history of an era").[21]

The ND was, and presently is, a complex phenomenon. To a certain extent, it never represented a homogeneous doctrinal movement, but rather, it acted as a sort of umbrella organization, especially for some heterodox and "nonconformist" intellectuals. Tamir Bar-On, for example, links the ND to interwar figures such as Georges Sorel and Valois (and, probably unintentionally, suggests a similarity with a typical fascist "pragmatism").[22] Moreover, even if the press had talked, since the summer of 1979, of a "new right," sympathizers preferred to label their initiatives, and consider their movement, as a "new culture." The label "right," as the GRECE national secretary, Guillaume Faye, once said to his Italian fellows, was "insufficient" to portray their movement.[23]

Setting aside the impact of the Algerian War and decolonization, the creation of the ND was sped up by both the failure of the extreme right in the 1967 legislative elections and the political and youth dissatisfaction at the end of the 1960s. May 1968, with its social implications and radical environment, had strong repercussions among these young neofascists.[24] According to de Benoist:

[20] On the importance of Mohler and the Conservative Revolution in general, see Roger Griffin, "Between Metapolitics and *apoliteia*: The Nouvelle Droite's Strategy for Conserving the Fascist Vision in the 'Interregnum,'" *Modern and Contemporary France*, 8(1), 2000, pp. 38–45. Duranton-Crabol traces that forty EA activists were involved in the foundation of the ND. See Duranton-Crabol, *Le Temps de l'OAS*, p. 253.

[21] *Diorama Letteraio*, 17, February 1979, p. 2; and *Diorama Letteraio*, 34, February 1981, pp. 3–4.

[22] Bar-On also suggests how Sorel and Valois "indiscriminately criss-crossed between the extreme-right and the extreme-left in order to defeat the detested parliamentarian system. ... De Benoist and the [ND] want the liberal democratic system to fall and they therefore assemble allies from all political camps in order to help the process along." Tamir Bar-On, *Where Have All Fascists Gone?* (Aldershot: Ashgate, 2007), p. 187. See also Tom McCulloch, "The Nouvelle Droite in the 1980s and 1990s: Ideology and Entryism, the Relationship with the Front National," *French Politics*, 4(2), 2006, p. 160.

[23] Guillaume Faye, "Nuova destra o nuova cultura?" in *Diorama Letterario. Ristampa anastatica integrale dei numeri 14/40 (settembre 1978–agosto 1981)* (Florence: La Roccia di Eric, 1998), p. 2; this essay was originally published in March-April 1980.

[24] See Jean-Claude Valla, "Pour une renaissance culturelle," in GRECE, *Dix ans de combat culturel pour une renaissance* (Paris: GRECE, 1977), pp. 59–60.

> when in May 1968, the New Right emerged ... there was a Left hegemony, quite evident within university circles and, generally speaking, among intellectuals. The [ND's] objective was to reconstruct ideas and concepts, developed through an encyclopedic process, to create a structured discourse in every domain of thought and knowledge.[25]

For him and others the key was to counter the extreme-left prominence in cultural activism. They became remarkably productive, founding a publishing house, the Éditions Copernic (and later the Éditions du Labyrinthe and the Éditions Pardès), and two periodicals, *Éléments* and *Nouvelle Ecole*. All this attracted a huge amount of interest among right-wing Europeans. Figures such as Armir Mohler, Konrad Lorenz, and Mircea Eliade were, for example, on the editorial board of *Nouvelle Ecole*.

GRECE and ND called for a "metapolitical," almost spiritual, engagement, which sought to enable them to gain hegemony and legitimacy.[26] For de Benoist this metapolitical strategy was based on three clear points: (1) definition of the goal (for example, cultural power), (2) definition of the dominant and prevailing ideals, and, finally, (3) definition of which of them the ND was to eventually replace with its own doctrine.[27] Indeed, after the independence of Algeria this group of activists basically renounced party activism. This was to avoid the colonial nostalgia of their neofascist associates, but this choice was mainly taken, to use Jean-Claude Valla's own expression in *Il Secolo d'Italia*, to "clarify beliefs on the base of the fundamental values of the European culture." The ambition was to forge those "intellectual weapons that would allow us to

[25] Alain de Benoist quoted in Frank Adler, "On the French Right – New and Old: An Interview with Alain de Benoist," *Telos*, 126, 2003, p. 113.

[26] It is beyond the scope of this book to discuss the overall ideology, the fascist/nonfascist roots, and the evolutions of the ND. For a discussion on the extremist, and eventually fascist, stance of the ND, see Joan Antón Mellón, "The Idées-Force of the European New Right: A New Paradigm?" in Andrea Mammone et al., *Varieties of Right-Wing Extremism in Europe* (London: Routledge, 2013), pp. 53–68; and Roger Griffin, "Plus ça change! The Fascist Pedigree of the Nouvelle Droite," in E. J. Arnold, ed., *The Development of the Radical Right in France: From Boulanger to Le Pen* (New York: St. Martin's Press, 2000), p. 240. However, there are also a number of works claiming the "nonfascist" connotation of de Benoist's doctrine. The approach here is that the ND, at least for the years discussed in the chapter, can be classified as an extreme-right phenomenon.

[27] Alain de Benoist, "Pour un 'gramscisme de droite,'" *Éléments*, 20, 1977, p. 7.

mount an assault to the political power."[28] There was an intellectual vacuum and delay to be filled, and this was exacerbated, for Valla, by the "distressing" intellectual silence of other French neofascist groups. Any debate, publication, and other cultural event were then useful to achieve this aim. The strategy was, in sum, to switch the debate from the political, party-centric, field – which was, for new rightists, an entity "empty of meaning" – to the metapolitical ground. This latter sphere was the place to design the concepts and visions of the world and the location where people were really in relation to one another.[29]

This led the movement to distance itself, at least officially, from contemporary political philosophies and from the right-left divide, and even to think of itself as representing a synthesis of opposite ideologies ("être en même temps la droite et la gauche," to quote de Benoist) – which, in many ways, and as mentioned, recalled some pre-1945 fascist figures and discourses.[30] As de Benoist put it, "the notions of Right and Left no longer adequately describe the present ideological groups or families of thought."[31] This third-wayism, leaning to a politically neutral and independent European continent, along with a coherent project for a regenerated society, was, for new rightists, the only possible future for France and Europe.[32]

The ND surely represents a specific cultural movement, which was characterized by an openness to the external world – and this was something not always common in the neofascist milieu. Over the years, the ND adopted some New Left themes, including "the valorization of regionalism, federalism and local communities."[33] In line with this, it backed certain ecologist

[28] Jean-Claude Valla interviewed in Maurizio Cabona, "Una 'società di pensiero' della nuova destra francese," *Il Secolo d'Italia*, June 10, 1978, p. 3. De Benoist considered Cabona, an animator of the Italian ND, as a "faithful friend." See De Benoist, *Dèrnière Annèe*, p. 73.

[29] Maurizio Cabona, "Incontro con Alain de Benoist, il 'nuovo filosofo' venuto da altrove," *Il Secolo d'Italia*, May 12, 1978, p. 3.

[30] Alain de Benoist, "Une droite qui soit à la fois *et* la droite *et* la gauche," *Éléments*, 24–25, 1977–78, p. 2.

[31] De Benoist quoted in Adler, "On the French Right," p. 114. It also evident, as Bar-On noted, that this "ideological mixture between what are viewed as polar opposite worldviews, namely, the revolutionary Right and New Left, constitutes the ND's major cultural and political ambiguity. This has created confusion for academics, concerned intellectuals, and political activists." Tamir Bar-On, "The Ambiguities of the *Nouvelle Droite*, 1968–1999," *The European Legacy*, 6(3), 2001, p. 337.

[32] François Dirksen, "Ni Washington, ni Moscou," *Éléments*, 26, 1978, p. 24.

[33] Bar-On, *Where Have All Fascists Gone?* p. 58.

and feminist thinkings that had developed in the 1970s.[34] It also supported some of the third worldist stances of the 1980s.[35]

It is enough here to argue that GRECE's fast-growing ideological productivity attempted to update the traditional neofascist philosophy, and also to play down verbal extremism, and give a sophisticated and theoretically refined façade to some classic themes. For example, it was the anti-egalitarian stance that became more noticeable – and with a greater future legacy – in the ND's discourse. Linked to this, the concept of "differentialism" – which promoted an unclear "right to difference" (in another sense the irreducible difference between people and cultures) – was quickly adopted as their main ideological innovation. All this seemed indissolubly tied with an elitist concept of society and the defense of a proper pan-European identity, but it also appeared to be closely related to some old rightist notions of social hierarchy.

The ND's ideological flexibility also made it possible that the pantheon of its opponents was very divergent: from the United States to the Christian Church, and from orthodox Marxism to liberalism.[36] This last – also following Evola's pedagogy and a well-established French tradition – was stoutly condemned for its related consumer society and the vision of modern life almost entirely based on economic values.[37] It was perceived as a Trojan horse for U.S. imperialism, as well as Western European colonialism. In addition, liberal beliefs were seen as being responsible for immigration to Europe, while colonialism allowed for the assimilation and integration of those who were previously colonized into the French

[34] See de Benoist, *Vu de droite*, pp. 323–37, and pp. 342–65, and *Éléments*, Special Edition on "Les équivoques de l'écologie," 21–22, 1977. Similarly, the ND had a more rational approach than the traditional extreme right toward others social issues and rights. See Jean-Claude Valla, "Le problème de l'avortement," *Nouvelle Ecole*, 10, 1969, pp. 9–18.

[35] See Alain de Benoist, *Europe, Tiers Monde, même combat* (Paris: Laffont, 1986), and also Anne-Marie Duranton-Cabrol, "La 'Nouvelle Droite' entre printemps et automne 1968–1986," *Vingtième Siècle*, 17, 1988, pp. 42–43.

[36] It is worth noting that, in 1974, a group of *nouvelle droitistes* left GRECE and founded the *Club de l'Horloge*, which was similarly anti-egalitarian and promoted the defense of French traditions but was economically in favor of liberalism and for the direct involvement in existing political parties (and acting more as a U.S.-type think tank) and promoted a traditional version of French Catholicism. For a brief account of the difference between the two streams, see Pierre-André Taguieff, "Origines and métamorphoses de la Nouvelle Droite," *Vingtième Siècle*, 40, 1993, pp. 17–20.

[37] Oliver Dard, "La Nouvelle Drote et la société de consommation," *Vingtième Siècle*, 91, 2006, pp. 125–35.

mainland.[38] From Guillaume Faye's standpoint, this free-market philosophy was linked with an economic reductionism: The liberal utopia was thereby more dangerous than egalitarian communism, as it was even more extremist and pragmatic.[39] The ND countered this with the need for a renaissance of the whole European continent. It was a regeneration enthusiastically based on "Indo-Europeanism," with reference to the Roman world, and especially to Celtic mythology.[40] This tells us how the modern extreme right, one willing to update doctrine, was, in any case, looking back at the past. Innovation, for the right-leaning world, could hardly avoid any reference to some tradition and its own history. It shows continuities with the old times (like the use of Evola, which will be mentioned). The same ideal of Europe was referring to a pre-Christian Europe that emphasized the oldest roots of the continent, such as Greek theater, the Roman epopee, Celtic poems, and the Germanic legends. Christian religion was (pragmatically), in fact, strongly criticized for its equality between human beings and within social and state communities, for the promotion of human rights, and, especially in the post-1968 context, for its "acceptance" of socialism.[41] As Pierre Vial suggested, "Christianity has introduced in the West a new 'anthropology' based on egalitarianism and totalitarianism."[42]

GRAMSCI, RIGHT AND LEFT

In one of his recent books de Benoist expressed warm consideration and sympathy toward Italy. He considered it as a place where he felt very comfortable and, probably, more than welcomed ("L'Italie est le pays

[38] Alberto Spektorowski, "The French New Right: Differentialism and the Idea of Ethnophilian Exclusionism," *Polity*, 33(2), 2000, p. 292.

[39] In this perspective, liberalism would, moreover, consider people as "intervenants abstraits sur un marché: clients, conommateurs, unités de main d'oeuvre," Guillaume Faye quoted in "Le G.R.E.C.E. prend la relève," *Éléments*, Special Edition devoted to "L'économie totalitarie," 28–29, 1979, p. 4.

[40] Jean-Claude Valla, "Une communauté de travail et de pensée," in Pierre Vial, ed., *Pour une renaissance culturelle: Le G.R.E.C.E. prend la parole* (Paris: Éditions Copernic, 1979), p. 34. On the importance of the Celtic world opposed to the contemporary western societies, see Pierre Lance, "Les occidentaux maladies de la peste," *Nouvelle Ecole*, 10, 1969, pp. 55–62.

[41] Robert de Herte, "Eglise: la fin du compromis," *Éléments*, 17–18, 1976, p. 2. Robert de Herte is the other pseudonym used by Alain de Benoist ("Fabrice Laroche" is another mentioned in the book).

[42] Pierre Vial, "L'église, l'Europe et le sacré," in Vial, *Pour une renaissance culturelle*, p. 194.

d'Europe où je me sens le mieux").[43] The Italian peninsula is, hence, a relevant nation for a reasonable number of ND activists. Moreover, a writer and journalist like Giorgio Locchi, whom readers have encountered, and who was a correspondent in Paris of the newspaper *Il Tempo*, had some marked impact on the early ideological education of many GRECE leaders. This also makes evident that some of the ND's philosophies and tactics were actually grounded in some Italian-based traditions.

In the cultural field, for example, ND ideologues realized the importance of confronting the strong activism and prominence of the extreme left. By borrowing a strategy developed earlier by Antonio Gramsci, Italy's most famous communist intellectual, on "cultural power" and "cultural hegemony," the ND became conscious that exclusively an authentic hegemony over society, the intellectual world, and political elites could aid their efforts to spread their ideals in public opinion.[44]

In fact, de Benoist believed that all revolutions in history were supported by a strong intellectual framework. This was, for the Frenchman, the "revenge of the ideologues," those who were, at least in his own view, usually perceived as history's losers. Gramsci, naturally, played a central role here. The ND leader suggested that the French right, however, had not properly understood Gramsci. Instead, a long-term strategy based on cultural hegemony was the key for French right-wing extremists. State structures were threatened by cultural power and not by ephemeral takeovers. By following Gramsci, de Benoist thought that this cultural power could bring about the required consensus to achieve and maintain political power.[45]

Gramsci had also showed some interest in the evolution of the French right. In some of his writings, the Italian theorist analyzed the developments and mixed fortunes of the traditional right and Charles Maurras.[46] In particular, he considered that the relative failure of the Action Française was due to its excessive sectarianism, being led by a small group of reactionary intellectuals and, thereby, was distant from everyday concrete life.[47] In this sense, the communist intellectual was used by the ND to criticize the classic extreme right, especially when it was unprepared to

[43] De Benoist, *Dèrnière Annèe*, p. 73.

[44] See, for example, de Benoist, "Pour un 'gramscisme de droite,'" pp. 7–8.

[45] Alain de Benoist, *Les idées à l'endroit* (Paris: Éditions Libres-Hallier, 1979), p. 62.

[46] Vito Catofiglio and Carmela Ferrandes, "Les aventures de la droite française et les avatars de Gramsci," *Mots*, Special Edition on "Droite, nouvelle droite, extrême droite. Discours et idéologie en France et en Italie," 12, 1986, p. 191.

[47] Ibid., p. 193.

undertake legitimate intellectual production (and, consequently, win in the intellectual world rather than the usual street fights) and to tackle bigger or unusual themes (for example, ecology) and contemporary processes (such as globalization) usually dominated by the left.[48]

In such a context, the ND paid high tribute to the Italian communist: It organized debates and promoted a "rightist Gramscianism." The sixteenth national conference of the ND, held in Paris in November 1981, seemed the greatest homage to Gramsci's strategy: Shamelessly, for a movement coming from a neofascist tradition, it was titled "Pour un 'gramscisme de droite'" (For a "Right-Wing Gramscianism").[49]

This was, in retrospect, a very pragmatic and practical use, interpretation, and readaptation of philosophical beliefs. The intention was basically to employ Gramsci's concepts of hegemony and power as a framework and as a veritable "method."[50] This approach was undertaken to replicate the success of the left.

The aims were probably to spread the ND's worldview within society and gain dominance in the cultural realm (and possibly in politics later). This Gramscianism was, in a sense, both the synthesis and the triumph of the "metapolitical engagement" *à la* de Benoist: ideals (elaborated) *à droite* and not only *à gauche*, culture over politics, and power through culture.[51] Especially after 1968, the right wing could not really leave the battle over ideologies to the youth-appealing left. In sum, doctrine also had to matter, and in a prominent way, for contemporary neofascism.

As suggested, there were, however, some ambiguities in the use of this famous communist writer. Dissenting voices on the borrowing from a left-winger like Gramsci were raised in some ND circles. This was, for instance, the case in Italy with a follower of the local ND, Marcello Veneziani, who is, as mentioned, a respected intellectual on Italian soil. In 1981, during one of the national conferences of the Italian ND (a movement that will be discussed shortly), Veneziani was skeptically

48 Ibid. 197; and Francesco Germinario, *La destra degli dei. Alain de Benoist e la cultura politica della Nouvelle droite* (Turin: Bollati Boringhieri, 2002), p. 30.

49 For the proceedings of the conference see GRECE. *Pour un 'gramscisme de droite'. Actes du XVIème colloque national du G.R.E.C.E.* (Paris: Éditions du Labyrinthe, 1982).

50 For de Benoist, "si l'on s'en tient aux aspects purement méthodologiques de la théorie du 'pouvoir culturel,' certains des vues de Gramsci se sont en effet révélées prophétiques." De Benoist, *Les idées*, p. 258. See also Catofiglio and Ferrandes, "Les aventures de la droite," p. 197.

51 To use some ND's words, "la *culture* . . . est le poste de commandement des valeurs et des idées." De Benoist, *Vu de droite*, p. 458.

outspoken on this point and wondered if Gramsci was the only source from which to organize and control culture and social forces. On the other hand, from Veneziani's very right-wing perspective, Gramsci borrowed some of Mussolini's tactics, especially in reference to the building of a consensus. In his estimation, it was an absurdity for the right to try to learn from Gramsci what he had previously digested from Italian fascism. Mussolini, along with other rightist and nationalist-focused themes, such as the importance of magic and myth, fatherland and heroism, had to become the real sources of inspiration for this generation of neofascists.[52]

This fascination with the communist thinker also led to some misunderstandings and omissions. The ND failed to properly acknowledge that the "metapolitical" PCI leader Gramsci was also very political, and that he was a leftist intellectual who had been imprisoned by the Italian fascist regime for his left-wing and anti-fascist beliefs. Gramsci's thinking was historically decontextualized, and the bizarre use of this imagined "methodological-only" version of him was deprived of its Marxist, materialist, and revolutionary connotations. Indeed, the struggle for hegemony was, in a real Gramscian sense, essentially a class struggle.[53]

This right-wing syncretism was, it would appear, justified with the opinion that the ND was beyond left and right, and that the existing political ideologies failed to cope with a post-1968 world that was irremediably changing. However, the French ND was deeply indebted to the old values of an archetypal European extreme right. Despite its pro-communitarian stance, post-nationalism, and pan-Europeanism, the role of culture, its paganism and anti-Catholic agenda, together with the use of some new left arguments, the ND was not an entirely new phenomenon.

[52] "L'organizzazione della cultura e più vastamente la conquista della società civile, sono progetti che possono essere approfonditi originalmente e senza ricorrere a Gramsci. E aggiungendo ciò che Gramsci, neoilluminista, non avrebbe capito: l'incidenza dei fattori non logici, il valore e l'uso del mito, del rito e del simbolo, il significato della Patria oltre il tema gramsciano e giacobino del 'nazionalpopolare,' la forza fascinatrice ed evocatrice della Parola, la vis eroica, la profondità del richiamo alle forze magiche, religiose e spirituali. In questo senso abbiamo più da imparare da un Mussolini che da un Gramsci: e lo stesso Gramsci imparò molto da lui, ed al fascismo si ispirò largamente quando descrisse il suo progetto di aggregazione, la sua fabbrica del consenso: sarebbe assurdo ora che si cercasse di assimilare da Gramsci quel che Gramsci ha assimilato dal fascismo." Marcello Veneziani, "Per una cultura dell'intervento," in Aa.Vv., *Al di là della destra e della sinistra. Atti del convegno 'costanti evoluzioni di un patrimonio culturale'* (Rome: L.ED.E., 1982), p. 45.

[53] See Guido Liguori, "Sinistra, perché non capisci più Antonio Gramsci?" *Liberazione*, May 11, 2007, p. 3.

Even the ND's interest in some leftist themes is something not completely novel in French history. The aforementioned features were not even a French rightist peculiarity. The interest in a type of leftism harkens back to the birth of fascist ideology and to the revolutionary roots of fascism (including in Zeev Sternhell's sense) and its (alleged) synthesis of opposite trends.[54]

A right wing aiming at being "né destra né sinistra" (neither right nor left) similarly existed in Italy. Historically, a part of the non-democratic right-leaning ideology attempted to position itself beyond the "right versus left" dichotomy. Currents within interwar fascism never accepted their rightist location in the political spectrum.[55] The *fascisti di sinistra* were a significant example of this tradition, even after 1945. Giuseppe Bottai and his fascist periodical *Critica Fascista*, for example, often rejected fascism as a capitalist-friendly movement. After the war, the neofascist MSI even experienced a debate on a possible leftist identity for the party, and this was mainly due to the experience of corporatism and the RSI.[56] Over the years, other figures such as Pino Rauti (in Italy), Jean Thiriart (in Belgium), and Christian Bouchet (in France), similarly, at times, questioned the alleged "rigid" left-right dichotomy (the last two also in the name of a "neo-communitarianism").[57]

METAPOLITICS: USING EVOLA

More than a full leftism of some right-wing circles, there was an adaptation (a "rightization") of some leftist themes.[58] In such a context, the ND could make its peculiar use of Gramsci. In Francesco Germinario's reading, the ND expressly engaged in a veritable "Evolianization" of the Marxist philosopher: This was the core of its desire to jettison politics "in the name of self-education."[59] It was, in fact, Evola's concept of *apolitia* that better fitted with the goals of the ND's *métapolitique*,

[54] On this, see also Spektorowski, "The French New Right," p. 285, footnote 4.

[55] Germinario, *Da Salò al governo*, p. 27.

[56] Ibid., pp. 26–27, and Tarchi, "L'impossibile identità."

[57] All of them are mentioned in the book.

[58] It is also worth mentioning that de Benoist generally believes that there is an existing cross-contamination and fertilization between the right and the leftist world. The left, culturally, had made some moves rightward, and the right moved leftward. See Alain de Benoist, *L'Écume et les Galets. 1991–1999: Dix ans d'actualité vue d'ailleurs* (Paris: Éditions du Labyrinthe, 2000), pp. 469–70; also quoted in Germinario, *La destra degli dei*, p. 20, footnote 40.

[59] Germinario, *La destra degli dei*, p. 30.

Apolitia, the Evolian notion of an irreversible detachment from contemporary times and their values, provided a more comforting and attractive myth to counter a society that these new rightists were fundamentally unable to subvert.[60]

All in all, this ND metapolitical enterprise did not follow a rejection of a hidden extreme-right core. Indeed, as Bar-On highlights:

> we should keep in mind that the [ND] intellectuals, whether they engage in metapolitics, *apoliteia* or eventually turn to political realm, seek the hasty arrival of anti-egalitarian, anti-liberal alternative to the hated materialism and decadence of liberal parliamentarism and global capitalism. ... All revolutionary and idealistic opposition to the existing system is essentially positive because it heralds the end of the old system and the arrival of an allegedly splendid age after the ruins.[61]

In other words, these up-to-date nonconformist ND intellectuals would have represented, to paraphrase one of the Italian baron's main scripts, the latest version of the "men among the ruins" of the modern society. As Valla spelt out, one of their main goals – which was Evolian in many ways – was to help Europe "to become aware of its decadence."[62]

We should, nonetheless, note that this use of Evola is well in line with this transnational story of interactions, and he is still the most read Italian neofascist thinker in France. This was also for the previously mentioned philosopher's collaboration with fascist and anti-modernist, and later neofascist, journals (for instance, *Défense de l'Occident*), together with his friendship with intellectuals such as Réne Guénon and Pierre Pascal, and finally for the links between the national-revolutionary extremist as well as the pan-European currents of the 1950s across the Alps (such as ON).[63]

Evola, hence, started to be portrayed as a spiritual guide. Indeed, he fascinated some French neofascist circles principally from the early 1970s onwards (when almost all his books were translated), including youth, and university-based, groups like the GUD, among others. This was undoubtedly for his analyses of the crisis of the modern world, for the need to have a right-wing philosopher to counter the Marxist gurus

[60] This point is well discussed in Bar-On, *Where Have All Fascists Gone?* p. 186. "Cos'è l'opzione debenoistiana per la metapolitica e il gramscismo di destra," Germinario similarly suggests, "se non la sconsolata constatazione che la milizia politica è ormai un'arma spuntata, inservibile per rovesciare la società liberale e l'Occidente?" Germinario, *La destra degli dei*, p. 31.

[61] Bar-On, *Where Have All Fascists Gone?* pp. 186–87.

[62] Cabona, "Una società di pensiero," p. 3.

[63] See also Milza, "Julius Evola," pp. 318–19.

(Almirante famously named Evola "our Marcuse"), but also for his influence on some MSI youth.[64] The publication in France of Evola's books, such as *Chevaucher le tigre* (1964), *Les hommes au milieu des ruines* (1972), and *Révolte contre le monde moderne* (1973), therefore contributed to the further spread of his doctrine. This led to the circulation of references to paganism, spiritualism, *Imperium* and *Regnum*.[65]

Like the Italian theorist Gramsci, Evola was especially read among the followers of the ND. Setting aside some differences in the meaning of concepts such as traditionalism, Alain de Benoist, remarkably, pointed out the importance of the Evolian thinking for the Nouvelle Droite:

> We think that some of Evola's criticisms in particular seem likely to inspire a reflection which pays attention to the evolution of the modern world. … The Evolian critique of the nation state, for example, maintains a strong relevance in an era where this political entity, which is emblematic of modernity, appears every day a little more struck by impotence and obsolescence. … Evola also had the great merit … to denounce any general conception of life or society based solely on economic terms strongly. … But ultimately, and as always with Evola, it is probably in the area of ethics which one can find his most inspiring considerations for our everyday thinking. … In these pages, both men and women can take some lessons.[66]

Some important and cross-national connective links may be observed between Evola's and de Benoist's intellectual and doctrinal productions along with the parallel *apolitia* and the criticism of the modern world, contemporary ideologies, and the Americanization of European societies. Similarities can, in fact, be found in a number of different domains. An example of this is the common Europeanism and the embracing of a post-national stance. Bar-On defined this as the "dream of a pan-European empire": a kind of transnational place where the objective was to preserve

[64] The GUD bulletin also welcomed the translation of *Gli uomini e le rovine* and hoped for the imminent publication of *Rivolta contro il mondo moderno* (and this would happen a year later). They appreciated Evola's findings on politics and the contemporary world: "Cet aspect de sa pensée qui a soulevé l'enthousiasme de milliers de jeunes du M.S.I. est fâcheusement méconnu en France; grâce à la traduction de 'Les hommes au milieu des ruines' cette erreur sera partiellement réparée et il faut espérer qu'un édition française de son titre principal: 'Rivolta contro il mondo moderno' nous permettra de comprendre mieux un mouvement intellectuel qui a pris une telle ampleur en Italie." "Notes de lecture: 'Les hommes au milieu des ruines,'" *GUD-OCCIDENTE-UNIVERSITE*, 1, December 1972, p. 3.

[65] See also Griffin, "Between Metapolitics and *apoliteia*," pp. 43–44.

[66] Alain de Benoist, "Julius Evola, réactionnaire radical et métaphysicien engagé: Analyse critique de la pensée politique de Julius Evola," *Nouvelle Ecole*, Special Edition on "Le Fascisme," 53–54, 2003, p. 169. For another account on Evola, see also De Benoist, *Vu de droite*, pp. 432–36.

a homogeneous European identity.[67] As we know from the previous chapters, this "Nation Europe" had fascinated part of the extreme right since 1945. However, this was also a spiritually defined and hierarchical Europe, and it represented another commonality between these ideologues. The state (and the community) itself had, in sum, to be possibly organized on sovereignty and a caste system (and probably not on theories of mass democracies).[68]

This hierarchical concept was innately elitist, with a consequent anti-egalitarian connotation.[69] All this was, for the ND, tied up with the ambiguous differentialism. The right to the "difference" (and to defend cultural specificities) also had, however, some implications for Evola. During his interwar fascist years, the Italian baron had discussed a sort of differentialism and how racism had to highlight differences against all egalitarian myths. All ethnicities were different, Evola claimed, with dissimilar and immutable features and peculiar cultural values. These differences, comprising the cultural ones, had to be preserved, while democracies generally worked with opposite goals wiping out diversities.[70]

Also strong was the common attack on the West and the Judeo-Christian paradigm, which was also made through the promotion of pagan thinking. It is well known that Evola was one the precursors of this paganism, and that the ND borrowed a considerable amount from this doctrine, even if there were differences in tone and understanding of it. Unsurprisingly, the new rightist *Éditions Pardès* had many contributions on this subject and on traditionalism, as well as some of Evola's manuscripts (such as *Impérialisme païen*).[71] For Evola and de Benoist, paganism went along with a concept of humankind based on a pre-Christian hierarchy, although also with an importance given to "magic," symbols, and the "myth" perceived as moving forces.[72]

[67] See Bar-On, "Fascism to the Nouvelle Droite."

[68] Thomas Sheehan, "Myth and Violence: The Fascism of Julius Evola and Alain de Benoist," *Social Research*, 48(1), 1981, p. 66.

[69] See also Julien Brunn, "La Nouvelle Droite. Le dossier du *"procès"* (Paris: Nouvelles éditions Oswald, 1979), p. 11.

[70] Germinario, *La destra degli dei*, pp. 117–21. According to the "differentialist" Evola: "L'umanità, il genere umano è un'astratta finzione. La natura umana è profondamente differenziata e le razze, i sangui, sono l'espressione più tangibile e immediata di questa differenziazione." Quoted in ibid., p. 119.

[71] See also Tamir Bar-On, "Transnationalism and the French *Nouvelle Droite*," *Patterns of Prejudice*, 45(3), 2011, pp. 205–6.

[72] See also Italo Mancini, *Il pensiero negativo e la nuova destra* (Milan: Mondadori, 1983), p. 78; and Sheehan, "Myth and Violence," p. 68.

HOBBIT CAMPS IN ITALY

Borrowing from Gramsci, and reading Evola, the Nouvelle Droite clearly had a palpable attraction for their sister country.[73] This was also a reciprocated "love." A similar movement directly inspired by the Konservative Revolution, Corneliu Codreanu, Julius Evola, Drieu la Rochelle, Ezra Pound, and, above all, the French ND, called Nuova Destra (New Right, IND), was established in Italy in 1977.[74] It was led by the Florentine youth leader of the MSI, Marco Tarchi, who was the nephew of RSI Minister Angelo Tarchi and is presently a respected professor of political science at the Università di Firenze (with no current links to extreme-right politics).[75] Additional important members were, among others, Stenio Solinas, Maurizio Cabona, Gennaro Malgieri, Giuseppe del Ninno, and Carlo Terracciano.

In contrast to the French prototype, at an early stage it officially developed in the framework of a party, the MSI, and in the stream led by Rauti. Given their backgrounds, and a certain intellectual vivacity, some of these youth activists were probably perceived as nonconformists and heretics when compared with classic MSI standards. They generally felt the necessity to explore different doctrinal constellations (from Brasillach to Primo de Rivera) and to revise the nostalgic "Back to the Future" policy. One of the ways to elaborate a more innovative rightist dimension was to be found in December 1974 with the publication of the first issue of the *La Voce della Fogna*.[76] This was a satirical-political periodical, featuring comic strips, irreverent (and derisive) articles on politics and society, music, and various vignettes. The goal was to contribute to the modernization of their political environment.

Interestingly, the transnational side of this story tells us that *La Voce della Fogna* was, in reality, born in Paris in summer 1974, when Tarchi,

[73] I should recall here de Benoist's words quoted at the beginning of this book: "On a beau dire, on a beau faire, parmi les Européens qui nous nous sont le plus proches, ceux avec lequels, nous autres Français, nous nous entendons le plus spontanément, ce sont les Italiens." De Benoist, *Dèrnière Annèe*, p. 73.

[74] See also Gennaro Malgieri, "Prefazione," and Marco Tarchi, "Ipotesi e strategia di una nuova destra," both in Aa.Vv., *Proviamola nuova. Atti del seminario "Ipotesi e strategia di una nuova destra"* (Rome: L.ED.E., 1980), respectively pp. 15 and 114.

[75] Nonetheless, Tarchi is still editing some journals that seem to be close to the French ND, and de Benoist appears in them.

[76] *La Voce della Fogna* (The Voice of the Sewer) possibly came also as a reaction to a famous slogan, "fascisti carogne tornate nelle fogne" ("fascist bastards go back into the sewers"), used by left-wingers to denigrate neofascists.

and a few companions, met de Benoist and other members of GRECE. In fact, these Italians had already become fascinated with reading *Nouvelle Ecole* – which they discovered through the pages of Pino Romualdi's journal *L'Italiano* – and that summer in Paris was really about to change their ideological perspectives. This meeting was promoted and organized by Jack Marchal, a French neofascist they had met the year before near Rome at one of the workshops of the MSI youth organizations.[77] Marchal was a leading member of Occident, GUD, and later FN (and Parti des Forces Nouvelles), but he was also an illustrator, cartoonist, and musician (in the extreme-right French identitary rock scene). He collaborated with the *Voce della Fogna*, for which he replicated some of its famous designs in comic strips and drawings previously produced for some of the GUD bulletins and for the French neofascist journal *Alternative*.[78] This latter, a similar satiric paper close to the GUD, was also a strong source of inspiration for Tarchi and his associates, as it was rooted in the metapolitics approach and the ideals promoted by de Benoist. Following on from this, the young neofascists started a really close and frequent mail correspondence with their French homologues, and they joined the GRECE annual conferences in Paris and its various summer *universités d'éte* in southern France.[79]

Some sectors of Italian neofascism looked with suspicion at this youth publishing project. In general, a contraposition with the "old" MSI was certainly due to a generational factor and age divide. All IND members were born in the 1950s and, like the ND, were, in some ways, influenced by 1968. The leftist year had, in fact, exerted a considerable impact on youth mentalities, mores, and habits.[80] A further breaking point with the nostalgic environment of the MSI was represented by Italy's "Movement of 1977." This was another moment of challenge to the existing system, which had witnessed some university occupations. It also proposed, again, divisions between the party and its youth milieu. The FUAN had, indeed, considered as legitimate this student protest, and numerous young neofascists started developing some 1968-like hypotheses of an alliance with extreme-left students, especially on the critique of the "regime," and on some concrete themes such as employment and quality of education. The MSI, on the other

77 Tarchi, "Postfazione. I Campi Hobbit, La Nuova destra e la "destra nuova." Una controversia politico-genealogica," in Tarchi, *La Rivoluzione Impossibile*, p. 445.

78 Marchal also designed the cover of the IND-edited volume *Proviamola nuova*.

79 Tarchi, "Postfazione," p. 445.

80 Marco Tarchi, "Alla ricerca della comunità. I Campi Hobbit fra tentazione della modernità e sindrome del ghetto," in Tarchi, *La Rivoluzione Impossibile*, p. 11.

hand, was, instead, more interested in strengthening its position in the political system. The result was a total closure, as in 1968, toward the demands and cultural ferments of the extreme-right youths.[81]

In such a context, we can observe how some sectors of the party youth wing (as previously mentioned, usually close to Rauti) prepared their response to this generational and political clash. This was the organization of a camp, almost like the ones organized by the communist groups, where they would gather all forces: They called this a Hobbit Camp. The first camp was organized in June 1977, and *La Voce della Fogna* invited its readers to attend it with its own typical youthful language well in line with the nonconformist approach:

> What do you think about ... a true, alternative, two-day musical event, with tents and sleeping bags (we cannot guarantee you some orgies: yet, our female readers might know us in person ... memorable experience?) [?] Well, the miracle is taking place. Mobilize relatives and male/female friends. Everyone at the Hobbit Camp 1 (and read Tolkien unwise people!).[82]

J. R. R. Tolkien's fantasy saga *The Hobbit*, in fact, served as a metaphor for these young neofascists rooted in an explicit tradition and, at the same time, willing to challenge a detested consumerist society. Colorfully, they perceived themselves like the creatures living in Tolkien's imagined land of Middle-earth and fighting against part of the contemporary world.[83] Their first and the third youth meetings especially (the latter was the last one in 1980) turned out to be quite representative of an extreme-right world that wanted to propose something different to the public. This was not the stereotypical picture of the neofascist militant with cudgel (and eventually "cudgel and double breast[ed coat]" as portrayed by Almirante).[84]

[81] Loredana Guerrieri, "*'All'Hobbit, all'Hobbit ... siam fascisti!'. La giovane destra italiana nei Campi Hobbit,*" *Giornale di Storia costituzionale*, 10(2), 2005, pp. 165–66.

[82] Quoted in Lanna and Rossi, *Fascisti immaginari*, p. 221.

[83] This is how one of the organizers of the first Hobbit Camp described the choice of Tolkien: "ricorrendo ai personaggi creati dalla fantasia di Tolkien e alle sue favole che assai bene adombrano la realtà, abbiamo voluto dimostrare e confermare che sì, non siamo nati certamente oggi, che abbiamo radici profonde, ma abbiamo anche voluto dire che questo monde così com'è non ci piace né lo accettiamo. Ed allora guardando al futuro evochiamo dalle favole di Tolkien quelle immagini che arricchiscono la nostra fantasia e appagano la nostra sete di contenuti. Sì, siamo anche noi abitatori della mitica Terra di Mezzo; anche noi siamo in lotta con draghi, orchi, ed altri personaggi." Generoso Simeone, "Perché Campo Hobbit," in Tarchi, *La Rivoluzione Impossibile*, p. 107.

[84] The second camp (1978) was a failure for innovation, proposals, and overall quality. The MSI tried to impose its line, and the more loyal youth, including the young leader Gianfranco Fini, were in charge of co-organizing it with the rebellious nonconformists.

The Hobbit Camps were, in another sense, a kind of opening to the leftist youth. They offered an outstretched hand to start a dialogue with former enemies. They also represented an attempt to get possession of other themes, for example, music, theater, poetry, cabaret, new media, graphic arts, cultural reviews, and ecology, that were usually associated with the post-1968 left. In other words, this generation of neofascists cried aloud that they did not want to live in cultural, and, at times, social, marginalization – not even in the backward-looking, and reassuring, one of their fathers. They wanted to look similar to their coetaneous left-wingers.

These gatherings led to the birth of the IND, which almost immediately produced journals such as *Diorama Letterario* and *Elementi*. Links with France were, again, intrinsic. There was an exchange of collaborations between journals across borders. For example, in 1979, *Elementi* set up an editorial agreement with its French homologue. From that point onwards, there were many cross-exchanges: Gennaro Malgieri wrote for *Eléments*, Stenio Solinas for *Nouvelle Ecole*, while Guillaume Faye, Michel Marmin, and Alain de Benoist featured articles in *Elementi*.[85] De Benoist, the founder of the, according to Cabona, "superb" cultural review *Nouvelle Ecole*, and his movement were thereby the unavoidable examples to follow.[86] At Easter 1980, furthermore, de Benoist went to Italy to promote the Italian translation of his main work of the time (*Visto da destra*). He had book launch events in Milan, Florence, Ancona, and Naples, with Tarchi and del Ninno, who also authored the two prefaces of the translated manuscript.[87] By following Tarchi, GRECE had, therefore, positively contributed to the development of some themes within the IND circles – and this helped Italian activists in their search for public legitimacy. It offered some tools to understand the contemporary world (including a book challenging the United

The party newspaper offered this time two full pages to promoting the "Campo Hobbit 2." See, for example, Gianfranco Fini, "Per un'alternativa senza nostalgismi," *Il Secolo d'Italia*, June 16, 1978, p. 6, where Fini tries (instrumentally, in my view) to use some of Tarchi's lexicon.

85 Anne-Marie Duranton-Crabol, *Visages de la Nouvelle Droite: Le G.R.E.C.E. et son histoire* (Paris: Presses de la Fondation Nationale des Sciences Politiques, 1998), p. 150.

86 See Cabona, "Incontro con Alain de Benoist," p. 3. What also impressed symphatizers in Italy was really the ND's attempt "to establish among its adherents a community." See Giovanni Perez, "G.R.E.C.E. e Nouvelle Droite'" in Aa.Vv., *Proviamola nuova*, p. 75.

87 Diorama Letterario, "La Nuova Destra e i suoi compiti," *Diorama Letterario*, 37, May 1980, p. 2.

States coauthored by de Benoist and Locchi in 1979) and enhanced the same IND overall policies beyond any narrow-minded Italian prism.[88]

The French think tank had, in sum, an influence that was, in the words of Tarchi, "comparable only to that of Evola – on distinct but adjoining fields."[89] Evola was, in fact, the old sage for this extreme right in Italy. The analysis of the contemporary era started from the Evolian concept of the "revolt against the modern world," but moved beyond Evola – there was not merely rejection, but also a partial interchange with the modern world.[90] In line with the *apolitia* doctrine of the philosopher, and just as its French counterpart, the IND also developed a metapolitics and right-wing Gramscianism.[91] As Tarchi suggested, "during the ten years since 1968 we have understood that cultural power is the primary engine, an indispensable tool."[92] This was naturally made for some pragmatic reasons. The political right was making a mistake in abandoning some themes because these were considered like being leftist. Neofascism could not just attract young people by suggesting they read books authored by rightist thinkers.[93] However, as in France, this also generated some outcomes. It led to the "methodologically-only" use of Gramsci (although without forgetting the other more genuinely right-leaning metapolitical projects of Evola and Adriano Romualdi).[94] All this went along with a criticism of the classic right. This latter was perceived to be an old enterprise that never tried to influence any of the prerequisites needed to achieve

88 See Alain de Benoist and Giorgio Locchi, *Il male Americano* (Rome: Libreria Editrice Europa, 1978). Tarchi enthusiastically reviewed this volume ("una guida sicura per non smarrirsi nelle pieghe di un mondo americanizzato"). See *Diorama Letterario*, 21, July-August 1979, pp. 2–3.

89 Tarchi, "Ipotesi e strategia," pp. 113–14.

90 Ibid., p. 111. On this point, see also Monica Zucchinali, *A destra in Italia oggi* (Milan: SugarCo, 1986), pp. 113–21.

91 On the theoretical and cultural influence of the French ND on the development of metapolitics, see also Marco Revelli, "La nuova destra," in F. Ferraresi, ed., *La destra radicale* (Milan: Feltrinelli, 1984), p. 170. However, Bar-On warns how later a "generational difference also led to a divergence between the *Nuova Destra* and French *nouvelle droite*, heirs of an older post-war, post-colonial generation of political memories and distinct national experience." Bar-On, *Where Have All Fascists Gone?* p. 145.

92 Tarchi quoted in Franco Sacchi, "The Italian New Right," *Telos*, Special Double Issue on "The French New Right: New Right-New Left-New Paradigm?" 98–99, 1993–94, p. 74.

93 See Simeone, "Perché Campo Hobbit," p. 106.

94 As we have noted with the ND, this shows the complexity of this political-cultural rightist movement (willing to use all possible means to gain cultural power, from cinema to scientific associations). See also Diorama, "Una scelta di campo," in *Diorama Letterario. Ristampa anastatica*, p. 2.

political power, including the systems of beliefs.[95] Historically, it was, for new rightists, a political right that was fundamentally syncretic and contradictory in its ideological and pragmatical stances.[96]

Ideologically, these Italian new rightists similarly rejected what they saw as the myths promoted by egalitarianism, neo-colonialism, liberalism, capitalism (the "market dictatorship"), developments based on the industrialist model, and, more generally, the predominant western modes of thinking. To the American-type lifestyle, they opposed, along with a post-national stance, a communitarian doctrine (as an Italian activist put it, "what I have really liked about GRECE is their communitarian spirit").[97] Specifically, a ND-like politically neutral Europe from the Atlantic to the Urals ("the empire") would have promoted "organic communities," avoided western globalized homogenization, and preserved some ethno-cultural features. Indeed, to avoid a would-be irreversible social disintegration, each society (the organic community) was to be based on a certain openness to new members, but also on shared values and distinct cultural differences and identities, and, finally, on the rediscovery of the "sacred as opposed to the materialism of consumerist societies."[98]

The transnational influence of the ND on this youth movement was more than evident, even if this, along with many other doctrinal elaborations (and also with an alternative communication style), generated great conflicts with the MSI and its ideals. The IND ideological demands were therefore rejected by the party, and many of its ideologues and leaders left, while others were essentially purged from the party.

CULTURE: A BRIDGE TOWARD THE NEW WORLD

The 1970s were, in sum, full of ferment for the extreme right in France and Italy. If the MSI experienced a relevant electoral result in 1972 and gathered other right-leaning and nationalist forces under its project, the French milieu welcomed this Italian enterprise and similarly built a party, the FN, that was going to have a strong impact on western right-wing extremism. At the same time, the cultural field experienced a similar activism after the student revolts. This was especially true for the youth

[95] Tarchi, "Ipotesi e strategia," pp. 119–20.

[96] Marco Tarchi, "Una cultura e uno stile," *Diorama Letterario*, 27, June 1980, p. 2.

[97] Aa.Vv., "Dibattito," in Aa.Vv., *Proviamola nuova*, p. 79.

[98] Marco Tarchi, "Le tre vie del radicalismo di destra," *Trasgressioni*, 4(1), 1989, p. 15. See also Sacchi, "The Italian New Right," pp. 78–79.

wings but also for some senior neofascists. It is, in fact, accepted that the ND brought to neofascism an interest on doctrines, cultural power, and hegemony. However, this was also developed through the editorial and publishing enterprise of Volpe, Plebe's anti-communist cultural initiatives, and with the launch of some of the mentioned journals and the neofascist rebranding of others such as *Il Conciliatore*, *Candido*, and *Pagine Libere*. In this sense, thinkers such as Bardèche and Evola, and groups such as EA, additionally represented early forms of an alleged right-wing Gramscianism. The ND, then, found a more fertile ground than one would imagine. In other words, as these pages have described, culture mattered for all sides of neofascism – albeit for some it mattered more for practical and electoral reasons than for ideological ones. All this showed that, in perspective, the extreme right could have produced some impact on society and politics.

ND's success might be, on the other hand, ascribed to a French environment. The reason was also the lack of a widespread diversity in Italy's neofascist milieu (as we have seen, this did not, nonetheless, stop collaboration across nations). This point is important, as the following few pages will also highlight the diverse fortunes of political extremism and the slow sunset of the MSI. The French scene was able to generate a movement like the FN, which was due to influence rightist politics for decades (including abroad), and possibly because it had less "orthodoxies" to respect.[99] In Italy, despite the presence of different streams, promoting some, even strong, external influences, the milestones for neofascism were often the fascist regime and the RSI (and, more generally, European fascism).

Although a complete acceptance of genuine innovative beliefs did not happen in France either, de Benoist was able to spread some more alternative themes, while the MSI basically rejected many of them – nor could the extreme right in the Italy of the late 1970s claim a somewhat public intellectual like the Frenchman. In this sense, the fragmentation of French forces and, historically, the presence of some different schools of thought, made possible the injection of ideals (including foreign ones) coming from various doctrinal elaborations. All this, as mentioned, was, nevertheless, to influence neofascist Italy. Indeed, what matters more here is, foremost, the transnationality and the ideological transfer. Moreover, the ND was important for its drive toward a genuine legitimization of the extreme right and some of its themes. It restored, for example, the credibility of that

[99] Germinario, *La destra degli dei*, p. 22.

revolutionary anti-liberal and anti-egalitarian discourse developed by the right in the 1920s and 1930s.[100] It was later reproposed by some other neofascists in the postwar years, even if they were largely unsuccessful.[101]

Most prominently, it also legitimated some discourses on the place and role of ethnicities, which later had a resonance on European multiethnic societies.[102] This was probably facilitated by the failure of liberal political elites to face multiculturalism and decolonization, the approach of some politicians on immigration, but also by the ND's initial impact on some media and the influence on senior figures of the mainstream French political right and on the FN. In truth, de Benoist attempted to distance himself from the FN and other neofascist parties around Europe. In summer 1990, *Le Choc du Mois* reported that he affirmed to perceive himself as a "stranger" in reference to Le Pen's party, with whom he did not share any policies. However, in the early 1980s, Pierre Vial and other prominent ND thinkers joined the FN, and the movement employed some of the ND's themes for its ideological and electoral platform. As has been noted, with the politicization of the immigration, it was exactly differentialism that was central to the rapprochement between Jean Marie Le Pen and the new rightist doctrine.[103]

Over the years this differentialism was refined, and another influence of the ND was the development of the concepts of ethno-pluralism and ethno-regionalism (with references to the glorification of cultural identities). "Culture" became, in other words, central. Ethno-pluralism and cultural racism then constituted some of the key elements that contributed to the rise of Western European right-wing extremists (and also characterized them). In such a context, cosmopolitans and anti-racists were seen as the true racists, as "they forced immigration to submit the rites of assimilation."[104] Such a discourse was obviously due to be used by contemporary parties across Europe to mask xenophobic ideals and promote debates on

[100] On this, and on the alleged democratization of the ND, see Tamir Bar-On, "Understanding Political Conversion and Mimetic Rivalry," *Totalitarian Movements and Political Religions*, 10(3–4), 2009, pp. 251–54.

[101] Today, this variegated revolutionary right-wing milieu is also made up by Third Positionists, National Bolsheviks and National Anarchists. Bar-On, "Transnationalism," p. 209.

[102] On this see also Richard Wolin, "Designer Fascism," in R. J. Golsan, ed., *Fascism's Return: Scandal, Revision, and Ideology since 1980* (Lincoln: University of Nebraska Press, 1998), p. 51; and Hans-Georg Betz, "Contemporary Right-Wing Radicalism in Europe," *Contemporary European History*, 8(2), 1999, p. 309.

[103] See also McCulloch, "The Nouvelle Droite," p. 165.

[104] Wolin, "Designer Fascism," p. 54.

the "danger of immigration," as well as to justify their own presence in mainstream politics and the mass media. On the other hand, the belief in a regionalist Europe, and an overall regional (rather than national) discourse, became popular among some extremist groups. The proposed "region" turned out to be a micro-ethnic and cultural community. In such a context, the ND, with its call for a post–nation-state Europe made up of cultural differences, has certainly offered a theoretically elaborated literature and philosophy for some extreme right-wing "regionalist" parties. An example of this is represented by the present influence on the LN in Italy. De Benoist has been also occasionally invited to some of its events, and he has been interviewed by the party newspaper and its youth wing's website. For these reasons, the French ND can be seen as a transmission belt between old fascism and the contemporary era.[105] (Indeed, for its nature and genesis, the LN has often been perceived as a different type of right-wing movement, often merely regionalist, though some of its themes are strongly influenced by a variegated right-leaning doctrinal environment with in many ways "traditional" extreme-right roots (and even more today, considering the recent history of the party).)

In sum, the ND, alongside the FN, the MSI-DN, editors such as Volpe, and a number of periodicals, showed how the extreme right elaborated a set of tactics after 1968 and how it entered the final decades of the twentieth century. Some groups started abandoning the defensive positions used to protect themselves in the anti-fascist postwar Europe and elaborated policies that would bear fruit during the decline of the traditional left, the post-communist context, the impact of European integration, and the society of immigration. However, much more needs to be said on these fruitful years, and the coming pages will discuss the interactions and interconnected stories of political neofascism in the 1970s and 1980s, from the influence of the MSI on extremism in France, and its building of a Euroright with French and Spanish forces, to the appeal of the overall Le Pen enterprise (including the ongoing political leadership of his daughter) with the anti-immigrant and anti-Islam propaganda that has characterized extreme-right forces up until today.

[105] For Alberto Spektorowski "an examination of the Lega Nord's political evolution provides us with an example of how the New Right's sophisticated neo-fascism is silently permeating and shaping the political ideology of what could at first be defined as a non-fascist regionalist movement." Alberto Spektorowski, "Ethnoregionalism: The Intellectual New Right and the Lega Nord," *Global Review of Ethnopolitics*, 2(3), 2003, p. 55.

6

From the Euroright to a Euro-leader

Despite the 1972 election, which represented a major achievement for the MSI, the environment surrounding 1968 had left a strong mark on Italian neofascism. Although the party had managed to create, at least politically, a larger container with which to contest elections, it was, on the other hand, losing its full hegemony in this political galaxy. Similarly, in France, after the initial enthusiasm stemming from the apparent unification of extremist fringes with the establishment of the FN, there followed another phase of splits, rapprochements, and then further divisions. In such a context, it was natural that until the mid-1980s at least, Italy and the MSI were, politically, still very attractive for their likeminded French associates. Culturally, as the previous pages have illuminated, right-wing Italy had been trying to make some progress in the intellectual environment, although, in reality, France was more innovative and productive in this field. It is evident that parties like the FN have interiorized, reelaborated, reinterpreted, and "exploited" the innovations brought about by some more intellectual streams. All this will make – as we shall see – France's becoming a landmark for many contemporary and recent western extreme-right movements in this new Europe.

The period from the late 1970s and early 1980s was certainly an interesting one, and from these years onwards European societies started to change, including culturally and ethnically. There were some shifting attitudes toward politics: from strong partisan loyalties – often based on class – to more volatile voting patterns, usually based on opinions about specific issues (and this seems to shift further today with a growing disillusionment with traditional politics). Socioeconomically, the changes were also apparent with the processes of post-industrialization and, in some historical phases, of increased unemployment. All this, along with the decline in the 1980s of some traditional political actors in France, the common program of the left, and the socialist François Mitterrand's victory in the 1981 presidential elections, unintentionally served, for example, to improve the prospects of the French extreme right. In other words, "the world of the 1980s and 1990s was a very different place than that experienced by the [extreme-right] fallen martyrs and surviving elders of the 1940s through the 1970s."[1]

Starting with a preliminary account of the historical development of neofascist parties from the very late 1960s to the early 1970s, the main objective in this section is, as usual, to focus on what, from a transnational perspective, unifies neofascism. There is already a very extensive literature on the recent history of the FN, but very little of this explores the cross-national transfer and the borrowing of foreign themes and "myths" – including for the whole French extreme-right environment (which, as I will mention in these pages, is currently strongly attracted by some contemporary neofascist movements and activities in Italy).

This perspective will be illustrated by noting the initial prominence of Italian neofascism and by exploring the MSI's interests in understanding political developments in extreme-right Paris and choosing their best potential ally in France, according to the different political conditions and strength. In such a context, the years surrounding the "Euroright project," which was an attempt to contest the first election for the European parliament and created some further networks with French, but also Spanish, forces, will be mentioned in these pages. Aside from the known international aspiration of the neofascist phenomenon, the Euroright proves how the extreme right attempted to adapt to the changing times of European politics. An alliance of European right-leaning forces in the parliament would have been, in fact, central in promoting their own vision of Europe. Moreover, it also represented a pragmatic reaction to the (previous) establishment of Eurocommunism – with leftists from the same countries, and where Italian communists from the PCI had a strong political and cultural leadership (like with the MSI on the rightist front).[2]

[1] Kaplan and Weinberg, *The Emergence of a Euro-American Radical Right*, p. 125.

[2] See among others, Michelangela Di Giacomo, "Identità eurocomunista: la traiettoria del Pce negli anni Settanta," *Studi storici*, 51(2), 2010, p. 461. The Euroright also represented another policy for the MSI to react to the difficulties in national politics and to the lost hegemony on the whole neofascist and youth environment after 1968. Intriguingly, this was similarly one of the reasons behind the Eurocommunist strategy and, this latter was also an attempt to refine political identities and adapt to the different social context, and

Moving from this international context, the following pages will not overlook the momentous (electoral) rise of the FN, its initial "subjection" to Almirante, and, later, some neofascist attempts to "borrow" Le Pen, and his party propaganda, for use in Italy. The French leader is being, in fact, labeled in Italy as the "new king" of European right-wing extremism and within the Franco-Italian network – and he was so up to January 2011 when his daughter, Marine, was acclaimed FN president. Her initial links with the extreme right, as well as mainstream right, in Italy are intriguingly highlighted – as they also confirm this continuous transnational web of exchanges. The FN's and Le Pen's leadership became even more evident, as will be described, with the process of fragmentation and reshaping of Italian neofascism since the 1990s. These pages of the book will also point out how, since the last decades of the past century, another link between the movements became a similar xenophobic ideology (and this will help us to trace a fascistic "continuity" to the present day). The anti-immigrant and then anti-Islam campaigns also show how neofascism has been able to exploit the sociopolitical circumstances. Unsurprisingly, some Eurobarometer surveys, for example, mention a substantial rise in anti-foreigner stances from 1988 to 2000 – specifically ethnic minorities and out-group populations – and these usually increase where and when extreme-right ideologies are stronger and mobilizing such exclusionary sensibilities.[3]

Since the 1980s, the "ethnic faces" of European societies were, in fact, dramatically changing due to some significant, and more noticeable, migratory fluxes. This led the extreme right to (re-)use a narrow concept of "community," which resembles some classic fascist themes of racial (and ideological, at least in my reading) purity, and that has been – although often implicitly – highlighted in some other parts of *Transnational Neofascism*. All this is also important for contemporary political observers: The rise of the extreme right in many European nations has been having an impact on ethnic relations, mainstream policies regarding immigration, and discussions on concepts such as citizenship and identity (including a wide European identity). This further shows how, for the recent era, we are really discussing a phenomenon that is at the center of Europe's life – and that is unlikely to disappear in the next few years.

react to its inability to control student protests and the social movements of the late 1960s and 1970s.

[3] Moshe Semyonov et al. "The Rise of Anti-foreigner Sentiment in European Societies, 1988–2000," *American Sociological Review*, 71(30), 2006, pp. 426–49.

Some of the extreme-right contemporary slogans seem, nonetheless, to be borrowed from more ancient times. As mentioned, the prominence of one's own group, the importance of white civilization, and the values of the fatherlands are not entirely new themes, and they are part of the long journeys of the extreme right since the interwar years. As Judt suggested,

> Visiting Vienna in October 1999 I found the Westbahnhof covered in posters for the Freedom party of Jörg Haider who, despite his open admiration of the "honourable men" of the Nazi armies, who "did their duty" on the eastern front, won 27 percent of the vote that year by mobilizing his fellow Austrians' anxiety and incomprehension at the changes that had taken place in their world over the past decade. After nearly half a century of quiescence Vienna – like the rest of Europe – had re-entered history.[4]

In some ways, some of the European "integralist sensibilities" mentioned in the Introduction survived and resurfaced again after the fall of the Berlin Wall had crushed communism, while (de)colonization and globalization contributed to change the demography of western communities as well as reframe the balance between national and global powers (with a deterioration of nation-states). These extreme-right sensibilities meant that, for some activists and political currents at least, history, and the past, mattered again.

THE NEOFASCIST ENVIRONMENT

Many outcomes of the late 1960s and 1970s were partially unexpected for neofascists. Apart from the policy of fronts and the reaction in the cultural and intellectual field (which were to have a marked impact in the following decades), these were also complex years for the extreme right. Indeed, the 1970s in France have been described by Jean-Marie Le Pen as the "crossing of the desert," years during which the FN "barely survived as a political entity."[5] During the same period, Italy was a nation that faced much more shocking problems with the realistic possibility of a radical neofascist coup.

[4] Judt, *Postwar*, p. 3.

[5] In retrospect, Le Pen's merit has been, above all, that of providing strong resistance to pitiable electoral scores. Paul Hainsworth, "The *Front National*: From Ascendancy to Fragmentation on the French Extreme Right," in P. Hainsworth, ed., *The Politics of the Extreme Right: From the Margins to the Mainstream* (London: Pinter, 2000), p. 19.

Some neofascists were, in fact, involved in so-called black terrorism.[6] An example of this political action was the December 1969 bomb attack in Piazza Fontana on a branch of the National Agricultural Bank in Milan. Pino Rauti, Guido Giannettini, and Franco Freda were, among others, suspected of being connected to it. In the eyes of public opinion and the media, all actions were carried out by extreme-right groups.[7] In spite of efforts to present a more respectable visage, the MSI, which was equipped with the notorious although controversial "bludgeon and double-breasted suit" strategy, was incontestably discredited. Moreover, for its rejection of the ferments of 1968, together with its backward-looking stance and the attempted policy of insertion in the mainstream political system, the MSI lost some appeal among the domestic extreme right.

Thinkers such as Freda, and groups such as the "Nazi-Maoist" Organizzazione Lotta di Popolo (People's Fight Organization, simply known as "Lotta di Popolo") and Terza Posizione, came to the fore and fascinated likeminded foreign movements (and, at the same time, overseas tendencies influenced them).[8] Freda was one of the most famous and controversial Italian extreme-right intellectuals, beguiled with rebellion and armed struggle. In 1969, he wrote a book on the "disintegration of the system" that had an impact on this "subordinate" period, and this strongly influenced the two earlier mentioned groups.[9] Arrested in 1972 (along with Rauti), for subversive attacks, he was immediately backed by *Défense de l'Occident*: "As it was with the case of Pino Rauti, the judge tries to amalgamate a strictly ideological cause with some of the alleged activities. And all this rests precariously on the testimony of a Marxist militant."[10]

[6] The reference is to the Strategia della Tensione (Strategy of Tension). Ferraresi, "The Radical Right," p. 90.

[7] Weinberg and Eubank, "Neo-Fascist," p. 536. On the neofascist narratives of events, see Anna Cento Bull, *Italian Neofascism: The Strategy of Tension and the Politics of Nonreconciliation* (New York: Berghahn Books, 2007); and Anna Cento Bull, "Casting a Long Shadow: The Legacy of *stragismo* for the Italian Extreme Right," *The Italianist*, 25(2), 2005.

[8] Italian Nazi-Maoism was a neofascist current of the late 1960s trying to combine the extreme right (including Evola) with some leftist stances (Maoist China). Lotta di Popolo was built by young activists such Ugo Gaudenzi, and by others previously in the Fuan-Caravella, Primula Goliardica, and the Italian section of Thiriart's Jeune Europe. Jean Thiriart also influenced some of the thinking of Freda, also for the (alleged) convergences of the left and right to subvert the system.

[9] See also Anna Cento Bull, "Neofascism," in R. Bosworth, ed., *The Oxford Handbook of Fascism* (Oxford: Oxford University Press, 2009), p. 600.

[10] "Documents: L'Affaire Freda," *Défense de l'Occident*, 106, 1972, pp. 77–79.

The FANE's publication *Notre Europe* similarly featured, over the years, a number of articles on Freda and Terza Posizione, the attacks on Italian neofascists, the imprisonment of black terrorists, and the various trials against them. All in all, the FANE maintained strong links with the whole Italian neofascist constellation (which were, once more, their most notable international contacts). This was particularly true for its local branches – and especially in southern France they had ties with the MSI, ON, and some of the most subversive anti-democratic activists.[11]

This confirms the continuous transnational story of transfer and similarity across some European lands. Moreover, in 1971 a carbon copy movement of Lotta di Popolo (which was instituted in 1968), named Organisation Lutte du Peuple (People's Fight Organization), was formed in Nantes by a group of young students and workers, initially linked with Ordre Nouveau and with the French section of the Belgian Jeune Europe. Lutte du Peuple was occasionally similarly labeled as Nazi-Maoist and was in contact with Lotta di Popolo.[12] The *trait d'union* between the two movements was Claudio Mutti, the most active member of Giovane Europa (the main Italian branch of Jeune Europe). Mutti was directly involved in *La Nation Européenne* (Jeune Europe's journal) and later joined Lotta di Popolo. As a prolific essayist, Mutti also had connections with the French quarterly *Totalité*. This latter publication was led by the founders of Cercles Culture et Liberté (close to both Thiriart's and Evola's doctrines) and had links in Italy with the rightist publishing house Edizioni all'insegna del Veltro.[13]

Given the number of these existing little groups, electorally the situation was not really impressive for the French extreme right. Despite this, the FN prepared for the March 1973 legislative election campaign, which, in Le Pen's ambitions, was supposed to offer the opportunity to merge the

[11] According to Ian Barnes, the FANE was "associated with the 1980 Bologna bombing. Credit for this incident was claimed by the ... NAR, an extreme right-wing movement comprising militants from *Ordine Nuovo* ... and *Avanguardia Nazionale*, all associated with past bombings in Italy. Certain NAR militants resident in southern France maintained links with FANE's Nice office. One, Marco Affatigato, was arrested ..., and another Durand, has admitted corresponding with him. In addition, Durand has associations with the ... MSI." Barnes, "Intellectual Processes," p. 11.

[12] By following Thiriart, Lutte du Peuple also called for the end of Americanization and Soviet imperialism and for a European revolution. For an analysis of this group, see Algazy, *L'extrême-droite*, pp. 150–51.

[13] X. Garaud and A. Courber, "The Book Trade on the French Far Right," *Patterns of Prejudice*, 16(3), 1982, pp. 44–45.

different currents into the "new front" and consolidate it.[14] However, unlike the MSI-DN policy of presenting, at least externally, a more innovative and plural party, the FN's campaign was enshrined in the usual propaganda. Moreover, the background of some members was probably not reassuring to conservative voters. People such as Alain Robert were closely monitored by the police because they considered him to be the leader of a clandestine group called Groupe d'Intervention Nationaliste (Nationalist Intervention Group), made up of fifty members and devoted to attacks against left-wing organizations.[15]

In addition, the young party was unable to attract foremost external personalities (like the MSI before 1972) and, as a consequence, potential voters who probably perceived the FN as an intersection of radical shibboleths. The insufficient electoral score provoked a clash between Le Pen and many Ordre Nouveau activists. Despite some difficulties, the former realized that the only possible way to escape a political backwater was to reinforce the image and structure of the party and to uphold the electoral strategy. The latter called for renewed militant activism. The reality, however, was that former Ordre Nouveau strategists were probably not completely aware of how difficult it would be to keep together such different figures and control Le Pen.[16]

These divergences opened a new political phase that was accelerated by an unforeseen event in June 1973, when Ordre Nouveau held a meeting to protest against what they termed uncontrolled and "savage" immigration. The meeting was followed by riots with the Ligue Communiste Révolutionnaire (Revolutionary Communist League). As expected, the government promptly outlawed both movements. In hindsight, the dissolution of the movement represented a stroke of luck for Le Pen, and the FN fell under his complete leadership, with the dream of transforming it into a real parliamentary force. However, initially, this did not change the political perspectives, and "pulverization" once more seemed to be the keyword. Indeed, the outlawed leaders, Brigneau and Robert, rejected Le Pen's plans. In late 1973, they founded the small group Faire Front

[14] J.-M. Le Pen, "Pour une candidature nationale," *Minute*, October 11–17, 1972, p. 20; and François Solchaga, "Nouvelles du 'Front,'" *Rivarol*, 1146, December 3, 1972, p. 5.

[15] BDIC, FJD, JD, "Ministre d'État Ministère de l'Intérieur, Direction Générale de la Police Nationale, Direction Centrale de la Police Judiciaire, Sous-Direction des Affaires Criminelles" (hereafter, "MI, DGPN, DCPJ, SDAC"), "'Note,' Object: Renseignements concernant le Mouvement clandestin 'Groupe d'Intervention Nationaliste' (G.I.N., 31 Oct. 1975)."

[16] See Hainsworth, "The Extreme Right in Post-War France," p. 36.

(Making the Front, also known as "Comités faire front") and then the Parti des Forces Nouvelles (Party of New Forces, PFN).

Some other political currents then joined the FN, affecting its ideology. This was the case, in particular, of François Duprat and the revolutionary nationalists. Being a large and combative group, they attempted to spread their hegemony over the FN. Consequently, the movement radicalized themes such as anti-capitalism and anti-Americanism, along with anti-Semitism.[17] In sum, in 1974 the FN was still relegated to the margins of the political system, lacking any real credibility. The presidential elections of May, with Le Pen as candidate, were a complete failure for the party (a mere 0.74 percent of the vote), while the extremists of Faire Front supported mainstream Valéry Giscard d'Estaing's presidential campaign.[18]

Divisions and difficulties can, however, also be observed on the other side of the Alps during the same period. The failure of the Christian Democrats' 1974 anti-divorce campaign, also promoted by the MSI, and the persistent refusal by the traditional right to participate in any electoral agreements were signs of poor credibility for neofascism.[19] These patterns, together with accusations of ties with anti-democratic groups and the resignations of Admiral Gino Birindelli from the party presidency, arguably contributed to the (re-)de-legitimization of Almirante's party.

The alarming result (with less of 2.6 percent of the vote) in the following legislative elections provoked a further clash between extreme-right internal streams. A more moderate current such as Democrazia Nazionale (National Democracy), represented by Ernesto De Marzio and Gastone Nencioni, challenged Almirante's leadership, as they seemed to propose an authentic doctrinal shift toward *defascistizzazione* and democratization. However, in December, they formed a distinctive parliamentary group. Indeed, some monarchists led by Alfredo Covelli, the "nonfascist" promoter of the MSI-DN culture, Plebe, and influential neofascist leaders such as the trade unionist Gianni Roberti and *Il Borghese* editor Tedeschi, along with Nencioni and De Marzio, all left the MSI. In total, twenty-six MPs abandoned the party. This was for the failure to

[17] Igounet notes that, at the time, the FN ideology embodied many of Duprat's negationist historiographical theses. Igounet, *Histoire du négationnisme*, p. 164.

[18] Forgetting the early criticisms of Le Pen's allegedly moderate political strategy, former ON activists, paradoxically, joined the mainstream right. Milza, *Fascisme Français*, pp. 343–44.

[19] Retrospectively, there were attempts over the years to pragmatically "use" the MSI when it was needed, but to generally isolate it in Italian politics.

insert the party into mainstream politics. In fact, the split deprived the party of some leading politicians, usually supporting the DN project, respected by other parliamentary groups, and more willing to adopt a policy of agreements with the moderate right.[20] Democrazia Nazionale lasted up to 1979 and with almost no grassroots activity, but it immediately tried to build some international collaboration, especially with French Gaullism.

THE EURORIGHT YEARS

For the MSI, the splitting away of Democrazia Nazionale and its somewhat respectable members seemed to be a blow to its ambitions, while the fragmentation of forces on the extreme-right spectrum had, instead, been a recurring feature in French history. This reinforced the transnational appeal of the MSI – which was still a role model despite some palpable predicaments.

This was certainly the case with the newly born Faire Front. A goal of this group, which simultaneously published the bulletin *Faire Front!*, was the launching of a "committee" for the establishment of a new "nationalist party."[21] In fact, Faire Front was ideologically grounded in this national revolutionary extremist wing. It professed "Europeanism" and the defense of the western world against communism.[22] There was also a virulent determination to stop foreign migrations: Indeed, an anti-immigration policy was perceived as a veritable "necessity," if not even a "national duty."[23]

In June 1974, Faire Front's committee (known as the Comité d'Initiative pour la Construction d'un Parti Nationaliste) started a permanent campaign of recruitment and propaganda that directly led to the creation of the PFN in November 1974. Obviously, the Faire Front's leaders (Robert and Brigneau and also Paul Gauchon and Jack Marchal) directed this movement – which, from March 1975, published a journal called *Initiative Nationale*. Naturally, the PFN used the same mobilizing themes of its immediate predecessor, but it also highlighted the need for a more proficient defense of "the fatherland, family, and the army."[24] In the

[20] Ferraresi, *Threats to Democracy*, p. 195.

[21] BDIC, FJD, JD, "MI, DGPN, DCPJ, SDAC," "Note: De la dissolution d'Ordre Nouveau à la création du Parti des Forces Nouvelles," p. 1.

[22] Ibid., p. 6.

[23] "Limiter l'immigration: c'est plus necessaire que jamais," *Faire Front!*, 6, April 1974, p. 6.

[24] BDIC, FJD, JD, "MI, DGPN, DCPJ, SDAC," "Note: De la dissolution d'Ordre Nouveau à la création du Parti des Forces Nouvelles," p. 19.

youth field, GUD and the Union et Défense des Lycéens (Alliance and Defense of High School Pupils) strongly backed its politics.[25] Nonetheless, these organizations were later directly controlled and coordinated by the PFN through its youth wing, the Front de la Jeunesse (Youth Front, FDJ).[26]

Transnationally, it was this youth arena that initially promoted and maintained links with the MSI. The FDJ, in fact, defined itself as an organization aiming to gather the best "youth nationalists" to proficiently oppose the existing power, as well as Marxism. This fight was placed in a wider context that, they claimed, would lead to the building of a "new Europe." According to the FDJ, this was chiefly a strategy to be developed together with other fraternal European groups – and among them, a prominent place was held by the MSI's wing, the Fronte della Gioventù, considered by the FDJ as the key example and "the most important organization of the European Youth."[27] The admiration for their Italian comrades was palpable. The label "Front de la Jeunesse" was a translation of Fronte della Gioventù (although it is impossible to assess how intentional the choice of the same name was). At the December 18, 1973, FDJ meeting, to which (allegedly) four hundred activists were invited, including some from abroad, *Faire Front!* proudly reported on a message from Marco Tarchi, which was read to the audience. He was described at the meeting as one of the leaders of the Fronte della Gioventù (as we know, he was also the ideologue of the Italian ND and a collaborator on MSI journals).[28] These cross-national links continued over the years and showed that Italy's young neofascists were well informed of the activities of FDJ, PFN, and GUD.[29]

The PFN's interest in Italian politics was, nonetheless, not limited to the youth milieu. *Faire Front!* analogously featured articles paying homage to the MSI. For example, some comments praised its huge mobilization of voters in the anti-divorce plebiscite (albeit this was, as

[25] In the 1970s, the GUD was active at the University of Paris II Panthéon-Assas and also in Amiens, Besançon, Bordeaux, Cleremont-Ferrand, Le Mans, Marseille, Nancy, Poitiers, Rouen, Saint-Etienne, and Toulouse. The Union et Défense des Lycéens was, instead, one of the few non-Marxist high school student associations of the time.

[26] BDIC, FJD, JD, "MI, DGPN, DCPJ, SDAC," "Note: De la dissolution d'Ordre Nouveau à la création du Parti des Forces Nouvelles," p. 27.

[27] "Fer de lance du nationalisme: le front de la jeunesse," *Faire Front!*, 6, April 1974, p. 14.

[28] "Front de la Jeunesse," *Faire Front!*, 4, January 1974, p. 3.

[29] Camus recorded that, in 1982, the Fronte della Gioventù had a poster from the GUD on their branch in Milan. Jean-Yves Camus, e-mail communication with the author, July 27, 2012.

suggested earlier, not exclusively organized by the MSI).[30] In a critical period for Italian politics and society, the journal also defended Almirante and his party: The radical anti-democratic groups were merely interested in attracting MSI young activists, the French neofascists reasoned, and the journal even wondered if some of them were, in reality, a deliberate fabrication of the police and the left. In sum, the final goal was mainly to prevent the political and electoral rise of the MSI.[31]

The PFN was, in the eyes of Almirante, a more serious partner than the FN. It was appreciated that the PFN developed an MSI-like policy of insertion in the political system and forging anti-communist alliances. This Italian perspective on France's extreme-right politics was relatively accurate, and contacts were developed largely with Gauchon, Robert, and Brigneau. *Il Secolo d'Italia* therefore sent journalists to France to interview PFN leaders and ran articles on the ideology and political programs of the party.[32] Once invited to attend a PFN national congress, Italians immediately felt at home:

> These are our people, and it is a wonderful surprise to find here the same expressions, the same thoughts, and the same problems that we have [in Italy]: finding all this here, in this extraordinary country, and in this [political] right which is young and rich, both fresh and storied.[33]

The belief was that the PFN offered a real magnet for the whole French neofascist movement, and, at the end of the 1970s, it effectively seemed to completely prevail over the FN. It also benefited from these links with the MSI and the Spanish Fuerza Nueva (New Force) and joined the Euroright project developed by the Italian leader.[34] Almirante was, in fact, looking for another international ally, and for the PFN was very relevant to be close to the Italian party.

30 "La faillite du système italien," *Faire Front!*, 7, June 1974, p. 12.

31 "Italie: d'une bombe à l'autre," *Faire Front!*, 8, October 1974, p. 15.

32 Siegfried Kessel, "La Nazione sociale come punto di riferimento: La giovane destra francese e il partito 'Forze nuove' – Intervista con Pascal Gauchon," *Il Secolo d'Italia*, March 1, 1978, p. 7.

33 "Il tono complessivo dei lavori dimostra che questo partito [il PFN] è veramente un partito di forze nuove, . . . moderne ma profondamente radicate nella storia e nella cultura di una delle destre più affascinanti di tutta l'Europa." Massimo Magliaro, "Nel segno dell'Eurodestra," *Il Secolo d'Italia*, June 18, 1978, p. 11.

34 For an overview of the European links of the extreme right (1960s–1980s), see Anne-Marie Duranton-Crabol, *Europe de l'extrême droite: de 1945 à nos jours* (Brussels: Complexe, 1991), pp. 167–81.

PFN officials rapidly organized a dinner debate in the restaurant of the Eiffel Tower, probably even falling into debt for the affair. Three hundred sympathizers paid tribute at the event to the special guest invited from Italy, Giorgio Almirante.[35] In Gauchon's view, Almirante's visit "left a mark."[36] From the first Euroright meeting in Rome in April 1978, joint conferences, meetings, and debates were organized across France, Italy, and Spain. A web among extremist forces in those "Latin sisters" was considered to be more than a simple necessity. In the words of neofascist sources, there was the need for a "Euroright" – "a modern, European, and Mediterranean right."[37] This project, which was envisaged as leading to a transnational coalition of neofascist forces in the European elections (and possibly within the European parliament), was viscerally anti-communist. In the long run, the hope was to create the usual "Europe of people, nations and states."[38] This obviously attracted the interest of a genuine early Eurofascist like Maurice Bardèche, who, interviewed by *Il Secolo d'Italia*, hoped that, at least, the Euroright would serve to organically unify the Western European extreme right.[39]

It is then evident how, in the 1970s, the FN was far from being considered a proper ally of the MSI – although, even if only as a matter of courtesy, the Italian party also maintained regular links with Le Pen. It appeared obvious to extreme-right observers in Rome that the FN was still struggling to find the balance between its internal currents, and that the unitary process was far from completion. This was very true: At the 1978 legislative elections, for example, Duprat's group represented almost one-third of the FN's candidates, but, at the same time, before the elections, Le Pen changed the electoral propaganda strategy of the FN (in some ways opposing Duprat).[40] However, the party was not rewarded by electors and scored a 0.8 percent, and Le Pen's line was strongly opposed by revolutionary nationalists. This provoked rifts in the party, but the mysterious assassination of Duprat in 1978 again shuffled the

[35] Charpier, *Génération Occident*, p. 302.

[36] Magliaro, "Nel segno dell'Eurodestra," p. 11.

[37] Cesare Pozzo, "Una destra moderna europea e mediterranea," *Il Secolo d'Italia*, February 23, 1978, p. 1.

[38] "'Europa, liberati,'" *Il Secolo d'Italia*, June 29, 1978, p. 1.

[39] Massimo Magliaro, "L'Eurodestra per il recupero morale dell'Europa. Intervista con Bardèche," *Il Secolo d'Italia*, June 23, 1978, p. 12.

[40] To attract voters, Le Pen thought that the party had to play the card of a new economic policy, embodying principles of economic liberalism and criticism of state economic interventionism. See Jean-Yves Camus, *Le Front National* (Toulouse: Editions Milan, 1998), p. 11.

cards on the table. This opened another phase in the political life of the FN, and, consequently, revolutionary nationalists lost influence over the movement.[41]

In such a context, the PFN and the FN even attempted to build a united front, the Union Française pour l'Euro-droite des Patries (French Union for a Euro-right of the Fatherlands), designed to contest the European elections in May 1979. This putative agreement disintegrated even before the elections, and, not surprisingly, the result was, as usual, insignificant. Predictably, this led to another internal rebalancing among the different party currents and saw the development of new more widespread and grassroots strategies.[42] Notably, the Union Solidariste (Solidarist Union), which had joined the FN in the late 1970s, increased its influence upon the party. This group stemmed from the Groupe Action Jeunesse (Youth Action Group) milieu, which was recognized for strong activism in the student field, especially for its attacks against left-wingers for "control" over some universities.[43] Eminent figures among the solidarist fringe included Jean-Pierre Stirbois and his wife Marie-France, Christian Baeckeroot, and Michel Collinot.[44]

It was, nevertheless, Stirbois, an astute politician, who left his mark indelibly on the FN, later playing some major roles in the party. He made much effort "to build up his own electoral base in Dreux, a dormitory town west of Paris," and, as general secretary, "his meticulous attention to detail helped build up the organization, membership and electoral strength of the party."[45] In retrospect, this was a proficient plan, and the solidarists gave considerable impetus, as well as doctrinal energy, to the FN. Their strategic line was to refuse arrangements with the mainstream rightist forces and, above all, to push hard for widespread local

41 However, as Shields argues, it is true that the "departure of the 'revolutionary nationalists' removed a major obstacle to electoral respectability and altered the complexion of the party. For the second time in its short history the FN had been purged of its most overtly radical elements." Shields, *The Extreme Right*, p. 184.

42 See also Michel Soudais, *Le Front national en face* (Paris: Flammarion, 1996), pp. 180–86.

43 BDIC, FJD, JD, "MI, DGPN, DCPJ, SDAC," "Note relative au 'Groupe Action Jeunesse' (G.A.J.)."

44 Michel Collinot was also the inventor of the FN's *Bleu-Blanc-Rouge* Day, which has taken place since 1981.

45 Fysh and Wolfreys, *The Politics of Racism*, p. 111. According again to Shields, Stirbois strengthened the party management and organization as a way of "maintaining order over the diverse factions, [and] tightening the links between the FN's local federations and its centralised decision-making machinery." Shields, *The Extreme Right*, p. 184.

implantation and presence in the nation. They also identified some forceful tools that could have a wider impact on rhetoric and on potential voters: Interesting, for example, was their insistence on a more openly xenophobic approach to the theme of immigration.[46]

In sum, the party, on the one hand, attempted to construct a more reassuring visage and, on the other hand, fully promoted the constant presence of immigration in its political discourse and as a mobilizing theme. Over subsequent years, this evolved into the most successful tactic ever implemented by a French neofascist movement, a strategy that benefited from some of the inner predicaments of French politics and society from the mid-1980s onwards and allowed the FN to become the most appealing extreme-right party in Western Europe.

LES FRANÇAIS D'ABORD!

At the 1982 cantonal elections the FN managed to attain more than 10 percent in five cantons. In 1983 Stirbois scored 12.6 percent of the vote in a by-election in Dreux. Similarly, in 1983 Le Pen, with the slogan "Paris to the Parisians," was elected *conseiller d'arrondissement* in the capital. Moreover, in the 1984 European elections, the FN scored about 11 percent of the vote and elected ten MEPs. In 1986 the proportional electoral system introduced by the new French president, Mitterrand, allowed the FN to gain thirty-five seats in the national assembly, while in the regional elections 135 regional *conseillers régionaux* were elected. Since then, the FN has managed to maintain considerable electoral results, including the incredible 2002 presidential elections in which Le Pen earned roughly 4,800,000 votes and was on the second ballot against Jacques Chirac (and even if Bruno Mégret with some of his Club de l'Horloge and ND associates formed the Mouvement National Républicain).[47]

[46] Solidarists popularized the famous FN slogan: "1 million de chômeurs, c'est 1 million d'immigrés de trop." It was noted how this slogan has some evident fascist roots: "l'équation est reprise d'une affiche à l'histoire lourde, issue de l'Allemagne des années 1930, mais son effet n'en reste pas sauvage, qui engendre l'insécurité. Un discours simple, voire simpliste, mais qui fera ses preuves au fil des années, jusqu'à devenir le centre des débats qui agiteront une bonne part de la société française au début des années 1980, et qui'n a pas fini de faire sentir ses effets." Erwan Lecoeur, *Un néo-populisme à la française. Trente ans de Front national* (Paris: La Découverte, 2003), p. 41.

[47] On the split and the movement led by Mégret, see also Gilles Ivaldi, "Les formations d'extrême droite: Front national et Mouvement national républicain," in P. Bréchon, ed., *Les partis politiques français* (Paris: La Documentation française, 2005), especially pp. 27–33.

The MSI also maintained acceptable electoral scores during the 1980s. This was analogously favored by some external factors such as the overall deradicalization of political conflict after the turbulent period of the 1960s and 1970s, the non–anti-fascist and "absolutory" readings of interwar fascism backed by the historian Renzo De Felice, and the somewhat positive approach of the socialist prime minister Bettino Craxi regarding the MSI.[48] Yet the Italian party was unable to capitalize on this opening up of the political system. Ideologically, Almirante kept playing some anti-system cards while proclaiming the "beauty" of corporatism, fascism, and Mussolini.[49] Italian neofascism, partly for some valid historical reasons, was still too embedded in its doctrinal orthodoxies to fully adopt the strategy of a more updated Western European extreme right. If the FN promoted its image as the "savior of France," calling for law and order and cleverly exploiting the predicaments of the political system (and society) – including the effects of party competition and organization and the growing fears toward North African immigration – the early MSI could not systematically adopt a sort of xenophobic stance.[50] In fact, as we shall see, when it tried to play this card it was mainly unsuccessful.

It is worth noting that the conditions in Italy were certainly less favorable than in France, starting with immigration. The politicization of this latter started quite belatedly in relation to other western nations. At that time, the processes of migration and ethnic diversification had exerted less impact in Italy than in France. In 1974, for example, France had 3,500,000 foreigners – and, among them, Algerians had obtained a privileged legal position following the Évian Accords in the era of decolonization.[51] At the time of the first electoral successes of Le Pen's party,

48 See also Piero Ignazi, *Extreme Right Parties in Western Europe* (Oxford: Oxford University Press, 2006), pp. 41–42.

49 At the thirteenth party congress in February 1982, the party prepared a pamphlet entitled *Alla riscoperta del Fascismo* (To the Rediscovery of Fascism), which brought together some book reviews and review articles which had previously appeared in *Il Secolo d'Italia* and referred to the literature of fascism. The front page highlighted a picture of Il Duce, while the preface opened with an original reproduction of the first program of the interwar Fasci Italiani di Combattimento (Italian Fasci of Combat). See Ufficio Propaganda del MSI-DN, ed., "XIII Congresso Nazionale del MSI-DN: Alla riscoperta del Fascismo," *I Quaderni dell'Alternativa*, Rome, 1982.

50 On the scholarship and the need to study the domestic political settings to understand the trajectories of the extreme right, see Antonis Ellinas, "Phased Out: Far Right Parties in Western Europe," *Comparative Politics*, 39(3), 2007, p. 353.

51 Patrick Weil, "Racisme et discrimination dans la politique française de d'immigration. 1938–1945/1974–1995," *Vingtième siècle*, 47, 1995, p. 99.

France had about four million resident immigrants, and Italy had a population of roughly two hundred thousand legal immigrants.[52] A change in the Italian public discourse may be observed from the very late 1980s when immigration was, henceforth, placed at the center of the public arena. By 1989–91, the terminology "shifted from multiple types of immigration used earlier to a single phenomenon of immigration of *extracomunitari*. This transformation facilitates the launching of immigration as a ... national problem and its politicization."[53] However, this was not yet enough to ensure the electoral success of a neofascist party adopting immigrants as the key theme in its electoral manifesto.

The overall situation in France was very different. The triumph of the socialists in the 1981 presidential elections had a considerable impact on political life, and the novel French leadership also aimed to undermine Gaullism. The FN turned out to be an effective "tool" in this process: It constituted a possible competitor for the mainstream right. In line with this strategy, in May 1982, Mitterrand called for a real pluralism in the television system. In theory, this would have offered tangible equal opportunities to all political actors. Immediately, Le Pen had access to a vast audience, and he was invited onto a number of TV programs. This allowed the FN to spread its themes and prepare future electoral achievements. In other words, "the media rise of ... Le Pen had anticipated his electoral growth."[54] This is, nonetheless, almost natural if we consider that media coverage may often have a strong impact on party politics, and especially on fringe movements.[55]

52 See, respectively, Fabienne Daguet and Suzanne Thave, "La population immigrée. Le résultat d'une longue histoire," *INSEE PREMIERE*, 458, June 1996, p. 2; A. Colombo and G. Sciortino, "Italian Immigration: The Origins, Nature and Evolution of Italy's Migratory Systems," *Journal of Modern Italian Studies*, 9(1), 2004, p. 54.

53 Giuseppe Sciortino and Asher Colombo, "The Flows and the Flood: The Public Discourse on Immigration in Italy, 1969–2001," *Journal of Modern Italian Studies*, 9(1), 2004, p. 103.

54 Emmanuel Faux et al., *La Main droite de Dieu. Enquête sur François Mitterrand et l'extrême droite* (Paris: Seuil, 1994), p. 26.

55 Antonis Ellinas purposely uses the FN to back this frame: "the trajectory of the French extreme right illustrates how the media can help marginal parties overcome their organisational weaknesses and enter the political mainstream with minimum organisational effort. ... Because the Dreux by-election was the only one held at the time, the FN's victory drew national media attention, amplifying the anti-immigrant message of the FN and granting it an even wider audience. Along with the politically-motivated exposure that public broadcasters gave the FN, the Dreux victory helped the party establish itself as a viable political force. A few months before the European parliament elections, in February 1984, Le Pen appeared on one of the most popular and sought-after French TV shows, L'Heure de la Verité (The Hour of Truth). As Le Pen recalls, the decision of

By this time, as we have noted, the discourses of FN candidates were fully premised on a virulent anti-communism and, above all, a rejection of ethnic minorities. The latter became useful as it potentially embodied all the preoccupations of the French extreme right: colonies, decadence, nationalism, xenophobia, and national and western values. Similarly, this mobilizing flag allowed candidates to offer an alternative vision of domestic society across class structure.[56] The FN theorized all this with the famous concept of *préférence nationale* (national preference). In essence, this stood for a systematic exclusion of migrants from economic opportunities and social benefits and the promotion of "fraternity and solidarity between fellow citizens."[57] From such a perspective, there was, in fact, no social and working place for immigrants, and it was, famously, claimed that "national citizens come first" (*Les Français d'abord!*).[58]

Theoretically, this *préférence nationale* was rooted in the very old approach that superior civilizations were natural.[59] The immigrant was, in this analysis, inassimilable. It was an external body, predominantly evoking "degradation" and "invasion."[60] France, and indeed Europe itself ("the most extraordinary civilization in the world," Le Pen argued), was an organic community that had to be culturally, ethnically, and

Antenne 2 to host him on this show transformed him into a respectable political leader and pushed him into the political mainstream. ... A survey carried out after the broadcasting of the programme showed that voting intentions for the FN doubled, from 3.5 percent to 7 percent." Antonis Ellinas, "Chaotic but Popular? Extreme-Right Organisation and Performance in the Age of Media Communication," *Journal of Contemporary European Studies*, Special Edition on "The Extreme Right in Contemporary Europe: History, Theory, Interpretations," 17(2), 2009, pp. 217–18. On this point, see also Nigel Copsey, "A Comparison between the Extreme Right in Contemporary France and Britain," *Contemporary European History*, 6(1), 1997, p. 208.

56 Jacques Le Bohec, *Sociologie du phénomène Le Pen* (Paris: La Découverte, 2005), p. 16.

57 Front National, *L'alternative nationale. 300 mesures pour la renaissance de la France. Programme de gouvernement* (Paris: Éditions Nationales, 1993), p. 37.

58 "National preference" essentially means, in Étienne Balibar's interpretation, "France belonging to the *true* French people" with the consequent exclusion of all non-Western European migrants that, instead, represent an apocalyptic "anti-France." Étienne Balibar, "De la 'préférence nationale' à l'invention de la politique: comme lutter contre le néofascisme?" in J. Viard, ed., *Aux source du populisme nationaliste. L'urgence de comprendre Toulon, Orange, Marignane* (La Tour d'Aigues: Éditions de L'Aube, 1996), pp. 209 and 211.

59 Jean-Paul Honoré, "La 'hiérarchie des sentiments,'" *Mots*, Special Edition on "Droite, nouvelle droite, extrême droite. Discours et idéologie en France et en Italie," 12, 1986, p. 130. For an extremist right-wing view on race, see Topoline, "La génétique est-elle raciste?" *National Hebdo*, October 2004, 7–13, p. 6.

60 See Honoré, "La hiérarchie," p. 131.

ideologically preserved.[61] It was unimaginable to envisage the same "democracy" without a homogeneously defined community of fundamentally native people sharing "language, culture, faith, and history."[62] All this seems to be also linked with an old fascist-like purity of one's own community and group.

The impact of immigration was then the difference across 1980s France and Italy. However, this belief in an immigration threat did not appear out of nowhere, nor was it merely popularized by the extreme right.[63] Since the late 1960s, French government policies had already "tended to treat immigration as an economic factor that can be controlled, manipulated, or even embraced – as an economic problem to be solved."[64] Later, it was portrayed as a social and often a national and security issue and as a source of authentic destabilization.[65] For example, tracing the process whereby immigration was gradually politicized in France during the presidency of Valéry Giscard d'Estaing in the 1970s is essential in regard to understanding how it became electorally available to the FN in the early 1980s (while the same thing did not happen for the MSI). In particular, Giscard d'Estaing's attempted forced repatriation of North Africans arguably established an unfriendly environment toward immigrants in some mainstream circles and a benevolence for anti-immigrant stances.[66] The FN capitalized on this and tied it up with the defense of national identity.

[61] Jean-Marie Le Pen, *Les Français d'abord* (Paris: Éditions Carrère, 1984), p. 158.

[62] Bruno Mégret quoted in René Monzat, *Les voleurs d'avenir. Pourquoi l'extrême droite peut avoir de beaux jours devant elle* (Paris: Les editions Textuel, 2004), p. 80.

[63] Jim Wolfreys, "'The Centre Cannot Hold': Fascism, the Left and the Crisis of French Politics," *International Socialism*, 95, 2002, p. 54.

[64] Paul A. Silverstein, *Algeria in France: Transpolitics, Race, and Nation* (Bloomington: Indiana University Press, 2004), p. 23.

[65] See also Max Silverman, *Deconstructing the Nation: Immigration, Racism and Citizenship in Modern France* (London: Routledge, 1992), p. 91; and Françoise Lionnet, "Immigration, Poster Art, and Transgressive Citizenship: France 1968–1988," *SubStance*, Special Edition on "France's Identity Crises," 24(1–2), 1995, pp. 94–95. For a brief account of the "immigration problem" in France since the Algerian war and its implications on national history, public memory, contemporary politics, and riots in the French *banlieues* in 2005, see also Geoffroy de Laforcade, "'Foreigners,' Nationalism and the 'Colonial Fracture.' Stigmatized Subjects of Historical Memory in France," *International Journal of Comparative Sociology*, 47(3–4), 2006, pp. 217–33.

[66] The equation "immigration = criminality" was not new, but in the middle of the 1970s it was "encouragée par les gouvernements de droite." Yvan Gastaut, *L'immigration et l'opinion en France sous la Vème République* (Paris: Seuil, 2000), pp. 481–82.

Part of the center-left similarly contributed to this politicization of foreign migrants.[67] In September 1984, for example, socialist Prime Minister Laurent Fabius controversially argued that the FN posed "good questions," to which it merely gave "wrong answers." Conservatives and the media went even further in pushing and legitimizing immigration on the political agenda. When the moderate right envisioned some local agreements with Le Pen's party, only a few commentators and politicians protested against these types of alliances. The press additionally injected ambiguities and sensitive slogans that, at times, worried public opinion and served in many people's eyes to dehumanize the immigrant. On August 3, 1984, *L'Express* carried reports on an alleged disappearance of white people.[68] Similarly, on October 26, 1985, *Le Figaro-Magazine* published a report likewise titled "Serons-nous encore Français dans trente ans?" (Will We Still Be French in Thirty Years?), which stirred up protests across the country. *Le Figaro* showed an opinion poll claiming that 71 percent of interviewees wanted to expel illegal immigrants.

A final point explaining the rise of the FN allows us to now draw a further transnational link across time and space. As with the MSI in the early 1970s with its DN project, for the first time in its relatively young life, Le Pen's movement was able to attract personalities outside the usual fascist groupings. Alongside Bruno Mégret, Jean-Yves Le Gallou, Jean-Claude Bardet, Yvan Blot, and other members of the ND and the Club de l'Horloge (the Clock Club), aristocratic figures such as Olivier d'Ormesson and Michel de Camaret, technocrats like Jean-Marie Le Chevallier (future FN major of Toulon from 1995 to 2001), and academics, such as Jean-Claude Martinez and Bruno Gollnisch (the latter will later be highly considered by the contemporary Italian activists), joined the FN.[69]

From the end of the 1970s, there was also the rapprochement of a strand of Catholic fundamentalism with Le Pen's party. This ultra-Catholic fringe had undergone a renewal since the second half of the

[67] Le Bohec highlights two meaningful examples: "la destruction d'un foyer d'immigrés par un bulldozer sur ordre du maire communiste de Clichy-sur-Seine le 24 décembre 1980; la campagne orchestrée à Marseille début 1983 par Gaston Defferre, maire PS sortant et ministre de l'Intérieur, téléguidant la liste raciste de Bernard Manovelli." Le Bohec, *Sociologie du phénomène*, p. 17. On this point, see also Frédéric-Joël Guilledoux, *Le Pen en Provence* (Paris: Fayard, 2004), p. 39. Fysh and Wolfreys noted that some socialists willing to defend immigrants and integration were viewed with suspicion. See Fysh and Wolfreys, *The Politics of Racism*, p. 45.

[68] Simone Bonnafous, *L'immigration prise aux mots. Les immigrés dans la presse au tournant des années 80* (Paris: Éditions Kimé, 1991), p. 12.

[69] Le Bohec, *Sociologie du phénomène*, p. 23.

1970s, most notably through groups under the leadership of Bishop Marcel Lefèbvre, who were initially located outside the FN's framework. However, through activists such as Bernard Antony (also known as Roman Marie, who officially joined the FN in 1984) and Jean Madiran, the movement Chrétienté-Solidarité (Christendom-Solidarity), and the newly founded journal *Présent*, key ultra-Catholic figures slowly joined the political extreme right (and the birth of *Présent*, after years in which the French extreme right had not been able to establish a noteworthy periodical, was especially welcomed by the Italian press).[70] This policy of recruitment showed itself to be fruitful and attracted voters who had previously belonged to the conservatives. Le Pen's party, in other words, looked increasingly attractive to a wider range of people, and, above all, it could now claim to be a more legitimate political actor: ideologically "plural," socially more acceptable, well structured, and properly funded. The "crossing of the desert" was finally ending.

A THRONE FOR THE NEW KING

From the late 1970s up to the first FN's success, the MSI's ally, as we noted when discussing the Euroright, was still the PFN. In fact, as early as January 1979, Almirante had visited Paris to promote and energetically recommend the unity of French neofascist forces in view of the forthcoming national elections.[71] Given the similarities between the two nations concerning the presence of strong communist parties, Almirante argued that the French electoral competition would have had repercussions in Italy. In such a context, from the pages of *Il Secolo d'Italia*, MSI journalist Massimo Magliaro (later head of the international channel of Italy's state-owned broadcaster, the RAI), criticized the FN as a party that, in his view, was willing only to promote its political autonomy and was not interested in a real political alternative and an anti-Marxist collaboration with moderate forces.[72]

This was, nonetheless, a feature of the past – and the FN's progression in the ballots changed the political landscape. The 1984 elections

[70] Marco Cuzzi, "L'Eurodestra: I rapporti tra il Msi-Dn e l'estrema destra francese (1968–1994)," in M. Antonioli and A. Moioli, eds., *Saggi storici in onore di Romain H. Rainero* (Milan: Franco Angeli, 2005), p. 228.

[71] Moreover, for the Italian leader, this election was a fundamental stepping-stone on the way to the following European elections.

[72] Massimo Magliaro, "Un voto contro l'incertezza," *Il Secolo d'Italia*, January 31, 1978, pp. 1 and 11.

cronache politiche

Sabato 16 giugno 1984

FRANCIA. *Jean-Marie Le Pen, leader del «Front National», punta a superare il 10 per cento dei voti*

«Voltiamo le spalle al socialismo» A Strasburgo insieme con il Msi-Dn

La rivoluzione tecnologica - sostiene - porta a destra; la destra non può non vincere - La Francia cerca un'immagine, io gliela do - Abbiamo rotto la monotonia della «banda dei quattro» ed ora puntiamo a riformare il sistema elettorale

Massimo Magliaro

Intervista di Giorgio Almirante a «Il Mattino»

Può fare molto l'Europa per il Mezzogiorno d'Italia

Quattrocentotrentaquattro i deputati che saranno eletti nei dieci paesi della Comunità

Verso la «costituente» dell'Unione politica

Il proposito dell'Europarlamento secondo il nuovo progetto di trattato

FIGURE 2: Jean-Marie Le Pen on *Il Secolo d'Italia*, 1984. Courtesy of Biblioteca Universitaria Alessandrina, thanks to the Ministero per i Beni e le Attività Culturali. Any reproduction is prohibited.

for the European parliament turned a page in the history of modern extreme-right movements. The present era was made up of some spectacular and unexpected victories by Le Pen. On June 16, 1984, *Il Secolo d'Italia*, for the first time, published an interview with Le Pen, entitled "'Let's Turn Our Backs on Socialism': In Strasbourg together with the MSI-DN."[73]

Immediately after these electoral exploits, Almirante sent a letter to congratulate Le Pen. The letter had some prominence on the front page of the party newspaper – and the picture of Le Pen was placed alongside an image of Almirante. The MSI leader argued that he felt that this was also an achievement of Italian neofascism, and he hoped that this was the first of a long series of electoral victories. In hindsight, Almirante was right, although he could not have imagined that this success was to change the political geography of the European extreme right.[74]

[73] Massimo Magliaro, "'Voltiamo le spalle al socialismo.' A Strasburgo con il MSI-DN," *Il Secolo d'Italia*, June 16, 1984, p. 2.

[74] Giorgio Almirante, "Per il Front National la prima di tante vittorie," *Il Secolo d'Italia*, June 19, 1984, p. 1.

In reality, the first rapprochement with the FN was probably in May 1984, when Magliaro, in an analysis of the prospects of French political forces before the European elections, reasoned that the FN's failures were possibly approaching an end.[75] In another article, he highlighted the fact that the FN was going full sail ahead with its political project. Significantly, he also remembered that the party was using the same MSI symbol (the tricolor flame), and he claimed that it was intensely touching to see that this flame with Italian roots was now being waved on the streets of Paris. For Magliaro, this proved that the MSI had been "the benchmark for many people, and not just in Italy, for forty years."[76]

At the beginning, precisely because it was only their first tangible victory, the FN showed a great respect for the MSI and paid homage to its leader. Italy was, predictably, once more the landmark. Indeed, in the interview with *Il Secolo d'Italia* mentioned previously, Le Pen used a political rhetoric that was markedly close to Almirante's. Furthermore, when invited to attend the fourteenth MSI national congress the following November 1984, the other FN leader, Stirbois, very much looked to the Italian party and its structure as a role model to be replicated in France. "I have been impressed by the MSI-DN organization," he said; "the FN is still young and it needs the example and experience of the MSI-DN."[77] The next day, it was Le Pen who greeted the MSI delegates with a warm "dearest MSI-DN comrades," calling Italy "our Latin sister" – and he closed the speech with a peremptory and fraternal "Viva il MSI-DN, viva il Front National, viva l'Italia, viva la Francia, viva l'Europa."[78]

The movements therefore started to collaborate at a supranational level. During a meeting organized in Paris in 1985, for example, the leaders decided on shared policies. According to an MSI activist such as

[75] Massimo Magliaro, "La locomotiva Chirac," *Il Secolo d'Italia*, May 13, 1984, p. 1.

[76] Massimo Magliaro, "Il 'Front national' va a gonfie vele," *Il Secolo d'Italia*, May 18, 1984, p. 1. Marco Cuzzi also quotes both this article and the one in the previous note. I am indebted to his chapter for the first links established in this period between the MSI and the FN. See Cuzzi, "L'Eurodestra," pp. 228–29.

[77] Quoted in Gennaro Malgieri, "Le destre europee guardano al Msi-Dn," *Il Secolo d'Italia*, December 2, 1984, p. 1.

[78] Jean-Marie Le Pen, "Il discorso di Jean Marie Le Pen, leader del Front National: L'Europa deve affrancarsi dalla minaccia comunista," *Il Secolo d'Italia*, December 3, 1984, p. 4. In line with this, among many other examples, at the launching of the Italian administrative elections of 1985, Le Pen from the Piazza del Popolo in Rome proudly stated: "Questa sera, il mio dovere è assicurare al Msi-Dn il fraterno appoggio del Front National, perché viva l'Europa." Jean-Marie Le Pen, "Verso la rinascita dell'Occidente," *Il Secolo d'Italia*, April 12, 1985, p. 2.

FIGURES 3: Jean-Marie Le Pen and Giorgio Almirante at a FN meeting, 1985. Courtesy of © Jacques Pavlovsky/Sygma/Corbis.

Mirko Tremaglia (former RSI, and later a governmental minister during Silvio Berlusconi's years), Le Pen and Almirante would "stick together in the tricolor flame, for a new Europe, and to help civilization to overcome communist imperialism."[79]

Nevertheless, neofascists did not have to wait long before noticing a change in the MSI's lexicon. Le Pen, indeed, became president of the extreme-right group in the European parliament. The PFN basically disappeared from *Il Secolo d'Italia*'s pages, while the FN was the main neofascist party on French soil.[80] From the end of 1984 onwards, Le Pen and the FN became the absolute overseas protagonists of *Il Secolo d'Italia*. Le Pen was quickly reaching the "throne." One year later, Magliaro summarized the Italian feelings on the FN. This movement was something that people had to be dealing with: "Le Pen's effect is so powerful," he wrote, "that it crosses, vertically, all other parties."[81]

[79] Mirko Tremaglia, "Msi-Dn e Front National per la Patria europea," *Il Secolo d'Italia*, February 5, 1985, p. 7.

[80] Gennaro Malgieri, "Le Pen: comune impegno con il Msi-Dn nell'edificazione dell'Europa-Nazione," *Il Secolo d'Italia*, December 3, 1984, p. 1.

[81] Massimo Magliaro, "I partiti francesi messi in crisi dal Front National," *Il Secolo d'Italia*, March 1, 1985, p. 1.

All in all, Le Pen was certainly "crossing" the MSI, especially when the Italian party experienced some difficulties. Almirante was forced to withdraw from the party leadership in 1987 because of health problems. The election of his successor became a difficult task. Rival groups, diverse ambitions, and opposing ideological stances clashed with each other. The young Gianfranco Fini, a close ally of Almirante, was elected as MSI secretary but resigned after only two years. However, this short tenure was characterized by a continuous friendship and research into collaboration with the extreme right in France. Fini (and Almirante) had immediately looked for recognition from the new "king" of Western European right-wing extremism. His first international appearance was at an electoral kermis organized by the FN in 1988. It was Almirante who took his youthful dauphin to France, and in his discourse from the tribune he reminded the youngster:

> Dear Fini . . ., the real and deep France is here; [a] country to whom Italy is linked by many, old and recent, fraternal ties. There is here a brave and coherent man, Le Pen, who represents today that part of Frenchmen that did not want to surrender to the decadence and the gradual lost of national identity.

In his own speech, a well-trained Fini reinforced this alliance with France, emphasizing that the MSI and the FN had a similar political and ideological line and shared the dream of a Europe of Fatherlands:

> The MSI is today led by a young man . . ., but today, as in the past, it is loyal to the national[ist] ideals. Today, as in the past, it is a good friend of France, and consequently of the greatest Frenchman, Le Pen! His battle does not concern exclusively France, but the whole of Europe.[82]

Admiration of the French leader was marked. At one point, Fini even tried to follow the FN strategy: Slightly anti-immigration propaganda had, in fact, permeated the MSI rhetoric after his appointment. At the same time, there was, more pragmatically, the impression (also developed in neofascist France) that the political left and the trade unions might mobilize this mass of people from the Third World.[83] However, this was not the sole preoccupation for some Italian neofascists. In their eyes, there was also the danger that migrants from North Africa – and the related problems of underemployment, exploitation,

[82] Both quoted in Alain Cochet, "Le Pen non finisce di stupire e i suoi avversari sono disorientati," *Il Secolo d'Italia*, January 12, 1988, p. 8.

[83] Raffaele Bruno, "Si aggrava lo sfruttamento dei lavoratori clandestini," *Il Secolo d'Italia*, January 19, 1988, p. 7.

and prostitution – would "change the face" of some big industrial northern cities.[84]

In such a context, *Il Secolo d'Italia* began defending Le Pen from accusations of overt xenophobia. "He argues that he loves a fellow countryman more than a foreigner – exactly like a father loves more his child than a stranger. Is this racism?" Magliaro reasoned.[85] Even a senior figure like Pino Romualdi argued that Le Pen could be classified "neither like a racist nor like a xenophobe" because he only had the courage to deal with a real French problem, notably the "indiscriminate mass immigration." Allegations against Le Pen were not taking into consideration that the FN leader was simply fighting to "save the jobs of French people and to avoid a transformation of French cities in Third World cities."[86] In line with this, the same MSI leader openly claimed the need for a shift in immigration. In a 1988 European conference of neofascist forces (a meeting that, de facto, concluded the experience of the Euroright), Fini backed the establishment of a strong Europe, which was also perceived as a way of preventing the potential "invasion" of non-European migrants, with Fini concluding "Wake up, Europe!"[87]

Nevertheless, it would be unfair to argue that immigration was brought into the MSI agenda only by Fini. A suspicious attitude toward black migrants had been in evidence in the pages of *Il Secolo d'Italia* since 1985 (before this era the party newspaper had almost overlooked the anti-immigration approach of parties like the PFN). In the same year, the party had organized, in conjunction with the FN, another European gathering in Rome, where they explicitly discussed demographic growth in Africa and the consequent risks of having "millions" of incoming migrants pushing at the borders of the European continent.[88] Some of the articles published during this period took a more philosophical stance, possibly being influenced by the ND, and referred to "organic

[84] Giuseppe Puppo, "La morsa della nuova immigrazione," *Il Secolo d'Italia*, March 31, 1988, p. 5.

[85] Massimo Magliaro, "I francesi guardano a Le Pen," *Il Secolo d'Italia*, April 24, 1988, p. 1.

[86] Romualdi continued that "Il che non vuol dire che non si vogliono i «colormen» ma che non li si vuole senza controllo, ad alimentare in maniera paurosa e delinquenziale la già pericolosa delinquenza nazionale." Pino Romualdi, "Scenario inedito," *Il Secolo d'Italia*, April 26, 1988, p. 1.

[87] Cuzzi, "L'Eurodestra," p. 236.

[88] Roberto Chiarini, "La tentazione della protesta anti-immigrati," in R. Chiarini and M. Maraffi, eds., *La destra allo specchio. La cultura politica di Alleanza Nazionale* (Venice: Marsilio, 2001), p. 173.

communities," "anti-egalitarianism," and "communitarianism."[89] In other essays, immigration was instead discussed like a mere "curse" and "scourge." The increasing number of immigrants was seen as a preoccupation for all of Europe. In Italy, according to the extreme-right press, this was exacerbated by some constitutional principles granting human equality. Nonetheless, the problem was also accentuated by illegal immigration and the cheap cost of labor. This would affect the very fabric of Italian society, with fewer "national jobs." Interestingly, one of the examples highlighted by a neofascist commentator reported that a small iron foundry had "20 Muslims out of 40 employees."[90]

These articles (probably) signified yet more homage to the FN's success and a fascination with its leader Le Pen rather than a full acceptance of the anti-immigration stance as an electoral platform. In a new Western Europe that was quickly, and ethnically, changing, this contributed to the loss of MSI "authority" over a future generation of extreme right-wing parties who remained fascinated with an overt xenophobia – because this was probably the right strategy to preserve western identities and attract voters. Fini's policy to popularize this theme from the FN then looked more like a half-hearted attempt that did not achieve any worthwhile electoral results, and his political line was, in fact, successfully challenged by the internal party opposition, led by Rauti.[91]

An unconcealed xenophobia in Italy would have to wait for the dissolution of the MSI and the adoption of the FN's national preference by the more contemporary movements. However, such fruitful years, along with the early influence of Le Pen, certainly later exerted an impact on the racialization of the ideological outlook of Italian symphatizers during the following decades.[92] Ultimately, in neofascist eyes, "the country of Saint Joan of Arc had given birth neither to any Nazi demon nor any racism. It simply said yes to the national preference."[93] The heirs of Mussolini, activists of the oldest neofascist party on the European continent liberated from the oppression of the fascist regimes, had essentially crowned Jean-Marie Le Pen as the modern king of right-wing extremism.

89 See, for example, Annalisa Terranova, "La 'Comunità' ritrovata," *Il Secolo d'Italia*, February 8, 1985, p. 5.

90 Raffaele Bruno, "Quella piaga dell'immigrazione clandestina," *Il Secolo d'Italia*, February 2, 1985, p. 7.

91 On this opposition and its ideological motivations, see Ignazi, *Il polo escluso*, p. 415.

92 On this, see also Chiarini, "La tentazione," p. 172.

93 Massimo Magliaro, "Ma è razzismo difendere l'identità nazionale?" *Il Secolo d'Italia*, April 28, 1988, p. 1.

ON THE ALLEANZA NAZIONALE

Italy had hence lost its hegemonic role in the European extremist party-politics universe. In the meantime, Fini had failed to keep the loyalty of a majority of his party, and Rauti gained the leadership in 1990. Under him, the MSI moved in the direction of a more national-revolutionary ideology, which, as we know, included third-wayism, anti-capitalism, and anti-Americanization among others, along with a blend of ND-like themes, such as differentialism, the critique of consumer society, and Third Worldism. Yet this was perhaps radical for some of the party electorate. After a defeat in the Sicilian election, another political phase opened with the reappointment of Fini as party leader in July 1991 (who, by that time, had famously claimed, "we are the fascism of the year 2000"), together with the symbolically very important election to parliament of Benito Mussolini's granddaughter, Alessandra, and, nostalgically, with the MSI commemoration of the seventieth anniversary of the March on Rome.

Following from this, at the 1995 Fiuggi Congress, the MSI controversially moved toward the center of the political spectrum and, thereafter, transformed into the Alleanza Nazionale (National Alliance, AN). This development occurred after Silvio Berlusconi's invitation to join his newly created rightist coalition in the 1994 electoral campaign. The party immediately progressed to winning approximately 13.5 percent of the vote, and this also opened the doors to government following the media tycoon's victory. With the change of name, some conservative and right-wing Christian Democrats also joined the AN, while some MSI activists led by Rauti founded the MSI-Fiamma Tricolore (MSI-Tricolour Flame, simply known as Fiamma Tricolore).[94] At the time of its formation, this latter party aimed to be the real heir of "traditional" neofascism, but then divisions became the routine. In late 1997, two of its members, Tomaso Staiti and, especially, Adriano Tilgher (a former FUAN-Caravella, MSI, and Avanguardia Nazionale member in the 1960s and 1970s), established a FN-inspired group, the Fronte Nazionale (National Front, which later became the Fronte Sociale Nazionale), which became a fringe movement.[95]

94 As a further example of the common vocabulary across French and Italian movements, one of the Fiamma Tricolore's internal bulletins, published in Enna (Sicily), was named *Fare Fronte* (Making the Front), which mirrors the name of the previously mentioned French periodical-movement of the 1970s.

95 Rao, *La Fiamma*, p. 337.

A few months later, Le Pen, however, gently greeted this latter movement. In November 1997, the French leader was, in fact, visiting Rome to back the mayoral campaign of one of his Italian friends, the right-wing aristocrat Lillio Sforza Ruspoli.[96] During this trip, Le Pen held a press conference attended by Tilgher and criticized Rauti for his ambiguous approach on the NATO and the Maastricht Treaty. In Rome, Le Pen was particular critical of Fini, who, in his eyes, had only the ambition to achieve power ("any compromise is acceptable [for Fini] to gain MPs and senior governmental positions"). In this reading of events, the AN leader had endorsed values that were antithetical to those promoted by the FN, but also by "Fini's masters, starting from Almirante."[97]

Despite these predictable criticisms, the AN kept its position as one of the foremost political forces in Berlusconi's center-right, and Fini was rewarded with some very prestigious institutional offices. The opportunities offered by Berlusconi probably saved the MSI from an inexorable decline, although all this was also linked to developments in domestic politics. Italy had faced a dramatic collapse of the political system: The 1990s opened with the Tangentopoli (Bribesville) corruption scandal, investigations by judges in Milan (famously known as the "clean hands"), and the disappearance of existing political forces such as the DC and PSI, which had followed the dramatic discovery of an enormous and widespread system of political bribery. This caused public consternation and many protests and contributed to the ending of the political exclusion of the *missini* (who were not perceived to be involved in this improper use of public funding). In a fashion similar to the 1980s coverage of the FN, the media (and public opinion) also showed a positive approach, and AN additionally benefited from "a generous compliance by the left-wing parties and opinion leaders. The reasons for this accepting attitude can be summed up in the desire to overcome, once and for all, the division in Italian politics provoked by the fascist regime."[98]

[96] Sforza Ruspoli, a prince and member of the Roman aristocracy, and well linked with the Italian and the Vatican high politics, perceives himself a friend of Le Pen – whom he had invited to his residence in 1994. The reason for his admiration toward the Frenchman was also because the FN president represented a symbol for those in Europe who supported tradition and the values of the fatherlands. "Palazzo Ruspoli: Cena riservata Le Pen da Lillo," *La Repubblica*, Cronaca di Roma, 1994, p. 2.

[97] Paola Di Caro, "'An traditrice, Rauti ambiguo': Le Pen boccia la destra italiana," *Corriere della Sera*, November 12, 1997, p. 7.

[98] Piero Ignazi, "The Extreme Right: Legitimation and Evolution on the Italian Right Wing: Social and Ideological Repositioning of Alleanza Nazionale and the Lega Nord," *South European Society and Politics*, 10(2), 2005, p. 336. According to Ignazi, this change of

These hectic times led to overlooking the fact that, in the first stages, the evolution of the AN was full of contradictions – including on themes like fascism and immigration.[99] Moreover, political socialization of activists did not really differ, also ideologically, from the neofascist MSI. Party visual propaganda, at times, referred to the iconography of fascism (which recalled, in some ways, the "Back to the future" strategy discussed in Chapter 4). This was particularly done for the use of traditional sympathizers and to preserve an original identity.[100] However, the party managed to maintain a more respectable approach and officially distanced itself from extreme-right movements.

To use Le Pen's and other neofascists' thought, with the birth of the AN, Fini "betrayed" his former beliefs – and then even almost attacked interwar fascism (although not all AN politicians, even when joining the mainstream right, really rejected neofascism and their links with the Italian and foreign extreme-right environment). Other genuine right-leaning figures mobilized their small forces to show that this political tradition had not disappeared, but what was clear is that part of neofascism in Italy had, instead, followed a peculiar pathway. It was also obvious that, probably, the previous decades had not prepared the Italian extreme right to (immediately) match the French extremism's achievements. This was the case, for example, in the cultural field. Volpe and

attitude toward the MSI was essentially generated by two factors: "firstly, the new plurality electoral system introduced a majoritarian logic splitting the political landscape into two distinct camps located on the left and the right. The political and electoral collapse of the centre and the constraint of the new electoral rule soft-pedalled the emotional intensity of the spatial labels, and in particular that of 'the right.' Secondly, the transformation of the MSI into the new *Alleanza Nazionale* ... dislodged the previous party's strict lineage from neofascism in the eyes of the mass public, de-polluting in this way the term 'right' from fascism." Ibid., p. 334.

[99] A discussion the AN's evolution, personnel and ideological platform is beyond the scope of my transnational study. On this see Carlo Ruzza and Stefano Fella, *Re-inventing the Italian Right: Territorial Politics, Populism and 'Post-Fascism'* (London: Routledge, 2009), pp. 141–82; Marco Tarchi, "The Political Culture of the Alleanza Nazionale: An Analysis of the Party's Programmatic Documents 1995–2002," *Journal of Modern Studies*, 8(2), 2003, pp. 135–81; Marco Tarchi, *Dal Msi ad An. Organizzazione e strategie* (Bologna: Il Mulino, 1997); Gianfranco Baldini and Rinaldo Vignati, "Dal MSI ad AN: una nuova cultura politica?" *Polis*, 10(1), 1996, pp. 81–101; Ignazi, *Il polo escluso*, pp. 445–52; Piero Ignazi, "From Neo-Fascists to Post-Fascists? The Transformation of the MSI into the AN," *West European Politics*, 19(4), 1996, pp. 693–714; and Piero Ignazi, *Postfascisti? Dal Movimento sociale italiano ad Alleanza nazionale* (Bologna: Il Mulino, 1994).

[100] Luciano Cheles, "Back to the Future: The Visual Propaganda of Alleanza Nazionale (1994–2009)," *Journal of Modern Italian Studies*, 15(2), 2010, pp. 232–311.

other publishers strongly contributed to the development of an extreme (and also ultraconservative) right-wing culture outside the usual environments, but they did not generate a context for an electoral breakthrough and to realistically influence public opinion – nor were there the sociopolitical conditions to do so. In some ways, this may leave readers wondering if some of the neofascist intellectual activities in Italy in the late 1970s and 1980s were less appealing and "innovative" than their French counterparts. The answer might be, at least partially, positive. Italy of the 1970s probably lacked an intellectual such as Alain de Benoist and the cultural movement surrounding him. His ND influenced the political discourse of extreme-right parties and of some mainstream political circles, especially with the concept of differentialism. Italian neofascists were unable to develop similar elaborations to justify concrete political actions and to lend a cloak of respectability to reactionary principles – although we know that the overall national settings were very different. However, we must understand that the reason for the sunset of the old MSI, and its renewal in almost respectable governmental clothing, was also evidently linked to the will to gain power after a long history of political marginalization (and the long and stable presence in parliament might have, at least partially, led to the conditions for a quick "institutionalization" of some of the party management). Power or renewed extremism? Some successors of Benito Mussolini opted for the former. After five decades in the political ghetto, once the possibility of joining the often dreamt-of government cabinet appeared, the party immediately dropped, at least publically, many references to its past (and to the racism promoted by the FN and the other Italian extremist fringes), and sought to maintain this political – and economic – power.

Yet even this was not the end of the story, and international observers are aware of how recent Italian politics is often full of surprises and *coups de théâtre*. After some years, in 2009 AN completely merged in one of Berlusconi's most recent political ventures, the Popolo della Libertà (People of Freedom, PDL), launched in 2007. From the beginning, this was not a mere cartel party. It led to the building of a single political force.[101] Fini even became president of the Chamber of Deputies. He later left Berlusconi's movement, although the latter in the winter of

[101] See Gianfranco Fini: "'An sciolta in autunno,'" *Corriere della Sera*, February 16, 2008, www.corriere.it/politica/08_febbraio_16/, accessed February 20, 2008. The majority of the AN activists seemed to have well accepted the dissolution of their "post-neofascist" party. Some AN-leaning party currents were, however, active within Berlusconi's party.

2013 reestablished his old Forza Italia (Go Italy) party (and a number of former AN politicians joined this group, while the PDL disappeared). Fini has instead turned out to be one of the media tycoon's most stringent opponents and seems to work for the creation of a centrist-conservative entity, also open to moderate Catholics previously aligned with the center-left. He backed Mario Monti's technocratic government in 2011–12, and was one of Monti's allies in the 2013 electoral campaign with his party Futuro e Libertà (Future and Freedom), a movement that, however, did not see good results in this election. Other former MSI members stepped down from Berlusconi's party for diverse reasons. For example, once the PDL experienced some trouble, the former minister of defense Ignazio La Russa, a very powerful political figure in past years, sponsored in 2012 the movement Fratelli d'Italia (Brothers of Italy) with other politicians from the right. The party dissociated itself from Europe's People Party and is getting closer to many of the positions of the FN, showing a strong admiration for Marine Le Pen. They ended up, however, being part of Berlusconi's coalition in the 2013 election and gaining nine MPs (and even if not in the government, probably their links with Berlusconi allowed La Russa to lead a parliamentary commission). This party also supported Gianni Alemanno, who was a significant politician in Berlusconi's PDL, in his (failed) attempt to be reelected as mayor of Rome in the spring 2013 election. Alemanno, a popular political figure, was another former senior minister and once leader of the MSI youth wing (and also of the Destra Sociale stream in the MSI/AN and the PDL). In October 2013, he founded his own little political group that joined Fratelli d'Italia and its forum to reunite all center-right entities outside Berlusconi's galaxy (named Officina per l'Italia) and especially the *missini*. It is useful to mention that Fratelli d'Italia has a logo including the labels Alleanza Nazionale and MSI, with the symbol of the latter (in fact, in 2014 its official name became Fratelli d'Italia-Alleanza Nazionale).

In other words, it appears that some neofascists have survived in various years in Berlusconi's political entities (and they will be mentioned here and in the Afterword). Some more genuine extremists are instead very active outside parliamentary politics, and they became very noticeable abroad. This is what the next section will discuss.

THE BLACKSHIRT ARCHIPELAGO IN ITALY

As suggested before, Italy lacked many political opportunities for the various neofascist movements, although we have seen a recent bizarre tolerance of some extreme-right leaders and the overall anti-immigration discourse. I will mention again how some of these neofascists are probably not even considered as "extreme right." This is probably also due to the ongoing historical revisionism on interwar fascism, the poor quality of public debates, and linked with the distinctiveness of some recent Italian politics and with the "banalization" of these movements.[102] Alessandra Mussolini, for example, is considered a folkloristic celebrity, a harmless and picturesque character, by the media. This may look paradoxical, as she never rejected fascism. After Fini's official visit to Israel in 2003 and his denunciation of some aspects of the fascist regime, Mussolini – at the time an European MP – left AN to form the party association Libertà di Azione (Freedom of Action), which, since 2005, has been known as Azione Sociale (Social Action).[103] However, she was not alone in leaving the AN, nor was she the only neofascist who benefited from such benevolent media and public opinion attitudes. In November 2007, the influential leader and former governor of Lazio (Rome's region) and minister in one of Berlusconi's governments, Francesco Storace, alongside the former European MP Nello Musumeci, plus the lifelong champion of the MSI in Rome and in parliament Teodoro Buontempo and a few other senators and deputies, all left AN and founded La Destra (The Right). If positive conditions will materialize, this party in the future might become one of the movements attractive for other forces, and the "prestige" of Storace allows good media coverage (although a similar role is being played by Alemanno and La Russa). Naturally, this party immediately tried to create contacts with the FN, especially through its youth organization. These are, nonetheless, really rapidly moving historical times, and La Destra is often (closely) collaborating with Berlusconi, while Azione Sociale disappeared and completely merged into the PDL. In fact, neofascist Mussolini is one of the "fathers" of this (vanished) "liberal" center-right party. However, this did not stop her followers from publishing on the internet a rather pompous letter sent

[102] On some of these themes, see Andrea Mammone, "Se l'onda razzista passa per folklore," *Reset*, 117, 2010, pp. 17–20; Mammone, "A Daily Revision of the Past"; Andrea Mammone, "Su politica, moralità e decadenza: note su destra, sinistra e (anti-) illuminismo," in A. Mammone et al., eds., *Un Paese normale? Saggi sull'Italia contemporanea* (Milan: Dalai editore, 2011).

[103] Fini's declarations on some negative features of interwar fascism hugely upset neofascist activists. In a 2003 press conference with other extremist leaders, Mussolini responded to Almirate's former protégé and suggested that it was instead the anti-fascist resistance that was a negative feature of Italian history. See Rao, *La Fiamma*, p. 347.

by the very influential FN vice-president and European MP Bruno Gollnisch to congratulate her on her election to the Italian parliament in 2008 (this letter is currently available in the archive of the same blog that is rebranded as being part of the PDL).[104] In some local areas, under their center-right collocation, these followers are, indeed, even promoting anti–anti-fascist and anti-immigration campaigns, which recalls, graphically, classic extreme-right propaganda.[105]

However, before this merger, in the early and mid-2000s, Mussolini's group surely represented one of the most visible and popular examples of xenophobic right-wing extremism in recent years.[106] The granddaughter of Il Duce, a former low-profile actress and singer, was for a while the main public figure in this nebulous world of neofascism – and more tolerable in people's eyes than other hardliners. She had a clear prominence also because of the attempts at federating the various extremist movements, such as during the European parliament elections of 2004 when she was elected under the umbrella organization of the Alternativa Sociale (Social Alternative), which acted as a magnet for fellow parties such as the mentioned Fronte Sociale Nazionale (which joined La Destra) and Forza Nuova (New Force).[107]

While Tilgher's movement disappeared in 2008, Forza Nuova is instead showing a significant activism in extremist politics.[108] The movement is led by the notorious Roberto Fiore, a neofascist "shielded" in Britain for many years due to accusations of ties with extreme-right subversive actions and who, in 2008, became a European MP.[109] Fiore plays an especially central role in maintaining and expanding the overseas

[104] Alternativa Sociale, "Il Front National ad Alessandra Mussolini." 2008, http://alternativasocialeschio.splinder.com/archive/2008–04, accessed October 25, 2010. The website to access the letter is http://alternativasocialeschio.iobloggo.com/archive.php?y=2008&m=04. After being published on the Azione Sociale website this letter also appeared in the French blog "Parole de France. Le Forum des Patriotes."

[105] See for examples some of the leaflets and posters used by the PDL in Veneto region. http://alexcioni-pdlschio.blogspot.co.uk/p/attivita-militante.html.

[106] This is usually neglected in academic studies. On the anti-immigration of Azione Sociale (also from a transnational perspective), see Mammone and Peace, "Cross-national Ideology," pp. 292–99.

[107] This lasted for roughly a couple of years, contesting some elections, including the 2006 general elections when it was (controversially) allied with Berlusconi's coalition. Fiamma Tricolore also briefly joined Alternativa Sociale in 2005.

[108] Tighler is in La Destra's various national and political bureaus.

[109] This was a gift from the Alternativa Sociale years. When Mussolini was elected to the Italian parliament with the center-right, she was replaced by Fiore.

links of Italian neofascism.[110] For example, in April 2009, his party organized a conference entitled "Our Europe" in Milan, with Simon Darby from the British National Party and the *frontiste* Bruno Gollnisch – a long-standing European MP who is also very regularly invited to Italy by the various extremist parties. This gathering stirred anti-fascist protests and involved Eastern European groups. Fiore has, in fact, been featured at the first International Boreal Festival in Hungary in 2012 with nationalists from many European nations. France was represented by Thibault de Chassey, president of Renouveau Français (French Renewal), a movement truly inspired by Forza Nuova. They discussed geopolitics and nationalistic history, along with the current state of Europe and the monetary sovereignty (some of these themes will be mentioned again in the Afterword). At this festival, it was, for example, decided to create a national-revolutionary shadow parliament that would serve as a political network and a platform to challenge the EU institutional frame.[111] The following festival was organized in Italy by Forza Nuova in September 2013, and Nick Griffin, the leader of the British National Party, was one of the speakers (although this event also generated some center-left and trade unionist protests, the major of Milan, and Giuliano Pisapia, did not allow it to take place in his city).

This blackshirt archipelago is in evolution also due to the uncertain and highly changeable political setting in Italy, but another movement should be mentioned for the curiosity that it is generating abroad.[112] The most interesting, and atypical in some ways, right-wing enterprise of these recent years is, in fact, represented by a "social" and political group named CasaPound, which took its name from Ezra Pound, the American poet who lived in Italy and admired Benito Mussolini's fascism.[113] It is led by Gianluca Iannone and was basically founded with the occupation of a state-owned building in Rome in 2003. Occupying public spaces for political activities also was meant to be a way to modernize activism and give a

110 Fiore is also the president of the European National Front. This is an association of movements from Spain, Poland, Greece (including the now well-known Golden Dawn), Romania, and Germany, along with affiliates from other nations.

111 Roberto Fiore, "Nasce in Ungheria il parlamento nazional-rivoluzionario," *Forza Nuova Comunicati*, July 22, 2012, www.forzanuova.org/comunicati/fiore-nasce-ungheria-il-parlamento-nazional-rivoluzionario, accessed July 23, 2012.

112 For a general assessment of the recent extreme right-wing environment in Italy, see Giovanni Fasanella and Antonella Grippo, *L'orda Nera* (Milan: BUR, 2009); and Tassinari, *Naufraghi*, pp. 175–277.

113 *Casa* means house and home.

fascist-inspired response to the traditional extreme-left squatted social centers.[114] This phenomenon is spreading in some other cities of Italy, and CasaPound also contested the 2013 mayoral elections in Rome.

The movement is known for its robust, at times violent, activism and the use of social and eco-friendly themes, which include generous social benefits for working mothers, a social mortgage for families, and a critique of global capitalism. To spread its doctrines, it has a youth wing that is active in a number of schools and universities (and it also is setting up a trade union). Its activities are followed by right-wing and "patriotic" blogs in France that often translate or reproduce articles on this group and interviews with Iannone. CasaPound also has a rock band – Iannone is a member – known as Zetazeroalfa. As with extreme-right music in general, this helps building international contacts and promotes further socialization.[115] The band is often featured in France, including in a tribute concert in Paris to the memory of a GUD militant. In addition, Zetazeroalfa recorded a mini-album ("Panique médiatique") with the French band Île de France – and both groups are included, according to some French websites, in the *musique identitaire* scene. Surprisingly, CasaPound officially backed "former" neofascist and then LN European MP Mario Borghezio (who was elected in center Italy) in the 2014 elections for the European parliament. This endorsment was, according to Iannone, because the LN was against immigration and for supporting

114 *Centri sociali* in Italy are traditionally known to be places for an alternative left-leaning social and political dissent. This form of neofascist activity attracted some new sympathizers – especially the young ones. To use Iannone's own words, CasaPound "works on dozens of projects and with various methods: from conferences to demonstrations, distribution of information, posters. The important thing is to generate counter information and to occupy the territory. It is fundamental to create a web of supporters other than focusing on elections. For election, you are in competition with heavily financed groups and with only one or two persons elected, you can't change anything. Politics for us is a community. It is a challenge, it is an affirmation. For us, politics is to try to be better every day. That is why we say that if we don't see you, it is because you are not there. That is why we are in the streets, on computers, in bookshops, in schools, in universities, in gymnasium, at the top of mountains or in the news stands. That is why we are in culture, social work and sport. That is a constant work." Collin Liddell, "In the House of Pound." *The Magazine*, February 5, 2012, www.alternativeright.com/main/the-magazine/in-the-house-of-pound, accessed July 24, 2012. This interview was also republished by the French blog zentropa.info.

115 On the extreme right and music, see Martin Langebach and Jan Raabe, "Inside the Extreme Right: The 'White Power' Music Scene," in A. Mammone et al., eds., *Varieties of Right-Wing Extremism in Europe* (London: Routledge, 2013), pp. 249–64.

economic protectionism, using a nationalist discourse, and, above all, for the alliance with the FN.

It is obvious how this is a galaxy populated by groups unable to elaborate a common political strategy and that are competing on the same themes (and this is reminiscent of neofascist France before the breakthrough of the FN).[116] As suggested, La Destra might potentially act as one of the political "federators" in the coming years – and his leader has been attempting to call for the formation of a right-leaning party including some of his former MSI and AN fellows. The project would be to establish what they call (using the English language) the "Next AN" – fundamentally another Alleanza Nazionale. Even if Fratelli d'Italia included this name in its official denomination, this policy of building a front for all forces is perceived as something significant especially because Berlusconi's Forza Italia is not really grounded in their right-wing tradition (and media tycoon's power is fading). In many circles (including mainstream ones and the media), the old *missini* Storace, La Russa, and Alemanno are seen as respected moderate politicians. Storace, for example, received a full endorsement and support from Berlusconi when he decided to run in 2013 with the aim to become again the regional governor of Lazio (the center-right coalition led by Storace achieved roughly 29 percent of votes). Musumeci similary ran for the presidency of Sicily in an electoral coalition made up of La Destra, Berlusconi's party, and other small movements (although the turnout was very low, and the center-left won the election, he was able to gain about 25 percent of the vote). The party has also inaugurated its new headquarters in the elegant area of the Parioli in Rome (at the time all this served to strengthen the impression of Storace as a mayoral candidate in the Rome election in spring 2013; in reality this movement, along with La Russa's Fratelli d'Italia, supported Alemanno). This inauguration also embodied a strong symbolic dimension. The property was owned by the old MSI. Donna

[116] To summarize, some of the predicaments of these little neofascist parties in contemporary Italy have been (1) the absence of a well-accepted leadership; (2) an excess of *personalismi* and a quarrelling attitude within movements and coalitions; (3) the presence of AN and Berlusconi's parties which attracted some traditional voters of neofascism; and, finally, (4) the influential LN (another of Berlusconi's allies), which became the leading right-leaning force in northern Italy and exploited the anti-immigrant themes. On the Lega, see also Martina Avanza, "The Northern League and its 'Innocuous' Xenophobia," in A. Mammone and G. A. Veltri, *Italy Today: The Sick Man of Europe* (London: Routledge, 2010), pp. 131–42; and Ignazi, "The Extreme Right," pp. 333–49.

Assunta Almirante, widow of the famous MSI leader, was invited to La Destra's home. "I am proud of having her here," said an excited Storace; "this gives us the moral heredity [of the MSI]."[117] Symbolism with a neofascist tradition was similarly kept alive with the candidature of Almirante's daughter, Giuliana de' Medici, as one of La Destra candidates for the regional assembly of Lazio in 2013. Fratelli d'Italia is also, and probably even more successfully, quickly attempting to back a federation with other AN activists, and its recent electoral perspectives are attracting voters and interest. It will depend on how these groups will eventully share a platform, what will happen to the Italian center-right, the results in the various elections, and especially if Fratelli d'Italia and its young party president, the former minister and PDL and AN member and respected figure Giorgia Meloni, will be able to take some of Berlusconi's electorate.

Setting aside the activity of these recent parties, the aim of federating and uniting the blackshirt archipelago indeed was, and remains, a policy shared by a number of extreme right-wingers – and the "winning" example of the FN often gives further impetus (exactly like it was the MSI in the past for the French forces). This was the case after Le Pen's huge success in the French 2002 presidential elections, when the Fiamma Tricolore, to give just one example, signed agreements with the FN for a common strategy for the European elections and, shortly thereafter, the new party secretary, Luca Romagnoli, backed the establishing of a national as well as international alliance of all European "national-popular forces."[118] The admiration for the FN is evident. Romagnoli, especially after he became a European MP in 2004, has been creating strong links with the French party, and his own movement proudly declared that it had opened a representative office in France. Apparently the two parties set some local transborder collaboration across the Italian regions of Piedmont and Valle d'Aosta and the French Rhone Alps. Fiamma Tricolore also often sided Jean-Marie Le Pen during commemorations, demonstrations, and marches.[119] France is therefore often a reference point for this fragmented *neofascismo;* Italian representatives today

[117] "Nuova sfida di Storace per tornare in parlamento. Il 'battesimo' non poteva essere più simbolico," *Il Tempo*, July 27, 2012, www.iltempo.it/2012/07/27/1354777-nuova_sfida_storace_tornare_parlamento.shtml, accessed July 28, 2012.

[118] Saverio Ferrari, *Da Salò ad Arcore. La mappa della destra eversiva* (Rome: Nuova Iniziativa Editoriale, 2006), p. 147.

[119] Fiamma Tricolore, "Parigi 1 Maggio 2005: L'Europa dice NO!" *Fiamma Tricolore Comunicati*, May 2, 2005, http://msibergamo.altervista.org/ft/?p=18, accessed July 23, 2012.

attend almost all most important FN events, and, occasionally, pictures of activists with Le Pen and at FN meetings are posted on their websites – even if, conversely, and I will point out this again, some smaller French groups look to these same Italian extremists to revitalize their political and cultural activism. In summary, transnationalism and transfer with right-wing France also continued for the post-MSI extreme right, and, as the next section will describe, after the first attempts made by the early Fini, many Italian rightists were clearly able to borrow Le Pen's anti-immigrant strategy.

BORROWING THE PRÉFÉRENCE NATIONALE

The previous pages have showed how since the 1980s the FN has constantly been an icon for all these modern right-wing extremists, and Le Pen was regularly invited to Italy, but this fascination also extends to the use of a specific party propaganda. It was, in fact, the *preferenza nazionale* (national preference) that became the most appealing mantra. The national preference, as argued earlier, is a theme characterized by "purity" and by idealized intertemporal communities in the shape of "the West," the "Indo-European," or "Judeo-Christian" civilization.[120] Almost all extreme-right parties across Europe borrowed this vision and often adopted identical programs and propaganda. Indeed, it is also exactly this rhetoric of exclusion that instantly characterizes the contemporary permutations of the extreme right in the eyes of many Europeans.[121] In other words, as was dreamed by some of the promoters of the fascist international associations in the 1950s, this xenophobia became another form of right-wing transnationalism. In this sense, the national preference also turned out to be an effective tool to adapt to the multi-ethnic world, and especially to the fears of white European citizens. As suggested in the Introduction, this as an example of the "contemporarization" of neofascism in a more global society.[122]

Nonetheless, the concept of nation and the primacy of "national citizens" were not, as we are well aware, novel themes in the vocabulary

[120] Étienne Balibar, "Y a-t-il un «néo-racisme»?" in É. Balibar and I. Wallerstein, *Race, Nation, Classe. Les Identités Ambiguës* (Paris: La Découverte, 1997), pp. 86–89.

[121] Mammone et al., "Introduction: Mapping the 'Right of the Mainstream Right,'" pp. 5–6.

[122] For a discussion of the anti-immigration stances of contemporary neofascist parties, the re-elaboration of fascist themes, and their approach toward democracies, see Mammone, "The Eternal Return?" pp. 178–81.

of the western European extreme right. For this reason, national preference simply corresponded to a new mask of xenophobia.[123] In fact, the FN's slogan of *La France aux Français* (France belonging to Frenchman) is not very different from the MSI's 1950s watchwords *L'Italia agli Italiani* (Italy belonging to Italians) – although the tone and goals might have been different (and not excessively racialized for the MSI at the time).[124] At the same time, this narrow stance may also take the suggested wider European significance and connotation – and especially when groups call for the prominence of European civilization and use slogans such as "Europe to us" and "Our Europe" (but once more, they often simply mirror some of themes that we encountered in Chapter 2 when discussing the postwar Eurofascist thinking of the 1950s onwards).

In other words, all this also constitutes a mere repetition of various other old French, Italian, and Western European slogans from the interwar and postwar years. There is indeed a direct link between old and novel racism. In 1964, for example, the EA leader, Dominique Venner, similarly (and already) rejected African migration to France and, in line with the extreme-right rhetoric of those years, summarized his vision of ethnic relations in an unambiguous manner:

> Our towns are going back to the dangerous times of previous centuries, women no longer dare to go out at night, parents worry when their children come in late, whole neighborhoods are taken over by hostile hordes, in our overstretched hospitals, we are paying for a bunch of skivers who abuse us whenever they get a chance. Crime rockets and diseases thrive, but on top of all this, we have got to pay for them! Soon there will be more than a million of them.[125]

Azione Sociale put this same rhetoric into practice in its local manifestos:

> Preference for social services run by the local authorities will be offered to Italian citizens ... we cannot disconnect the fact that those who have roots in an area have contributed through successive generations to the creation of these services over the years. On the other hand, foreigners can obviously not claim the same rights to such services.[126]

123 Balibar, "De la préférence nationale," p. 197.

124 See, for example, the 1950 leaflet "L'Italia agli italiani," in AFUS, FMC, Serie 2 "Attività nel Movimento sociale italiano, 1930–1990," Sottoserie 2 "Propaganda e documentazione," UA 49 "Manifesti e volantini."

125 Dominique Venner, "Bientôt ils seront 1 million," *Europe Action*, 22, October 1964, p. 1

126 Azione Sociale, *Programma politico delle Elezioni Amministrative comunali (Maggio 2006)* (Ravenna: Azione Sociale Pubblicazioni, 2006), p. 12; also quoted in Mammone and Peace, "Cross-national Ideology," p. 297.

In a similar way, Fratelli d'Italia, La Destra, Fiamma Tricolore, and Forza Nuova, for example, generally called for the use of national preference in the allocation of jobs, the use of the welfare system, and all social benefits.[127] Storace's La Destra, among others, even argued that in these fields Italians are now "invisible," and the *preferenza nazionale* would be needed to give national citizens more chances to get city council and state-funded houses and nurseries.[128] Fiamma Tricolore extended this request to the whole state education, where Italians should have a clear priority over immigrants.[129] In 2014, Fratelli d'Italia organized a number of events against the operation Mare Nostrum, led by the Italian Navy and established by the government the year to provide humanitarian help to the huge number of migrants landing on the southern Italian coasts. The right-wing party virulently asked to stop this operation and the illegal immigration, with slogans and leaflets suggesting how Italians come "first." In sum, the successors of the MSI (and some also of AN) played the card of a politicization of an ethnic and cultural (and religious) identity, which, in turn, became one of the main ideological components of their manifestos. By following the FN, they developed – although with different degrees – the ideal that national identity had to be ethnically and culturally homogeneous. Like in France, this essentially meant a rejection of the multicultural society. Across nations, the common denominator was the defense of *this* identity through the promotion of the true domestic culture, tradition, and the virtues of the community, alongside family, and kinship.[130] In Italy, because of its cultural background this also meant a very strong defense of Catholicism and its related values.[131]

[127] See La Destra, "La Destra per l'Italia. Contro tutte le 'caste,'" *Assemblea Costituente per La Destra*, Rome, November 10–11, 2007, p. 8; Movimento Sociale-Fiamma Tricolore, *Programma politico*, 2006, pp. 4–5; and Forza Nuova, *Manifesto politico di opposizione*, 2006, pp. 8 and 15.

[128] Dipartimento Organizzazione Movimento Politico La Destra, ed., *Manuale della Sovranità: i 10 punti dell'Italia di domani* (Rome: La Destra, 2012), pp. 6–7.

[129] Movimento Sociale-Fiamma Tricolore, *Programma politico*, p. 5.

[130] See, for instance, Azione Sociale, *Il Decalogo dei valori di Azione Sociale*, 2008; Front National, *Programme du Front National*, 2006; Front National, *Les Argumentaries. Les dérives du droit de la nationalité*, 2004, www.frontnational.com/argumentaries/derive_droit_nationalite.php, accessed January 15, 2004; and, on the academic side, Maryse Souchard et al., *Le Pen, le mots. Analyse d'un discours d'extrême droite* (Paris: La Découverte/Poche, 1998), p. 95.

[131] This is also related to the preservation of a traditional Italian (as well as European) culture. Forza Nuova, in its document on the "style" that activists should follow, highlights the importance of religion, the need to "love God" and of being religious. This should give party members some further inner strength (as they should also know

The immigrant (the "other"), and especially the Muslim in recent years, is, according to this worldview, one of the main reasons for national decadence: He has no place in white European societies, and he challenges the notion of a needed narrow identity and a closed belonging. "Identity," as Luca Romagnoli wrote in 2009, "also means defending the *ius sanguinis* and national primacy."[132] Migrants from Islamic nations may, in this reading backed by Fiamma Tricolore, even turn in the direction of, or be influenced by, fundamentalism, and this would be a reason why they would be also perceived as a danger in many European societies.[133] After the Jew, the immigrant became the opponent.

TRANSNATIONAL WEBS: FRENCH MOVEMENTS AND MARINE LE PEN

As highlighted in this chapter, the continuous exchanges, transfer, and similarities that have occurred since the 1970s up to the present time showed, once more, some significant cross-fertilization – in a word, of "transnationalism" – across geographical borders. When the old MSI no longer represented the ideal type of the extreme right in a globalized world, the FN was immediately able to occupy the vacant throne. Up to the first electoral breakthroughs of the FN, the MSI was, however, still the main source of inspiration (and of possible financial help) for the French neofascists. The FANE, Lutte du Peuple, the PFN, and the FN all looked to Italy as a benevolent nation. However, Le Pen's electoral impetus, and an overall world that was changing at a rapid pace, shuffled all the cards, mainly in the FN's favor. In such a context, these pages mentioned how the French leader became a genuine role model. To borrow the words used by the (former) FN national youth leader and then a high officer and politician, David Rachline, during a national camp organized by La Destra's young members in Naples in

that a life discipline was similarly relevant for the greatness of the ancient Rome and Roman-Germanic Christianity). Forza Nuova, *Lo stile forzanovista*, 2012, www.milano.forzanuova.info/blog/stile-forzanovista, accessed July 27, 2012. It is worth mentioning that in France as well some parties and movements take a very similar approach.

132 Luca Romagnoli, "Per l'Italia Sociale," *Mozione per il V Congresso Nazionale MSFT*, Rome, December 5–6, 2009, p. 4.

133 Movimento Sociale-Fiamma Tricolore, Dipartimento Nazionale per le Riforme, *Immigrazione (cause, problemi, vantaggi, soluzioni)* (Rome: MSFT, 2011), p. 4.

October 2010, Jean-Marie Le Pen "is a somewhat mythical figure in the minds of these Italian nationalists."[134]

When some encouraging sociopolitical conditions appeared in Italy, it was late, as previously noted, for a strong anti-immigrant party – and the LN had monopolized this theme and electorate. "Political offices," "governments," "respectability," and "fragmentation" were (at least up until the downturn of Berlusconi) the words that could describe the MSI's environment. Le Pen, on the other hand, did not really receive any realistic offers inviting him to join national and regional governments: He instead convincingly played the card of activism and politically incorrect propaganda, becoming a role model for some Western Europeans. Yet after his efforts in the creation of the FN, the long crossing with no electoral visibility, and then the years of some considerable rise and successes, the old leader stepped down. In January 2011 at the Congress of Tours, Le Pen basically left the party in the hands of his daughter Marine, who was already a top FN officer, after she won the vote of the party members in a campaign in which she was opposed to Gollnisch. As readers will recall, the latter was (and is) also quite powerful in maintaining the international contacts of the French movement, and Italy seemed to have a great place in his transnational and pan-European activity (as he also speaks some Italian).

Gollnisch was the representative of the party old guard, and probably a more secure option for some traditional sectors of the extreme right. In fact, Marine Le Pen's strategy worried some hardline neofascists (and she has been recently having disagreements with her father, presently suspended from the party). She immediately tried to give a more modern and less radical image of the FN, playing down, for example, some of the anti-Semitic themes, and this may have, at least initially, upset part of the wider extremist environment, especially outside the French party. However, these grassroots groups in France, as suggested earlier when discussing the blackshirt galaxy in contemporary Italy, are looking abroad for some policies, and possibly at the activism and politics of movements like CasaPound and Forza Nuova.[135] In such a context, it is not really

[134] Loic Baudoin, "À Naples, David Rachline dialogue avec les jeunes patriotes italiens," *Nations Presse Info,* October 6, 2010, www.nationspresse.info/?p=112553, accessed November 15, 2011.

[135] The small group Bloc Identitaire prefers instead to consider the political example offered by a party such as the LN. They are strongly anti-Islam and promote a "triple identity:" regional ("physical"), French ("historical"), and European ("civilization"). See Bloc Identitaire, "La ligne politique du Bloc Identitaire," 2012, www.bloc-identitaire.com/bloc-identitaire/ligne-politique, accessed June 25, 2012.

surprising that Renouveau Français mirrors Forza Nuova in some of its policies. The French group is, for example, similarly promoting a nationalistic rebirth and the forceful defense of civilization by establishing a "nationalist, social, and Christian state."[136] In 2012, these parties jointly organized protests against a theater play directed by the Italian Romeo Castellucci because this was considered morally offensive.[137]

It is, nevertheless, CasaPound that is quickly becoming an attractive enterprise for a number of foreign activists. The widely distributed French quarterly magazine *Réfléchir & Agir*, among others, pays lots of attention to this new Italian phenomenon, and its collaborators and sympathizers are probably among the few abroad who can "really understand what a centro sociale di destra is."[138] *Réfléchir & Agir*'s press, the Éditions Auda Isarn, translated the novel *Nessun dolore* (No Pain), written by Domenico di Tullio.[139] This mostly autobiographical book, originally published by the important mainstream Italian press Rizzoli, is a journey within CasaPound and its members' passions and sentiments. According to Auda Isarn's book description, the experiences of these "twenty-first century pirates" should represent a "lesson of life and hope."[140]

136 Renouveau Français, "Présentation," 2012, http://renouveau-francais.com/?page_id=626, accessed July 31, 2012. Renouveau Français is also very active in promoting pro-French Algeria and OAS demonstrations. This included participating to commemorations for the honor of the French army of Algeria, including the Grand Rassemblement Patriotique organized on June 30, 2012, in Paris by the Cercle National des Combattants led by Roger Holeindre (former OAS, and, as described in Chapter 4, a member of the first FN political bureau in the early 1970s).

137 Forza Nuova and Renouveau Français attend together many international meetings and are creating links with Central and Eastern European likeminded groups.

138 Jean-Yves Camus, personal e-mail communication with the author, July 27, 2012. *Réfléchir & Agir* was founded in 1993 and considers itself an openly European, pagan, *identitaire*, socialist, and anti-capitalist review (see the website for more details: www.reflechiretagir.com). It may be, in some ways, put in line with the mentioned journal *Europe-Action*. Indeed, it featured articles from EA leader Venner, Christian Bouchet, and some ND ideologues.

139 Interestingly, Auda Isarn also publishes *La Maîtresse du cardinal*, the French version of the novel written by Benito Mussolini.

140 "Dans ce roman largement autobiographique, Domenico di Tullio nous parle de son irruption au sein de la planète CasaPound. Une planète toutefois non martienne mais solidement arrimée dans l'Urbs éternelle. Dans les éclats de rire et les bastons sévères, entre un verre au Cutty Stark et une virée en vespa, comment ces pirates fascistes du XXIe siècle ont-ils pu conquérir les cœurs et s'imposer durablement dans le paysage romain et italien? Foisonnant d'invention et de créativité, les garçons et les filles du Capitaine (surnom de Gianluca Iannone dans le livre) montent à l'assaut d'un monde en perdition et hissent bien haut le drapeau frappé de la tortue. Cette nouvelle île de la Tortue n'est qu'à une heure d'avion de chez nous, et vous allez découvrir dans ce roman

This transnational web was reinforced when, in November 2014, the group GUD organized with CasaPound a European conference in Paris (entitled "Le réveil des nations"), inviting the Greek Golden Dawn and some little extremist movements. Apparently this was also made to publicize the Italian group internationally and in France. A number of sources are also suggesting that some ongoing links with CasaPound are presently being established by Frédéric Chatillon. He is a former GUD in Paris, close to Marine Le Pen, who does some work for the FN. He opened an Italian quarter of his media agency, the Riwal, and he seems to use the networks of CasaPound for some of his business activities.

All this may be surprising given the presence of a strong party like the FN that should attract all domestic attention from fellow minor groups. Nonetheless, the reason that some of the little groups and associations look toward Rome is possibly because the intellectual production of the FN is quite modest, while, culturally and theoretically, neofascist Italy at least offers a good number of right-leaning publications and publishing houses.[141] Moreover, some Italian periodicals are directly sold in France, and many extreme-right books are currently translated in French. Ideologues such as the Italian Gabriele Adinolfi and the French Christian Bouchet additionally play a strong role in promoting *fascismo* in France. With a past militancy in Third Position, Adinolfi was initially and briefly in the MSI in the 1960s before joining some extra-parliamentary groups such as Avanguardia Nazionale and Lotta di Popolo. Along with Roberto Fiore, he was also accused of extreme-right subversion in the 1980s and fled to France. Over the years, he became an influential voice, and he is very active in publishing books in different languages, leading cultural and political reviews, and study centers in Paris and Rome (where he is close to CasaPound). The national-revolutionary Bouchet was previously influenced by both Evola and Thiriart, and despite being very far from Marine Le Pen's alleged "normalizing" line, he was still a FN candidate in the 2012 general elections and maintains a significant party role at the local level. A former member of Organisation Lutte du Peuple and Troisième Voie (Third Way), and founder in 1991 of the (now disappeared) pan-European and national-revolutionary Nouvelle Résistance

jubilatoire ce qui se cache derrière les mots CasaPound, Blocco Studentesco, Cinghiamattanza ou Area 19. Une leçon de vie et d'espérance." Réfléchir & Agir, "Les Éditions Auda Isarn: Domenico di Tullio, *Nessun dolore*," 2011, www.reflechiretagir.com/auda.html#nessun, accessed June 27, 2012.

141 Jean-Yves Camus, e-mail communication with the author, July 27, 2012.

(New Resistance), this French activist has been constantly spreading the works of Evola, Mutti, Adinolfi, and many others.[142] Bouchet is also behind the Librad, an online bookshop that has French, German, and Italian translations and sells volumes in various languages.[143] His own books are also translated into Italian, and he was the French correspondent of the Italian daily and website *Rinascita* led by Ugo Gaudenzi, notably one the former leaders of Lotta di Popolo (*Rinascita* also had a section of its website in French and covered many of the political developments occurring in France).[144]

These groups aim to represent a purer version of political (and cultural) extremism. Yet, it would be wrong to consider Marine Le Pen and her Front National like a version of Gianfranco Fini's adventure and a potential change toward a more moderate and governmental political right. The younger Le Pen has not made any real change to the party ideology: It is more about some of the external image. Party rhetoric is, once more, on themes like anti-Euro, rejection of Islam, and anti-immigrants – as she admitted in an interview with a blog owned by a local youth branch of La Destra, both France and Italy should use their navies to stop African migrants from arriving on the national coasts.[145] All this is certainly not comparable to the Congress of Fiuggi where the MSI was converted into the AN. Indeed, Jean-Marie Le Pen's daughter rejected Fini's move as well. Interviewed by *Il Giornale*, a major

[142] On the Nouvelle Résistance see Bale, "National revolutionary groupuscules," and Jean-Yves Camus, "Une avant-garde populiste: 'peuple' et 'nation' dans le discours de Nouvelle résistance," *Mots*, 55, 1998, pp. 128–38. Almost all the movements and activists quoted here have been also discussed somewhere else in the book.

[143] See www.librad.com.

[144] *Rinascita* has been accused of anti-Semitic propaganda. It claimed to be a non-party daily, providing a vision of the national and European identity that is (allegedly) outside the usual circles and against the current forms of capitalism and globalization. See Rinascita, "Manifesto," www.rinascita.eu/?action=manifesto, accessed May 5, 2012. This publication is, in some ways, in line with the "left-wing fascists" tradition discussed in the book, and which also envisioned a third way between capitalism and socialism. It is also linked with Lotta di Popolo's stances mentioned in these pages. *Rinascita* is being investigated in an alleged fraud. It seems to have exaggerated the number of sold copies in 2009 to obtain roughly two million Euros of state funding for the publishing sector. See Lavina di Gianvito, "'Rinascita,' vendite gonfiate per ottenere i contributi per l'editoria: truffa da 2,3 milioni," *Corriere della Sera*, May 23, 2013, http://roma.corriere.it/roma/notizie/cronaca/13_maggio_23/truffa-contributi-editoria-sequestro-2221279615235.shtml, accessed May 25, 2013.

[145] Giovane Destra Lecco, "Una sola al comando. Intervista a Marine Le Pen (Front National)," *Pensiero Nazionale* (blog), March 25, 2012, http://blog.libero.it/GiovaneDestra/, accessed June 18, 2012.

newspaper owned by Berlusconi's brother, the new leader warned how a parallel between the two party congresses (Fiuggi and Tours) could not be made. She would have not acted like Fini, who, in her words, made a choice "so radical that he shifted to the left. ... Moreover, he was allied with Berlusconi, while we will never go with the [Nicolas Sarkozy's] UMP (the French center-right party)."[146]

Italy was also among the first international trips that Marine Le Pen made to establish contacts with like-minded movements (a bit like Almirante with the young Fini).[147] In March 2011, she landed at Lampedusa, a tiny Sicilian island facing Tunisia and one of Europe's gates for migration. Le Pen was there with Borghezio to protest against the EU's inability to stop immigration.[148] The main occasion to reinforce the Franco-Italian transnational web came, nonetheless, when the once popular Edizioni Il Borghese translated into Italian her book *À contre flots* (Counter Currents), with a preface by right-wing journalist Fabio Torriero.[149] This publisher had already organized in Rome a round table on "Islam, Europe and the new European right," with Le Pen and Borghezio (during her trip in March). However, the journey to promote the volume remarkably turned out to be a very fruitful occasion to forge links with Italy.[150]

[146] Redazione, "Marine Le Pen nuovo leader del Fronte nazionale," *Il Giornale*, January 16, 2011, www.ilgiornale.it/news/marine-pen-nuovo-leader-fronte-nazionale-non-far-fini.html, accessed April 23, 2012.

[147] In Italy Le Pen is also benefiting from the ties of former GUD members, the mentioned Chatillon and Jildaz Mahé O'Chinal, who are her communication and media experts.

[148] Borghezio has a history in neofascist groups like Ordine Nuovo and Jeune Europe, but he joined Bossi's movement beginning in its early days. He has strong links with France, including with Bloc Identitaire. As recorded by a French channel Canal+ documentary entitled *Europe: Ascenseur pour les faschos*, Borghezio advised activists from Bloc Identitaire and Nissa Rebela how to infiltrate into society and local and regional assemblies by using a "regionalist" or "Catholic" camouflage ("this is a good way not to be classified as nostalgic fascists") but probably maintaining a concealed fascist spirit. Nissa Rebela is the local permutation of Bloc Identitaire in the area of Nice (in southern France). See Canal+, *Europe: Ascenseur pour les faschos* (documentary directed by Barbara Conforti and Stephane Lepetitt, 2009), www.youtube.com/watch?v1/4lk8vpuajKGc, accessed March 5, 2009.

[149] The review *Il Borghese* and its press are historical rightist publications, and they are mentioned and quoted many times here. They have also restarted their activity in contemporary Italy (although with less success and influence than in the past). According to the newspaper *Il Fatto Quotidiano*, Luciano Lucarini, editor of *Il Borghese*, is one of Le Pen's "main contacts" in Italy. Torriero is instead a journalist involved in a number of magazines that are also very close to the mainstream right. See Leonardo Martinelli, "Il viaggio in Italia di Marine Le Pen. Tra Santanchè, Borghezio e la destra sociale," *Il Fatto Quotidiano*, October 21, 2011, www.ilfattoquotidiano.it/2011/10/21/marine-le-pen-viaggio-in-italia-tra-santanche-borghezio-e-la-destra-sociale/165394/, accessed March 27, 2012.

In particular, on October 20, 2011, she flew to Verona, in northern Italy, invited by Massimo Mariotti, a politician very close to Alemanno. After a sightseeing tour led by an official city council political delegation, Le Pen attended a dinner in a prestigious villa with some entrepreneurs.[151] The next day she had a round table with Berlusconi's cabinet undersecretary Daniela Santanché, also a former La Destra prime minister candidate in the 2008 parliamentary election (in alliance with Fiamma Tricolore), and a noticeable, popular, and very "noisy" leader of the mainstream PDL and Forza Italia.[152] The event, chaired by a rather famous journalist like Vittorio Feltri, was entitled *Europa che verrà: Deux femmes pour l'Europe des nations* (Europe's Future: Two Women for the Europe of the Nations). After the debate, Le Pen admitted how Santanché shared "many similar views."[153] Indeed, the Italian politician was, possibly, trying to use some of Le Pen's themes and influence the policies of her own center-right party. This conference was (at least partially) prepared by a visit in France that Diego Zarnieri, a close associate of Santanché (and also the candidate in Brescia's 2008 mayoral election for La Destra and Fiamma Tricolore, and a candidate for Berlusconi's party in the 2013 parliamentary elections), made in September 2011. The FN hosted him, and he apparently joined Le Pen's electoral campaign and met the French leader to discuss Europe, immigration, foreign policy, banks, globalization, and other related themes. This was also because,

150 This meeting was held in the local quarters of the EU parliament in Rome on March 15, 2011. Intriguingly, it was criticized by part of the right leaning toward Fini's positions, and also by the former MSI daily, *Secolo d'Italia* (a newspaper almost fully controlled of the former AN's group merged into Berlusconi's party), which accused Torriero of having a debate with a politician like Le Pen. Other currents of the PDL immediately reacted against Fini and this type of criticism. See, for example, Fabio Torriero, "Il 'Secolo' è a fondo: ha paura delle idee," *Il Giornale*, March 13, 2011, p. 2; and Alfonso Piscitelli, "L'anatema del 'Secolo' contro Fabio Torriero," *Il PreDelLino*, March 14, 2011, www.ilpredellino.it/online/prima-pagina/78-articoli/4044-lanatema-del-qsecoloq-contro-fabio-torriero, accessed March 15, 2011.

151 "Incontri importanti in Italia per Marine Le Pen," *L'Italiano*, October 23, 2011, p. 5.

152 In the 2008 elections, La Destra and Fiamma Tricolore ran together with Santanché as main candidate, but this coalition was not able to enter parliament. However, Santanché immediately left La Destra, being very loyal to Berlusconi. She was indeed rewarded with the mentioned cabinet position.

153 Marine Le Pen quoted in Abel Mestre and Caroline Monnot, "Marine Le Pen en Italie: l'ombre portée du MSI," *Droite(s) Extrême(s) (Le Monde.fr Blog)*, October 22, 2011, http://droites-extremes.blog.lemonde.fr/2011/10/22/marine-le-pen-en-italie-lombre-portee-du-msi, accessed May 25, 2012. This French daily *Le Monde*'s blog closely followed Le Pen's activity in Italy.

FIGURE 4: Donna Assunta Almirante and Marine Le Pen in Rome, 2011. Courtesy of © Riccardo Vanorio/Demotix/Demotix/Demotix/Corbis.

as Zarnieri suggested, Marine Le Pen was not "alone" in Europe and they were closely looking at her project.[154] This second Italian trip ended up with a book launch in Rome on October 22. The discussants were the usual journalist Torriero, Luciano Lucarini (book editor, *Il Borghese*), Musumeci (at the time a governmental undersecretary and, as mentioned,

[154] According to Zarnieri, his visit was "un'occasione importante di confronto su temi mai come oggi attuali: in un periodo di crisi internazionale interrogarsi sull'idea di Europa, sul suo assetto attuale e sul suo destino è una passaggio fondamentale. Il successo in termini di consenso di Marine Le Pen dimostra che su questi temi c'è molta più attenzione da parte dell'elettorato di quanto si pensi." Zarneri also suggested that he was about to host Le Pen in Italy for a debate, and that, meanwhile, he was going to collaborate to her electoral campaign. See Redazione, "Il bresciano Zarneri in Francia incontra la candidata alle presidenziali francesi Marine Le Pen," *Bsnews.it*, September 30, 2011, www.bsnews.it/notizia/10813/30_09_2011_Il_bresciano_Zarneri_in_ Francia_incontra_la_candidata_alle_presidenziali_francesi_Marine_Le_Pen_, accessed May 23, 2012. The event in Milan was, in fact, organized by the very little known Associazione Vox Populi directed by Roberto Perticone and Zarneri's Fondazione Radici Europee, and backed by Roberto Jonghi Lavarini. As suggested, these activists have political experiences in the various extreme-right and center-right movements (including AN and the PDL). Perticone is considered by some blogs as a personal friend of Le Pen's family. Jonghi Lavarini had links with France and Le Pen's environment, established when he was in the MSI youth wing in the 1980s.

a ruling figure of La Destra), and MP Francesco Aracri (from the PDL national bureau).

It attracted representatives from many of Rome's extreme-right groups, including the national youth leaders of La Destra. Jean-Marie Le Pen's old friend, Sforza Ruspoli, was among the spectators and was interviewed by the French daily *20 minutes*, and he also appeared excited about the prospects to gather together political forces to build Europe.[155] Donna Assunta Almirante also attended the event and celebrated the French leader. "I am happy to see her," she said, and nostalgically remembered when Marine's father traveled to Rome to meet her husband.[156] "History" mattered again, and, in fact, it did not end with the former neofascist leaders.

These journeys might be considered as only the first and most noticeable examples of some attempts to consolidate and strengthen the existing links with Italian politics. This is because Italy is, in many ways, culturally, politically, and symbolically, often at the forefront of the European extreme right. The Afterword will also mention how neofascist Italy is, for example, backing some international networks that try to exploit Europe's new social circumstances and the current predicaments of nation-states (although Le Pen's activity will be also mentioned there). These following pages will then discuss the activities and perspectives of the (European) extreme right in an age characterized by austerity policies, but they will also highlight how the French 2012 presidential elections confirmed the ongoing transnational trend across France and Italy with the consolidation of a right-leaning web, intriguingly including Marine Le Pen, the neofascist forces, and some of the Italian mainstream right.

[155] Anne-Laëtitia Béraud, "La droite dure italienne botte Marine Le Pen," *20 minutes*, October 24, 2011, p. 8.

[156] Donna Assunta Almirante quoted in Mestre and Monnot, "Marine Le Pen en Italie."

Afterword – On the Recent Old Europe

This book has recounted how the story of transfer between France and Italy did not vanish with the fragmentation of the Italian neofascist milieu. If the Euroright's adventure led by Almirante saw the keen interest of French forces, the political landscape changed in the 1980s, and the FN and its policies became an appealing model to be followed, while the pan-European networks are, once more, back and influencing recent European history, politics, and society. This represents another segment of this fruitful history of interactions, which started well before 1945 and strongly continued after the war. As I suggested earlier, historians should play a central role in the understanding and mapping of Europe's postwar extreme right. There is, in fact, the necessity to change the ahistorical approach for the modern history of this European phenomenon essentially has to be written after the electoral successes of the FN. Readers have noticed, for example, how rich the Cold War years were for the development of neofascism and its political and cultural interconnections across nation-states.

This may also open some other questions. Do historical events, processes, and movements really repeat themselves across time? Do they also need to be completely similar to be considered as a transnational entity? The Introduction mentioned how exact replicas of the past and cross-national identical copies rarely exist – perfect duplications are probably merely robotic-like artificial creations for fantasy movies. An example may be more illuminating here: Chapter 5 discussed the similar extreme-right patterns in the intellectual field following the left-leaning rebellions of 1968. However, even the Italian Nuova Destra, a clear permutation of France's Nouvelle Droite, was not a full copy of its French counterpart.

Although the latter movement had success in Italy (and, equally, Italian ideologues influenced Alain de Benoist), even this think tank has some natural peculiarities that were not fully shared by all other similar movements. Nonetheless, interactions, commonalities, and cross-influences very often played a significant role in the making and shaping of ideals and identities. This also shows another facet of this story: In this case, the "transnational" and "international" really merge, and the ND might, at this point, be also conceptualized as a variegated entity with ramifications in different geographical areas (and, in some ways, this might recall Finchelstein's reading of a global and transnational fascism).[1]

As this book shows, these dimensions may be traced and highlighted through the transnational method. The flexibility of transnational history allows us not simply to go beyond the limitations of national (but also European) borders. It also helps to link the international sphere with a more local dimension – and explore the correlation between the two. *Transnational Neofascism* is full of these examples and stories: from the deterritorialization of nationalist ideology in the early Cold War years (with the development of a Europeanism and its use among domestic activists) to the decolonization (with, among others, the interests of Italian neofascists in Franco-Algerian relations), along with the other very recent Europe-wide international and political projects that will be narrated in the coming pages. At the same time, additionally, many other similarities and trans-border associations in Italy and France were highlighted. These have ranged from the analogous resurgence of a nostalgic right after 1945 to the use of a similar electoral propaganda in the contemporary age and included the various attempts to revitalize nationalism, the years of the foundation of political fronts as a reaction to 1968, and the analogous development of a cultural activism since the 1970s. All this evidence should at least offer some more fruitful interpretations and, as I will be suggesting again later, encourage studies of the interconnected history of the right-wing movements. In this sense we should be more prepared to perceive the core of the postwar extreme right also as a transnational ideology, potentially interpreted and reformulated in different geographical and cultural landscapes, at times tied up with a pan-national dimension and a common (imagined) space.

This also means that it is possible to observe some cross-national "continuities" and some historical recurrences across time. Chapter 6

[1] On this point see especially Jean-Yves Camus, "La Nuova Destra: bilancio provvisorio di una scuola di pensiero," *Trasgressioni*, 21(1), 2006, pp. 3–9.

has described the recycling and reshaping of some old themes since the 1990s to fit (and exploit) a fluctuating historical socioeconomic environment. The FN was Europe's key example here, but after the demise of the MSI, it was also transnationally relevant to recollect that Italian neofascism was back again, and this time it also wore the xenophobic guise of an FN-inspired *préférence nationale*. This means that strands of neofascist right-wing extremism survived in contemporary times, and they will do so in the Europe to come. Since the 1980s, a society characterized by immigration, multiculturalism, globalization, and post-materialist values has burst onto the political scene, placing politicians under ever-greater pressures. This has actually generated other unexpected challenges and opened up opportunities for the extreme right. Leaders in some nations exploited these cleavages and the fears of people toward a world that they did not completely understand. They have sought to gain electorally from the sense of social and political exclusion felt by many citizens (especially the white working class) and have attacked mainstream politicians for their apparent indecision when faced by the predicaments posed by a fast-changing world. Movements like the FN took electoral advantage of this popular sense of exclusion and powerlessness by proposing a romantic model of representation and a narrow self-identification, a policy that offers protection to members of the nation, the region, the community, and the group.

The sociopolitical context of this millennium appears slightly different, although with similarly favorable chances. Recent European politics and society have been, in fact, offering some additional opportunities to the rise of nationalist, anti-EU, and right-wing forces. "The battle for France has just started," declared a triumphant Marine Le Pen after her impressive results in the first round of the French 2012 presidential election. She immediately added that her party was ready to defend French identity. This "battle" is, however, wider than this and, perhaps, involves the same future of the European Union and, in some ways, international relations as well. In a historical era facing economic uncertainty, austerity budgets, and a perceived international markets and German- and EU-led interference in national lives, the possibility is to strengthen domestic nationalisms and anti-EU forces and experience the further growth of extreme-right movements along with old and novel resentments among nations – and the electoral achievements of Le Pen and the hardline neofascist right in Greece up to 2015, confirm this possible trend. Some Euro-elites should therefore realize that this is also the outcome of cuts in public spending, fears for the collapse of welfare systems threatened by some supranational powers' hidden agendas, the (unachieved) EU political unity, high levels of unemployment, a supposed weakness of the West, and the impression of a "fortress Europe" assaulted by banks, financial markets, immigration, and Muslims. It is unsurprisingly that Le Pen and Geert Wilders, the leader of the extreme-right and anti-Islam Freedom Party in Holland, supported a pan-European anti-EU alliance of movements (with the Lega Nord for Italy) running in the May 2014 elections for the European parliament with the hope to have a strong group and undermine the EU institutions (the group was then established in 2015 including the LN). The FN won the elections in France (although the turnout was low), with 25 percent of votes, with propaganda supporting the nation-states and backing national sovereignties.

It is evident that this socioeconomic and political environment is included in a wider framework and refers to bigger questions such as sovereignty, national identities, impact of ethnic and cultural diversity on public opinion, creation of a European public sphere, and, consequently, the role of nation-states. Some in the rightist galaxy have been trying to understand this changing western world and adapt to it accordingly. During a *lectio magistralis* in a small literary festival held in southern Italy in 2007 and partially published in advance on the cultural pages of the right-leaning daily *Libero*, de Benoist, for example, argued that nations do not guarantee such "feeling of unity" among the members of the community, and this would be particularly true in an era characterized by the lack of many other (social and political) reference points. This had, in de Benoist's view, an influence on the recognition of the same meaning of identity.[2] It also probably led, as Chapter 6 and this Afterword suggest, to a radicalization of an explicit form of identitary politics and certainly contributed to an updated activism based on the (re)proposition and projection of an ethnic-based pan-European or western solidarity among some narrowly defined political groups and values. All this naturally transcends the geopolitical boundaries of Europe's states. It is seriously further unifying contemporary neofascists and, eventually, helping to forge links with anti-Islam and xenophobic fellows in other continents. As I argued earlier, this seems especially mixed with the troubled EU and national economic measures and the rising tensions among ordinary citizens who feel that there is no clear democratic

[2] Alain de Benoist, "Lo Stato nazione in crisi cede alle identità locali," *Libero*, November 15, 2007, p. 29.

legitimacy for these types of reforms.[3] This is also facilitating the reorganization of the whole extreme-right environment and beyond the usual better known parties, and especially because it is furthermore used like a powerful flag for mobilizing and electoral purposes.

Virtually all Italian right-wing movements are, predictably, using this anti-EU, anti-Euro, anti-banks, and anti-austerity rhetoric. The leader of Fratelli d'Italia in the 2014 European elections, Meloni, along with Alemanno, had a meeting with Marine Le Pen and used a very similar FN discourse against EU institutions and European policies (they saw no MPs elected, although they received roughly one million votes). The link with the FN was reinforced with Rachline visiting Fratelli d'Italia in Rome before the elections in May 2014. La Destra is also one of the most active movements using this political propaganda. Storace's group was criticized by the Roman Jewish community for attempting to (apparently) unify some (small) national-revolutionary forces to build an anti-system and anti-EU party. They, in fact, took part in a meeting called "Aprite le porte ai ribelli" (Open the doors to the rebels), which was attended by some hardliner neofascists, historical revisionists, anti-Semitic figures, former MSI supporters, leaders of the old Avanguardia Nazionale, and activists from a number of other parties (as usual in recent Italian politics, some of them have connections with mainstream politics).[4] In early March 2012, Storace's group organized a demonstration in Rome against the "plutocratic government" led, at that time, by the EU-backed Mario Monti. The perspective was to reestablish Italy's "national, popular and monetary sovereignty." La Destra pompously claimed that thirty thousand "patriots" attended the gathering, and this, proudly for the organizers, included historical symbols such as Donna Assunta Almirante and Prince Sforza Ruspoli. This approach is hardly surprising if one considers that La Destra's manifesto criticizes the Euro and the European Central Bank (in their words, a "private bank"), and it proposes a rather confusing call for the return to the Italian lira until European political unity would be achieved (and then using the Euro for international exchanges and the

[3] Even one of the promoters of this European policy like Dutch Prime Minister Mark Rutte was forced to resign in late April 2012, after Wilders, one of his political allies, rejected what was perceived as an imposed budgetary plan, which was, in Wilders's view, not in national citizens' interests.

[4] Benedetta Argentieri and Valerio Renzi, "La Destra vuole unire le forze 'nazionalrivoluzionarie,'" *Corriere della Sera*, July 26, 2012, www.corriere.it/politica/12_luglio_26/destra-forze-rivoluzionarie_4496819a-d735-11e1-a7bb-b1b271585285.shtml, accessed on July 27, 2012.

lira for national ones).[5] In 2014, La Destra supported candidates from Berlusconi's Forza Italia in the elections for the European parliament.

This propaganda mirrors the Front National's criticism of the EU and ultra-liberalism. Rachline, speaking at a national camp organized in the past by La Destra (mentioned in Chapter 6), in fact reminded his Italian audience how he was in favor of a broad unity of young European "patriots" in the framework of their common struggle against globalization, and to preserve national identities against the EU. This also meant, in his words, borrowing Jean-Marie Le Pen's motto: *Patriotes de tous les pays, unissez-vous!* (Patriots of all countries: unite!).[6] Indeed, the old leader had often been very clear about these themes. During a trip to Italy in November 1997, for example, when journalists questioned him about the Schengen Agreement – a settlement that projected the realistic image of a Europe with no borders – he simply replied that this treaty was only a "sheet of paper."[7] His daughter Marine continued with this tradition. After a meeting with Storace, she criticized all ultra-liberalist outlooks along with this globalization "with no rules."[8] Along the same lines, in a recent interview with an Italian news channel, she accused Monti, then leader of government, of being a bank employee and urged the necessity of going back to national currencies.[9]

As suggested before, these are not at all isolated cases. In an attempt to exploit the social and economic situation, there is, in fact, a proliferation of international networks and gatherings, often with the use of the same slogans. On February 25–26, 2012, activists from Italy, Spain, France, Greece, and other nations, for example, met in Rome to set up a European coordination. Among the promoters was featured the tiny and virtually unknown Movimento Sociale per l'Europa (European Social Movement for Europe, although they also label themselves the "MSE"). This young group, founded in late 2011, has its headquarters in Rome in a location that has a significant historical lineage with a local branch of the MSI (this

[5] La Destra, ed., *Manuale della Sovranità*, p. 3.

[6] Baudoin, "À Naples." Rachline is one the most important FN's official ties in Italy and is highly regarded by Italian activists.

[7] Di Caro, "'An traditrice," p. 7.

[8] "Storace incontra Marine Le Pen," *Corriere della Sera*, April 15, 2012, p. 16.

[9] Forza Nuova, "Francia, Marine Le Pen: Mario Monti è un impiegato di banca e farà gli interessi delle banche, tornare alle monete nazionali," *Forza Nuova News*, May 3, 2012, www.forzanuova.org/attualita/francia-marine-le-pen-mario-monti-%C3%A8-un-impiegato-di-banca-e-far%C3%A0-interessi-delle-banche, accessed June 18, 2012.

quarter is shared with the fellow movement Lotta Europea).[10] As was described in Chapter 2, we know that an international association with the same name (MSE) was formed in 1951, and Rome similarly played an important role in this historical event. Also in this case the basic shared watchword became "Europe belongs to us!" This "Europe" was, again, a spiritual, economic, and political space. In truth, even for a more practical approach of rapproachment with AN (with whom it was associated since 2001) and the center-right, the same name Movimento Sociale Europeo was used in 2000 by a different movement led by Roberto Bigliardo, a European MP for the Fiamma Tricolore, after some electoral disagreement with Rauti. The party was backed by Jean-Marie Le Pen (who attended the party founding congress) and the group of *Rinascita*.

In the case of this very recent Movimento Sociale per l'Europa, their political activism is instead against capitalism and liberalism, Americanization, globalization, and the EU strategies on the economic crisis. Romagnoli, the leader of Fiamma Tricolore, was among the speakers at their Rome meeting in 2012. CasaPound attended the event, and among the groups in this network there was the French Troisième Voie led by the former skinhead Serge Ayoub (until its dissolution in 2013). This latter movement had an extended web of contacts with likeminded anti-capitalist and anti-global extreme-right groupings in Europe and in the United States (with an American organization called New Resistance, and they also seemed to have a local branch in Quebec). Additionally, they were very active in organizing debates and demonstrations. Links with Italy were dynamic as usual. A group named Sinistra Nazionale (National Left – which should be probably close to Gaudenzi's *Rinascita*) was often one of the invited representatives in their events.[11] The group's monthly *Salut Public* also featured a contribution from Adinolfi in a special issue on the "conservative revolution."[12] Troisième Voie should, however, not be confused with other movements that used the same name in French

[10] The Movimento Sociale per l'Europa and Lotta Europea seem to be very active in organizing events in a local pub named Fortezza Europa (Fortress Europe). Marco Pasqua, "Il movimento nel nome di Miki Mantakas. MSE, i neofascisti che vogliono l'Europa" *La Repubblica*, June 5, 2012, http://inchieste.repubblica.it/it/repubblica/rep-it/2012/06/05/news/nel_nome_di_miki_mantakas_la_nuova_internazionale_neofascista-36592593/?inchiesta=%2Fit%2Frepubblica%2Frep-it%2F2012%2F06%2F28%2Fnews%2Fneonazismo_in_europa_-_italia-36683873%2F, accessed June 15, 2012.

[11] The Sinistra Nazionale's link on the website of the U.S.-based New Resistance leads directly to *Rinascita*'s own website.

[12] Some local branches of Troisième Voie have, from time to time, also web links to CasaPound.

history. It is, in any case, well in line with a tradition of neofascism, *solidarisme*, national-revolutionary stances, and rebellion.

"Rebellion" is, in fact, the other powerful watchword in these years of strict budgetary measures. On their website, the novel MSE claimed that a Euro-rebellion started, specifically in November 2012, with the waves of protests across the European continent and the demonstrations organized by right-wing extremists. In their reading, in those days people were expressing their anger toward technocracies and the EU bureaucrats, their financial and social policies, and against the "American occupation" of Europe, while also showing, once more, their "brotherhood with Russia."[13] According to the important newspaper *La Repubblica*, for these modern-day MSE activists, Paris and Berlin are respectively the cultural and economic capitals of this imagined pan-European land, while Rome is the political center. However, it is Moscow – in their words, the "third Rome" – that would have a world leadership, bringing also "peace and prosperity."[14] The international dimension and perspectives are then something well developed also for these neofascists of the new century. In fact, a few days later, two leaders of this MSE were among the speakers at the VII Jornadas de la Disidencia (Seventh Dissidence Days), organized in Madrid by the Spanish Círculo de Estudios La Emboscadura and the Ediciones Nueva República (both tied to the Movimiento Social Republicano) and attended by a number of European extremists.

It may appear that there is, at times, an excessive activism and even competition on themes such as Europe, austerity, and globalization among these movements recently. However, this mostly shows how rich and probably growing these right-leaning transnational webs are, and France and Italy are, as we are noticing here, at their center. Gollnisch was, to mention another example, the president of the European Alliance of National Movements (AEMN), while Luca Romagnoli and Valerio Cignetti (Fiamma Tricolore), along with Nick Griffin (British National Party) and Belá Kovács from the Jobbik (the powerful Hungarian extreme-right party), are in the political bureau. This association was initially established in 2009 and gathers parties from different nations. It was officially recognized as a pan-European party association in the

[13] Movimento Sociale per l'Europa, "L'Euroribellione è iniziata," *Articoli*, 2012, www.movimentosocialeeuropeo.eu/?p=461, accessed November 22, 2012. One of the posters of their demonstration held in Rome on November 2012, had a single sentence ("Europe, Russia, Solidarity") written in a number of languages, starting with Russian.

[14] Pasqua, "Il movimento."

European parliament in early 2012, and they were possibly about to receive an EU subsidy of roughly 289,000 euros.[15] On July 2012, the AEMN organized a conference in Milan, where all invited parties planned the creation of a European think tank (also to "preserve the national identities") and signed a common political declaration.[16] Along with the leaders mentioned earlier, the conference had speakers from other European areas. As a slogan Gollnisch borrowed a Le Pen–like motto: "Nationalists of all European countries: unite!"[17] Setting aside this rhetoric, and the very astonishing references made to Evola's doctrine during the event (in order, I would suggest, to disapprove of the modern era), the platform was very similar to the other cases here described. Indeed, during the discussion Romagnoli highlighted how this meeting was created to discuss the role of the EU and the challenge to nation-states' sovereignty. Other speakers suggested the (usual) reappropriation of the no longer used national currencies, criticized all governmental technocracies, the European Central Bank, globalization, and liberalism, along with a rejection of the usual communism, multi-culturalism, immigration, and Islam.[18] All this was mixed with the promotion of a specific Europeanism,

[15] On the AEMN organization, see also Bruno Gollnisch, "Réunion de l'AEMN à Hédervár: une profession de foi pour l'Europe des patries," *Bruno Gollnisch Blog*, October 24, 2012, http:///2012/10/24/reunion-de-laemn-a-hedervar-une-profession-de-foi-pour-leurope-des-patries, accessed October 25, 2012.

[16] AEMN-Coordinamento Nazionale Italiano, "Lanciato in Italia il nuovo partito europeo: sostegni e adesioni anticipano le nuove iniziative," *Comunicato Stampa*, www.aemn.it/comsto3.pdf; and AEMN, "Dichiarazione Politica. Alleanza dei Movimenti Nazionali Europei," www.aemn.it/dichiarazioneaemn.pdf, accessed July 30, 2012.

[17] Benedetta Argentieri, "La destra nazionalista europea a Milano," *Corriere della Sera*, June 29, 2012, http://milano.corriere.it/milano/notizie/cronaca/12_giugno_29/destra-nazionalista-201811703498.shtml, accessed June 29, 2012; Gollisch quoted in Giovanna Faggionato, "Crisi, la ricetta dell'anima nera d'Europa," *Lettera 43*, July 7, 2012, www.lettera43.it/politica/crisi-la-ricetta-dell-anima-nera-d-europa_4367557103.htm, accessed July 7, 2012. Jean-Marie Le Pen backed the AEMN and sent a message to these activists ("Je tiens à saluer vos efforts pour coordonner votre action tendant à la défense du patrimoine matériel, moral et spirituel de chacune de nos nations, dont la diversité, l'indépendance et l'égale dignité est l'un des plus précieux apports de la civilisation européenne."). See Bruno Gollnisch, "Le message de soutien de Jean-Marie Le Pen à l'AEMN," *Bruno Gollnisch Blog*, October 24, 2012, www.gollnisch.com/2012/10/24/le-message-de-soutien-de-jean-marie-le-pen-a-laemn, accessed October 25, 2012.

[18] See AEMN, "Dichiarazione Politica"; and Luca Romagnoli, "Per un'altra Italia per un'altra Europa," *Discorso. Presentazione italiana dell'Alleanza Europea dei Movimenti Nazionalisti*, Milan, July 7, 2012, www.aemn.it/romagnoli01.pdf, accessed July 30, 2012.

or better, to use Romagnoli's words, a concept of Europe "which is different from the current one."[19]

This challenge to the international organizations is also in line with the traditional extreme-right tendency to reject the EU frame. The call was and is then for a reasonably different Europe – a Europe of free nations, fatherlands, and people, which is the pan-national continent that, as readers are well aware, some Italian and French neofascists have attempted to build and envisage all over the postwar years. As we know, criticisms of liberalism and capitalism are, moreover, hardly a fully recent story – at least in historical terms. There have been generations of third way doctrines and anti-capitalist extreme-right streams, which, among others, influenced the shape of international networks in the 1950s.[20] However, Europe and the international relations are, once more, appealing themes for neofascists. Some of these extreme "nationalists" may, in fact, attract new sympathizers across almost all European states, and specifically with the previously highlighted adoption of a political agenda openly against globalization, financial markets, and the EU economic policies and the measures on southern Europe. Their rhetoric made by references to national securities, narrow forms of territorial belonging, and the defense of local identities, and more pragmatically, of jobs and welfare systems, might generate some interest in these troubled times. This is certainly an additional burden for the Euro-elites, even if the evidence shows that they are probably not focusing on these things properly. This approach may, perhaps, change in the near future – otherwise Le Pen's votes in recent elections in France will merely represent the small sign of a growing political anti-EU frame that is going to influence Europe's life even further for years to come.

[19] Romagnoli quoted in Argentieri, "La destra nazionalista."

[20] In some cases, this critique to ultra-liberalism and the role of the United States were even seen to be in line with some peculiar, although mainstream, national attitudes. Journalist Umberto Bianchi, from the webpages of *Rinascita*, for example, a bit pompously linked Marine Le Pen with De Gaulle's "anti-Americanism" ("La Francia non ha prodotto solo la Rivoluzione Francese, ma anche ... uomini come De Gaulle che, nel generale clima di asservimento europeo ai voleri d'oltreoceano, mostrò di avere il coraggio di dire 'no' al totale asservimento della Francia agli USA. E, senza dubbio, Marine Le Pen, si sta avviando sulla strada giusta"). It is mentioned in another note how *Rinascita* was known for its anti-global stances. In the same article, Bianchi even hopes for the unification of all opponents of this liberal globalization, with the creation of a "wide front" including all (anti-global) political ideologies. This approach was also shared, among others, by Christian Bouchet's Nouvelle Résistance (see Chapter 6). See Umberto Bianchi, "'Destra' italiana e 'Front National' francese," *Rinascita*, May 16, 2012, www.rinascita.eu/index.php?action=news&id=14905, accessed June 18, 2012.

"Neofascism" will also survive in the cosmology of recent movements because the FN and its fellows are not something completely novel in European history. They are rooted in a right-leaning tradition, as the background and socialization of some members as well as the core of their ideals demonstrate. It was, for example, suggested how the same contemporary anti-immigration stance is certain not a new theme. There are, in sum, historical lines that should not be easily overlooked. In other words, just like the MSI was the natural development of the political ferment born with the 1943 Italian armistice and the establishment of the RSI, so the FN showed a degree of continuity with some pages of French history. Similarly, Italian rightist groupings such as Fratelli d'Italia, La Destra, Fiamma Tricolore, and Forza Nuova, which are currently strongly influenced by the FN's political discourse, represent the continuation of the neofascist tradition (the MSI).

Moreover, despite the adoption, in some cases, of a modernized façade, and the MSI-DN-inspired "double breasted suit" approach, neofascism survives also because the same "contemporarized" FN owes a debt to the old MSI. This book has identified an important fact that the literature tends to neglect, namely, that the Italian activists, including people such as Giorgio Almirante and Julius Evola, were a vital force in the European extremist milieu. They acted as a source of inspiration (and a magnet) for other movements and activists, especially in France. In other cases, it was fascist France that influenced Italy: The fertilization worked both ways and favored a shared transnational web and a common (ideological in many ways) space. When discussing the nature of parties, we should then not forget the proximity of the FN with the MSI and Italian neofascism – and Chapter 4 did show the fundamental Italian influence on the establishing of Le Pen's movement in 1972. The same French extremists, at times, remember this fact. In the late 1980s, when the FN had become the example to follow for many *missini*, the French journalist Alain Cochet, writing in the pages of the MSI newspaper *Il Secolo d'Italia*, acknowledged the relevance of Almirante's movement for the French extreme right: "a party [the MSI] that, starting from the 1970s, gave a tremendous contribution to write the difficult, but fascinating, history of the French right. The [MSI] represented, more or less unconsciously, a role model for French right-wing activists."[21]

[21] Cochet, "Le Pen non finisce di stupire," p. 8.

Given this, it can be argued that if one insists on the exceptionality of the FN and its national-populist-only stance (which I discussed in the Introduction), then an analogous approach should be (wrongly) followed for the MSI and its successors in Italy. This is because of the inner transnationality and the similarities between right-leaning France and Italy. If we accept that the FN borrowed from the neofascist MSI, while Italian movements have recently adopted the FN propaganda but they do not even dispute the neofascist label, how should we consider this extreme-right galaxy? Populist and merely new and, therefore, different from the past? More attention should be consequently given to a wider European history made of interrelated values – in other words, to the transnational history of Europe and of its political movements. The reality is also that, for the recent era, we are facing a new right-wing party family with a dual face. Extremism may be considered as an entity with one face looking backward and the other forward to the future. This is what I label the contemporarization of neofascism.[22] This should leave enough room for historians and other social scientists to further explore the inner nature of the extreme right, rather than analyzing exclusively manifestos, voters, and elections.

It is not even really central here to understand if this contemporarization is a genuine recurrence of interwar fascism. What is relevant to highlight, however, for the recent years, is that the borrowing of the FN's national preference ideology in Italy is a reshaping of some older themes and a relevant example of transfer and transnationalism. In this sense, the cross-border analysis (and possibly for all disciplines) elucidates processes, such as xenophobia, among others, that are often treated in specific contexts and as by-products of single nation-states. This shows that the history of the extreme right in France and Italy was effectively interconnected again – exactly like in the earlier mentioned honeycomb structure where the web keeps working. On the other hand, much more needs to be written on other significant geographical areas and on the extreme right's use of the internet, its international gatherings, and on the opposition to globalization, Americanization, and Islam. All these developments are often ways to spread doctrines and membership, share resources, and strengthen links across borders.

Islam, in particular, represents today another essential mobilization flag (and Chapter 6 has also mentioned this issue), although we should

[22] Mammone, "The Eternal Return?" See also the discussion on this theme included in the introductory pages.

also remember that the defense of European native traditions, religions, and civilization – as described in Chapter 3 – was, for example, a right-wing theme at least since the Algerian War. There is, in general, a perception that the media and western governments accord Islam a better and more respectful treatment than the various Christian faiths. This is because they do not want to hurt some disadvantaged ethnic minorities and, possibly, for the fear of radical Islamists. The controversies surrounding the case of the Danish newspaper that published some cartoons caricaturing the Prophet Mohammed were a symptom of this situation. The problem is not exclusively how to integrate non-European cultures and religions in the western landscape, but how to make modern societies work appropriately. As readers know, some have offered an answer: "Stop the Islamization of Europe." Indeed, Denmark really proved to be a crossroads for this extremist stance. A right-wing movement like the English Defence League, for example, organized a gathering in Aarhus on March 31, 2012, with some newly similarly formed leagues from all over Europe, and all worried about the decline of western civilization and the growing presence of Islam. They wanted some coordination at the supranational level and to implement transnational activism and strategies, for the establishment of a genuine European Defence League. The meeting was, in reality, a genuine failure, although it seems that some (very unknown and possibly tiny) French and Italian activists showed some interest in this project. For what matters here, this shows that the extreme right is trying to mobilize forces well beyond the usual most famous movements.

However, for the story narrated in the pages of this book, it may be handy to observe even further the direct developments of the Franco-Italian network in this new old Europe. As we are well aware, in the contemporary era, this web had for a long time a principal actor like Jean-Marie Le Pen, and it would be worth seeing whether his daughter, Marine, also fully takes on this mantle. I mentioned that, since the 1980s, the French FN adapted its discourse to the sociopolitical environment, reshaping its mobilization strategies – and basically replaced the MSI as a leading figure in this imagined transnational structure. It maintained a genuine extreme rightist identity, and this made possible its appeal in right-wing circles overseas. It became the guiding light for the Italian activists, and this also seems to be case under the ongoing FN leadership, and with an unexpected appeal even outside the neofascist figures – and the closing part of Chapter 6 especially suggested this. There are, in sum, signs that this transnational web may go ahead. The French politician is naturally interested in keeping these links and expanding extreme right-wing politics in Europe. In February 2015, she sent a video message to fully back the LN leader Matteo Salvini, also a fellow European MP, in a demonstration in Rome against Italy's government, with references and, above all, insults to Prime Minister Matteo Renzi, immigration, and the EU. Representatives from the Bloc Identitaire, the rising German anti-Islam Pegida, and the Greek Golden Dawn also attended it. A slogan from the organizers suggested their hopes for the event: "We will make History, do not miss it!" It is interesting here to note how this demonstration emblematically assumes a great significance. Berlusconi's troubles are leading to a fragmentation of the center-right with the necessity of a new leader, while right-wing policies are gaining popularity across Europe. If Marine Le Pen is the rising star among disillusioned French voters, the LN is, according to surveys (and also May 2015 regional elections), presently numerically above Berlusconi's Forza Italia in an eventual election. A party characterized by the belief in the superiority of northern Italy is trying to spread its influence in southern areas with the establishment of Salvini-inspired little leagues fundamentally criticizing the authority of the central state. In Rome they were joined by the fascist CasaPound. The respectable right-leaning façade was, instead, represented by Fratelli d'Italia. Overall, roughly 25,000 activists marched, probably for the first time with such numbers and media exposition, in Rome. They gathered in the very central Piazza del Popolo, and, along with the green flags of the LN, some groups were performing Roman salutes and slogans for the Duce. In a significant democratic phase for Italy, with EU economic pressure, unemployment, asylum seekers, and governments giving, for the various Remembrance day, honors and awards to interwar fascist soldiers because of their fights against Tito's communist partisans, more attention should be on this potential coalition between the LN and the extreme right linked to the fascist tradition. The main electoral and political opposition to Renzi might be therefore represented by this xenophobic and nationalist network – one that is nationally organized by Salvini, internationally led by Le Pen, and politically opposing Islam, backing Russia, and rejecting the EU and the United States.

It is then evident that, like her father in the 1980s, Marine Le Pen's ongoing electoral growth in the recent years is generating lots of attention. In April 2012, for example, immediately after the French elections, Le Pen's breakthrough was a reason for some concern in the western world and among the international media. Yet, it was also very well received by some sectors of European politics and society. In Italy some members of

Silvio Berlusconi's PDL backed the French extreme-right leader.[23] La Russa, the politician and former minister of defense who had not yet established his own party, said that he sent a message of congratulations to Le Pen on her "prestigious electoral result," and he was hoping to congratulate her in person (as he was wishing to be invited to Le Pen's speech on May 1, 2012).[24] This was, in one of the future leaders of Fratelli d'Italia's reading, the success of a "modern, European, and democratic right," one that, La Russa added, "loves its own country" and is worried about the preservation of national identity and the current excessive taxation. In his view, the FN had received "four to five percent" of extremist votes, and the dimension of its electoral share made it look more like a "moderate party."[25]

La Russa was not alone in expressing this appreciation for the French leader. We know how Le Pen is fascinating many other former *missini*. Some cultural and political associations and websites backing the Italian center-right (but, as mentioned, probably close to the MSI-AN's tradition) and the extreme right launched an online campaign to "use" Marine to regenerate the Italian right-wing environment. A number of them claimed that the FN did not have a xenophobic platform. At a local level Le Pen is also generating significant interest in many Italian regions. To mention a useful example, Isabella Rauti, the then Lazio regional councilor (for the PDL), daughter of Pino Rauti, and wife of Rome's former mayor Alemanno, claimed that she would have voted for Le Pen. This was for her electoral campaign, and also because the two women had, in her words, "something in common on a family and personal level."[26] Interestingly, also in the cultural field, respected intellectuals such as Angelo Mellone, a journalist and prolific writer who has also been working in universities and for the state television and radio, admitted this fascination with Le Pen. According to Mellone, she would represent an innovator. Apparently, this is for the work she did on the FN image and political platform. In such a context, Le Pen would

[23] It is also worth pointing out that this proximity with the extreme right also caused some criticism within the party.

[24] As La Russa put it, "se Le Pen . . . invitasse esponenti italiani, sarei felice di ascoltare cosa ha da dire ai francesi, sarà molto interessante." Ignazio La Russa, "Francia: Senza la destra non si vince," *Blog di Ignazio La Russa*, April 23, 2012, www.ignaziolarussa.net/?p=1972, accessed April 25, 2012.

[25] Ibid. At the same time, the political right is fundamental, according to La Russa, to win elections, while the "centrist coalitions" cannot represent a proper political answer in the current European sociopolitical climate.

[26] "L'Europa si preoccupa? Entusiasmante," *Il Tempo*, April 24, 2012, www.iltempo.it/2012/04/24/1336530-europa_preoccupa_entusiasmante.shtml, accessed April 25, 2012.

represent "a product of a postmodern and television politics, but in a positive sense."[27] Almost the same story happened in 2014 with the French administrative elections and the EU elections, with La Russa, for example, suggesting that they have historical affinities and the same symbol, and Alemanno and Meloni using this to strengthen their anti-Euro discourse.

Comically, all this looks, at times, also like a race for the (best) friendship with the French star. A remarkable case is here represented by the "mainstream" Daniela Santanché. Interviewed in 2012 by *Il Giornale*, Santanché warned – with some great exaggeration, though, as we know with some little truth – that she was the only politician "inviting Marine Le Pen in Italy, while now all pretend to be her friends." She therefore proudly admitted that she invited Marine for dinner at her house in Milan during the discussed Italian trip of late 2011 (in which they had the debate on Europe chaired by the journalist Feltri) and contributed to introducing her French fellow to some representatives of Italy's high society. The PDL had to, Santanché claimed,

> think hard about Le Pen's policies. ... I agree with her. ... We need to defend our identity, sovereignty, our companies. ... And on immigration is she not right? Our party should change its name, consider the adoption of a more powerful political program, ... one more distant from the centrist [ideological] positions.[28]

Ironically enough, when asked about the reactions of Berlusconi, her leader, on Le Pen's previous trips to Italy and the meetings with center-right politicians, she also said, "he agreed. ... He always believed in women."[29] In a more serious tone, and aside from his famous Bunga Bunga scandal, this also shows how Berlusconi has been able to maintain a gray link with the Italian extreme-right cultural environment.

This mainstream approach toward the FN is probably also symptomatic of the politics and political system in recent years in Italy.[30] For a

[27] Angelo Mellone, "Marine Le Pen è la vera vincitrice: la sua destra parla ai giovani," *Il Tempo*, April 23, 2012, www.iltempo.it/2012/04/23/1336310-angelo_mellone_vero_fenomeno_primo_turno_presidenziale_francia_volto_donna_marine.shtml.

[28] Manila Alfano, "Daniela Santanchè: 'In Italia ero l'unica a invitare Marine, ora tutti amici,'" *Il Giornale*, April 24, 2012, www.ilgiornale.it/interni/il_cavaliere_era_daccordo_crede_donne_lei_non_ha_preconcetti/24-04-2012/articolo-id=584512-page=0-comments=1, accessed April 25, 2012.

[29] Ibid.

[30] On the political situation in Italy, see generally Andrea Mammone and Giuseppe A. Veltri, "Un Paese smarrito," and Mammone, "Su politica, moralità e decadenza" in A. Mammone et al., eds., *Un Paese normale? Saggi sull'Italia contemporanea*

while Santanché was even considered Berlusconi's likely choice as party leader for the 2013 parliamentary elections, and then an eventual vice-leader in an electoral ticket with the tycoon. As suggested here, other politicians like La Russa, Alessandra Mussolini, and Alemanno are not considered as belonging to an extremist fringe. They are, or were, all part of Berlusconi's center-right, which, at the EU parliamentary level, is in the moderate European People's Party group. This should lead us discuss the fact that, probably, in some cases the line of demarcation between some of the mainstream and extreme right is more porous and flexible than imagined. This similarly shows how fascism has been, at least partially, legitimized in Italian society. Second, this also tells us that Berlusconi has undoubtedly managed to attract some of the extremist electorate (setting aside the merger with AN and the *missini* joining the government). This happened also for his anti-communist rhetoric and because it represented the most significant and powerful figure on the right-wing side of the political spectrum.

It is also useful to underline that Marine Le Pen is also enjoying a more favorable environment in France, and recent electoral results seem to confirm this. Surveys at the beginning of 2014 showed an acceptance of Le Pen's image in part of the French society. Fifty-six percent of the interviewees thought that "she understands the daily predicaments of the French people," while forty-six percent seemed to believe that she represents "a patriotic right linked with the traditional values." Voters of the traditional center-right were also becoming attracted by the FN politician (as they are lacking strong political leadership at this stage). Forty-four percent of them would consider some alliances with Le Pen's movement at a local level. This does not mean a full recognition of the FN discourse (a very high number of people still believe that she is a "danger for democracy"). However, it suggests how Le Pen's approach, image, and appeal are at least partially working.

However, if we keep again our transnational story in focus, Le Pen unsurprisingly was similarly taken as a key example by the other usual right-wing political forces. After the French elections, an excited Storace announced that his party put thousands of posters up in Rome. These

(Milan: Dalai editore, 2011), pp. 21–46 and 452–77; Andrea Mammone and Giuseppe A. Veltri, "'A Sick Man' in Europe," in A. Mammone and G. A. Veltri, eds., *Italy Today: The Sick Man of Europe* (London: Routledge, 2010), pp. 1–15; and Andrea Mammone, "Italy's Moral Crisis," *Soundings: A Journal of Politics and Culture*, 46(3), 2010, pp. 64–75.

were banners, showing big picture of Marine Le Pen with the La Destra logo, along with a celebration of her partial victory. The hope was that "the right-wing wind blowing from the Alps" was, to use Storace's argument, arriving in Italy.[31] The French politician had clearly gained the leadership of an ideal "front of Europe's nations," and, in the eyes of Italian neofascists, this may generate some advantageous opportunities for a European right led by Le Pen. Indeed, this electoral achievement represented, Storace continued, the starting point of the type of "Europe that we want, Marine Le Pen's Europe, our Europe."[32]

Just as La Russa was not the only politician on the (would-be) moderate right to praise Le Pen and the FN in 2012, Storace had many other likeminded followers on the extreme right-wing front. Forza Nuova leader Fiore also sent a personal note of congratulations.[33] In a statement he mentioned how the victory of the FN represented a reaction to the lack of national and monetary sovereignties and essentially mapped out the way for a national renaissance.[34] However, it is La Destra's activism (and presently Fratelli d'Italia's one) that may potentially generate some other links also at a more institutional level. This recent strong interest in Le Pen's activity, and her promotion in Italy, looked like another step of a friendship that Storace's party is currently trying to establish with the FN. Just before the election on March 30, a La Destra youth-wing delegation

[31] Francesco Storace, "Vince la coerenza," *Blog di Francesco Storace*, April 24, 2012, www.storace.it/2012/04/24/vince-la-coerenza, accessed April 25, 2012.

[32] Francesco Storace, "Oui, La France," *Blog di Francesco Storace*, April 23, 2012, www.storace.it/2012/04/23/oui-la-france, accessed April 23, 2012; Tommaso Caldarelli, "Vi racconto Marine Le Pen e la nuova destra europea," *Giornalettismo*, April 23, 2012, www.giornalettismo.com/archives/270892/vi-racconto-marine-le-pen-e-la-nuova-destra-europea, accessed April 25, 2012. In February 2015, Marine Le Pen tried to distance the FN from her father and his usual stances about European and French history and the role of fascism. This also meant started opposing Jean-Marie Le Pen's eventual candidature in a regional election, with the hope for her of running in a more moderate guise in the presidential election. However, I would suggest that there are no huge differences in their actual policies, including immigration and European integration. See my article "Don't Be Fooled by 'Moderate' Marine Le Pen: Front National's More Toxic than Ever," *The Guardian*, February 11, 2015, www.theguardian.com/commentisfree/2015/apr/10/dont-be-fooled-by-marine-le-pen-front-national-toxic, accessed February 15, 2015.

[33] This message was sent through Bruno Gollnisch. This politician has regular contacts with Forza Nuova (and Fiamma Tricolore). He was also scheduled to appear at the 2012 mayoral campaign in Verona to back the local candidate from Fiore's party.

[34] Roberto Fiore, "La vittoria del Front National traccia il cammino per la Rinascita Nazionale," *Forza Nuova Comunicati*, April 23, 2012, www.forzanuova.org/comunicati/fiore-fnla-vittoria-del-front-national-traccia-il-cammino-la-rinascita-nazionale, accessed April 25, 2012.

was, for example, sent to a FN meeting to back Le Pen's candidature. According to their own press release, they had the chance to get together with many FN officers and with Rachline.[35] This continued with invitations to the FN national summer convention (the *université d'été*) and other debates during the parliamentary election and meetings with Jean-Marie Le Pen and other politicians. On April 13, 2012, Storace traveled to Nanterre, near Paris, to meet Marine Le Pen. This was the first meeting with the French leader, and they discussed the economic and international situation and the opportunities to push further right-wing party politics in Europe.[36]

What has been described so far in this Afterword was also necessary to remind us again that, although there were reasons for an apparent divergence (in the sense of the political trajectories of the FN and AN, Jean-Marie Le Pen and Gianfranco Fini), this by no means represented the end of the transfer that developed since the immediate postwar years. It confirms that transnationalism has not, in fact, vanished. Intriguingly, Fini's enterprise was probably taken as an example across the Alps. When Bruno Mégret established the Mouvement National Républicain, he played, at least initially, the card of an insertion into mainstream politics, exactly as Fini had been able to do with AN. Another similarity is, in recent years, the role of women like Marine Le Pen, Alessandra Mussolini, and Daniela Santanché – who are often perceived as the modern (even acceptable) faces of the right-wing galaxy. These are other examples of the neofascist commonality, networks, and shared history.

It is then obvious how the neofascist right can be studied as single domestic unit and as a larger whole. It is, nonetheless, exactly this latter that can enrich our understanding of European political history (and, once more, the transnational historical frame is allowing us to specifically observe the extreme right like a phenomenon not strictly and merely related to defined territorial spaces). There is really, in this sense, the need to place the developments of the extreme right in more openly European

[35] Gioventù Italiana, "Gioventù Italiana sostiene Marine Le Pen," *Gioventù Italiana – Informazione,* www.gioventuitaliana.org/?p=4574, accessed April 24, 2012.

[36] It was Storace who expressively asked for this meeting with Le Pen. See "Storace incontra Marine Le Pen," *Corriere della Sera*, April 15, p. 16, and Abel Mestre and Caroline Monnot, "Marine Le Pen a rencontré Francesco Storace, figure de l'extrême droite italienne," *Droite(s) Extrême(s) (Le Monde.fr Blog)*, April 15, 2012, http://droites-extremes.blog.lemonde.fr/2011/10/22/marine-le-pen-en-italie-lombre-portee-du-msi, accessed April 15, 2012.

frameworks, and by considering mutual influences, interactions, and transfer between nations. For these reasons, *Transnational Neofascism* has suggested a focus on some political entities as a whole, on their interrelated histories, on forms of socialization, and on their similar ideology.

Consequently, and very fascinatingly, this right-leaning tradition may be taken as a transnational, and even international, actor, such as the "joint" Franco-Italian enterprise explored in the book. This will hopefully further open gateways on the non-national dimensions of the extreme right's politics – a subject that, as we know, has often been studied solely in the limits of a geographical territory and nationalist ideological landscape. However, if one looks at the French and Italian materializations of this phenomenon, the galaxy of rightist nationalism is made by interactions, from the borrowing of the Destra Nazionale project by the activists of Ordre Nouveau to the Italian fascination with French fascists like Pierre Drieu la Rochelle and Robert Brasillach, from the use of Julius Evola in France to Giorgio Almirante's Euroright project with the Parti des Forces Nouvelles, from the ND-inspired Hobbit Camps in Italy to Maurice Bardèche's admiration for the Salò Republic, from the *Europe-Action* interest in Italian neofascist themes to Ordine Nuovo promoting French organizations, and so on.

The transnational frame may be borrowed by other types of studies (including outside the extreme-right field). France and Italy are not isolated cases. The history of the extreme right, and nationalism, in Europe is very rich with "encounters." Setting aside the extreme-right wind blowing from the west in the direction of other regions of Europe, exchanges are, for example, very evident between Italy and the other southern European and Mediterranean areas, in the Germanic world, across the Francophone and the French-speaking areas, between the British and the Italian extreme right, in many borderland regions, through international gatherings, associations of soccer hooligans, and, last but not least, by means of collaboration at the EU parliamentary level. It would be impossible to list here all of the ongoing academic studies in these fields, but more research is needed by scholars to fully understand the evolution of some nationalistic tendencies in the postwar years, as well as the richness of the European political cultures.

It is true that the wheel is not being reinvented. Europe itself is old and porous, and the use of "a transnational perspective on European history, and the concern for connections and circulations, was certainly advocated, albeit in a different wording, many decades ago."[37] Something more and novel, nonetheless, may be said. Contributions such as this book should encourage researchers to look across national boundaries when they explore the different dimensions of politics in postwar Europe: by considering, for example, the foreign influences on national phenomena, the movement of ideals, the fascination with non-domestic paradigms, the reelaboration of external strategies, the reformulation of overseas events, the borrowing of foreign thinkers, and the sharing of philosophies. To put it simply, we should attempt to highlight the transnational dimensions and the intersections of national and international phenomena.

In sum, what these pages have tried to offer is a more fruitful reading of the past, shedding light on political strategies, and hopefully setting the agenda for future studies. It is, in fact, possible, and very rewarding, to write and trace historical trajectories and journeys across times and, above all, space. The book has therefore been one of these long journeys, one that has lasted more than half a century. It has been a journey where we have encountered passions, ideals, and activists throughout the postwar history of the extreme right, and it has involved the crossing and recrossing of the lands of a long-standing interrelated Europe.

[37] Saunier, "Learning by Doing," p. 177.

Bibliography

Periodicals

Azione
Charta Minuta
Corriere della Sera
Corrispondenza Repubblicana
Creatività
Défense de l'Occident
Diorama Letterario
Éléments
Europe Action
Europa Sociale
Europe Action Hebdomadaire
Faire Front!
Fraternité Française
Gerarchia
GUD-OCCIDENTE-UNIVERSITE
I Quaderni dell'Alternativa
Il Borghese
Il Conciliatore
Il Fatto Quotidiano
Il Giornale
Il Machiavelli
Il Piccolo
Il Secolo d'Italia
Il Tempo

Imperium
Italia Tricolore
Je suis partout
Jeune Nation
L'Italiano
L'Ordine Sociale
L'Orologio
L'Uomo qualunque
La Rivolta Ideale
La Sentinelle
La Sfida
Le Choc du Mois
Le Figaro-Magazine
Le Monde
Liberazione
Libero
Meridiano d'Italia
Milano-sera
Minute
National Hebdo
Nazionalismo Sociale
Notre Europe
Nouvelle Ecole
Ordine Nuovo
Politica
Quaderni di Ordine Nuovo
Rataplan
REL
Rivarol
Rivista Italiana di Studi Corporativi
20 minutes
Union

Special collections

Archivio Centrale di Stato (Rome), Ministero dell'Interno, Direzione Generale di Pubblica Sicurezza, Divisione Servizi Informativi Speciali

Archivio Fondazione Ugo Spirito (Rome), Fondo Mario Cassiano and Fondo Movimento Sociale Italiano

Bibliothèque de Documentation Internationale Contemporaine (Nanterre, Paris), Fonds Jacques Delarue

Other sources

Aa.Vv., "Dibattito," in Aa.Vv., *Proviamola nuova. Atti del seminario "Ipotesi e strategia di una nuova destra"* (Rome: L.ED.E., 1980)

La guerra rivoluzionaria. Atti del Primo Convegno organizzato dall'Istituto Pollio (Rome: Edizioni Giovanni Volpe, 1965)

Adler, F., "On the French Right – New and Old: An Interview with Alain de Benoist," *Telos*, 126, 2003

AEMN, "Dichiarazione Politica. Alleanza dei Movimenti Nazionali Europei," 2012 (online: www.aemn.it/dichiarazioneaemn.pdf)

AEMN-Coordinamento Nazionale Italiano, "Lanciato in Italia il nuovo partito europeo: sostegni e adesioni anticipano le nuove iniziative," *Comunicato Stampa*, 2012 (online: www.aemn.it/comsto3.pdf)

Affron, M. and Mark Antliff, "Art and Fascist Ideology in France and Italy: An Introduction," in M. Affron and M. Antliff, eds., *Fascist Visions: Art and Ideology in France and Italy* (Princeton: Princeton University Press, 1997)

Albanese, M. and Del Hierro, P., "A Transnational Network: The Contact between Fascist Elements in Spain and Italy, 1943–1968," *Politics, Religion & Identity*, 15(1), 2014

Algazy, J., *L'extrême-droite en France de 1965 à 1984* (Paris: L'Harmattan, 1989)

La tentation néo-fasciste en France de 1944 à 1965 (Paris: Fayard, 1984)

Alternativa Sociale, "Il Front National ad Alessandra Mussolini," 2008 (online: http://alternativasocialeschio.iobloggo.com/archive.php?y=2008&m=04)

Ariès, P., *Un historien du dimanche* (Paris: Seuil, 1980)

Aron, R., (in collaboration with G. Elgey), *Historie de Vichy. 1940–1944* (Paris: Fayard, 1954)

Art, D., *Inside the Radical Right: The Development of Anti-Immigrant Parties in Western Europe* (New York: Cambridge University Press, 2011)

The Politics of the Nazi Past in Germany and Austria (New York: Cambridge University Press, 2006)

Avanza, M., "The Northern League and Its 'Innocuous' Xenophobia," in A. Mammone and G. A. Veltri, *Italy Today. The Sick Man of Europe* (London: Routledge, 2010)

Azione Sociale, *Il Decalogo dei valori di Azione Sociale*, 2008

Programma politico delle Elezioni Amministrative comunali (Maggio 2006) (Ravenna: Azione Sociale Pubblicazioni, 2006)

Baudoin, L., "À Naples, David Rachline dialogue avec les jeunes patriotes italiens," *Nations Presse Info*, October 6, 2010 (online: www.nationspresse.info/?p=112553)

Baldini, G. and Vignati, R., "Dal MSI ad AN: una nuova cultura politica?" *Polis*, 10(1), 1996

Bale, J. M., "'National Revolutionary' Groupuscules and the Resurgence of 'Left-Wing' Fascism: The Case of France's Nouvelle Résistance," *Patterns of Prejudice*, 36(3), 2002
Balibar, É., "Y a-t-il un 'néo-racisme'?" in É. Balibar and I. Wallerstein, eds., *Race, Nation, Classe. Les Identités Ambiguës* (Paris: La Découverte, 1997)
"De la 'préférence nationale' à l'invention de la politique: comme lutter contre le néofascisme?" in J. Viard, ed., *Aux source du populisme nationaliste. L'urgence de comprendre Toulon, Orange, Marignane* (La Tour d'Aigues: Éditions de L'Aube, 1996)
Baldoni, A., *La Destra in Italia. 1945–1969* (Rome: Editoriale Pantheon, 2000)
Il Crollo dei Miti. Utopie, Ideologie, Estremismi (Rome: Settimo Sigillo, 1996)
Bar-On, T., "Transnationalism and the French *Nouvelle Droite*," *Patterns of Prejudice*, 45(3), 2011
"Understanding Political Conversion and Mimetic Rivarly," *Totalitarian Movements and Political Religions*, 10(3–4), 2009
"Fascism to the Nouvelle Droite: The Dream of Pan-European Empire," *Journal of Contemporary European Studies*, 16(3), 2008
Where Have All Fascists Gone? (Aldershot, Hampshire: Ashgate, 2007)
"The Ambiguities of the *Nouvelle Droite*, 1968–1999," *European Legacy*, 6(3), 2001
Bardèche, M., "Introduction," in F. Duprat, ed., *Les journées de Mai 68. Les dessous d'une révolution* (Paris: Nouvelles Éditions Latines, 1968)
"Post-Face," in F. Duprat, ed., *Les journées de Mai 68. Les dessous d'une révolution* (Paris: Nouvelles Éditions Latines, 1968)
Che cosa è il fascismo? (Rome: Edizioni Giovanni Volpe, 1963)
Qu'est-ce que le fascisme? (Paris: Les Sept Couleurs, 1961)
Nuremberg ou la terre promise (Paris: Les Sept Couleurs 1948)
Lettre à François Mauriac (Paris: La Pensée Libre 1947)
Barnes, I., "A Fascist Trojan Horse: Maurice Bardèche, Fascism and Authoritarian Socialism," *Patterns of Prejudice*, 37(2), 2003
"Intellectual Processes on the French Far Right," *Patterns of Prejudice*, 16(1), 1982
Berlin, I., *Against the Current. Essays in the History of Ideas* (London: Hogarth Press, 1979)
Bertagna, F., *La patria di riserva. L'emigrazione fascista in Argentina* (Rome: Donzelli Editore, 2006)
Betz, H.-G., "Contemporary Right-Wing Radicalism in Europe," *Contemporary European History*, 8(2), 1999
Bianchi, U., "'Destra' italiana e 'Front National' francese," *Rinascita*, May 16, 2012 (online: www.rinascita.eu/index.php?action=news&id=14905)
Bihr, A., *L'actualité d'un archaïsme. La pensée d'extrême droite et la crise de la modernité* (Lausanne: Page deux, 1998)
Binet, R., *Théorie du racisme* (Paris: Éditions des Vikings, 1950)
Birnbaum, P., "The French Radical Right: From Anti-Semitic Zionism to Anti-Semitic Anti-Zionism," *Journal of Israeli History*, 25(1), 2006
Bloc Identitaire, "La ligne politique du Bloc Identitaire," 2012 (online: www.bloc-identitaire.com/bloc-identitaire/ligne-politique)

Bonnafous, S., *L'immigration prise aux mots. Les immigrés dans la presse au tournant des années 80* (Paris: Éditions Kimé, 1991)

Borne, D., *Petits-bourgeois en révolte? Le mouvement Poujade* (Paris: Flammarion, 1977)

Bosworth, R. J., "War, Totalitarianism and 'Deep Belief' in Fascist Italy, 1935–43," *European History Quarterly*, 34(4), 2004

Brunn, J., *La Nouvelle Droite. Le dossier du " procès"* (Paris: Nouvelles éditions Oswald, 1979)

Buton, P. "Occupation, Liberation, Purges: The Changing Landscape of French Memory," in A. Knapp, ed., *The Uncertain Foundation: France at the Liberation, 1944–47* (Basingstoke: Palgrave Macmillan, 2007)

Caciagli, M., "The Movimento Sociale Italiano-Destra Nazionale and Neo-Fascism in Italy," in K. Von Beyme, ed., *Right-Wing Extremism in Western Europe* (London: Frank Cass, 1988)

Cacciola, B., *Appunti per una storia del M.S.I.* (Rome: Fuan, 1990)

Caldarelli, T., "Vi racconto Marine Le Pen e la nuova destra europea," *Giornalettismo*, April 23, 2012 (online: www.giornalettismo.com/archives/270892/vi-racconto-marine-le-pen-e-la-nuova-destra-europea)

Cambadélis, J.-C. and Osmond, E., *La France blafarde. Une histoire politique de l'extrême droite* (Paris: Plon, 1998)

Camus, J.-Y., "La Nuova Destra: bilancio provvisorio di una scuola di pensiero," *Trasgressioni*, 21(1), 2006

"Nostalgia and Political Impotence: Neo-Nazi and Extreme Right Movements in France, 1944–64," in E. J. Arnold, ed., *The Development of the Radical Right in France. From Boulanger to Le Pen* (New York: St. Martin's Press, 2000)

Le Front National (Toulouse: Editions Milan, 1998)

"Une avant-garde populiste: 'peuple' et 'nation' dans le discours de Nouvelle résistance," *Mots*, 55, 1998

and Monzat, R., *Les Droites nationales et radicales en France* (Lyon: Presses Universitaires de Lyon, 1992)

Canal+, *Europe: Ascenseur pour les faschos* (documentary directed by Barbara Conforti and Stephane Lepetitt), 2009 (online: www.youtube.com/watch?v1/4lk8vpuajKGc)

Caprettini, A., *La nuova destra. E quindi uscimmo a riveder le stelle...* (Palermo: Arbor, 1995)

Carocci, G., *Destra e sinistra nella storia d'Italia* (Rome: Laterza, 2002)

Carter, E., *The Extreme Right in Western Europe: Success or Failure?* (Manchester: Manchester University Press, 2005)

Cassata, F., *A destra del fascismo. Profilo politico di Julius Evola* (Turin: Bollati Boringhieri, 2003)

Catofiglio, V. and Ferrandes, C., "Les aventures de la droite française et les avatars de Gramsci," *Mots*, 12, 1986

Cento Bull, A., "Neofascism," in R. Bosworth, ed., *The Oxford Handbook of Fascism* (Oxford: Oxford University Press, 2009)

Italian Neo-Fascism. The Strategy of Tension and the Politics of Non-Reconciliation (Oxford: Berghahn Books, 2007)

"Casting a Long Shadow: The Legacy of *stragismo* for the Italian Extreme Right," *The Italianist*, 25(2), 2005
and Cooke, P., *Ending Terrorism in Italy* (London: Routledge, 2013)
Centre de regroupement des informations universitaires, ed., *Quelle Université? Quelle Société? Textes réunis par le Centre de Regroupement des Informations Universitaires* (Paris: Seuil, 1968)
Charpier, F., *Génération Occident. De l'extrême droite à la droite* (Paris: Seuil, 2005)
Chebel d'Appollonia, A., *L'extrême-droite en France. De Maurras à Le Pen* (Brussels: Editions Complexe, 1988)
Cheles, L., "Back to the Future. The Visual Propaganda of Alleanza Nazionale (1994–2009)," *Journal of Modern Italian Studies*, 15(2), 2010
"Il '68 nella propaganda figurativa del Movimento Sociale Italiano," in S. Casilio and L. Guerrieri, eds., *Il '68 diffuso. Contestazione e linguaggi in movimento* (Bologna: Clueb, 2009)
"'Nostalgia dell'Avvenire.' The New Propaganda of the MSI between Tradition and Innovation," in L. Cheles et al., eds., *Neo-Fascism in Europe* (London: Longman, 1991)
"Le 'new look' du néo-fascisme italien," *Mots*, 12, 1986
Chiarini, R., "Anti-Zionism and the Italian Extreme Right," *Modern Italy*, 13(1), 2008
"La tentazione della protesta anti-immigrati," in R. Chiarini and M. Maraffi, eds., *La destra allo specchio. La cultura politica di Alleanza Nazionale* (Venice: Marsilio, 2001)
"La fortuna del gollismo in Italia," in E. Decleva and P. Milza, eds., *Italia e Francia: I nazionalismi a confronto* (Milan: Franco Angeli, 1993)
"'Sacro egoismo' e 'missione civilizzatrice.' La politica estera del Msi dalla fondazione alla metà degli anni Cinquanta," *Storia contemporanea*, 21(3), 1990
and Corsini, P., *Da Salò a Piazza della Loggia. Blocco d'ordine, neofascismo, radicalismo di destra a Brescia (1945–1974)* (Milan: Franco Angeli, 1983)
Choate, M. I., *Emigrant Nation. The Making of Italy Abroad* (Cambridge, MA: Harvard University Press, 2008).
Clavin, P., "Time, Manner, Place: Writing Modern European History in Global, Transnational and International Contexts," *European History Quarterly*, 40 (4), 2010
"Defining Transnationalism," *Contemporary European History*, 14(4), 2005
Coakley, J., "Mobilizing the Past: Nationalist Images of History," *Nationalism and Ethnic Politics*, 10(4), 2004
Collovald, A., *Le 'Populisme du FN'. Un dangereux contresens* (Broissieux: Éditions du Croquant, 2004)
"Le 'national-populisme' ou le fascisme disparu," in M. Dobry, ed., *Le mythe de l'allergie française au fascisme* (Paris: Albin Michel, 2003)
Colombo, A. and Sciortino, G., "Italian Immigration: The Origins, Nature and Evolution of Italy's Migratory Systems," *Journal of Modern Italian Studies*, 9 (1), 2004

Conniff, M. L., "Introduction: Toward a Comparative Definition of Populism," in M. L. Conniff, ed., *Latin American Populism in Comparative Perspective* (Albuquerque: University of New Mexico Press, 1982)

Conti, G., "La RSI e l'attività del fascismo clandestino nell'Italia liberata dal settembre 1943 all'aprile 1945," *Storia contemporanea*, 10, 1979

Coogan, K., "Lost Imperium: The European Liberation Front (1949–54)," *Patterns of Prejudice*, 36(3), 2002

Dreamer of the Day. Francis Parker Yockey and the Postwar Fascist International (New York: Autonomedia, 1999)

Copsey, N., "'Fascism ... but with an Open Mind.' Reflections on the Contemporary Far Right in (Western) Europe. First Lecture on Fascism – Amsterdam – 25 April 2013," *Fascism: Journal of Comparative Fascist Studies*, 2(1), 2013

"A Comparison between the Extreme Right in Contemporary France and Britain," *Contemporary European History*, 6(1), 1997

Corner, P., *The Fascist Party and Popular Opinion in Mussolini's Italy* (Oxford: Oxford University Press, 2012)

"Everyday Fascism in the 1930s: Centre and Periphery in the Decline of Mussolini's Dictatorship," *Contemporary European History*, 15(2), 2006

"Consenso e coercizione. L'opinione popolare nella Germania Nazista e nell'Italia fascista," *Contemporanea*, 6(3), 2003

Cowans, J., "French Public Opinion and the Founding of the Fourth Republic," *French Historical Studies*, 17(1), 1991

Cuzzi, M., *Antieuropa. Il fascismo universale di Mussolini* (Milan: M & B Publishing, 2007)

L'Internazionale delle Camicie nere. I CAUR, Comitati d'azione per l'universalità di Roma 1933–1939 (Milan: Mursia, 2005)

"L'Eurodestra: I rapporti tra il Msi-Dn e l'estrema destra francese (1968–1994)," in M. Antonioli and A. Moioli, eds., *Saggi storici in onore di Romain H. Rainero* (Milan: Franco Angeli, 2005)

Daguet, F. and Thave, S., "La population immigrée. Le résultat d'une longue histoire," *INSEE PREMIERE*, 458, 1996

Dard, O., "La Nouvelle Drote et la société de consommation," *Vingtième Siècle*, 91, 2006

De Benoist, A., *Dèrnière Annèe. Notes pour conclure le siècle* (Paris: L'Âge d'Homme, 2001)

L'Écume et les Galets. 1991–1999: Dix ans d'actualité vue d'ailleurs (Paris: Éditions du Labyrinthe, 2000)

Europe, Tiers Monde, même combat (Paris: Laffont, 1986)

Les idées à l'endroit (Paris: Éditions Libres-Hallier, 1979)

and Locchi, G., *Il male Americano* (Rome: Libreria Editrice Europa, 1978)

Vu de droite. Anthologie critique des idées contemporaines (Paris: Copernic, 1977)

De Caprariis, L., "'Fascism for Export'? The Rise and Eclipse of the Fasci Italiani all' Estero," *Journal of Contemporary History*, 35(2), 2000

De Grand, A. J., *Fascist Italy and Nazi Germany: The 'Fascist' Style of Rule* (New York: Routledge, 1996)
De Laforcade, G., "'Foreigners,' Nationalism and the 'Colonial Fracture.' Stigmatized Subjects of Historical Memory in France," *International Journal of Comparative Sociology*, 47(3–4), 2006
DeClair, E. G., *Politics on the Fringe. The People, Policies, and Organization of the French National Front* (Durham: Duke University Press, 1999)
Del Boca, A. and Giovana, M., *Fascism Today. A World Survey* (London: Heinemann, 1970)
De Troia, M., *Fronte della Gioventù. Una militanza difficile tra partito e società civile* (Rome: Settimo Sigillo, 2001)
Dély, R., *Histoire secrète du Front National* (Paris: Grasset, 1999)
Di Giacomo, M., "Identità eurocomunista: la traiettoria del Pce negli anni Settanta," *Studi storici*, 51(2), 2010
Diorama, "Una scelta di campo," in *Diorama Letterario. Ristampa anastatica integrale dei numeri 14/40 (settembre 1978–agosto 1981)* (Florence: La Roccia di Eric, 1998)
Dipartimento Organizzazione Movimento Politico La Destra, ed., *Manuale della Sovranità: i 10 punti dell'Italia di domani* (Rome: La Destra, 2012)
Dobry, M., ed., *Le mythe de l'allergie française au fascisme* (Paris: Albin Michel, 2003)
Dorril, S., *Blackshirt: Sir Oswald Mosley and British Fascism* (London: Penguin/Viking, 2007)
Drake, D., *Intellectuals and Politics in Post-War France* (Basingstoke: Palgrave, 2002)
Duggan, C., "Italy in the Cold War Years and the Legacy of Fascism," in C. Duggan and C. Wagstaff, eds., *Italy in the Cold War. Politics, Culture and Society. 1948–1958* (Oxford: Berg, 1995)
Dunwoodie, P., "Postface: History, Memory and Identity – Today's Crisis, Yesterday's Issue," *French History*, 20(3), 2006
Duprat, F., *Droite Nationale en France: de 1971 à 1975* (Paris: Éditions de l'Homme Libre, 2002)
Les Mouvements d'extrême-droite en France depuis 1944 (Paris: Albatros, 1972)
L'Ascension du M.S.I (Movimento Sociale Italiano) (Paris: Les Sept Couleurs, 1972)
Les journées de Mai 68. Les dessous d'une révolution (Paris: Nouvelles Éditions Latines, 1968)
Duranton-Crabol, A.-M., *Visages de la Nouvelle Droite: Le G.R.E.C.E. et son histoire* (Paris: Presses de la Fondation Nationale des Sciences Politiques, 1998)
Le Temps de l'OAS (Brussels: Éditions Complexe, 1995)
Europe de l'extrême droite: de 1945 à nos jours (Brussels: Éditions Complexe, 1991)
"La 'Nouvelle Droite' entre printemps et automne. 1968–1986," *Vingtième Siècle*, 17, 1988
Eatwell, R., *Fascism: A History* (London: Pimlico, 2003)

"The Rebirth of the 'Extreme Right' in Western Europe," *Parliamentary Affairs*, 53(3), 2000
Edgar, D., "Much like the 1950s," *London Review of Books*, 29(11), June 7, 2007
Eley, G., "When Europe Was New: Liberation and the Making of the Post-War Era," in M. Reina and G. Schaffer, eds., *The Lasting War. Society and Identity in Britain, France and Germany after 1945* (Basingstoke: Palgrave Macmillan, 2008)
Ellinas, A., "Chaotic but Popular? Extreme-Right Organisation and Performance in the Age of Media Communication," *Journal of Contemporary European Studies*, 17(2), 2009
"Phased Out. Far Right Parties in Western Europe," *Comparative Politics*, 39 (3), 2007
Evola, J., *Apolitia. Scritti sugli "orientamenti esistenziali" 1934–1973*, R. Paradisi, ed. (Rome: Controcorrente, 2004)
Orientamenti (Rome: Settimo Sigillo, 2002)
"I due volti del liberalismo," in Julius Evola, *Idee per una Destra*, Alessandro Barbera, ed. (Rome: Fondazione Julius Evola, 1997)
"Idee sulla destra," in Julius Evola, *Idee per una Destra*, Alessandro Barbera, ed. (Rome: Fondazione Julius Evola, 1997)
Cavalcare la Tigre. Orientamenti esistenziali per un'epoca della dissoluzione (Rome: Edizioni Mediterranee, 1995)
Revolt against the Modern World (Rochester, VT: Inner Traditions International, 1995)
"The True Europe's Revolt against the Modern World," in R. Griffin, ed., *Fascism* (Oxford: Oxford University Press, 1995)
Il fascismo visto dalla destra. Note sul Terzo Reich (Rome: Edizioni Giovanni Volpe, 1974)
Gli uomini e le rovine (Rome: Edizioni Giovanni Volpe, 1972)
Faggionato, G., "Crisi, la ricetta dell'anima nera d'Europa," *Lettera* 43, July 7, 2012 (online: www.lettera43.it/politica/crisi-la-ricetta-dell-anima-nera-d-europa_4367557103.htm)
Fasanella, G. and Grippo, A., *L'orda nera* (Milan: BUR, 2009)
Faux, E. et al., *La Main droite de Dieu. Enquête sur François Mitterrand et l'extrême droite* (Paris: Seuil, 1994)
Faye, G., "Nuova destra o nuova cultura?" in *Diorama Letterario. Ristampa anastatica integrale dei numeri 14/40 (settembre 1978 – agosto 1981)* (Florence: La Roccia di Eric, 1998)
Ferrara, O., *Il mito negato. Da Giovane Europa ad Avanguardia di Popolo. La destra eretica negli anni Settanta* (Sarno: Centro Studi I Diòscuri, 1996)
Ferrari, S., *Da Salò ad Arcore. La mappa della destra eversiva* (Rome: Nuova Iniziativa Editoriale, 2006)
Ferraresi, F., *Threats to Democracy. The Radical Right in Italy after the War* (Princeton: Princeton University Press, 1996)
"The Radical Right in Postwar Italy," *Politics and Society*, 16(1), 1988
Fiamma Tricolore, "Parigi 1 Maggio 2005: L'Europa dice NO!" *Fiamma Tricolore Comunicati*, May 2, 2005 (online: msibergamo.altervista.org/ft/?p=18)

Fieschi, C., *Fascism, Populism and the French Fifth Republic. In the Shadow of Democracy* (Manchester: Manchester University Press, 2004)
Finchelstein, F., *Transatlantic Fascism. Ideology, Violence, and the Sacred in Argentina and Italy, 1919–1945* (Duke: Duke University Press, 2010)
Finotti, S., "Difesa occidentale e Patto Atlantico: la scelta internazionale del Msi," *Storia delle Relazioni Internazionali*, 2(1), 1988
Fiore, R., "Nasce in Ungheria il parlamento nazional-rivoluzionario," *Forza Nuova Comunicati*, July 22, 2012 (online: www.forzanuova.org/comunicati/fiore-nasce-ungheria-il-parlamento-nazional-rivoluzionario)
"La vittoria del Front National traccia il cammino per la Rinascita Nazionale," *Forza Nuova Comunicati*, April 23, 2012 (online: www.forzanuova.org/comunicati/fiore-fnla-vittoria-del-front-national-traccia-il-cammino-la- rinascita-nazionale)
Forza Nuova, *Lo stile forzanovista*, 2012 (online: www.milano.forzanuova.info/blog/stile-forzanovista)
"Francia, Marine Le Pen: Mario Monti è un impiegato di banca e farà gli interessi delle banche, tornare alle monete nazionali," *Forza Nuova News*, May 3, 2012 (online: www.forzanuova.org/attualita/francia-marine-le-pen-mario-monti-%C3%A8-un-impiegato-di-banca-e-far%C3%A0-interessi-delle-banche)
Manifesto politico di opposizione, 2006
Front National, *Programme du Front National*, 2006
Les Argumentaires. Les dérives du droit de la nationalité, 2004 (online: www.frontnational.com/argumentaries/derive_droit_nationalite.php)
L'alternative nationale. 300 mesures pour la renaissance de la France. Programme de gouvernement (Paris: Éditions Nationales, 1993)
Fysh, P. and Wolfreys, J., *The Politics of Racism in France* (London: Palgrave, 2003)
Gabaccia, D. R. and Ottanelli, F. M., eds., *Italian Workers of the World: Labor Migration and the Formation of Multiethnic States* (Urbana: University of Illinois Press, 2001)
Galli, G., *I colonnelli della guerra rivoluzionaria* (Bologna: Il Mulino, 1962)
Garaud, X. and Courber, A., "The Book Trade on the French Far Right," *Patterns of Prejudice*, 16(3), 1982
Gasparetti, A., *La destra e il '68* (Rome: Settimo Sigillo, 2007)
Gastaut, Y., *L'immigration et l'opinion en France sous la Vème République* (Paris: Seuil, 2000)
Gentile, F., "Fra vissuto e scelta politica. I fascisti napoletani da Salò al Movimento sociale italiano 1943–1948," *Italia contemporanea*, 237, 2004
Germani, G., *Authoritarianism, Fascism, and National Populism* (New Brunswick, NJ: Transaction Books, 1978)
Germinario, F., *Da Salò al governo. Immaginario e cultura politica della destra italiana* (Turin: Bollati Boringhieri, 2005)
La destra degli dei. Alain de Benoist e la cultura politica della Nouvelle droite (Turin: Bollati Boringhieri, 2002)
Estranei alla Democrazia. Negazionismo e antisemitismo nella destra radicale italiana (Pisa: BFS Edizioni, 2001)

"Giovanni Volpe e 'Intervento': Storia di una rivista di cultura della destra (1972–1984)," *Studi Piacentini*, 30, 2001

Giannettini, G. and Rauti, P., *Le mani rosse sulle forze armate* (Rome: Savelli, 1975)

Giovane Destra Lecco, "Una sola al comando. Intervista a Marine Le Pen (Front National)," *Pensiero Nazionale (blog)*, March 25, 2012 (online: blog.libero.it/GiovaneDestra)

Giovane Nazione, *Consuntivo di un anno di attività 1960–61*, Milan, 1961

Gioventù Italiana, "Gioventù Italiana sostiene Marine Le Pen," *Gioventù Italiana – Informazione* (online: www.gioventuitaliana.org/?p=4574)

Gobille, B., "La vocation d'hétérodoxie," in D. Damamme et al., eds., *Mai-June 68* (Paris: Éditions de l'Atelier, 2008)

Goeschel, C., "*Italia docet*? The Relationship between Italian Fascism and Nazism Revisited," *European History Quarterly*, 42(3), 2012

Gollnisch, B., "Réunion de l'AEMN à Hédervár: une profession de foi pour l'Europe des patries," *Bruno Gollnisch Blog*, October 24, 2012 (online: www.gollnisch.com/2012/10/24/reunion-de-laemn-a-hedervar-une-profession-de-foi-pour-leurope-des-patries)

"Le message de soutien de Jean-Marie Le Pen à l'AEMN," *Bruno Gollnisch Blog*, October 24, 2012 (online: www.gollnisch.com/2012/10/24/le-message-de-soutien-de-jean-marie-le-pen-a-laemn)

Goodwin, M. J., "Grandpa's Fascism and the New Kids on the Block: Contemporary Approaches to the Dark Side of Europe," *Ethnopolitics*, 6(1), 2007

GRECE, *Pour un 'gramscisme de droite'. Actes du XVIème colloque national du G.R.E.C.E.* (Paris: Éditions du Labyrinthe, 1982)

Gregor, J. A., *The Search for Neofascism: The Use and Abuse of Social Science* (Cambridge: Cambridge University Press, 2006)

Griffin, R., "Plus ça change: The Fascist Pedigree of the Nouvelle Droite," in E. J. Arnold, ed., *The Development of the Radical Right in France: From Boulanger to Le Pen* (New York: St. Martin's Press, 2000)

"Between Metapolitics and *apoliteia*: The Nouvelle Droite's Strategy for Conserving the Fascist Vision in the 'Interregnum,'" *Modern and Contemporary France*, 8(1), 2000

Guerrieri, L., '*... Essere fascisti in democrazia': Destra ed estrema destra in Italia (1956–1969)* (PhD dissertation, Università degli Studi di Macerata, 2007)

"'All'Hobbit, all'Hobbit... siam fascisti!' La giovane destra italiana nei Campi Hobbit," *Giornale di Storia costituzionale*, 10(II), 2005

Guiat, C. "Le choix du beau et du vrai. La politique culturelle du FN/MNR à Vitrolles: entre néo-classicisme et invention de la tradition, 1997–2002," *e-France*, 1, 2007

Guilledoux, F.-J., *Le Pen en Provence* (Paris: Fayard, 2004)

Guland, O., *Le Pen, Mégret et le Juifs. L'obsession du 'complot mondialiste'* (Paris: La Découverte, 2000)

Hajek, A., "*E se il '68 fosse (anche) di destra? Media and Identity Formation: Rereading the Protest Movement of 1968 from the Right*," ASMI Conference, 2008

Hainsworth, P., "The Front National: From Ascendancy to Fragmentation on the French Extreme Right," in P. Hainsworth, ed., *The Politics of the Extreme Right. From the Margins to the Mainstream* (London: Pinter, 2000)

"The Extreme Right in Post-War France: The Emergence and Success of the Front National," in P. Hainsworth, ed., *The Extreme Right in Europe and the USA* (London: Pinter, 1992)

and Mitchell, P. "France: The Front National fromCrossroads to Crossroads?" *Parliamentary Affairs*, 53(3), 2000

Hansen, H. T., "A Short Introduction to Julius Evola," in J. Evola, ed., *Revolt against the Modern World* (Rochester, VT: Inner Traditions International, 1995)

Harrison, T., *Of Passionate Intensity. Right-Wing Populism and the Reform Party of Canada* (Toronto: University of Toronto Press, 1995)

Hillman, N., "'Tell Me Chum, in Case I Got It Wrong. What Was It We Were Fighting during the War?' The Re-emergence of British Fascism, 1945–58," *Contemporary British History*, 15(4), 2001

Hoffman, S., *Le mouvement Poujade* (Paris: Armand Colin, 1956)

Holmes, D. R., *Integral Europe. Fast-Capitalism, Multiculturalism, Neofascism* (Princeton: Princeton University Press, 2000)

Honoré, J.-P., "La 'hiérarchiedes sentiments,'" *Mots*, 12, 1986

Horn, G.-H., *Western European Liberation Theology, The First Wave (1924–1959)* (Oxford: Oxford University Press, 2008)

The Spirit of '68: Rebellion in Western Europe and North America, 1956–1976 (Oxford: Oxford University Press, 2007)

"The Working-Class Dimension of 1968," in G.-R. Horn and P. Kenney, eds., *Transnational Moments of Change. Europe 1945, 1968, 1989* (Lanham, MD: Rowman and Littlefield, 2004)

European Socialists Respond to Fascism: Ideology, Activism and Contingency in the 1930s (New York: Oxford University Press, 1996)

House, J., *Antiracism and Antiracist Discourse in France from 1900 to the Present Day* (PhD dissertation, University of Leeds, 1997)

House, J. and MacMaster, N., *Paris 1961. Algerians, State Terror, and Memory* (Oxford: Oxford University Press, 2006)

Husbands, C. T., "How to Tame the Dragon, or What Goes around Comes around: A Critical Review of Some Major Contemporary Attempts to Account for Extreme-Right Racist Politics in Western Europe," in M. Schain, A. Zolberg, and P. Hossay, eds., *Shadows over Europe: The Development and Impact of the Extreme Right in Western Europe* (New York: Palgrave Macmillan, 2002)

Ignazi, P., *Extreme Right Parties in Western Europe* (Oxford: Oxford University Press, 2006)

"The Extreme Right. Legitimation and Evolution on the Italian Right Wing: Social and Ideological Repositioning of Alleanza Nazionale and the Lega Nord," *South European Society and Politics*, 10(2), 2005

Il polo escluso. Profilo storico del Movimento Sociale Italiano (Bologna: Il Mulino, 1998)

"From Neo-Fascists to Post-Fascists? The Transformation of the MSI into the AN," *West European Politics*, 19(4), 1996

Postfascisti? Dal Movimento sociale italiano ad Alleanza nazionale (Bologna: Il Mulino, 1994) and Ysmal, C., "New and Old Extreme Right Parties: The French Front National and the Italian Movimento Sociale," *European Journal of Political Research*, 2(1), 1992

"La cultura politica del Movimento Sociale Italiano," *Rivista Italiana di Scienza Politica*, 19(3), 1989

Igounet, V., *Histoire du négationnisme en France* (Paris: Seuil, 2000)

Iriye, A. and Saunier, P.-Y., eds., *The Palgrave Dictionary of Transnational History* (Basingstoke: Palgrave Macmillan, 2009)

Ivaldi, G., "Les formations d'extrême droite: Front national et Mouvement national républicain," in P. Bréchon, ed., *Les partis politiques français* (Paris: La Documentation française, 2005)

Ivarsflaten, E., "What Unites Right-Wing Populists in Western Europe? Re-Examining Grievance Mobilization Models in Seven Successful Cases," *Comparative Political Studies*, (41)1, 2008

Jackson, J., "The Mystery of May 1968," *French Historical Studies*, 33(4), 2010

France. The Dark Years. 1940–1944 (Oxford: Oxford University Press, 2001)

Jarausch, K. H. and Lindenberger, T., "Contours of a Critical History of Contemporary Europe: A Transnational Agenda," in K. H. Jarausch and T. Lindenberger, eds., *Conflicted Memories: Europeanizing Contemporary Histories* (New York: Berghahn Books, 2007)

Jenkins, B., ed., *France in the Era of Fascism. Essays on the French Authoritarian Right* (Oxford: Berghahn Books, 2005)

Jesi, F., *Cultura di destra* (Milan: Garzanti, 1979)

Judt, T., *Postwar. A History of Europe Since 1945* (London: Pimlico, 2007)

Kaelble, H. and Passerini, L., "European Public Sphere and European Identity in 20th Century History," *Journal of European Integration History*, 8(2), 2002

Kaiser, W., *Christian Democracy and the Origins of European Union* (Cambridge: Cambridge University Press, 2007)

"Transnational Western Europe Since 1945," in W. Kaiser and P. Starie, eds., *Transnational European Union: Towards a Common Political Space* (London: Routledge, 2005)

Kaplan, J. and Weinberg, L., *The Emergence of a Euro-American Radical Right* (New Brunswick, NJ: Rutgers University Press, 1998)

Kastoryano, R., "Vers un nationalisme transnational: Redéfinir la nation, le nationalisme et le territoire," *Revue Française de Science Politique*, 56(4), 2006

Kenney, P., "Borders Breached: The Transnational in Eastern Europe Since Solidarity," *Journal of Modern European History*, 8(2), 2010

and Horn, G.-R., "Introduction: Approaches to the Transnational," in G.-R. Horn and P. Kenney, eds., *Transnational Moments of Change. Europe 1945, 1968, 1989* (Lanham, MD: Rowman and Littlefield, 2004)

Knapp, A., "Introduction: France's 'Long' Liberation, 1944–47," in A. Knapp, ed., *The Uncertain Foundation: France at the Liberation, 1944–47* (Basingstoke: Palgrave Macmillan, 2007)

Krikorian, N., "Européanisme, nationalisme, libéralisme dans les éditoriaux de Louis Pauwels (*Figaro-Magazine*, 1977–1984)," *Mots*, 12, 1986

Kumar, K., "The Idea of Europe: Cultural Legacies, Transnational Imaginings, and the Nation-State," in M. Berezin and M. Schain, eds., *Europe without Borders: Remapping Territory, Citizenship, and Identity in a Transnational Age* (Baltimore: Johns Hopkins University Press, 2003)

La Destra, "La Destra per l'Italia. Contro tutte le 'caste,'" *Assemblea Costituente per La Destra*, Rome, November 10–11, 2007

Langebach, M. and Raabe, J., "Inside the Extreme Right: The 'White Power' Music Scene," in A. Mammone, E. Godin, and B. Jenkins, eds., *Varieties of Right-Wing Extremism in Europe* (London: Routledge, 2013)

Lanna, L. and Rossi, F., *Fascisti immaginari. Tutto quello che c'è da sapere sulla destra* (Florence: Vallecchi, 2003)

La Russa, I., "Francia: Senza la destra non si vince," *Blog di Ignazio La Russa*, April 23, 2012 (online: www.ignaziolarussa.net/?p=1972)

Le Pen, J.-M., *Les Français d'abord* (Paris: Éditions Carrère, 1984)

Le Bohec, J., *Sociologie du phénomène Le Pen* (Paris: La Découverte, 2005)

Lecoeur, E., *Un néo-populisme à la française. Trente ans de Front national* (Paris: La Découverte, 2003)

Ledeen, M. A., *Universal Fascism: The Theory and Practice of the Fascist International* (New York: Howard Fertig, 1972)

Liddell, C., "In the House of Pound." *The Magazine*, February 5, 2012 (online: www.alternativeright.com/main/the-magazine/in-the-house-of-pound)

Lionnet, F., "Immigration, Poster Art, and Transgressive Citizenship: France 1968–1988," *SubStance*, 24(1–2), 1995

Lipman, J., "National Front Thugs Mount Anti-Jewish Attack in Paris," *Jewish Chronicle Online*, March 2, 2012 (online: www.thejc.com/news/world-news/64469/national-front-thugs-mount-anti-jewish-attack-paris)

Lipstadt, D. E., *Denying the Holocaust. The Growing Assault on Truth and Memory* (New York: Penguin, 1994)

Long, I., "L' Épuration: The Intervention of Simone de Beauvoir," in J. Wardhaugh, ed., *Paris and the Right in the Twentieth Century* (Cambridge: Cambridge Scholars Press, 2007)

Lucci Chiarissi, L., *Esame di coscienza di un fascista* (Rome: IRSE, 1978)

Macklin, G., *See Very Deeply Dyed in Black: Sir Oswald Mosley and the Postwar Reconstruction of British Fascism* (London: I. B. Tauris, 2007)

Madiran, J., *Brasillach* (Paris: Club du Luxembourg, 1958)

Mak, G., *Europe: Travels through the Twentieth Century* (London: Vintage, 2008)

Malgieri, G., "Prefazione," in Aa.Vv., *Proviamola nuova. Atti del seminario «Ipotesi e strategia di una nuova destra»* (Rome: L.ED.E., 1980)

Mammone, A., "Il British National Party e l'ideologia neofascista nell'Europa contemporanea," *Studi Storici*, 52(2), 2011

and Peace, T., "Cross-national Ideology in Local Elections: The Case of Azione Sociale and the British National Party," in A. Mammone, E. Godin, and B. Jenkins, eds., *Mapping the Extreme Right in Contemporary Europe: From Local to Transnational* (London: Routledge, 2012)

Godin, E. and Jenkins, B., "Introduction: Mapping the 'Right of the Mainstream Right' in Contemporary Europe," in A. Mammone, E. Godin, and B.

Jenkins, eds., *Mapping the Extreme Right in Contemporary Europe: From Local to Transnational* (London: Routledge, 2012)
"Su politica, moralità e decadenza: note su destra, sinistra e (anti-)illuminismo," in A. Mammone, N. Tranfaglia, and G. A. Veltri, eds., *Un Paese normale? Saggi sull'Italia contemporanea* (Milan: Dalai editore, 2011)
and Veltri, G. A., "Un Paese smarrito," in A. Mammone, N. Tranfaglia, and G. A. Veltri, eds., *Un Paese normale? Saggi sull'Italia contemporanea* (Milan: Dalai editore, 2011)
and Veltri, G. A., "'A Sick Man' in Europe," in A. Mammone and G. A. Veltri, eds., *Italy Today: The Sick Man of Europe* (London: Routledge, 2010)
"Italy's Moral Crisis," *Soundings: A Journal of Politics and Culture*, 46(3), 2010
"Se l'onda razzista passa per folklore," *Reset*, 117, 2010
"The Eternal Return? Faux Populism and Contemporarization of Neo-Fascism across Britain, France and Italy," *Journal of Contemporary European Studies*, 17(2), 2009
"The Black-shirt Resistance: Clandestine Fascism in Italy, 1943–1950," *The Italianist*, 27(2), 2007
"A Daily Revision of the Past: Fascism, Anti-Fascism, and Memory in Contemporary Italy," *Modern Italy*, 11(2), 2006
"Gli orfani del Duce. Fascisti dal 1943 al 1946," *Italia contemporanea*, 239–240(2), 2005
Mancini, I., *Il pensiero negativo e la nuova destra* (Milan: Mondadori, 1983)
Massi, E., *L'Europa e la crisi africana*, Milan: Istituto Editoriale Sociale, 1960
"La funzione delle 'Internazionali,'" in E. Massi, ed., *Nazione Sociale. Scritti Politici, 1948–1976* (Rome: ISC, 1990)
"Per una politica sociale ed economica al servizio dell'unità europea," in E. Massi, ed., *Nazione Sociale. Scritti Politici, 1948–1976* (Rome: ISC, 1990)
Marwick, A., "Six Novels of the Sixties — Three French, Three Italian," *Journal of Contemporary History*, 28(4), 1993
McCulloch, T., "The Nouvelle Droite in the 1980s and 1990s: Ideology and Entryism, the Relationship with the Front National," *French Politics*, 4(2), 2006
Mellón, J.-A., "The idées-force of the European New Right: A New Paradigm?" in A. Mammone, E. Godin, and B. Jenkins, eds., *Varieties of Right-Wing Extremism in Contemporary Europe* (London: Routledge, 2013)
Mendras, H. (with A. Cole), *Social Change in Modern France: Towards a Cultural Anthropology of the Fifth Republic* (Cambridge: Cambridge University Press, 1991)
Mestre, A. and Monnot, C., "Marine Le Pen a rencontré Francesco Storace, figure de l'extrême droite italienne," *Droite(s) Extrême(s) (Le Monde.fr Blog)*, April 15, 2012 (online: droites-extremes.blog.lemonde.fr/2011/10/22/marine-le-pen-en-italie-lombre-portee-du-msi)
"Marine Le Pen en Italie: l'ombre portée du MSI," *Droite(s) Extrême(s) (Le Monde.fr Blog)*, October 22, 2011 (online: droites-extremes.blog.lemonde.fr/2011/10/22/marine-le-pen-en-italie-lombre-portee-du-msi)

Milza, P., "Julius Evola et la 'Nouvelle Droite' française," in E. Decleva and P. Milza, eds., *Italia e Francia: i nazionalismi a confronto* (Milan: Franco Angeli, 1993)
Fascisme français. Passé et présent (Paris: Flammarion, 1987)
Monzat, R., *Les voleurs d'avenir. Pourquoi l'extrême droite peut avoir de beaux jours devant elle* (Paris: Les éditions Textuel, 2004)
Movimento Sociale-Fiamma Tricolore, *Dipartimento Nazionale per le Riforme, Immigrazione (cause, problemi, vantaggi, soluzioni)* (Rome: MSFT, 2011)
Movimento Sociale per l'Europa, "L'Euroribellione è iniziata," *Articoli*, 2012 (online: www.movimentosocialeeuropeo.eu/?p=461)
Neglie, P., "Il Movimento sociale italiano fra terzaforzismo e atlantismo," *Storia contemporanea*, 25(6), 1994
Núñez, X.-M., "Nations and Territorial Identities in Europe: Transnational Reflections," *European History Quarterly*, 40(4), 2010
Özcan, A. K., "Nationalism: Distilling the *Cultural* and the *Political*," *Nationalism and Ethnic Politics*, 11(2), 2005
Palmowski, J., "The Europeanization of the Nation-State," *Journal of Contemporary History*, 46(3), 2011
Parlato, G., *Fascisti senza Mussolini. Le origini del neofascismo in Italia, 1943–1948* (Bologna: Il Mulino, 2006)
Paxton, R., *The Anatomy of Fascism* (New York: Vintage, 2005)
"The Five Stages of Fascism," *Journal of Modern History*, 70(1), 1998
Vichy France: Old Guard and New Order. 1940–1944 (New York: Knopf, 1972)
Petitfils, J.-C., *L'extrême droite en France: De Maurras à Le Pen* (Paris: Presses Universitaires de France, 1983)
Perez, G., "G.R.E.C.E. e Nouvelle Droite," in *Aa.Vv., Proviamola nuova. Atti del seminario 'Ipotesi e strategia di una nuova destra'* (Rome: L.ED.E., 1980)
Pervillé, G., "L'Algérie dans la mémoire des droites," in J.-F. Sirinelli, ed., *Histoire des droites en France. 2. Cultures* (Paris: Gallimard, 1992)
Piscitelli, A., "L'anatema del 'Secolo' contro Fabio Torriero," *Il PreDelLino*, March 14, 2011 (online: www.ilpredellino.it/online/prima-pagina/78-articoli/4044-lanatema-del-qsecoloq-contro-fabio-torriero)
Plebe, A., *Il libretto della Destra* (Rome: Il Borghese, 1972)
Poujade, P., *J'ai choisi le combat* (Saint-Céré: Société Générales des Editions et des Publications, 1955)
Prisco, M., Giannettini, G. and Romualdi, A., *Drieu La Rochelle: Il mito dell'Europa* (Rome: Edizioni del Solstizio, 1965)
Rao, N., *La Fiamma e la Celtica* (Milan: Sperling & Kupfer Editori, 2007)
Neofascisti! La Destra italiana da Salò a Fiuggi nel ricordo dei protagonisti (Rome: Settimo Sigillo, 1999)
Rauti, P., *Le idee che mossero il mondo* (Rome: Edizioni Europa, 1976)
Redazione, "Il bresciano Zarneri in Francia incontra la candidata alle presidenziali francesi Marine Le Pen," *Bsnews.it*, September 30, 2011 (online: www.bsnews.it/notizia/10813/30_09_2011_Il_bresciano_Zarneri_in_Francia_incontra_la_candidata_alle_presidenziali_francesi_Marine_Le_Pen_)
Réfléchir and Agir, "Les Éditions Auda Isarn: Domenico di Tullio, *Nessun dolore*," 2012 (online: www.reflechiretagir.com/auda.html#nessun)

Rémond, R., *La droite en France. Vol. II: 1940–Juin 1968* (Paris: Aubier, 1980)
The Right Wing in France: From 1815 to de Gaulle (Philadelphia: University of Pennsylvania Press, 1971)
Renouveau Français, "Présentation," 2012 (online: renouveau-francais.com/?page_id=626)
Revelli, M., "La nuova destra," in F. Ferraresi, ed., *La destra radicale* (Milan: Feltrinelli, 1984)
Rinascita, "Manifesto," 2012 (online: www.rinascita.eu/?action=manifesto)
Rioux, J.-P., "Des clandestines aux activistes (1945–1965)," in M. Winock, ed., *Histoire de l'extrême droite en France* (Paris: Seuil, 1993)
Roberti, G., *L'opposizione di destra in Italia, 1946–1979* (Naples: Gallina, 1988)
Romagnoli, L., "Per un'altra Italia per un'altra Europa," *Discorso. Presentazione italiana dell'Alleanza Europea dei Movimenti Nazionalisti*, Milan, July 7, 2012 (online: www.aemn.it/romagnoli01.pdf)
"Per l'Italia Sociale," *Mozione per il V Congresso Nazionale MSFT*, Rome, December 5–6, 2009
Romualdi, A., *Una cultura per l'Europa* (Rome: Settimo Sigillo, 1986)
Julius Evola: l'uomo e l'opera (Rome: Edizioni Giovanni Volpe, 1966)
Romualdi, P., *Filippo Anfuso e l'idea d'Europa-nazione: Discorso commemorativo nel 20. anniversario della scomparsa* (Palermo: I.S.S.P.E., 1984)
Rosenbaum, P., *Il nuovo fascismo, da Salò ad Almirante* (Milan: Feltrinelli, 1975)
Ross, K., *May '68 and Its Afterlives* (Chicago: University of Chicago Press, 2002)
Rossi, G. S., *La destra e gli ebrei: Una storia italiana* (Soveria Mannelli: Rubbettino, 2003)
Rousso, H., "La Seconde Guerre mondiale dans la mémoire des droites françaises," in J.-F. Sirinelli, ed., *Histoire des droites en France. 2. Cultures* (Paris: Gallimard, 1992)
The Vichy Syndrome: History and Memory in France Since 1944 (Cambridge, MA: Harvard University Press, 1991)
Ruzza, C. and Fella, S., *Re-inventing the Italian Right: Territorial Politics, Populism and 'Post-Fascism'* (London: Routledge, 2009)
Sacchi, F., "The Italian New Right," *Telos*, 98–99, 1993–1994
Saint-Loup (Marc Augier), *I volontari europei delle Waffen SS* (Rome: Edizioni Giovanni Volpe, 1967)
Saunier, P.-Y., "Learning by Doing: Notes about the Making of the *Palgrave Dictionary of Transnational History*," *Journal of Modern European History*, 6(2), 2008
"Going Transnational? News from Down Under," *History: Transnational*, January 13, 2006 (online: geschichte-transnational.clio-online.net/forum/type=artikel&id=680)
Sciortino, G. and Colombo, A., "The Flows and the Flood: The Public Discourse on Immigration in Italy, 1969–2001," *Journal of Modern Italian Studies*, 9(1), 2004
Semyonov, M., Rajiman, R., and Gorodzeisky, A., "The Rise of Anti-Foreigner Sentiment in European Societies, 1988–2000," *American Sociological Review*, 71(30), 2006
Setta, S., *La Destra nell'Italia del dopoguerra* (Rome: Laterza, 2001)
L'Uomo Qualunque 1944–1948 (Rome: Laterza, 2000)

Sheehan, T., "Myth and Violence: The Fascism of Julius Evola and Alain de Benoist," *Social Research*, 48(1), 1981
Shields, J. G., *The Extreme Right in France. From Pétain to Le Pen* (London: Routledge, 2007)
"The Poujadist Movement: A Faux 'Fascism,'" *Modern & Contemporary France*, 8(1), 2000
Silj, A., *Malpaese: Criminalità, corruzione, e politica nell'Italia della prima Repubblica. 1943–1994* (Rome: Donzelli Editore, 1994)
Silverman, M., *Deconstructing the Nation. Immigration, Racism and Citizenship in Modern France* (London: Routledge, 1992)
Silverstein, P. A., *Algeria in France: Transpolitics, Race, and Nation* (Bloomington: Indiana University Press, 2004)
Simeone, G., "Perché Campo Hobbit," in M. Tarchi, ed., *La Rivoluzione Impossibile. Dai Campi Hobbit alla Nuova destra* (Florence: Vallecchi, 2010)
Sommier, I., *La violence politique et son deuil. L'après 68 en France et en Italie* (Rennes: Presses Universitaires de Rennes, 1998)
Souchard, M., Wahnich, S., Cuminal, I., Wathier, V., *Le Pen, le mots: Analyse d'un discours d'extrême droite* (Paris: La Découverte/Poche, 1998)
Soucy, R., *French Fascism: The Second Wave, 1933–1939* (New Haven, CT: Yale University Press, 1995)
French Fascism: The First Wave 1924–33. (New Haven, CT: Yale University Press, 1986)
Fascism in France. The Case of Maurice Barrès (Berkeley: University of California Press, 1972)
Soudais, M., *Le Front national en face* (Paris: Flammarion, 1996)
Spektorowski, A., "Ethnoregionalism: The Intellectual New Right and the Lega Nord," *Global Review of Ethnopolitics*, 2(3), 2003
"The French New Right: Differentialism and the Idea of Ethnophilian Exclusionism," *Polity*, 33(2), 2000
Sternhell, Z., *La droite révolutionnaire (1885–1914). Les origines françaises du fascisme* (Paris: Gallimard, 1998)
(with M. Sznajder and M. Asheri), *The Birth of Fascist Ideology: From Cultural Rebellion to Political Revolution* (Princeton: Princeton University Press, 1994)
Ni droite ni gauche: L'Idéologie fasciste en France (Paris: Seuil, 1983)
Maurice Barrès et le nationalisme francaise (Paris: Armand Colin, 1972)
Storace, F., "Vince la coerenza," *Blog di Francesco Storace*, April 24, 2012 (online: www.storace.it/2012/04/24/vince-la-coerenza)
"Oui, La France," *Blog di Francesco Storace*, April 23, 2012 (online: www.storace.it/2012/04/23/oui-la-france)
Streccioni, A., *A destra della destra: Dentro e fuori l'MSI, dai FAR a Terza Posizione* (Rome: Settimo Sigillo, 2000)
Sturzo, L. "Has Fascism Ended with Mussolini?" *Review of Politics*, 7(3), 1945
Taggart, P., *Populism* (Buckingham: Open University Press, 2000)
Taguieff, P.-A., *L'illusione populista. Dall'arcaico al mediatico* (Milan: Mondadori, 2003)

"Un programme révolutionnaire?" in N. Mayer and P. Perrineau, eds., *Le Front National à découvert* (Paris: Presses de Sciences Po, 1996)
"Origines et métamorphoses de la Nouvelle Droite," *Vingtième siècle*, 40, 1993
"La doctrine du national-populisme en France," *Études*, 364, 1986
"La rhétorique du national-populisme (I)," *Cahiers Bernard Lazare*, 109, 1984
"La rhétorique du national-populisme (II)," *Mots*, 9, 1984

Tarchi, M., "Alla ricerca della comunità. I Campi Hobbit fra tentazione della modernità e sindrome del ghetto," in M. Tarchi, ed., *La Rivoluzione Impossibile. Dai Campi Hobbit alla Nuova destra* (Florence: Vallecchi, 2010)
"Postfazione. I Campi Hobbit, La Nuova destra e la 'destra nuova.' Una controversia politico-genealogica," in M. Tarchi, ed., *La Rivoluzione Impossibile. Dai Campi Hobbit alla Nuova destra* (Florence: Vallecchi, 2010)
"The Political Culture of the Alleanza Nazionale: Ananalysis of the Party's Programmatic Documents 1995–2002," *Journal of Modern Studies*, 8(2), 2003
Dal Msi ad An: Organizzazione e strategie (Bologna: Il Mulino, 1997)
Cinquant'anni di nostalgia: La destra italiana dopo il fascismo (Milan: Rizzoli, 1995)
Esuli in patria. I fascisti nell'Italia repubblicana (Parma: Guanda, 1995)
"L'impossibile identità: Il neofascismo tra destra e sinistra," *Trasgressioni*, 4(2), 1989
"Le tre vie del radicalismo di destra," *Trasgressioni*, 4(1), 1989
"Ipotesi e strategia di una nuova destra," in AA.VV., *Proviamola nuova: Atti del seminario "Ipotesi e strategia di una nuova destra"* (Rome: L.ED.E., 1980)

Tassani, G., "Le culture della destra italiana tra dopoguerra e centrosinistra: Gentilianesimo, cattolicesimo ed evolismo a confronto e in concorrenza," *Nuova Storia Contemporanea*, 7(2), 2003

Tassinari, U. G., *Naufraghi: Da Mussolini alla Mussolini: 60 anni di storia della destra radicale* (Naples: Immaginapoli, 2007)

Tauber, K. P., "German Nationalists and European Union," *Political Science Quarterly*, 74(4), 1959

Tedeschi, M., *Fascisti dopo Mussolini* (Rome: Settimo Sigillo, 1996)
Destra Nazionale: Sintesi di una politica nuova (Rome: Il Borghese, 1972)

Temkin, M., "'Avec un certain malaise': The Paxtonian Trauma in France, 1973–74," *Journal of Contemporary History*, 38(2), 2003

Te Velde, H., "Political Transfer: An Introduction," *European Review of History-Revue Européenne d'Histoire*, 12(2), 2005

Thelen, D., "The Nation and Beyond: Transnational Perspectives on United States History," *Journal of American History*, 86(3), 1999

Thurlow, R., "The Guardian of the 'Sacred Flame': The Failed Political Resurrection of Sir Oswald Mosley after 1945," *Journal of Contemporary History*, 33(2), 1998

Tranfaglia, N., *Come Nasce la Repubblica: La mafia, il Vaticano e il neofascismo nei documenti americani e italiani 1943–1947* (Milan: Bompiani, 2004)

Tucker, W. M., "Politics and Aesthetics: The Fascism of Robert Brasillach," *Western Political Quarterly*, 15(4), 1962
Turcato, D., "Italian Anarchism as a Transnational Movement, 1885–1915," *International Review of Social History*, 52(3), 2007
Tyrrell, I., *Transnational Nation. United States History in Global Perspective Since 1789* (New York: Palgrave Macmillan, 2007)
Ufficio Propaganda del MSI-DN, ed., "XIII Congresso Nazionale del MSI-DN: Alla riscoperta del Fascismo," *I Quaderni dell'Alternativa*, Rome, 1982
Valla, J.-C., "Une communauté de travail et de pensée," in P. Vial, ed., *Pour une renaissance culturelle: Le G.R.E.C.E. prend la parole* (Paris: Éditions Copernic, 1979)
"Pour une renaissance culturelle," in GRECE, ed., *Dix ans de combat culturel pour une renaissance* (Paris: GRECE, 1977)
Vander Velpen, J., *Les voilà qui arrivent! L'extrême droite et l'Europe* (Brussels: EPO, 1993)
Varvaro, P., "European Travellers in Italy," *European Review of History–Revue Européenne d'Histoire*, 4(2), 1997
Veneziani, M., *68 pensieri sul '68. Un trentennio di Sessantottite visto da destra* (Florence: Loggia De'Lanzi, 1998)
"Per una cultura dell'intervento," in Aa.Vv., *Al di là della destra e della sinistra: Atti del convegno «costanti evoluzioni di un patrimonio culturale»* (Rome: L.ED.E., 1982)
Venner, F., *Extrême France: Les mouvements frontistes, nationaux-radicaux, royalistes, catholiques traditionalistes et provie* (Paris: Grasset, 2006)
Veugelers, J., "After Colonialism: Local Politics and Far-Right Affinities in a City of Southern France," in A. Mammone, E. Godin, and B. Jenkins, eds., *Mapping the Extreme Right in Contemporary Europe: From Local to Transnational* (London: Routledge, 2012)
Vinen, R., *France, 1934–1970* (London: Macmillan, 1996)
Von Beyme, K., "Right-Wing Extremism in Post-war Europe," in K. von Beyme, ed., *Right-Wing Extremism in Western Europe* (London: Frank Cass, 1988)
Weil, P., "Racisme et discrimination dans la politique française de d'immigration. 1938–1945/1974–1995," *Vingtième Siècle*, 47, 1995
Weinberg, L. and Eubank, W. L., "Neo-Fascist and Far Left Terrorists in Italy: Some Bibliographical Observations," *British Journal of Political Science*, 18 (4), 1988
Wieviorka, O., "Replacement or Renewal? The French Political Élite at the Liberation," in A. Knapp, ed., *The Uncertain Foundation: France at the Liberation, 1944–47* (Basingstoke: Palgrave Macmillan, 2007)
Winock, M., *Nationalisme, antisémitisme et fascisme en France* (Paris: Seuil, 2004)
"Populismes Français," *Vingtième Siècle*, 56, 1997
Wolfreys, J., "'The Centre Cannot Hold': Fascism, the Left and the Crisis of French Politics," *International Socialism*, 95, 2002
"An Iron Hand in a Velvet Glove: The Programme of the French Front National," *Parliamentary Affairs*, 46(3), 1993

Wolin, R., "Designer Fascism," in R. J. Golsan, ed., *Fascism's Return: Scandal, Revision, and Ideology Since 1980* (Lincoln: University of Nebraska Press, 1998)

Yeoh, B. S. A., Willis, K. D., and Khader Fakhiri, S. M. A., "Introduction: Transnationalism and Its Edges," *Ethnic and Racial Studies*, 26(2), 2003

Zucchinali, M., *A destra in Italia oggi* (Milan: SugarCo, 1986)

Index

Lightning Source UK Ltd.
Milton Keynes UK
UKHW040938280219
338171UK00001B/81/P

9 781108 705851